BREAKTHROUGH

ALSO BY MOSHE DAYAN

Diary of the Sinai Campaign (1966)
Story of My Life (1976)
Living with the Bible (1978)

MOSHE DAYAN

BREAK-THROUGH

A Personal Account of the Egypt-Israel Peace Negotiations

WEIDENFELD AND NICOLSON
LONDON

First published in Great Britain by
George Weidenfeld & Nicolson Limited
91 Clapham High Street, London SW4 7TA

ISBN 0 297 77916 8

Printed and bound in Great Britain by
Butler & Tanner Limited
Frome and London

Contents

ILLUSTRATIONS   vii

1 The Appointment   1
2 The Start   17
3 Secret Meetings   26
4 Rendezvous in Morocco   38
5 Preparatory Talks   55
6 Sadat in Jerusalem   75
7 Meeting in Marrakesh   91
8 The First Steps   98
9 The Short Life of the Political Committee   109
10 No Ease in Washington   115
11 Leeds Castle   138
12 Camp David   149
13 The Proposals   160
14 Touch-and-Go   169
15 The Signing   181
16 The Home Front   191
17 Blair House   199
18 Change of Mood   222
19 Crisis   244
20 Camp David II   259
21 Half the Battle   268
22 Celebration at the White House   279
23 Cancer   285
24 Resignation   303

Appendices

1 The Camp David Accords   321
2 The Peace Treaty with Egypt   332
3 Memoranda of Agreement   356
4 Self-rule for Palestinian Arabs, Residents of Judaea, Samaria and
  the Gaza District, which will be instituted upon the Establishment
  of Peace   359

Index   362

Illustrations

Between pages 120 and 121

Moshe Dayan with President Sadat in Jerusalem (© *Contact, Jerusalem*).

Premier Begin visits Dayan in hospital (© *Shalom Bar-Tal*).

With President Ne Win in Burma.

With the Prime Minister of Singapore (© *Singapore Ministry of Culture*).

With the King of Nepal.

Moshe and Rahel Dayan are received by the King and Queen of Thailand (© *Government of Thailand Press Office*).

King Hassan of Morocco.

US Secretary of State Cyrus Vance at Dayan's home in Zahala, near Tel Aviv.

US Vice-President Walter Mondale with Dayan in Washington.

Former US Secretary of State Henry Kissinger and Moshe Dayan before one of their Washington meetings (© *Associated Press*).

President Sadat with Dayan during the Camp David negotiations.

The Israeli delegation to the Camp David Conference (© *Israel Government Press Office*).

With President Carter at the White House (© *The White House*).

Between pages 216 and 217

Premier Begin, President Carter, President Sadat and Moshe Dayan on a visit to Gettysburg during the Camp David talks (© *Israel Government Press Office*).

The US and Israeli delegation heads at Camp David (© *Israel Government Press Office*).

Egypt's Dr Hassan Tuhami and Butros Ghali with Dayan at Camp David (© *Israel Government Press Office*).

With Egypt's Prime Minister at the time, Mustapha Khalil.

The Egypt-Israel-US delegations at Washington's Blair House Conference (© *Robert A. Cumins*).

Sadat, Carter and Begin at the White House after signing the Peace Treaty.

Egypt's Minister of State for Foreign Affairs in the Dayan garden (© *Shalom Bar-Tal*).

Egyptian Defence Minister General Kamal Hassan Ali greeted by Dayan at a party in the Dayan home (© *Israel Government Press Office*).

Dayan with Egypt's Foreign Minister Muhammad Ibrahim Kamel (© *Zoom 77*).

With Rahel in Burma.

Dayan at the podium in the Knesset (© *Israel Sun*).

The backbencher (© *Sunphot*).

In the 'archaeological corner' of his garden (© *Yossi Roth*).

Maps

Israel and the borders after the Six-Day War 13

Sinai: phased withdrawal under Egypt-Israel peace treaty 283

Appendix 2: Map 1 Sinai Peninsula 337

Map 2 Sinai Peninsula 341

Map 3 Sub-Phases of Withdrawal to the El Arish–Ras Mohammad Line 343

Map 4 Sinai Peninsula 349

CHAPTER ONE

The Appointment

On Saturday morning, 21 May 1977, Menachem Begin telephoned and offered me the post of Foreign Minister in the Cabinet he was in the process of forming. His party, which had been in opposition for twenty-nine years, had gained an astonishing victory in the general elections held that month, and he would be heading the next coalition Government. My own Labour Party, which had been in office without interruption since the establishment of the State in 1948, had lost. I myself had been returned to the Knesset (Israel's parliament) on the Labour list. For Begin to ask a member of the Opposition to assume a key post in his Government was without precedent.

I told the Prime Minister that if he could reassure me there and then on two policy issues, I would weigh his offer and give him my reply three days later, on the following Tuesday.

The first concerned the limits of Israeli sovereignty – I was against extending it to the territories Israel had captured in the 1967 Six Day War which we now administered. Begin clarified this point to my satisfaction.

The second concerned my parliamentary seat. If I accepted his offer, I might decide to give up my membership of the Knesset since I had been elected on the Labour Party ticket. I would not be breaking precedent if I retained my seat, but I would wish to consider the matter. Begin said he was not proposing that I join his Cabinet in order to gain an additional parliamentary vote for his coalition. His offer stood even if I resigned my seat, and under our Basic Laws, Knesset membership was not a prerequisite for a ministerial appointment.

With that our telephone conversation ended.

The inner struggle over whether to accept or refuse the appointment, which engaged me for the next three days, was the toughest I had ever known. Abandoning my party and joining the Government of our rival would mean a final break with my remaining Labour friends. Moreover, if I decided not to give up my Knesset seat so that it could be returned to the Labour Party, I would be accused of impropriety towards the public and treachery to my party. The fact that other Labour Knesset members in the past had done the same – left the party and retained their seats as independents – would not stand me in good stead. What would be forgiven Mordechai Ben Porat, Yonah Kesse, Liova Eliav and Channa Lamdan would not be forgiven me. There would be renewed demonstrations against me by bereaved parents whose sons had fallen in the Yom Kippur War. Such demonstrations in the past had not been entirely free of political motivation, and this would assuredly be the case now: I would be denigrated from all directions.

There was another aspect to consider: how would I get on with the group I would be joining? Would I find a common language with Begin and his associates in the Government? True, I was closer to his views on political matters than I was to those of the Labour Party leadership at that time; but I was not with him on all issues. And as for our social outlook, I was part of the very fibre of the socialist farm-settlement movement. How could I share collective responsibility in a Begin Government when we shared no common basis in this social and economic sphere?

The key factor favouring my acceptance of his offer was the belief that as Minister for Foreign Affairs in his Cabinet I could significantly influence Israel's moves towards achieving a peace arrangement with our neighbouring Arab States and with the Palestinian inhabitants of Judea and Samaria (the West Bank) and the Gaza Strip. Would I indeed have such influence? Did I have anything positive on this subject to propose to Begin, to the Arabs, to the Americans?

There was a leaden atmosphere about the house in Zahala. On the surface, we went through the routine motions of day-to-day living; but not for one moment during the seventy-two hours following the telephone call was I free of the problem of how to respond to the Prime Minister's offer. I asked my wife Rahel what she thought, but all she would say was that it was indeed a hard decision, and she was confident I would make the right one. However, the reply was in her eyes. She would prefer me not to take the post, with its heavy responsibilities. And she would not wish me to be exposed once again to the shafts of vilification and abuse as had happened after the Yom Kippur War, though the report of the Agranat Commission had exonerated me and laid the blame for the mishap on the Chief of Staff and several senior officers.

I, too, was not unmindful of the personal aspects of the problem; but for me the main question was whether my appraisal of the situation was correct. It seemed to me that Israel was about to be faced with a crucial set of circumstances. I judged that Sadat was sincere when he expressed his willingness to attend the Geneva Peace Conference. I thought the Egyptian President wanted peace, and I had said so in the Knesset and on other public platforms. Was I right? If I was, then it might well be that the permanent frontiers of Israel would be established in the near future. The United States was bound to be involved in this peace process, and it would be a testing time for US–Israel relations, with concomitant implications for the relations between American Jewry and the State of Israel.

If indeed we were moving towards the stage of peace-making, the further question was whether I had a firm perception of the issues involved which could be translated into practical proposals that Begin could accept. Ten years earlier, in 1967, when Begin and I were fellow ministers in the National Government of Levi Eshkol – we had both been invited to join his Cabinet on the eve of the Six Day War – our views on the subject of our borders with Egypt and Syria were more moderate than those of the Labour Party. We both held that frontier negotiations with those two countries should be based on the national interests of both parties. On the delineation of our border with Egypt, we said, our interest was security, and freedom of navigation through the Gulf of Eilat. On the Israel–Syria border, our interest was security, and protection of the sources of the River Jordan. As to the West Bank, however, Begin and I took a more extreme position than that of the Labour Party, which envisaged a solution through territorial compromise – the division of the West Bank between the Kingdom of Jordan and Israel. We did not reject such a solution if it were proposed by the Arabs. We said we were prepared to give it serious consideration, but we did not believe in that course. The Likud election platform stated that Israeli sovereignty should cover the entire territory 'between the Mediterranean and the River Jordan', while I favoured an arrangement based on co-existence without the imposition of sovereignty by either side upon the other.

In earlier years, when I served as Chief of Staff of the Army and later as Minister of Agriculture under the premiership of David Ben Gurion, and subsequently as Minister of Defence in the Governments of Levi Eshkol and Golda Meir, I never went to them simply to put questions and request instructions. I always brought my own proposals on national issues, political or military, which required a solution. My suggestions were sometimes accepted and sometimes not. But at no time did I consider that anyone – even Ben Gurion, whom I admired more than any other of our leaders – understood our situation and what we should do about it better than I did, and so I never considered myself relieved of the responsibility of thinking out the correct course for us to follow.

Now, too, I trusted my judgment. I was confident that my political diagnosis was correct. I judged that Israel would soon have to take critical decisions which would shape her future, and that if I were to participate in determining policy, I could exert considerable influence on those Government decisions.

Begin was taken ill on the Monday following the telephone call, so that our promised meeting at which I was to give him my answer took place at his bedside in the Ichilov hospital. His doctor asked me to keep our talk short, and I did. I wanted to be clear about Begin's position on certain subjects that I considered basic, which could give rise to a clash in the Cabinet if I took office.

One was the issue of sovereignty, which we had discussed on the telephone. I had reminded him then that this topic had come up in the talks we had held before the parliamentary elections on the possibility of my appearing as a candidate under the banner of his Likud ('Unity') group of parties. He had known at the time, since it was no secret, that I was disenchanted with the Labour Party and some of its new leaders. My relationship with that party had been uneasy ever since I had followed Ben Gurion out of its ranks in June 1965 and formed our breakaway party called Rafi. Six months after the Six Day War, Rafi rejoined a united Labour Party (though Ben Gurion himself stayed out), and I had served in the Governments under Levi Eshkol and Golda Meir. I resigned when she did in April 1974, and did not join the new Labour coalition headed by Yitzhak Rabin in June of that year. On the eve of the 1977 elections, therefore, I had been approached by Begin's people to join them.

I had told them I would do so if the Likud platform contained the declaration that as long as there were peace negotiations with the Arab States, we would not extend Israeli sovereignty to the administered territories.

When I had said this during our Saturday morning telephone talk, Begin had cut in with the comment that this was past history. Not at all, I had replied, for he had then refused my demand, and I had therefore not run for election on his ticket. This was a subject which would surely recur, and I had not changed my mind. He should know this when offering me a ministerial post. Begin's reply had been that following our eve-of-election talks, he had finally agreed to a formula which stated that there would be no sovereignty over the territories 'while' peace negotiations were in progress. Thus, the difference between us was simply his 'while' instead of my 'as long as'. I frankly saw no distinction – but no one had told me of his formula before the elections. Begin explained that this had been due to a technical hitch. I had no interest in burrowing into the past, so I simply asked him if I could regard his proposed formula as committing the Government he was about to form. In that telephone conversation he had given an affirmative reply.

Now, at his hospital bedside, I said I was ready to accept his wording on sovereignty, but this fact should be published. He agreed that I could quote him.

I then raised the question of the Geneva Peace Conference, which had begun during the term of the previous Government. Did Begin agree with our position that the two sides were prepared to participate without prior conditions, and that the basis for peace negotiations would be Security Council Resolution 242? To my astonishment, Begin not only agreed, but added that his Government would honour all international commitments which earlier Governments had undertaken.

Another issue was the preservation of the *status quo* for the Arabs in the administered territories. Begin agreed that they could continue to send their representatives to the Jordanian parliament in Amman, and to receive financial help from the Arab States through Amman.

I also received a reassuring reply on my fourth point: he would maintain the practice of the Governments of Golda Meir and Yitzhak Rabin in not allowing organized Jewish prayer services on Jerusalem's Haram esh-Sharif, the Moslem compound on the original site of the sacred Jewish Temple built by Solomon in the tenth century BC. He would also leave unchanged the Jewish and Moslem prayer arrangements in Hebron's Tomb of the Patriarchs, held sacred by both faiths, where the building above the caves contained both a synagogue and a mosque.

The doctor was chafing by now and urged me to bring our talk to an end. I told Begin that I accepted his offer of the Foreign Ministry, and we agreed on a brief official statement: 'Begin asked Dayan to serve as Foreign Minister in his Government, and Dayan accepted the offer in principle.'

With the official announcement that I was accepting the appointment came a wave of public obloquy and disparagement. Newspaper editorials, letters to the press and personal letters to me deprecated my action. Rahel, silent, tight-lipped, found it hard to bear. I, who had expected it, was more immune. I was also hardened by the wounds and scars of past experience. I withdrew into myself, drawing the curtains and closing the shutters between the inner me and the outside voices. It was with reluctance that I responded to requests that I explain my move.

I appeared on television, gave some press interviews, and replied to a few personal letters. One of them was to Yehuda Tubin, a kibbutznik from Bet Zera in the Jordan Valley. We had been in correspondence for several years

and had also met on occasion for political talks. His long letter to me was full
of diatribe and denunciation. But I knew him as a sincere man, and I knew
that what he had written about my leaving the party and going over to the
Opposition expressed what many felt. Here is part of my reply:

I responded to Begin's offer because I did not have the courage to flinch from the
difficulties, the insults, the humiliation and the isolation that my acceptance will bring
down upon me and my family. I was concerned solely with what I saw as the situation
of our country and our people: that the borders and character of Israel were about to
be determined.... The alternative to a peace arrangement with the Arabs could well
be war. Would a Begin Government without me be better for Israel? And if I joined it,
would there be a chance of gaining our aims – as I see them? Do I, in fact, have a
solution to the problem of our conflict with the Arabs, and would I be able to act
according to my perceptions in such a government? If the answer to this last question
is positive, should I, despite that, reject Begin's proposal?

I also replied to Gad Yacobi, one of the leaders of the Labour Party,
whose letter dealt mainly with the party aspect of my action. He, too, of
course, did not spare the lash, and he explained at length why I had tarnished
party ethics. To him I wrote:

One word is curiously missing from your letter – Israel. That, and that alone, was at
the centre of my considerations when I decided to accept Begin's offer. I thought that
everyone would see, as I see, the gravity of the developments which the State of Israel
is likely to face. I am not absolutely certain that this is indeed the case – I shan't go into
detailed explanation – and it may be that you and other friends are right in
thinking that the sole subject of importance is the maintenance of normalcy in our
party and parliamentary life.
    The fact is that an Israeli Government headed by Begin (with his political out-
look, his personality, and the people close to him), plus the attitude of the United
States to the Israeli–Arab conflict, plus the military, political and economic power
of the Arabs – these are the factors which have brought Israel to the most critical
hour of decision since 1948, a decision which will determine our boundaries and
much else ...
    The question which I myself had to face was whether my acceptance of Begin's
proposal and working with him could materially change the situation for the good
of Israel, as against my refusal, and the appointment of someone else as Foreign
Minister.
    You may be right in thinking that I should have refused. But to do that I would
need to see things differently from the way I see them, or to cherish Israel less.

The formal procedures that followed my decision were simple. I notified
the Labour Party that I was leaving it; I did not resign my seat in the Knesset;

and I requested and received from the House Committee 'the accepted rights of a one-man party'.

Begin completed the formation of his Cabinet and presented it to the Knesset for approval on 20 June 1977. The coalition Government consisted of the Likud, with 45 members in the 120-seat Knesset; the National Religious Party, 12; Agudat Yisrael, 4; and myself. Some weeks later, the Democratic Party, with 15 members, joined the coalition.

After the usual debate, the vote of confidence in the new Government was carried by 63 to 53. Premier and ministers, one by one, then stepped up to the podium, took the oath of office, and proceeded to their places at the Cabinet table in the centre of the Chamber.

The debate preceding the vote had followed immediately on the Prime Minister's opening statement naming his ministers and outlining the broad policy of his Government. After him came the Leader of the Opposition and speakers from all parties. I pondered whether to take part or not. I had no formal obligation to do so, nor had any of the other ministers, and I, as a one-man party, could certainly remain silent. I had also told Begin that my participation in the debate was uncertain.

At the start of the Knesset session, however, I had been told that Opposition members were preparing demonstrative interruptions if I spoke, and it was even possible that there would be a mass walk-out by members of the Ma'arach grouping of Labour parties. Then came the rumour that there would be harassment as I took the oath of office. In the light of such reports, my friends advised me not to speak, recommending that I wait a few weeks until tempers had cooled.

I might have listened to them had I not been seized by the thought that if I followed their suggestion, it might conceivably be to escape an unpleasant and difficult situation. I therefore resolved to take part in the debate come what may. Difficulties had to be faced, not evaded.

I prepared my speech with care. I even approached Begin to ensure that I correctly interpreted his views on two of the policy issues we had discussed, even though I would be speaking in my name alone: that Israel would attend the Geneva Conference on the basis of UN Resolution 242, as agreed to by previous Governments; and no step would be taken to annex the administered territories while we were conducting peace negotiations with our neighbours. If the Government were ever to take such a step, it would require a minimum Knesset vote of 61 out of 120, and ministers would not be obliged to vote for the Government's motion.

When I rose to speak, no one left the Chamber. But during the first part of my address I was hardly allowed to complete a sentence. The interruptions were systematic. Continuous calls of 'return your Knesset seat', 'shame' and 'resign', were screamed from the Labour benches, particularly from the left-wing Mapam. Most vociferous, however, were members of the tiny party known as Sheli, whose leader had been a Labour Knesset member, had left the party – and retained his Knesset seat!

Though it was not at all pleasant, I went on with my speech, and felt no psychological stress. I withdrew within myself, a sensation familiar to me from the battlefield, when I would cut myself off emotionally from reality. What was happening in the Knesset was happening in a fog and was unreal to me, like the burst of shells when crossing a field of fire.

The main theme of my address was my judgment that we were approaching a decisive period in which the boundaries of Israel would be determined. This, then, was the moment when we should all seek a consensus. However, though I was speaking objectively of the national aspects of this important issue, the cries of 'resign' made me think more acutely of the personal question: was it right and proper of me to have joined the Begin Government?

I knew better than any of my critics what was involved in the step I had taken. From the forthcoming talks we would be holding in Washington, I would not be returning with a laurel crown. The sole privilege I was granted by my function as Foreign Minister was the opportunity of fighting for our future. Refusal to accept the ministerial position would mean, for me, running away from the most important campaign in our national life.

I was also well aware of the impact on my personal life. I was cutting myself off from my friends and from the circle to which I belonged. I had no interest in merging with my new political colleagues, and I was separating myself from my associates in the Labour Party. I could not say that this social and personal factor was of no consequence to me. But as I stood at the podium of the Knesset, the focus of hostile looks and angry cries, the recognition that I had chosen the correct path was in no way diminished, and so it was not difficult for me to continue saying what I had to say.

A week after the Knesset formalities, and shortly before we were to hold our first Cabinet meeting, the new Government assembled at the presidential residence to be presented to the Head of State. The ceremony was brief and, to me, familiar. The President offered his good wishes, the Prime Minister responded, glasses were raised, hands were shaken, and we then formed a semi-circle, with the President and the Prime Minister in the middle, for the official photograph. Minister of Health Shostak tried to draw me towards the centre, so that I would be next to the Prime Minister; but I refused. I preferred to stand at the edge, next to Ezer Weizman and Arik Sharon. In our personal relations we had much in common, far more than the political differences that divided us. The three of us had spent many years in the army, and had fought together in every one of Israel's wars, and on all fronts.

The President, Ephraim Katzir, told me he was impressed by what I had said in the Knesset about there being time enough to quarrel among ourselves and indulge in splits and schisms when the Arabs were ready to accept the Labour Party's plan for the territorial division of the West Bank. Until then, however, we should be united. He added that he had been present in the Knesset during the bout of heckling, but this in no way lessened the aptness of my words. I wondered, as he spoke, whether he could not see, or did not wish to see, that the aim of the Opposition parties was to bring down the Begin Government, even at the expense of the country.

In the Cabinet room, for our first meeting, I found I had been given the seat I had occupied when I had served in earlier Governments - opposite the Prime Minister. The main items on the agenda were reviews by the Defence Minister and by me. I confined myself on this opening session to Israel-US relations and the Prime Minister's forthcoming visit to the United States.

The meeting was conducted with efficiency, though not without a certain tenseness. Begin is a good chairman. He speaks succinctly and to the point, and hints that others should do the same. The less positive aspect was that ministers did not feel free to challenge the Prime Minister even when they disagreed with him. Begin informed us - it was an instruction, not a suggestion - that all ministers were to attend the Knesset sessions on Mondays and Tuesdays. This was not to ensure a voting majority, but to reassure the public: they watched the Knesset proceedings on television, and were bitterly critical when they saw so many empty seats in the Chamber and at the Government table. I scribbled a note to Begin telling him that his order was not feasible. Some ministers had also to be present in the Knesset on Wednesdays, the day set aside for members' questions. And added to these three Knesset days were the Sundays earmarked for Cabinet meetings, leaving ministers little time to run their offices. I therefore recommended that half the Cabinet attend the Knesset on Mondays and the other half on Tuesdays. Begin accepted this without demur, and everyone was relieved.

Another suggestion of mine which was accepted at that first meeting, though outside my ministerial field, concerned Israel's national airline, El Al, which was stricken with labour troubles. I was against the proposal of the ministers directly involved, and it was dropped. They had recommended Government intervention, which I considered hasty and shortsighted, failing to take account of the resultant complications with the National Labour Federation and the El Al staff.

The fact was, of course, that most members of this Government were novices. They had to learn to put more thought into the proposals they brought up for Cabinet decision, otherwise the consequences could be grave. This applied also to Begin: he did not give sufficient study to every subject. It was this, perhaps, that prompted him to listen carefully to what others said, and at times take decisions different from those he had proposed.

The composition and character of this Cabinet were poles apart from the previous Governments in which I had served. Yet I felt neither strange nor uncomfortable. Nor, I confess, was I moved by any sense of excitement, as perhaps I should have been, at being back at the Government table.

A few days before that first Cabinet session, Begin had asked me for a memorandum setting out the principles on which I thought we should base our position on peace negotiations with the Arabs. This was required in preparation for the Geneva Peace Conference. The Security Council had adopted the celebrated Resolution 338, which called for the immediate opening of negotiations between Israel and the Arab States, and the parties had agreed. Representatives of the United States and the Soviet Union were to be the joint chairmen, and Geneva was selected as the venue. United States President Jimmy Carter worked energetically and pressed the parties to convene the conference quickly. Begin and I both believed that the peace process might indeed be launched in the near future.

While composing the memorandum, I weighed the alternatives – whether to formulate our position in ideal terms, expressing what we would really like, or whether to present only the minimal conditions that Israel considered essential for a just and lasting peace. I decided to follow the second course: to give the Prime Minister my frank views, and not to make proposals which I did not believe the Arabs would accept.

This was particularly true of Syria. For example, I did not feel that the Syrians, the most extreme nationalists, who also enjoyed the support of the Soviet Union, would agree out of goodness of heart to a change in the international boundary which would leave the Golan Heights as part of the State of Israel. The Golan was not Sinai. It had been a settled strip of territory before the 1967 war, with some 60,000 villagers who were now living in refugee camps in the area of Damascus. Since then we had established farm settlements in the Golan, which put us under an obligation to find an arrangement for them agreed to by ourselves and the Syrians, if indeed Syria was prepared to sign a peace treaty with us.

I recognized that Begin, like his three predecessors in the premiership,

Eshkol, Golda and Rabin, might not accept my views. But it was my duty to let him have my sincere judgment.

I wrote to the Prime Minister on 24 June 1977, summing up my thoughts on the subjects which would no doubt come up at Geneva. Since these were the very ones which were to be argued over interminably at negotiation parleys in the three years that followed – some even to this day – I offer them here as background to the later developments.

I told Begin that to secure a permanent peace with the Arabs, we had first to reach agreement on a variety of complex subjects, notably, the permanent boundaries with the four neighbouring Arab States, special arrangements for Jerusalem, and the settlement of the Palestinian refugees. There were also the questions of the nationality of the inhabitants of the Gaza Strip and their relationship with the Arab countries, as well as the connection of the West Bank inhabitants to the Kingdom of Jordan. It did not seem to me possible to solve these problems simultaneously and quickly, in a single stage. The refugee problem, for example, would take time to study, and more time to plan and implement whatever solution was agreed upon after reaching an overall accord. I therefore proposed to the Prime Minister that we show willingness to deal separately with each item, and not hold up the settlement of some only because others still proved intractable.

There were cases, I wrote, where the value of proposed solutions could be judged only after they had been carried out. A good example was the reopening of the Suez Canal in accordance with the Separation of Forces Agreement we signed with Egypt after the Yom Kippur War. It was expected that the cities in the Canal zone would be rehabilitated and industrial plants established, creating thereby a climate of normalcy and peace along the demarcation line between Egypt and Israeli forces in Sinai. But a signature alone at the bottom of an agreement was not enough to make it happen. We had to wait several years before discovering whether what had been planned had indeed been realized. We should therefore favour an approach that called for the implementation of the agreement in stages, with satisfactory results in the early stages being the condition for taking the next step. I added that it was probably not possible to reach a final peace agreement in the situation that existed then. At the most – if we were thinking of all fronts – we might gain accord on an end to the state of war. But, of course, in such an agreement we would not concede territory that we would be prepared to give up within the framework of a permanent peace treaty.

I then touched on the subject of security guarantees by the United States. The possibility of such guarantees had been mooted by various American spokesmen, but only in vague and hypothetical terms. I told the Prime

Minister that I doubted very much whether the United States would be ready to enter into the firm and long-term commitment of a defence treaty. If she were, I would regard it as an achievement of the utmost importance for the State of Israel.

I well recognized that such a prospect, hinted at by the Americans, was conceived by them as a substitute for the territories we would be asked to give up. Without going into the merits of a 'deal' of this kind, I ventured the view that we should consider positively the possibility of including a US–Israel defence treaty as a basic plank in an Israel–Arab peace arrangement. The subject was worth a thorough study.

In negotiating the border between Israel and Egypt, I said, we would be guided by Israel's interests in ensuring freedom of navigation in the Red Sea and the Gulf of Eilat, in certain boundary changes, and in securing a buffer zone in Sinai. The military possibilities for the buffer zone could include demilitarization, reduction of forces, or control by UN forces. The minimal boundary changes should be such as to leave within Israeli hands the Eitan and Etzion airfields near the Negev–Sinai frontier, together with an appropriate area around them, as well as the Jewish settlements within the approaches to Rafah. This meant an Israeli-controlled territorial strip from the Mediterranean to Eilat, west of the international boundary.

To ensure freedom of shipping, I recommended that we should not lay down hard and fast terms in advance, but rather display a readiness to listen to suggestions for its solution. However, the proposal that seemed feasible to me, within the framework of a final peace treaty, was the retention of military posts along the west coast of the Gulf of Eilat which would give us control of a territorial strip several miles wide from Eilat to Sharm e-Sheikh.

The Israel–Syria border required a different approach. There, Israel's interests were protection of the water sources of the River Jordan, and defence of Israel's northern Galilee farm settlements. The Jewish settlements established on the Golan Heights since 1967 were an additional factor in this border issue. I suggested that in any negotiations with Syria, Israel should present the water and defence problems, and invite proposals for their solution. On changes in the international border, however, we should insist only on Israeli military posts on the Golan and Mount Hermon – again, within the framework of permanent peace.

I next dealt with the Palestinian refugees. Getting them settled was the key to the solution of what is known as the Palestinian problem. Their political and military standard-bearers were the terrorist movements grouped under the PLO, the Palestine Liberation Organization, who were themselves refugees, and not the permanent residents of the West Bank or the Gaza District.

Israel and the borders after the Six-Day War

Mediterranean

Sea

LEBANON

SYRIA

Kuneitra

Haifa

Tiberias

ISRAEL

Tel-Aviv

Nablus

Jericho

Jerusalem

Gaza

Hebron

Dead
Sea

JORDAN

Beersheba

El-Arish

Abu Awugeila

Bir el Hasana

Bir Gifgafa

Gidi Pass

Bir eth Themada

Suez

Sinai

Mitla Pass

Ras es Sudar

Eilat

EGYPT

Gulf of Suez

Nuweiba

Gulf of Eilat

SAUDI

Abu Rudeis

St. Catherine's
Monastery

Dahab

ARABIA

Et-Tur

Strait of Tiran

Area occupied
in Six-Day War

Cease fire line 1967

Armistice line 1949

Snapir

| 0 | 10 | 20 | 30 miles |
| 0 | 20 | 40 km | |

© carta, JERUSALEM

Suez Canal

The total number of refugees was about one million: some half a million in Jordan, three hundred thousand in Lebanon, and one hundred and ninety thousand in the Gaza Strip. The status of 'refugeedom' was basically expressed by three factors: lack of citizenship; residence in a refugee camp, which created – and denoted – an inferior way of life; and lack of work, or even a work permit. Officially, a refugee who had a permanent job lost his rights to aid from the international relief agencies.

The refugees in Jordan had both Jordanian citizenship and jobs. Thus, the only problem for them was to get out of the refugee camps and into suitable homes, which called for housing projects of the type common in Jordanian villages. As far as I knew, the Government of Jordan was anxious to see this accomplished, and had even approached the United States Government for assistance. (One of Jordan's main reasons for wanting to see its refugees properly settled was prompted by the events of 'Black September'. Arafat's PLO had become a power in Jordan, virtually a 'State within a State', and in September 1970, the Jordanian army, in a full-scale battle with the PLO, defeated them, and drove them out. They fled to Lebanon.)

Actually, if the half-a-million refugees could be recognized as permanent citizens of Jordan, the notion of Jordan as the Palestinian homeland would be strengthened; and so would the links with that country of the inhabitants of the West Bank and the Gaza District. I therefore proposed to the Prime Minister that we support the permanent settlement in Jordan of the refugees already there.

The refugees in the Gaza Strip differed from their counterparts in Jordan in that they had no State nationality – the document they carried was a local identity card. Most lived in camps, but all had jobs, working in Israel, the West Bank and the Strip itself. I saw no possibility of moving them to another territory. I therefore recommended that we work towards the provision of suitable housing projects for them in the region in which they now lived. As for the question of citizenship, I suggested that it should not be raised for the moment. They had no wish to receive Israeli citizenship; and within the framework of a peace agreement, or even of an interim arrangement with Jordan, they might be able to obtain Jordanian citizenship on the model of the Palestinians in the West Bank.

In Lebanon, the refugees lacked Lebanese citizenship, though some had Jordanian papers; most of them were in camps; and there were work opportunities in the country. I proposed that they be offered the alternatives of remaining permanently in Lebanon or emigrating to another Arab country, and in either case they should receive compensation.

The permanent settlement of the refugees in the regions they now inhabited was to my mind also the answer to the problem of 'a Palestine home-land'. If their present condition were to continue, there would be mounting pressure to recognize the West Bank as their country. And if this became the Palestine State, while the refugees in Jordan and Lebanon remained un-settled, it would serve as a military, political and ideological springboard for the conquest of Israel and its conversion into 'Palestine'. To prevent this – and I assumed that even those in the United States administration who favoured a Palestinian State in the West Bank would agree – the permanent settlement of the refugees in the lands where they were now resident should be accomplished before any declaration of Palestinian statehood for the West Bank. Unless this were done, I envisaged the growth of three evils. A Pales-tine State would be proclaimed, even though it would be a 'non-State'. The refugee problem would remain. And the 'option' to conquer Israel would be given a territorial basis, which would encourage and strengthen those who harboured this objective.

The future of the West Bank and the Gaza Strip was bound to figure prominently in any Israel–Arab negotiations, and I set out our position on these territories. It was important for us to stress the fundamental meaning of biblical Judea and Samaria – the West Bank – for Israel. They were part of our ancient homeland, and it was inconceivable that, with the rebirth of Israel and the Return to Zion, Jews should be prohibited from settling there, or that they should be considered strangers. We might be driven from this territory by force of arms, but never by an attempt to compel us 'voluntarily' to cut ourselves off from it.

Even from the Arab point of view there was no substance to the proposal of a Palestine 'homeland' with the status of statehood in the administered territories. The narrow thirty-mile stretch of the West Bank between the River Jordan and the frontier of Israel could not constitute a viable State. It was also geographically disjointed. The Gaza Strip was isolated from the Hebron hills. The northern part of the West Bank, with its towns of Nablus and Jenin, was separated from the southern part by Jerusalem. Moreover, Bethle-hem and Ramallah did not wish to be disconnected from Jerusalem.

The only possible arrangement for these territories was co-existence be-tween the Israelis and the Palestinian inhabitants, which was the situation in Jerusalem, with the Palestinians retaining both their Jordanian citizenship and their ties with Jordan. It was my considered view that we should not propose the application of Israeli law to the West Bank or the Gaza Strip. We should confine ourselves simply to the announcement that we rejected the transfer of these territories to an Arab State, be it Jordan or some future Palestinian State; that this portion of the Arab–Israeli problem required

further consideration and negotiation towards an eventual solution; and that
we should be satisfied for the moment with seeking an interim arrangement.
Such an arrangement for the West Bank should give its Palestinian inhabitants more independence than they now enjoyed, as well as closer links with
Jordan. As for Israel's role, we should not diminish the military control and
governmental authority we currently maintained in these areas.

Bound up with the problem of the West Bank was that of Jerusalem. (The
advocates of a West Bank Palestine State included East Jerusalem within its
borders.) If the basic situation in the West Bank were maintained, with the
functional improvements I suggested in an interim arrangement, there would
need to be a distinction between secular and religious affairs. All that per-
tained to the secular sphere should be handled by a mixed Arab–Jewish
municipal council. In the religious sphere, a special status should be granted
to the Christian and Moslem Holy Places.

My final proposal concerned the boundaries with our neighbouring Arab
countries. United States representatives often spoke of possible 'secure boundaries' which would be different from the political frontiers. They had in
mind early-warning stations and advanced observation posts. This suggestion did not seem feasible to me. (Even less feasible was the Arab approach:
they would make their agreement to such a device conditional on such posts
and stations being established on *both* sides of the frontier.) I regarded the
place for such a system to be in the buffer zone, such as the area in Sinai
which was under the control of UN forces. Elsewhere – if we should agree to
army posts (other than those along the international border) such as at
Sharm e-Sheikh, on Mount Hermon and the Golan Heights – such positions
had to remain Israeli.

CHAPTER TWO

The Start

The first nudge that set the wheels of the Israel–Arab peace negotiations moving came from Jimmy Carter, President of the United States.

Premier Begin had spoken of peace when he addressed the Knesset on 20 June 1977, seeking parliamentary approval for his new Cabinet. He called on the heads of the neighbouring Arab States to meet with him with the object of establishing a true peace. 'If, however, this appeal is rejected, we shall take note thereof.'

On the same day President Carter cabled his congratulations to Begin on his election as Prime Minister. The important part of the signal, however, was not the polite goodwill message but a practical appeal to Begin to start peace negotiations with the Arabs. For this purpose, Carter invited Begin to come to Washington the following month to discuss the principles which could bring about a just settlement. Carter added that he, the US President, felt himself deeply committed to help Israel and her neighbours resolve the conflict between them.

Two days earlier, before the Cabinet was sworn in, the American Ambassador to Israel, Samuel Lewis, asked to see me. He told me then that he was going to Washington for consultations, and that Begin would be invited to meet Carter. Lewis asked if I would be joining Begin, since it was customary for Foreign Ministers to accompany their Prime Ministers on such official visits. I said that Begin had not proposed that I go (and I did not), and what was 'customary' did not apply to Begin. I gathered from what the Ambassador said that the main theme of the Washington talks would be Carter's wish to bring Israel and the Arabs to Geneva as soon as possible in order to reach a peace agreement.

My session with the Ambassador was heavy going. He wanted to hear my views on peace arrangements with the various Arab countries, and particularly on the solution to the Palestinian problem. He kept asking specific questions, and I could only tell him that I had not yet consulted with the Prime Minister on these subjects. I assured him, however, that his hosts would find Begin constructive.

Begin left for the United States on 15 July and reached Washington two days later, to be received with full ceremonial honours. The President had sent a special plane to bring him and his party from New York, and Secretary of State Cyrus Vance awaited them at Andrews Air Force Base. From there they proceeded to the White House, through streets bedecked with Israeli flags. The welcoming ceremony began at 10.30 a.m. with a nineteen-gun salvo and the playing of the two national anthems. Carter, Begin and their wives mounted the podium, the President and Prime Minister made their brief speeches, and that was that.

These ceremonial diplomatic rites inevitably bear the mark of routine, yet this one was particularly festive, despite the oppressive heat. Carter spoke to Begin with great cordiality, and underlined the special relationship between the United States and Israel. Begin, speaking with emotion, began his reply with a Hebrew sentence: 'Mr President, I come to you from Zion in the name of an ancient people.' He then continued in excellent English and made a very good speech.

Immediately after the ceremony, the two leaders retired with their senior aides to hold their first working session, which lasted two hours. Carter went directly to business. The main subjects of their discussions, he said, were the steps to be taken to achieve peace between Israel and its Arab neighbours. To this end, it was the US wish to convene the Geneva Conference as quickly as possible. For this conference to be fruitful, it was necessary to establish in advance the principles that would be acceptable to both parties. US representatives had already met with leaders of the Arab States, and he now wanted to consider those principles with the Prime Minister of Israel. Carter emphasized that in talking to the Arab leaders he had used the same language and the same connotations he proposed to use in his talk with Begin, so that nobody could say that the US had proposed a different formula to Israel from that offered to the Arabs.

The first principle was the acceptance of UN Security Council Resolution 242, as agreed by the parties. The United States had widened the meaning of this resolution, and proposed that it be regarded as obliging the parties to conclude a full peace agreement and not, as the original text stated, merely 'an end of belligerency'. It was the American view that the peace should include open borders, free movement of peoples and cargoes, diplomatic ties, and the establishment of completely normal relations between Israel and the Arab countries. Carter said that the Arab leaders had found it difficult to accept this approach, but none had rejected it out of hand.

(When I read the cabled report of the talks a few hours later in Jerusalem, I was much heartened by Carter's words, and thought them of the highest

significance. The importance of the new American position lay not only in its
view of the essence and quality of the desired peace, but also in its interpretation of Resolution 242. I had no doubt that 242 would continue to be the
legal basis of peace with the Arabs, and the wider and constructive meaning
given to it by the Americans would help us greatly in achieving a full solution
to the conflict.)

Continuing his presentation to Begin, Carter moved on to the territorial
problem. The Americans, he said, were not drawing maps, but they held to
the principle that the borders ultimately decided upon had to be secure,
recognized and agreed to by all the parties. There was also a territorial aspect
to the refugee problem: were the Arab refugees from 1948 onwards to have
territory which would be under their exclusive control? The Arab position
was that the Palestinian refugees constituted an independent nation and had
to have their own State. 'We, the Americans,' said Carter, 'used the term
"Homeland".'

Another question was how the Palestinians were to be included in the
deliberations at Geneva. President Sadat and King Hussein felt they should
be part of the Jordanian delegation, while President Assad of Syria preferred
a united Arab delegation at the Geneva Conference that would include the
Palestinians and would conduct the negotiations with Israel on behalf of all
the Arabs.

Carter then asked Begin to state Israel's position. The Prime Minister had
with him a paper that had been formulated by the Israeli Cabinet, the first
part of which dealt with questions of procedure for convening the Geneva
Conference. Israel was prepared as from 10 October 1977 to take part in the
conference in accordance with Security Council Resolution 338, and this
resolution also included Resolution 242. The participants were to be the
accredited representatives of Israel, Egypt, Syria and Jordan, and they were
not to present preconditions of any kind for their participation. At the
inaugural session, the representatives of all the parties would make public
opening addresses. Thereafter, three separate mixed committees would be
established: an Egypt-Israel, a Syria-Israel and a Jordan-Israel committee.
These three committees would negotiate and finalize the peace treaties between Israel and her neighbours.

The second part of the paper on Israel's proposals dealt with the substantive subjects of borders and the West Bank. Begin did not refer to it at the
large morning meeting with all the aides present. He read it to Carter at their
first private talk which was held that night after the State dinner. It consisted
of three brief articles. The first, on the Israel-Egypt border, stated that in
view of the large area separating the two countries, Israel was prepared,

within the framework of a peace treaty, 'to make a significant withdrawal of her forces in Sinai'. The second was concerned with the Israel–Syria border. It said that Israel would remain on the Golan Heights; 'but within the framework of a peace treaty, we shall be prepared to withdraw our forces from their present lines and redeploy them along a line to be established as the permanent boundary'. The third article was headed 'The West Bank', and stated that 'Israel will not transfer Judea, Samaria and the Gaza District to any foreign sovereign authority'. There was a dual basis to this position: 'the historic rights of our nation to this land'; and 'the needs of our national security, which demand a defence capability of our State and the lives of our citizens'.

Anyone familiar with Begin's long-held traditional points of view cannot but be impressed by the flexibility reflected in the document which he presented. True, there was no surrender of Judea, Samaria and Gaza to a foreign sovereignty; but neither was there the claim for Israeli sovereignty. On Sinai, there was a declaration of readiness for a deep withdrawal. As for Golan, Israel was prepared to make a partial withdrawal. Israel was also very forthcoming on matters of principle. Entering into negotiations with no preconditions covered all parties and all subjects, which meant that any item could be brought up for discussion, even Jerusalem and the West Bank, which Begin had always held were non-negotiable. Another example of flexibility was his acceptance of UN Resolutions 338 and 242 as the basis for negotiations.

The main cause for Begin's change of stand was undoubtedly the fact that he was now Prime Minister. The burden of responsibility had had its effect. He had affirmed in the Knesset, when outlining the Government's programme, that all parties to the peace negotiations would have the right to propose any subject they wished for discussion, and we had held internal deliberations to determine our attitude to those that were bound to be raised. One of them was the West Bank territories of Judea and Samaria, and Begin's position at first was that we should 'claim the West Bank'. Only after protracted argument did he agree to the formula I suggested that 'the West Bank shall not be under foreign sovereignty'.

We also had a long discussion over the status of the Holy Places in Jerusalem. The Government's outline programme, which was written by Begin, stated that 'the Jerusalem Holy Places will be preserved for all creeds'. I argued that this formula did not go far enough, and I proposed the statement that every religion should have full control over its religious institutions in Jerusalem. Begin finally agreed to my formulation on condition it was made clear that the control of the religious institutions would be administrative. I readily accepted the amendment. I, too, had not intended that they be given sovereignty.

After Begin had spoken at the morning meeting with the aides present, Shmuel Katz took the floor. He was the foreign press adviser in the Prime Minister's Office, and the purpose of his contribution now was to give the Israeli position an ideological wrapping. His main 'ideological' argument was that most of the Palestinian Arabs were really new immigrants who had come to Palestine only in the last hundred years. The silliest part was his 'proof' that the Arabs were strangers in the land of Israel. It was almost certain, said Katz, that that was the reason why so many Arabs had fled so easily in the 1948 war. Farmers rooted in their soil did not behave that way. The only Arabs who really belonged to the country were those who stayed, despite the war.

Katz's words were also in the cabled report, and when I read them I did not even try to guess what the Americans must have thought when they heard them. According to this criterion, the Arabs in the Golan Heights fled in the Six Day War because they lacked a deep attachment to their soil, whereas the Arab refugees in the Gaza Strip, who had been there less than twenty years when the 1967 war reached them, remained during that war because their hearts beat with the feeling that the miserable camps in which they lived was their homeland!

After his talks with Carter, Begin left for New York in high spirits. It appeared to him that he had established personal ties with the President, and that on the political issues he had not only avoided a confrontation between the United States and Israel but had even achieved mutual understanding. He gave expression to this judgment at a public meeting in New York of leading supporters of State of Israel Bonds. He declared to this gathering of two thousand friends of Israel that he had met many statesmen, authors, scientists and humanists in his life; but never had he met a man of the stature of President Carter.

The Americans were also happy with their talks, and favourably impressed by Begin; but they knew that the central purpose had not been attained – to pave the way for convening the Geneva Peace Conference. Many problems had not yet been solved, among them Palestinian representation, withdrawal from the West Bank, and a united Arab delegation.

The Prime Minister returned to Israel on 25 July 1977, and on the same day the US Ambassador to Israel, Samuel Lewis, handed us a memorandum intended to serve as a basis for the discussions at the Geneva Conference. It contained five articles, and the Americans hoped they would be acceptable to both parties. We had no objection to the first three: that the purpose of the negotiations was to reach peace agreements; that the basis for the conference were Resolutions 242 and 338; and that the aim of 242 was not only an end to belligerency but the establishment of completely normal relations.

However, Israel was not prepared to accept the last two, as formulated. Article 4 spoke of an Israeli withdrawal from all fronts; and Article 5 stated that the arrangement reached at Geneva had to include a directive about 'a Palestine entity', enabling the Palestinians to gain self-determination in their future status.

We told the Americans that if they intended to negotiate with the Arabs on the basis of this memorandum, they had to make it clear that these two articles were not acceptable to us. We rejected Article 5 entirely. On Article 4, concerning withdrawal, we proposed the deletion of the words 'from all fronts', so that it would now read that it was understood that the withdrawal called for in Resolution 242 would be 'to mutually agreed, secure, and recognized borders', and would not include an undertaking for Israel to withdraw on all the fronts.

The reason for our objection to the American formulation was apparent. The Begin Government was prepared to withdraw from the Egyptian and Syrian fronts, but not the Jordanian front, namely, the West Bank territories of Judea and Samaria.

The controversy over the five-article memorandum continued both in Washington, between our Ambassador and the State Department, and in Jerusalem, between us and the United States Ambassador. Each side sought to convince the other of the justice of his stand; but in vain. The differences remained unresolved.

On the 9th of August, some two weeks after Premier Begin returned from his visit to the United States, Secretary of State Cyrus Vance arrived in Israel. It was his last stop on a round of visits to the Arab States in the Middle East. He had been to Egypt, Saudi Arabia, Jordan, Syria and Lebanon, met with the leaders of these countries and talked with them about convening the Geneva Conference and the conditions for a peace agreement with Israel. He had two meetings in Israel, one with me on the day of his arrival and one with the Prime Minister on the following day.

At the session with me in the Foreign Ministry, Vance was accompanied by Philip Habib, Under-Secretary for Political Affairs; Alfred Atherton, Assistant Secretary for Near Eastern and South Asian Affairs (later, ambassador-at-large); William Quandt, staff member of the National Security Council; and US Ambassador to Israel, Samuel Lewis. My own senior staff members included my Director-General, Ephraim Evron, and Israel's Ambassador to Washington, Simcha Dinitz.

It was my first meeting with this Washington group. Vance was the only one who spoke, though his aides handed him notes from time to time. The main subject was their impression of their talks with the Arab leaders. Vance spoke with clarity and economy. I did not imagine that he told us all the Arabs had said nor all that he had told them, but I had not the slightest doubt that what he told us was accurate. It was a civilized talk, for Vance is a man of integrity, and there was nothing vague or evasive about his answers to my questions.

From our point of view, the information he brought us was disappointing. All the Arab States demanded the participation of the PLO in our deliberations. America's response to this demand was that she would be prepared to talk to the PLO if its leaders announced their acceptance of Resolution 242. America did not insist that the PLO cancel the article in its charter which calls for the liquidation of Israel. According to Vance, this was not necessary, for acceptance of 242 implied recognition of Israel and thus automatically cancelled the offending article. He went on to say that 242 defined the Palestinians as refugees, but the PLO demanded that they be regarded as a nation with aspirations for their own State. The Americans thought this problem could be met if the PLO announced that its acceptance of Resolution 242 was conditional upon recognition of the Palestinians' right to a homeland.

This formula had presumably emerged from what the heads of the Arab States had said; but Vance confirmed that there was no certainty that the PLO itself would accept it. Thus, the question of PLO participation in the Geneva Conference was not mentioned. When I raised it, Vance reminded us that Begin had told Carter that Israel would not examine the credentials of the Palestinian Arabs who would be attached to the Jordanian delegation. He gathered from this that Israel would not investigate whether the Jordanian delegation would, in fact, include PLO representatives.

Turning to the principles upon which the peace negotiations were to be based, Vance said he had tried to reach an agreed formula with the Arab leaders but had failed. All their proposals were extreme, and he had not found them reasonable. Egypt demanded that Israel return to the pre-1967 borders and the Gaza Strip be restored to Egyptian control. In time it would be handed over to the Palestinians. With Israel's withdrawal from the West Bank, the UN forces would take Israel's place, and after some years, the inhabitants would express their will in a referendum as to the regime they wanted. This referendum would include the option for self-determination.

The problem of the 1948 Palestinian refugees was raised, said Vance, by only one Arab country, but he had no doubt that all the Arabs considered that these refugees should be given the right to choose between returning to their place of origin, namely Israel, or settling elsewhere and receiving compensation.

Vance said he found a unity of views on the procedural question: there was no point in going to Geneva without advance preparation. Thus, it was impossible to open the conference before November or December. The preliminary clarification could take place in New York during September, when the UN General Assembly would be in session. The deliberations should be undertaken through the medium of the United States by the system of 'proximity talks', since the Arabs were not prepared to sit with the Israelis face to face. This was also the intention of Sadat when he said, in a joint press conference with Vance, that a committee should meet in New York to prepare the ground for the Geneva Conference.

These Arab suggestions for preliminary talks appealed to Vance, and he had asked their leaders to present a draft proposal for a peace agreement as a basis for consideration at these talks. Vance requested that I, too, should come to New York in September to take part in these preliminary deliberations.

I told Vance that the gap between our position and that of the Arabs was very wide, and that in any case I was convinced that only one Arab State, Egypt, was perhaps ready, in principle, to come to terms with Israel. As for the other Arab countries, I suspected that any talk of peace with Israel was illusory. Syria wanted Israel destroyed, and her President would never sign his name to any document that gave recognition to her right to exist. Lebanon had no voice since she was under conquest by the Syrian army. Jordan was a small kingdom without courageous leadership. Hussein wished to preserve his throne and would fear an uprising from elements in the army and the Palestinians in his country. After the Rabat Conference's recognition by the Arab States of the PLO as the authorized representative of the Palestinian people, Hussein would prefer to remain on the sidelines.

Vance agreed that the positions taken by the Arabs were rigid and very far from ours. Nevertheless he spoke with no trace of weakness or despair. It was up to all parties, he said, to stop talking in generalities and enunciating principles and get down to practical proposals. If we did this, it might be possible to localize the differences of approach and to search for ways of bridging them.

Vance's meeting with the Prime Minister took place the following morning, with the participation, apart from Begin and myself, of five ministers: Deputy Premier Yigael Yadin, Defence Minister Ezer Weizman, Finance Minister Simcha Ehrlich, Interior Minister Yosef Burg, and Agriculture

Minister Arik Sharon. Also present were Legal Adviser Aharon Barak, Foreign Press Advisor Shmuel Katz, Chief of Staff General Motta Gur, and Chief of Operations General Raphael Eytan.

The first part of the meeting was given over to military affairs - the situation in Lebanon, and arms supplies to Israel. The generals then left and we moved on to political matters. We wished to build housing estates for the Palestinian refugees in Gaza who were living in crowded camps and tottering buildings, and we asked Vance for American financial help. The project was costly and Israel could not undertake it alone. Vance listened but said nothing. Nor did he accept our suggestion that he visit the Gaza Strip and see the camps for himself. He was no more forthcoming about our next proposal. Begin had asked that while the peace negotiations were under way the United States should refrain from repeating her view that Israel should return to the pre-1967 borders, with slight modifications. Vance confirmed that this subject had come up during his visits to the Arab countries and that he had been obliged to state that the United States' long-held position had not changed. That, he said, was the truth, and when he was asked about it he could not avoid giving them that answer.

The last subject we discussed was an American guarantee for the security of Israel. The Prime Minister emphasized that he was not asking for such a guarantee, but since various stories had appeared in the press, he would like to know Washington's position. Vance replied that this, too, had been raised by the Arab leaders he had just been meeting, and his reply had been that if a peace agreement were reached between Israel and the Arabs, and if, to consummate it, an American guarantee were required, he assumed it would be given. It would need a decision of the American Congress, but Vance thought the President would recommend it and Congress would approve.

The meeting ended at noon and Vance left the same day for Washington. He said he would report to the President on the stands of both sides and he hoped that the Foreign Ministers of both the Arab States and Israel would come to the United States as soon as possible so that they could begin the negotiations.

Vance had just completed two arduous weeks of travel from one capital to another, with long and tiring deliberations by day, followed by nightly consultations with his aides. Yet he showed no signs of fatigue. When I saw him off at the airport, I shook hands with a man full of energy, who was determined to bring the Arabs and Israel together in peace.

CHAPTER THREE

Secret Meetings

I would be seeing Vance again a month later, in Washington. That month, from mid-August to mid-September, was marked by a series of secret meetings which took me to India, Iran, England and Morocco. The first was somewhat odd, and not very important. The fourth augured the eventual peace treaty with Egypt.

I flew to New Delhi on 14 August 1977 for talks with India's newly elected Prime Minister, Moraji Desai. Israel has no diplomatic relations with India (though we maintain a consulate in Bombay), and it was not through diplomatic channels that the meeting was arranged. It came about through a chance encounter between two businessmen in an unlikely spot remote from the corridors of international politics.

An Israeli friend of mine, Azriel Eynav, is rather plump, and he had gone to England two months before and signed in at a 'health farm' in an effort to lose weight. (He lost more than forty pounds in five weeks, telling me later that all he had been allowed to eat was one grapefruit a day. He vowed never again to set foot in that accursed place!)

During his penance, he met there an Indian businessman with a more positive approach to shedding weight. He had been there thirteen weeks (and dropped from three hundred to two hundred pounds). This Indian, he said, had many visitors, most of them fellow Indians who held important positions in their country. One, indeed, was Finance Minister in the Government of Indira Gandhi, who was in power at the time. The Indian was quite frank about the reason for their visits: they wanted him to contribute handsomely to the election campaign funds of their political parties. He said he was close to the leaders of both parties in India, and if Indira lost the current elections, which he predicted, an associate of his would be given a key portfolio in the new Government.

During the weeks they were at the 'farm', Eynav and his Indian companion considered the possibility of doing business together. When the 'health' course was over, Eynav went to India and found that his acquaintance had made an accurate forecast. There *was* a change of Government, Indira Gandhi was out, Moraji Desai was the new Prime Minister, and the Indian took my friend to see him. At that talk, the Prime Minister said he would like to help Israel and the Arabs make peace. Eynav suggested that I come to India to meet him, and Moraji Desai agreed.

When Eynav returned to Israel and told me of the invitation, I said I would need it in writing. Soon after, I received a signal from New Delhi saying that the Prime Minister would be pleased to receive me at his home on 14 August.

I had two purposes in meeting the Indian Premier. One was to explain Israel's views on possible peace arrangements to be discussed at the projected Geneva Conference. The other was to seek an improvement in India–Israel diplomatic relations. Premier Begin approved my journey, and reported it to the Cabinet at its session the previous day. It was, of course, to remain secret – at India's urgent request.

I boarded an Alitalia plane – since there was no El Al service to India – and after a six-hour flight landed in Bombay. There I was awaited by the Prime Minister's personal plane (a Tupolev 114 jet) for the onward journey to New Delhi. The aircraft was full of Indian secret servicemen. Indeed, the security arrangements were tighter than any I had known. They told me this was both to protect me – and to ensure the secrecy of my visit! So careful were they that when we took off, we flew low, and left the main air corridor, to give the impression that we would be landing at a local airfield. Only a little later did we gain height and proceed to our destination. The land looked beautiful from the air, an expanse of green criss-crossed by networks of canals and ditches. But when we landed, the sight near the airport was dismal – a jungle of hovels crowded with exhausted, emaciated and bedraggled humanity.

It was 4 in the afternoon when we reached the secluded private guest-house, commodious and well furnished, with only a single fault: the mattresses in the bedrooms were stiff boards. True, they were innocent of nails, but they were harder than the earth in the fields of Israel.

The meeting with the Prime Minister was set for 7.30 that evening at Government House, a quarter of an hour's drive away. Moraji Desai was waiting for me in the visitors' room, a bare chamber of demonstrative modesty, the walls unadorned, the floor uncarpeted, and only a small table, a sofa and a few ordinary chairs for furniture. There was also a simplicity about the dress of my host and of the Foreign Minister, who joined us a few minutes later. Both wore the traditional plain white gown.

The Prime Minister asked me to sit next to him on the sofa, and after we were served tea, I gave him greetings from Premier Begin and also a copy of a book of mine that had been published shortly before I took office. Moraji Desai looked at the cover, and before opening it asked me the price. I replied ten dollars. 'Oh,' he exclaimed, 'expensive'.

We settled down to our talk. During the plane flight, I had prepared in my mind how to broach the subjects I was anxious to discuss. I would review the problems of attaining peace with our Arab neighbours, and I would then urge the strengthening of ties between our two countries, with the establishment of diplomatic relations, and the opening of an Indian embassy in Israel and an Israeli embassy in India.

But I never got to utter my preliminary remarks. As soon as I thanked him for receiving me, Moraji Desai began his talk. 'Why do you think I was anxious to meet you?' he asked, and immediately followed with the answer. It was because he was interested in peace in our region. Sadat had been to see him and had explained the situation, so that there was no need, he said, for me to go over it again. The facts were known to him. But he wanted to give me his views. 'You must make peace with the Arabs. The Israelis have suffered from the Nazis and from persecution in Europe, but the Palestinians should not be made to pay for that.' The refugees had to be settled, and we had to withdraw from the occupied territories, which would then be proclaimed a Palestinian State.

The Prime Minister continued:

I told Sadat that one could not turn the clock back, that Israel was now an established fact, and that you, the Arabs, must guarantee her existence; but Israel must make possible the rise of a Palestinian State. Yasser Arafat, head of the PLO, wanted to return to Israel, but this should not be done, for it would mean the liquidation of the State of Israel. Incidentally, how many are you? Two million Jews? Therefore, the solution is to establish a Palestinian State in the Arab territories which you will evacuate.

It was clear that on Israel's withdrawal and the emergence of a Palestinian State, he had reached final conclusions.

The Prime Minister was equally firm about the question of India–Israel relations. India, he said, was unable to take any step, however insignificant, to improve them. The Indian people would rise up against any such step. Only after Israel managed to reach a peace agreement with the Arabs would India establish full diplomatic relations with us. India had been mistaken, he said, in not having done this at the very outset, when Nehru had come to power with India's independence. But this mistaken policy could not now be changed. He could not even allow a second consulate – in addition to the one we had in Bombay – to be opened in New Delhi. India had seventy million Moslems, and even the non-Moslems were not sympathetic to Israel. If the news of my visit to him now were to be published, he said, he would be out of office. He had taken the risk of inviting me only because he was anxious to advance the prospect of Arab-Israel peace.

It was now my turn. I explained why we could not agree to a Palestinian State, and why the solution to the Arab refugees was to settle them in the lands where they dwelt at present – in the same way as we had absorbed and settled the 850,000 Jews who had come to Israel from the Arab States in which they had lived. I then reacted pretty sharply to what he had said about India-Israel relations. If he was so anxious to help in the achievement of Arab-Israel peace, he should ensure equality of relations with both parties. Otherwise, there was no point in discussing the matter with him, for his words would have no influence upon us. Now, when his help was needed on behalf of peace, he could do nothing, since he had no diplomatic relations with Israel; and once peace was attained, and India were to establish such relations, its help would no longer be necessary.

The Prime Minister smiled when I said this, but his mind remained unchanged. I suggested that his Foreign Minister pay a visit to our region, to both the Arab States and Israel. No, he said, his Foreign Minister could not visit Israel, even anonymously. The only thing he agreed to was further talks with him, as well as meetings between his Foreign Minister and me when we would both be in Europe or the United States in September and October of that year. It was agreed that I would be in touch with them at the appropriate time.

Although we found no accord on a single subject, the atmosphere was cordial.

We turned to world affairs, and he had some interesting things to say about the Soviet Union and his meetings with Khrushchev, Brezhnev, Kosygin and Gromyko, stressing that he was not a communist but a democrat. He sought to strengthen ties with the United States. When I mentioned Burma, he said he wished to do the same with that country, and in fact his Foreign Minister was leaving next day for Rangoon.

As he saw me to the car at the end of the meeting, he expressed the hope that we would meet again soon. His English, incidentally, was excellent, but the Indian accent was strange to my ears, and at times it was difficult to catch what he was saying.

Despite his age – he was eighty-two – he was alert and sharp. He knew what he wanted and showed a certain impatience when listening to counter-arguments, for he knew that anyway he would not accept them. His aides told me without any embarrassment that for many years now he had isolated himself from women and had thus kept his vigour. The only relative close to him and who was always with him was his forty-eight-year-old son, who said that when they walked together he found it hard to keep up with his father.

I did not know what the people of India thought of him, but I was impressed by his personality, though not by his intellectual integrity. When he spoke of Israeli matters, he took a moralizing tone, insisting that 'peace is more important than anything else', and demanding that the Palestinian refugees should be given a homeland. He airily dismissed any practical counter-argument. But when it came to diplomatic relations with Israel, he did not hesitate to resort to practical arguments and take the easy way out. To his credit, however, it must be said that he made no attempt to delude me, nor did he indulge in ambiguities. Simple, modest and unpretentious in his ways, he wore an air of sanctity, but with it all he was tough and practical, with his feet firmly planted on the ground. Incidentally, I noticed that when he resorted to arguments which he knew to be insincere, he signalled the fact by a mischievous smile.

When we returned to our quarters, we were served with what one could call an Anglo-Indian dinner – drinks in the English manner and spicy Indian food. I felt my innards burning, but the fire was quenched by the Cassata ice-cream.

August in India is the hottest month of a hot year, and though my room was air-conditioned it was scarcely noticeable. The main cooling came from giant fans, like aircraft propellers and almost as noisy, that spun, though more slowly, from an attachment to the ceiling. The way to keep cool was to sleep without sheets or pyjamas, and expose the body to the breeze from the fans. Sleep was difficult, and I tried to get the BBC wave-length on the radio, but without success. The only audible station was something called 'The Voice of the Covenant' (I think from Amsterdam) that explained in excellent Hebrew that the Jews should understand correctly the biblical Book of Daniel, accept the New Testament and convert to Christianity. With the help of this Dutch programme – and a pill – I slept.

Early in the morning, and in the finest British tradition to which India clings to this day, I was awakened with a cup of strong tea. Over breakfast I listened to the local radio news and heard of increased fighting in Lebanon (with the Christians in their enclave supported by Israeli artillery). There was also a statement by President Carter that the United States would help, influence, advise and put forward her own programme to resolve the conflict in the Middle East. The same bulletin carried a review of the world press, and quoted the report from a Jordanian paper of an eight-point proposal by

Cyrus Vance, the key point being what Moraji Desai had kept thrusting at me the previous evening: Israel's withdrawal, and the establishment of a Palestinian State. Even if this report were incorrect, I had no doubt that we would face very grave differences with the United States. However, I considered that our situation was sound. The territories were in our hands; and our relations with the Arab inhabitants were such that we could continue to live with them even without a peace agreement. Our bargaining position was strong as long as we kept our nerve.

That day happened to be the thirtieth anniversary of India's independence, and it was celebrated with an address by the Prime Minister followed by an official reception to which, of course, I could not be invited. The speech was delivered before a crowd of 80,000 in the stadium at seven o'clock in the morning, the very hour at which, thirty years earlier, the British had handed over their rule to the Indians themselves. My hosts observed wryly that the point of the British saying that they ruled 'an empire on which the sun never sets' was that 'in the dark you can't trust the British'. Britain, they said, now held second-class rank in India; but I wondered how they felt about her prime place being taken by the United States and the Soviet Union.

I had to wait until dusk before returning to Israel, so I spent the afternoon on a brief drive round the city and its environs. But I did not enjoy it as much as I might have done had I been allowed to get out of the car, walk the streets and mingle with the people.

At dusk I flew to Bombay, again in the Prime Minister's plane, and from there by commercial flight to Israel. Before leaving, my hosts wished to give me a parting gift – ancient silver tableware – but I refused to accept it, and hope they were not insulted.

The only useful thing about meeting India's Premier was the fact of our having met. As far as I knew, the only other time an Israeli minister had talked to an Indian Prime Minister was twenty-one years earlier, in 1956, when Moshe Sharett and Mordechai Bentov had met Jawaharlal Nehru at an international socialist conference. Moreover, if indeed Moraji Desai meant what he said, this meeting would be followed by others, if not with him at least with his Foreign Minister during the UN General Assembly meeting in New York.

It was an interesting visit, but it seemed to me that if I had spent my life as a professional diplomat I would have felt frustrated. Not that I or Israel was demeaned or humiliated, but the fact could not be ignored that I had asked India to establish diplomatic relations with us and she had refused. However, the unpleasantness was soon stifled by switching my mind to the abundant, positive, Israeli experiences that have given us rich and creative lives of achievement and victory, building a land and a society with our own hands and relying on our own strength – without being patronized by India.

On the return journey, as on the outward flight, I wore dark glasses and a large straw hat of the kind often seen on an American golf course, satisfied in my mind that I would not be recognized. Of course there was no logical reason for such a hat on a night flight from Bombay, but who would notice? I had barely settled myself down for a nap, confident in the effectiveness of my 'cover', when one of the passengers without any show of surprise came up to me with a 'Good evening, Mr Dayan' and asked for my autograph. I regret to record that I sent him packing, and he left rather embarrassed. How could I explain that my anger was directed not at him but at myself for having failed in my 'Operation Disguise', which I had thought was perfect.

I was off again two days later, this time to Teheran for meetings with the Shah to clarify certain economic and political matters. We had met before, when I was Minister of Agriculture and Israel was providing technical aid for the development of several branches of farming in Iran. (This was not publicized, as the Iranians did not wish our relationship to be official – or even known. We had an ambassador, but he was called 'the diplomatic representative', and our embassy bore no plaque on the gate. Nor was it listed in the diplomatic handbook of the Iranian Foreign Office.)

I left Israel after dark in a military aircraft on 18 August and reached Teheran shortly before midnight. The Minister for Protocol received us at the airport and took us to our quarters, where waiters dressed in white soon appeared in the central lounge to serve us fragrant tea and replenish the bowls of fruit and the country's celebrated pistachio nuts on the side tables. Despite the hour, I met with our ambassador and some of his staff to review the subjects I would be discussing with the Shah.

As I drove to the palace in the morning for our meeting at ten, I recalled our earlier meetings, and remembered how interested he was in raising the standards and output of his farmers, and how knowledgeable about the new crops we were helping him to introduce. There was one occasion when his Agriculture Minister, who had joined us, produced figures of the quantity of water required to raise cotton. They happened to be wrong. Before I could open my mouth, the Shah corrected him, giving the proper amount.

At the palace I was shown into a study and was soon joined by the Shah, who greeted me like an old friend. He seemed to have changed little. He was lean and upright as ever, his face unwrinkled. Only the streaks of grey in his hair betrayed the passage of time.

There were just the two of us at this meeting, and he spoke with complete frankness. The first topic was a proposal we had put up for a joint Iranian–Israeli industrial project, and I wanted to know where it stood. The Shah said that the US Ambassador had told him he knew of it and had received Washington's approval in general terms. However, the Ambassador had also said that Israel had not yet supplied the Americans with the required specifications, and so America could not yet determine its final position on the matter. I told the Shah that I had myself reported the proposal to Secretary Cyrus Vance. The Shah's response was that co-operation between Israel and Iran was a political not a technical matter. He had discussed it with his ministers and it was clear that he could not enter into any joint undertakings with us without the blessing and support of the United States. Thus, until it was certain that the Americans had no objection, he could not conclude any joint arrangement with us. He had instructed his officials to clarify the issue with the American Ambassador, but he wished me to know that if the Americans were opposed to such Iranian–Israeli co-operation, his reply to me would have to be negative.

'Your Majesty,' I said, 'you will certainly realize that if, as a result of such co-operation, your country acquires the technical knowledge of industrial production, you will have taken a very constructive step – laid the foundations for a modern industry – and you will have done it yourselves.' His eyes lit up: this was what he wanted desperately. But then they clouded over. 'You must understand', he said sadly, 'that we are in the same position as Israel, dependent upon the United States; and I must be sure of their support before taking a step which might involve us in serious political risks.'

There was little point in continuing with this subject. I had said all there was to say, and the decision now rested with him. We moved on to more general matters.

The Shah told me he had problems with Turkey over the Kurds. He himself was willing to help the Kurds secure autonomy, and even more, but the Turks objected. They had a large Kurdish population, and feared an upsurge of nationalist sentiments.

He then had some advice for me. On no account should we agree to a Palestinian State, he said, even if Yasser Arafat was the 'good man' some Arab leaders maintained. One could not know who would succeed him. The whole PLO was a bad institution, not to be trusted.

He was equally scathing about the Saudis. Everything in Saudi Arabia was riddled with bribery and corruption. The Americans, he added bitterly, depended on them, not knowing that they were a broken reed. Indeed, US policy in the Middle East in general was shortsighted. 'If I thought the Americans might seek Saudi agreement before supplying me with planes, I'd fling the aircraft back in their faces. If they don't want to sell me arms, they can go to the devil. I can always renew my ties with the Soviet Union.'

He was in a fury, and his words sprang from resentment and humiliation rather than sober political evaluation. When he had cooled down, he repeated what he had said earlier. 'I know I have no option, and in spite of all I must go with the United States.'

He was also bitter about Europe. The press there was full of libellous articles about Iran, he said, and it was particularly vicious over the electric power difficulties the country was experiencing. This was true. Even Teheran was inadequately served, and entire quarters were left for hours without lighting. 'But who is responsible?' he asked. 'We paid vast sums to European companies to build us power stations. They signed contracts, received the cash, but failed to deliver the goods.' This was also true of the great American corporations. 'There are contracts, but no electricity. They take money, fail to do the job, and then their newspapers make fun of us. They attack the regime in Iran for being backward, and say the Shah is incapable of doing anything for his country.'

The Shah this time was different in one major respect from the man I remembered at our meetings several years earlier. He now seemed remote from the day-to-day problems of his own country, yet very much concerned with developments in other countries. I listened intently to all he said, and this apparently encouraged him to give me a world political tour, speaking at length on what was happening in Africa, in the Far East – Vietnam, China, India – and, of course, in the oil States of the Persian Gulf. I cannot say I was impressed. He was a man of undoubted intelligence. He read widely, travelled extensively, and had met the leaders of East and West. Yet, as against his expert knowledge of the Middle East, his political analysis of the situation in other regions of the world was shallow, and accompanied by criticism and complaint.

This was directed particularly against the United States. The Americans failed to foresee or grasp the implications of Russia's moves and her growing influence, and had taken no counter-measures. The Shah did not explain what he thought America should do. Nor, to my mind, did he understand the character and popular mood of the American people, and the weight of their influence on their Government, especially after the *débâcle* in Vietnam. The Shah also had little praise for the heads of the European Governments and of the Arab States. Listening to him, one might have imagined that all they needed to do to impose their will was wave a wand.

I left Teheran with the feeling that his many years on the throne had left the Shah with only a tenuous grasp of reality.

*   *   *

Three days after the talk in Teheran, I flew to England for a meeting with King Hussein of Jordan. After an exchange of messages through indirect channels, the King agreed to meet me in London, which he was about to visit, and we set the date for Monday, 22 August, so that I could attend our weekly Cabinet session on the Sunday. It was just as well that the appointment was arranged for 9.30 in the evening, for my plane developed engine trouble after leaving Israel on a direct flight, and was diverted to Paris. There we had a delay of several hours because of a strike by the air control staff at London's Heathrow airport. I managed to get to the rendezvous just in time.

The holding of the meeting was to be secret – not for my benefit but for that of the King. (I am at liberty to disclose it now only because it has since been published.) As I was advised that the secret was to be kept even from the British – which also meant officers of the Special Branch assigned as my bodyguards – I unfortunately had to mislead them. I drove from my hotel to a house, where I stayed a few moments, and left by a back door to another car that awaited me. I then continued to a private home where Hussein and I were to meet. I had been there some years before, on a similar purpose, and already knew the owner.

King Hussein was late, and he apologized as he greeted me with a handshake and a broad smile. He had had guests, he explained, and could not get away until they had left. I found him greatly changed, not in appearance but in spirit. It was not the same man I had last seen. He was now withdrawn, subdued, without sparkle, and the political topics I raised did not seem to touch him deeply. His language was clipped, his answers to my questions often monosyllabic, rarely more than Yes and No, without clear explanatory enlargement. His depression may have been due to the tragic death of his wife, who had been killed shortly before in a helicopter crash. Or it may have sprung from one of the decisions of the Rabat Conference of Arab States, of which he was bitterly critical. This was the decision to recognize the PLO as the sole authorized representative of the Palestinians and withdraw that role from Hussein. Now, he said, he was concerning himself exclusively with administering the East Bank of the river – his Kingdom of Jordan. He was neither able nor anxious to clash with the Arab countries and the PLO on this matter. If they did not want him, they could run the affairs of the Palestinians without him.

Was Hussein, I wondered, still the King of Jordan or only the shadow of a ruler? Was he really looking after his country or was he spending most of his time gallivanting abroad? At all events, his attitude towards the subject of our discussion – the attempt to find a suitable and agreed arrangement for the problem of the West Bank and the Gaza Strip – seemed to be one of indifference.

We parted after about an hour and a half, and I did not expect to see him again for some time. To my surprise, our host of the evening telephoned me the next morning to say that the King would like to continue our talk, and we met again at 4 that afternoon. There was nothing particularly new in what he had to say this time, but he probably felt that he might not have been sufficiently explicit in our first talk, and in order to avoid any misunderstanding on my part he had decided to make his position clear.

He did. He had no intention of taking any initiative on matters relating to the Palestinians. He felt a deep obligation to help them. Most of the inhabitants of Jordan were Palestinians, with strong family, economic and sentimental ties with the West Bank: thus, if they were to turn to him, he would respond. But he was no longer their representative, and he would not try to force himself upon them.

Yet for me, this second talk turned out to be very important; for apart from repeating his approach to the Palestinians, he also clarified for me his stand on the possible division of the West Bank between Jordan and Israel. Did he think such a plan might serve as the basis for an Israel–Jordan peace treaty? I asked and received not only an unequivocal answer but also an instructive lesson. He rejected it out of hand. A peace arrangement based on the division of the West Bank would mean that he, Hussein, would agree that part of it was to be joined to the State of Israel. I had to understand, he said, that he, as an Arab monarch, could not propose to the people of even a single Arab village that they cut themselves off from their brother Arabs and become Israelis. His agreement to such a plan would be regarded as treachery. He would be charged with 'selling' Arab land to the Jews so that he could enlarge his own kingdom.

Moreover, he continued, we had to know that not a single Arab in the West Bank or Gaza would willingly seek to become an Israeli. Anyone who sought to introduce such a plan could do so only by force of arms. Was it not clear to us that those Arabs in that part of the West Bank which would be attached to Israel were not the only ones who would rise up against us? All the Arab States would do so too. The sole solution in order to attain peace, he said, was for Israel to return to the pre-June 1967 borders.

He could not give up any part of the West Bank that Jordan had controlled (since his grandfather, King Abdullah, had annexed it). He could not even concede Mount Scopus, the original site of the Hebrew University campus and the Hadassah Hospital, which had always been within Israel's control. He added, however, that it was possible to find suitable practical arrangements whereby the Israelis could have access to these institutions and run them without interference. But on the question of sovereignty, we had to restore to Jordan all the territory we had captured in the 1967 Six Day War.

I raised the question of the PLO and of the establishment of an independent Palestine State. I said I assumed that such a State would be inimical to his interests, since the PLO would undermine his throne. Hussein did not refute my assumption, but he showed no inclination to discuss it. He simply said, with frankness, that his representative at the United Nations would not say anything different from what was said by the other Arab ambassadors. Jordan's official position on the Palestinians was the same as that of all the Arab States. In the past, Jordan had been the official spokesman of the Palestinians, and the West Bank was under her authority. This function and status had been cancelled at the Rabat Conference.

What then, I asked, would he like to see happen in the West Bank? 'Let the Palestinians do what they want,' he replied. He could live without them. He had no ambitions, and would take no measures, direct or indirect, to get involved. His watchword, in replies to all my other questions on this topic, was that the Palestinians could do what they wished without him.

An Israel–Jordan peace treaty was the central subject of our talk, but we also had an exchange on another matter. I asked him about the future of the half-a-million Palestinian refugees in his country, living in camps outside Amman, his capital. He replied that he was prepared to absorb them as permanent settlers in Jordan, but that required vast means for huge housing projects as well as the creation of sources of employment. He himself lacked the resources, and America's financial aid was inadequate.

I finally asked Hussein about the refugees in Lebanon. Did the Palestinians there disdain Lebanese citizenship or did the Lebanese refuse to grant it? Both, he replied. The Palestinians did not want Lebanese papers, and were themselves not wanted by the Lebanese.

I returned to Israel with no tidings of salvation in my knapsack. But I now knew better what we could expect from Jordan – or rather what we could not expect. I was to have a more fruitful experience two weeks later, after a secret meeting with another Arab ruler, which heightened the prospect of a peace arrangement with a neighbouring country more important than Jordan – a prospect that was eventually fulfilled.

CHAPTER FOUR

Rendezvous in Morocco

On the bright and sunny afternoon of Sunday, 4 September 1977, I set out on what was to be the first of three secret visits to an Arab ruler, King Hassan of Morocco. It was not his first meeting with a representative of the Israeli Government; but now that there was a new Government in office, headed by Menachem Begin, the earlier contact was being renewed, and I received an invitation from the King. Begin approved my journey and we agreed on the points I was to present at the meeting. Our principal purpose was to try to secure Hassan's help in arranging for us to meet directly and hold peace talks with Egyptian representatives.

I attended the regular weekly Cabinet meeting as usual on that Sunday morning, and stayed almost to the end. I then excused myself, left Jerusalem and drove to a military airfield. Somewhere *en route* we stopped and I changed cars, getting into a large station wagon with curtained windows. There, under expert hands, I was transformed out of all recognition. Pressed upon my skull was the mane of a beatnik; my upper lip was adorned with the moustache of a dandy; and on the bridge of my nose rested large dark sunglasses. It was beneath this outrageous disguise that I reached the airfield, stepped out of the car and into the plane.

First stop was Paris, where I emerged from the Israeli aircraft and boarded a Moroccan plane that was standing by. We took off without delay. Inside the comfortable, executive-type jet, I raised the arm rests, tilted the seat back and dozed. I was so tired that not even the French cheeses and red wine we were offered could tempt me out of the blanket in which I had wrapped myself.

We landed at Fez, and from there were driven to a resort city in the Atlas mountains where the King has his summer residence. We reached the guest-house, close to the palace, at 10 p.m., so it was only at dawn next morning that I could see the surroundings. The resort is beautiful, set amidst forest and greenery, and bearing something of the style of a Swiss mountain village, with the buildings and cottages topped by red-tiled gabled roofs which extend in a steep angle beyond the walls almost to the ground. The altitude of the Atlas range and the cool climate – there is much snow and rain in winter – give the scenery a European appearance, as though it were part of another planet flung by magic into an arid region. The guest-house was pleasant and spacious. I was much taken by the furniture of heavy, rough-grained cedar wood, matching the rafters and the window frames, and exuding a pleasing aroma. Cedar retains its perfume even after the wood has dried.

I was to meet the King that night, and so we could spend the day sight-seeing. We drove back to Fez and were flown from there to Marrakesh. Greeting us as we stepped down from the plane was the regional governor. He had no idea who we were, but he had been told to expect the guests of the Crown, and after the traditional coffee he took us on a tour of the area. We passed extensive groves of olives and palm trees, skirted a huge pool, and came upon the ruins of past palaces and the rose-red walls that enclose the city and its suburbs. Rose is the prevailing colour, for the bricks are fashioned from the reddish soil of the region, and even the modern concrete buildings were painted in this colour. We lunched handsomely in the hotel, the royal treatment well up to the highest traditions of Arab hospitality, although our host did not himself partake of food. It was the month of Ramadan, when pious Moslems are allowed to eat only after the sun goes down.

We spent the afternoon at the bazaar. I had first been there twenty-four years earlier, in 1953, when I was on my way to England to attend a senior army officers' course and had stopped off in Morocco to see the country. My impression of the Marrakesh bazaar had remained etched in my memory, and when I saw it now as a much older man I was in no way disillusioned. I thought then, and I saw now, that it was indeed the most interesting bazaar and market-place I had ever seen, larger and more vibrant than those in Teheran or Damascus. Despite the fast of Ramadan, it hummed with people, great crowds of them, filling and moving down the alleys in endless streams. The Berbers, men of the mountains, are tall and handsome, the young women erect and slender, their unveiled faces bright and clear. Sitting in the arts and crafts shops set in the alley walls were young children weaving carpets and embroidering galabiyas (cloaks), beating out copper, shaping and engraving silver vessels, and carving wood from the scented cedar.

The wide and open market centre was thronged with men and women ranged in circles round the varied wonder-workers, story-tellers, and fast-talking bargain salesmen offering embroidered gowns, strings of beads and bangles. One old man attracted a crowd with a cobra that rose slowly from its basket as he played a tune on his flute. Near by, a withered Berber in tattered clothes kept a group spellbound with a gripping tale of suspense, recited in an unexpectedly powerful voice with accompanying histrionic gestures. But the ones which drew the largest audiences were the fortune-tellers and the sellers of amulets, talismans, special perfumes and lucky charms guaranteeing romance, pregnancy, success – and evil to one's enemies. I could not always follow the Moroccan Arabic, but the expressions of curiosity, eagerness, or joy on the faces of the crowds made verbal explanations superfluous.

Reluctantly I dragged myself away shortly before dusk, bade farewell to my host, and emplaned for the royal guest-house in the mountains.

The opening meeting with the King was held at 8.30 in the evening, when I was ushered into his presence for a private talk which lasted an hour and a half. We were then joined by our aides, and sat down to a festive, though one-sided, meal, for it was only we, the Israelis, who ate heartily. The Moroccans, having fasted during the day, had had their dinner at sundown, which took the edge off their appetite. Despite the royal presence – perhaps because of it – the talk was free and informal, without the restraints of protocol, though it was not entirely candid.

Far more candid had been our private pre-dinner meeting, when we were alone, without an interpreter. The King was open, amiable, articulate and direct. Though I had not mentioned it, he apparently felt it necessary to explain his special position, and problem, as an intermediary between us and the Arabs, and as host to an official representative of the Government of Israel. Perhaps to make me feel more at ease, he opened with the following remark: 'If it became known that you were here, my throne would not topple. I have a large Jewish community in Morocco. I am popular with them, and to me they are loyal Moroccan citizens. I speak openly about my contacts with the Jews and my earnest desire for peace between the Arab States and Israel.' He also thought it necessary to apologize for the absence of his Foreign Minister. He was away, he said, in Cairo, attending a meeting of Arab Foreign Ministers. At the same time, when the conversation turned to the 1973 Yom Kippur War, he emphasized that a Moroccan brigade had fought together with the Syrians against us in the Golan Heights, and he was taking a considerable risk by meeting with members of the Israeli Government.

Even after he had offered his explanations, it was not clear to me what special reason – if there was one – had prompted him to undertake his peace efforts, for after all there was no confrontation between his country and mine. I got the impression that he was a do-gooder by nature, and though Western-educated, he was thoroughly conversant with, and active in, the affairs of the Arab world.

No effort was required on my part to raise the subject that was the purpose of my visit. After his preliminary remarks, it was the King himself who said he had looked forward to our meeting in order to hear my views on the central and decisive issue in the Middle East: 'How do we make peace?' I told him we had problems with Arab groups who differed among themselves in their approach to this issue. There were, for example, the Syrians. It was my basic assumption that President Assad, because of his radicalism, did not in his heart of hearts wish to make peace with Israel, and did not wish to see the Israeli flag fluttering from the staff of an Israeli embassy in Damascus.

This brought me to the principal point of the discussion. I explained to the King that there seemed to be two contradictory problems. On the one hand, not a single Arab country would wish to make peace with us on its own, namely, without the other Arab States. Even if a feasible solution were found, for example, for the problems between us and Egypt, Egypt would be unwilling to sign a separate peace. On the other hand, securing a comprehensive peace in the whole of the Middle East was so complex that it was impossible to achieve a simultaneous peace arrangement with all the Arab States. We were thus enclosed in a vicious circle. To my mind, I said, we could break out of the ring by concluding an agreement with some of the Arab States, perhaps not publicly at the beginning, perhaps at first without an exchange of ambassadors, and seeking gradually to meet the other problems one by one until we reached open, comprehensive peace treaties with all. The form of this first step would be a kind of gentleman's agreement, accompanied by an exchange of letters with the Americans. These letters, addressed to the President of the United States, would commit the parties to fulfil the agreement between them.

The King thought this idea had practical possibilities, but what I felt was particularly important was his promise to do all he could to arrange a meeting between us and an Egyptian political representative. I told him we would welcome a meeting at the highest level. It could be with Hosni Mubarak, Sadat's Vice-President, or even with Sadat himself, but whoever it was, it had to be someone with authority who was conversant with the subject. The counterpart on our side would be the Prime Minister or myself.

The King promised a reply within five days. He would send a trusted emissary to Cairo immediately to examine the prospects, so that if the Egyptians agreed, the meeting could take place before my visit to Washington and New York (to attend the UN General Assembly) later that month, or on the way back.

During dinner, at which our aides were present, the King referred to the possibility of such a meeting and he was optimistic. He then expressed his conviction that Syria's Assad, too, would eventually agree to meet us; but that, he quickly added, had to be kept strictly secret. I gathered that King Hassan thought highly of Assad. I told him that we had had no contact with him so far, and that all our attempts to meet him had failed. I mentioned the Arab representatives at the United Nations, and the King agreed that they were of no real calibre and that talking to them was of no practical value. It would not lead to negotiations.

As to the Palestinians, it was Hassan's judgment that we would be unable to reach an arrangement with them. If a Jordinian–Palestinian federation were to arise, the Palestinians would be in the majority, and they would soon kick out King Hussein. Indeed, any solution of the Palestine problem within the framework of the Kingdom of Jordan would lead to the loss of the throne, and so Hussein would assuredly withhold his agreement. It was evident that Hassan regarded himself as belonging to 'the League of Arab Kings', and his approach to this issue was primarily monarchic.

We also spoke of wars and weaponry. I asked Hassan why he had despatched an expeditionary force to fight with the Syrians against us in the Golan Heights, and what had happened to the Moroccan unit in the Yom Kippur War. He replied that he was part of the Arab nation. The Egyptians had turned to him and he had responded. In another context, he said that Nasser had not been a man of integrity, and had misled both his friends and his enemies; but Sadat was different.

I returned to Israel next morning, reported to the Prime Minister on my talk, and we awaited Hassan's signal on a possible meeting with a representative from Egypt.

It came quickly. The King had been as good as his word, and on 9 September, four days after I had left Morocco, we received his message that the Egyptians agreed to a high-level meeting as soon as possible. The proposed participants could be Egypt's President Sadat and Israel's Prime Minister Begin, or Egyptian Deputy Premier Hassan Tuhami and me. I thought both levels had their advantages and drawbacks. If we started at the lower rung and reached an impasse, it could be dealt with at the higher level, whereas an immediate impasse at the top would be more difficult to break. On the other hand, a President–Prime Minister meeting could be immediately fruitful since both leaders had the authority to take decisions on the spot. I could hardly propose to the Prime Minister that he leave it to me and Tuhami, and so I recommended that he meet Sadat.

That was the signal that was sent to King Hassan: the meeting would be between Israel's Prime Minister and Egypt's President. But the Egyptians then said they would prefer it at the lower level. My meeting with Egypt's

Deputy Premier was accordingly set for the night of 16 September in Morocco, so that I could proceed from there to Washington where talks had been previously scheduled with the State Department.

I left Israel the day before, together with my wife Rahel and officials from the Foreign Ministry, and flew to Brussels. There I met first with representatives of the Jewish community, and later conferred with our ambassadors in the European capitals. Next morning I had a breakfast meeting with the Belgian Foreign Minister, and then called on General Alexander Haig, the NATO commander, who was an old friend. We had first met in 1966 when I spent a month in Vietnam. He was then a battalion commander, and I visited his unit, and even went out on a jungle patrol with his men. Some years later, he took over from Haldeman (who was forced to leave after the Watergate revelations) as Chief of Staff to President Nixon. I was then Minister of Defence in Golda Meir's Government, and we had had frequent opportunities to discuss the problems of Israel and the Middle East. He left the White House upon his appointment to the NATO command, and we saw each other in Europe from time to time to exchange views on current political and military events. We did the same now. Haig wanted to know about the character of the Begin Government and the prospects of peace with the Arabs. I told him I was optimistic as far as Egypt was concerned, adding that I thought Sadat now wanted peace rather than another war.

From Haig's office I went before the television cameras for interviews with Belgian and French correspondents, and then, with Rahel and the rest of my party, set off for the airport – and on an evasive operation. While they continued to the air terminal and boarded a plane for New York, my car turned off the highway into a side street and I was taken to a private house. There I was again submitted to wig, moustache and sunglasses, taken out through a back door, driven to where another car was waiting, brought by that car to yet another vehicle, and after a further exchange of cars we set out for Paris. Since it had been arranged for us to reach the French capital only after 4 p.m., at dusk, we could take the journey slowly. We even had time to stop for a picnic lunch. It would indeed have been a pleasant drive through the countryside had it not been for the beastly wig and moustache. They irritated my skin, as they had on the first occasion, and above all affected my eye, which went red and kept watering. The inflammation persisted despite the frequent use of eyedrops, and gave me cause for anxiety.

Our Moroccan friends were waiting for us when we reached Paris and they drove us straight to their plane. I was given my familiar seat, and we took off on the three-hour flight, this time not to Fez but to Rabat. There I was installed in a guest suite of the royal palace, a spacious affair decorated from floor to rafters in oriental style. The huge rose-red bathroom had matching towels, and cupboards and shelves filled with a variety of cologne and perfume bottles and creams. The bedroom, too, lacked nothing (except for books, journals or writing paper, of which there was no trace), the tables laden with a variety of bonbons, cakes and fruits, impressive in colour and fragrance.

I showered, shaved, replaced my disguise, and went to join my aides in one of the palace drawing rooms. Our meeting had been scheduled for 8 p.m., but we were then informed that it would be a few minutes later as the Egyptian representative, Dr Hassan Tuhami, wished to have a private talk with the King before we met. The 'few minutes' lasted an hour, and we were then driven to another royal building where the meeting, and dinner, were to be held. When we got there, I slipped into a side room, removed my disguise, replaced my eye-patch, and breathed with relief. I then entered the meeting-chamber to find myself in the company of the King, Dr Tuhami, and a distinguished group of top-ranking Moroccans. I had only one other Israeli with me, our liaison man with Morocco.

The King welcomed me warmly, and after the exchange of greetings I presented him with a Canaanite sword and an arrowhead of bronze, both from the second millennium BC. As he examined them, I remarked that before the invention of the Phantom and the Mig, empires were conquered by those weapons. And it was with such weaponry that the Israelites, some forty years after their Exodus from Egypt, had subdued the petty Kingdoms of Canaan and the neighbouring countries in the late thirteenth and early twelfth centuries BC. The King thanked me with an appropriate and felicitous observation: 'These weapons are a reminder of past wars. The time has now arrived to make peace.'

I was formally introduced to Dr Tuhami, a man of impressive appearance, with a neatly clipped silvery beard that belied a youthful ebullience. Exuding an air of self-confidence and authority, and using a tone that verged on the aggressive, as though he were reacting to an affront, he said he had a message from President Sadat that he wished to read to me. He did so, in clear and precise diction. It contained the overall conditions for an Egyptian peace proposal. He ended the message with his own abrupt declaration, which he repeated for emphasis: 'That's that.' We could accept it or reject it, but there was no room for bargaining. I said nothing.

We then adjourned for what is known as a 'working dinner' which lasted four hours, ending at 2 a.m. Some time during the talks the King excused himself on the plea that he had to visit his mother, and we were left alone. We could now embark on an informal exchange, and there was an evident softening in Tuhami's attitude when I began asking questions. The impression grew on me as the talks proceeded that Tuhami was definitely interested in securing peace. On the other hand, he showed a singular unfamiliarity with what was happening in the administered territories in the West Bank and the Gaza Strip, and the pattern of co-existence between the Jews and Arabs in Jerusalem. He was guided by one overriding principle: peace in exchange for our complete withdrawal from the territories we had occupied since the Six Day War. Arab sovereignty should be absolute and the Arab flag should fly in all these territories, including East Jerusalem. He emphasized how dangerous was this step they had now taken – a direct Arab–Israel meeting – and he added that Sadat and Vice-President Hosni Mubarak were the only Egyptians who knew he was meeting me. He stressed the importance of secrecy. Not even the Americans were to be told. His life depended on its not being known.

I sensed, however, that his request for secrecy at the time was also prompted by what I can only describe as a crisis of the soul. For him to be meeting an official representative of the Israeli Government to discuss peace was an emotional shock. As I listened to him and observed his expression, he seemed to reflect the very apotheosis of Egyptian pride. He told me that in the army he had served in a commando unit, and it was evident that on no account could he reconcile himself to the idea that the Egyptians, with a population of forty million, together with Syria, Jordan and other Arab States, had been defeated by Israel, with its population of only three million Jews, most of them immigrants. He had therefore devised a simple explanation for the rout of the Arabs in their wars with Israel. In the 1956 Sinai Campaign and the 1967 Six Day War, Egypt's President Nasser betrayed his own people, and intentionally brought his own country to its knees. As for the 1973 Yom Kippur War, when Nasser was already dead, he had another explanation: the superpowers prevented the Egyptian army from advancing. His face fell only when, after asking my opinion of the Egyptian army, I referred to the records of our rival air forces. In air-to-air combat the results were fifty to one in Israel's favour; not a single Egyptian aircraft managed to cross the lines into Israel, whereas our pilots roamed at will over Egyptian skies. He then told me that his brother, a pilot, had been shot down in the Yom Kippur War.

The King had returned during this informal talk, and he and his aides tried on the whole to be helpful. They urged Tuhami not to be so rigid. He could surely understand that one could not speak to Israel about peace in peremptory terms and lay down preconditions. Israel's guarantees of security and her very existence, they said, were the territories she held, and how could she be expected to give them up without suitable safeguards?

When we reached the coffee stage, the King proposed that we get down to orderly discussion, with each side presenting his case. At first, however, as our host, he wished to make some preliminary remarks.

He opened by presenting Dr Tuhami as a man who enjoyed the complete trust of President Sadat, as one who was moved by the noble purpose of securing peace, and who had come to hold informal and secret talks to that end. This could well mark the start of a new era of direct contacts between the two parties in which they could clarify all the points related to a peace arrangement. After the parties had reached agreement on the main issues, he said, they could both present their proposals in writing to the United States, both out of respect for the American Government, and also to let it appear that it was America who had brought about an agreement between the Arabs and Israelis. Once the principal problem of withdrawal from the territories was settled, it would not be difficult to find appropriate solutions for most of the other urgent issues, including the question of full and normal peace relations between Israel and her Arab neighbours.

These direct contacts, the King continued, were of supreme importance, and agreement could be accomplished only through regular working meetings which should be undertaken at the highest level from now on. It was up to Tuhami and me to prepare the way for Begin to come and talk to Sadat. The King urged me not to widen the circle of those who were in on the secret, and not to bring additional aides when I came to the next meeting.

He went on to observe that the most important problem was the return of territories to their sovereign owners, and added, with his eyes on Tuhami, that these lands now in the possession of Israel were the exclusive guarantee of her security. Therefore, alternative guarantees had to be sought by mutual agreement. Similarly, an acceptable solution had to be found for Jerusalem, which was holy to both faiths, so that this problem would not prove a stumbling-block on the path to peace.

As for the Palestinians, the King continued, this was the most difficult of all the issues. He said he accepted my argument that the Palestinians were likely to prove a danger to Israel's future, just as they endangered the position of the King of Jordan. This problem had accordingly to be dealt with and settled in a reasonable manner: the Arab States should assume collective responsibility for the Palestinians, maintain supervision over them, and devise security measures which would satisfy Israel. The Palestinian problem, after all, was basically an Arab problem; it should therefore be considered and solved by the Arab countries, and not by Israel or the United States. President Assad of Syria, said the King, would ultimately be persuaded to join in the pursuit of peace despite his extremist anti-Israel declarations, but this would come about only after the achievement of a peace treaty with Egypt's Sadat.

The King was followed by Tuhami, who presented the Egyptian position. Speaking with emotion in choice literary English, he said that meeting me here under the roof of the Moroccan King was a source of deep satisfaction to him. He had long thought we would one day meet, either on the battlefield or under the circumstance of a political *débâcle*. (This enigmatic phrase became clear to me later, when we met privately. The *débâcle* was to be Israel's.) Yet here we were together, in a search for peace, thanks to the efforts of the King and to the trust which Sadat placed in Begin and in me. We were strong and courageous leaders, he said, and Sadat was confident that we would be bold enough to take fateful decisions for a full and just peace. Sadat had had no faith in previous Israeli Governments but he had faith in us.

Sadat was deadly serious in his quest for peace. 'Let us, therefore, consider together how we may achieve it. But let us keep it between ourselves, without the United States. Later, when we reach agreement, we can tell them.' He added that Sadat thought the time had now arrived to discuss all the details. Some time earlier, Romania's President Nicolae Ceausescu had suggested that he meet Begin, but Sadat had not believed anything would come of such a meeting. He had changed his mind, thanks to the mediation of the King of Morocco and his trust in Begin's Government. Sadat now agreed to open a dialogue with us; but only after Begin agreed to the principle of total withdrawal from the administered territories would Sadat meet with Begin and shake his hand. Israel's withdrawal was the basic problem. Its solution was the key to peace, for involved in it were the questions of sovereignty, of national honour, and of Sadat's own continuance in office. If it remained unsolved, it could lead to deadlock. But if Begin were prepared to accept the principle, it would then be possible to negotiate all the other important issues, including guarantees for Israel's security in place of the territories she would be abandoning.

As to the danger from Palestinian extremists, Tuhami said they would become a more potent force if their nationalist ambitions remained unfulfilled, and would open the way for a renewed Soviet penetration of our region. But once they gained 'nationhood' (Tuhami's term), the Arab countries were for the most part capable of controlling them. It was within the power of Jordan and Egypt to counter communist influence on the Palestinians, just as Soviet influence in Egypt had been halted. He added that even in their efforts towards peace, the Egyptians wanted no contact with Soviet Russia, only with the United States.

Turning to the specific territories, Tuhami said that the Palestinian enclave west of the River Jordan (the West Bank) could be linked to the Kingdom of Jordan, and Saudi Arabia and Egypt together could keep the Palestinian extremists under control and also keep the King of Jordan on his throne. In the Gaza Strip, Egypt could give us guarantees that we would have no trouble from the Palestinians there. Egypt would ensure this, operating from Cairo, without exercising direct rule over the Strip.

'It is our solemn request', said Tuhami, 'that you accept Sadat's word that he will respect all commitments and obligations as written. He is a man of principle, of honour, of nobility. If presented with a formula to which he can agree, Sadat will go with you all the way, for both you and we have vital interests in common.'

Tuhami added that Sadat would discuss with us all possible sureties. If we wanted United Nations forces stationed on both sides of the border, it would be done. If we wanted guarantees from the United States or the Soviet Union, Egypt would have no objection, though 'it would be better to avoid the latter and secure guarantees from America alone'.

Tuhami then proposed that there, in Morocco, with the help of the King, and before the Geneva Conference, we should conclude our negotiations, and reach agreement on all the factors which concerned us. We would then proceed to Geneva merely to affix our signature. Such an agreement would have its impact on Syrian President Assad. Of course he would oppose it at first, but later, when King Hussein would join us, Assad, too, would get on the peace wagon.

He suggested that we each draw up peace documents, show them to the United States, study them carefully, meet again and discuss them. 'If only Begin would agree to the principle of withdrawal for the sake of peace between our peoples,' said Tuhami. Without that, all their sincere intentions would be doomed, for that was the exclusive key that would open the gates to a brighter future.

He urged that the next meeting should be a working session between the two of us. This would be the beginning of official relations. A relationship of full peace would need to develop gradually, and could take three, four or five years. (At this point the King interrupted him with: 'You must say "a certain period" without specifying so many years.') We should be interested in a complete package deal with all the difficulties smoothed out, not a partial arrangement, not in public, and not at Geneva, but there, between our two sides.

Tuhami touched on a few additional points. One was Jerusalem. The Holy City was an important issue. He said that we should come with a constructive plan which would satisfy the religious feelings of the Arab States. A sympathetic solution to this problem would be proof of our sincerity. An acceptable proposal on this matter would lessen Arab anxiety and draw the sting from Arab hostility.

Returning yet again to what he called the central problem, that of the occupied territories, he quoted Sadat's declaration that he was 'a soldier whose land has been conquered'. Sadat wanted peace without having to surrender. When he received Begin's word that Israel would withdraw from the territories she had captured, Sadat's honour would be restored and this would enable him to conduct negotiations on the other items. For Sadat, 'sovereignty over his land' was not a subject for discussion.

Although he would not sign a final peace treaty alone, without the participation of his friends, Sadat was convinced that he would succeed in persuading Jordan and Syria to follow suit, and that would include solving the Palestinian problem. That problem could probably be settled along the lines of a collective covenant by the Arab States. But that could be considered in due course. So could the question of the Jewish settlements which would find themselves in the territories reverting to Arab sovereignty.

Tuhami concluded his presentation with the proposal that we should meet there again after each side had studied the other's peace document, and that I bring with me Begin's reactions to Sadat's request. He thought the meeting could take place in about a fortnight.

It was now my turn. The hour was late, and I tried to be brief, being principally concerned, I told them, with reporting to Prime Minister Begin what I had heard that evening. I said I well appreciated the importance of our meeting, and I understood from all that had been said that what would be agreed upon here would also be acceptable to the other Arab States. I stressed that I was here only as the emissary of Begin, and so I could not myself react to the points they had raised without his instructions. It was necessary, however, for me to be clear about their position. Was I to understand from Tuhami that Sadat's request for a Begin commitment to withdraw from the territories was a precondition for subsequent discussions, or was it to serve as guidance to Begin in future meetings that would be held here? I would also need to know whether Egypt would agree to meetings at the highest level, namely, between Begin and Sadat, even if Begin did not agree to total withdrawal.

I paused here, awaiting a reply.

The response was clouded. While Tuhami said that what was required from Begin was a specific commitment to withdraw from the territories, the King broke in with: 'Allow me to correct my friend.' Then, in a pointed reference to Tuhami's remark about Sadat's handshake, he said: 'From what

I know of Sadat's thinking, and after his talks with me, I give my word of honour that Sadat will meet Begin and shake his hand if Begin can offer his personal undertaking that the basis of the bilateral talks will be the under-standing that Israel will withdraw from the territories.'

After these replies, I said that whatever Begin proposed to do would need to be brought before his Government for decision and the Knesset for ratifi-cation. No Israeli Prime Minister could take such a crucial decision without the endorsement of the Knesset. Those were the procedures of our demo-cratic regime. As an example, I cited the case of the Israeli Government's refusal to accept Egypt's precondition of our withdrawal during the period of Gunnar Jarring's mediation mission.

Another item on which I sought clarification was whether the Egyptians wished basic subjects to be discussed by representatives like Tuhami and myself, or whether it would not be more effective for the highest levels to meet face to face in a frank talk. They could then prescribe by mutual agreement the guideline principles which would govern the continued discus-sions between lower-level representatives.

I turned to Tuhami and said that I placed full trust in his word, just as Sadat had put his trust in our leaders. I would regard any gentleman's agreement with him to have the validity of a written obligation – which was not the case with some of our other adversaries. On the principal question of withdrawal from territories, I could not tell whether Begin would respond to his request. He might, or might not. But he would certainly, without commit-ting himself to anything, wish to meet at the highest Egyptian level to discuss the overall subject of peace. I was saying this, I added to Tuhami, even though he had stated that Sadat would first need a commitment from Begin on territorial withdrawal, after which all other items would then be open for discus-sion. Withdrawal was no light matter. For nineteen years before the 1967 Six Day War our population centres had been attacked from the hills. What guarantee was there that this would not happen again? And how could we ensure freedom of navigation for our ships through the Red Sea? Perhaps together we might find the answers. We had certain recognized rights in the territories; but what would their status be once these territories were trans-ferred to the sovereignty of Arab States? What of our settlements in the Golan Heights? What of the Western Wall and the Jewish Quarter of the Old City, the Mount of Olives and the Hebrew University on Mount Scopus? And what of the new population centres in the south, in Sinai, if we with-drew? Would they be allowed to live as foreigners under Arab sovereignty? Satisfactory solutions had to be found for each of these items.

Another point I referred to was Tuhami's insistence that we had to withdraw from all the territories we occupied in 1967, including those formerly ruled by Jordan and Syria, and that a peace agreement had to be reached with the collection of Arab States with whom we had been in military conflict. There had never been a case in history, I said, in which a collective peace agreement had been signed with an organization. It was not an organization that had waged war against us, but individual Arab States, and each should now be dealt with on an individual and separate basis, according to conventional international procedures. Anything else would be both unacceptable and impractical. Moreover, UN Resolution 242 spoke of the various countries and named them one by one. There was no mention in that resolution of a 'collective organization of Arab States' nor even of the Palestinians as a party to a peace treaty.

Speaking of the Palestinians, I called attention to their slogans, and to such declarations by Syria's President as 'All the Palestinians shall return to their homes'. What would happen if they were indeed to return? They would not be satisfied with living only in the comparatively small enclaves of the West Bank and the Gaza Strip. There was not enough room and work for them there. They would stream into Israel, and this would be a demographic catastrophe for us. Some other solution would need to be found; they would have to be settled elsewhere.

In conclusion I said that though the problems were difficult and complex, I was convinced they could be settled by negotiation with Egypt and with Jordan. I had doubts about Syria. The problems associated with religion in Jerusalem, I thought, would be solved with comparative ease to the satisfaction of all parties. This was also true, as far as Egypt was concerned, of the south and the Red Sea area. I also thought we could reach a settlement on all the issues between Israel and the King of Jordan, though there would be no sovereign Palestine State. Turning to Tuhami, I expressed my firm belief that we could arrive at a suitable arrangement with Egypt. We relied on Sadat. We did not trust the President of Syria. We should therefore begin serious and immediate discussions of the issues affecting Israel and Egypt. I accepted his suggestion that we exchange our respective documents of peace proposals for mutual study as quickly as possible, so that we could meet again within a fortnight. I could fly back to Morocco on my way home from the United States towards the end of the month.

With the King's blessing, Tuhami and I agreed to the following three moves:

1. Both parties would report immediately to their heads of government in order to receive their approval for a further meeting between us. I would

report to Begin the request of Sadat that Israel make the commitment to withdraw from the administered territories as a prior condition for a continuation of the talks.

2. The peace documents which both sides were proposing would be exchanged and studied by each party before our next meeting, and shown to the United States.

3. If these proposals were approved by the heads of government, our next meeting would take place in Morocco within two weeks.

Although, as they knew, I had stopped off here while on my way to the United States, I would now fly back to Israel to report to Begin and receive his directives, and then go to America.

Several interesting topics, unrelated to the peace talks, cropped up during the informal part of the dinner meeting when the conversation was less inhibited. The King asked me at one point whether Israel was involved in the war then going on in Ethiopia, and if so why? I told him that we were not involved in the war but only in aid to Ethiopia, towards whom we had moral obligations. Ethiopia had helped us in the past with port and air facilities when our ships and planes were in desperate straits. We would not refuse them now when they were in trouble and asked us for arms. The King argued that times had changed, that Ethiopia would soon be left without any ports, and perhaps we would do better to try to get closer to the moderate wing of the liberation movement along the Red Sea coast. I told him there was no chance of that. The liberation movement was already affiliated to the Arab League and would not come to our assistance in time of need.

Tuhami told me a story about the 1967 Six Day War. He said that Egyptian military intelligence had a spy 'in place' at the time in a strategic position: he was 'a senior officer in the Israeli Army', and he had sent back the information that the attack would begin between the 3rd and 6th of June! Why, then, had the Egyptian High Command and particularly the Egyptian Air Force not been on the alert? Tuhami looked at me and asked seriously: 'Tell me frankly, did not Nasser conspire together with you at that time? Otherwise, how could such a catastrophe have befallen us? And why did Nasser send Egypt's army commander Abd el Hakim flying into Sinai to visit units exactly on the day you opened your attack?' As he spoke of Nasser, Tuhami's lips quivered in anger and contempt. He indicated that he was about to write a book on Nasser which would tell 'the whole truth' about 'this madman who had brought Egypt to the brink of collapse'.

I invited Tuhami to come and visit Israel, and see for himself the relations between the Jews and the Arabs, and how a return to the geographical division of Jerusalem and the cutting off of the West Bank were no longer practicable. Tuhami responded with a smile of satisfaction, and said he took note of the invitation and would remind me of it at an appropriate time. When we parted, he said again that he had never imagined we would ever meet under such circumstances. He had conceived that we might meet in battle or when Israel was caught in a national crisis and I would come to Egypt on an official mission. (Though he did not say it in so many words, the implication was that I would be arriving on a mission of surrender or to plead for mercy.) Nevertheless he shook my hand firmly and said he looked forward to seeing me again in two weeks. He also asked me to send him a copy of my book *Story of My Life* and I promised to do so.

I returned to the guest suite. Though I would be leaving an hour and a half later, I stretched out on the bed. An hour's sleep is after all an hour's sleep. I was awakened at 3.30 a.m., drove to the plane, and flew to Paris. Despite my fatigue, I did not even manage to doze. On arrival, I was driven to a hotel near Orly airport, and on the way I removed the cursed wig and moustache. A breakfast of hot coffee, buttered rolls and the *Herald Tribune* brought me back to the world of reality. I read that my sudden disappearance had caused something of a sensation and promoted all sorts of speculations as to where I had been – all of them far from the truth.

Three hours later I was on an El Al plane flying back to Israel, and on arrival I drove straight to Jerusalem to see the Prime Minister. I reported on the meeting and received Begin's approval to my three suggestions:

1. That we exchange our respective proposals for a peace treaty for mutual study. (Begin insisted that we notify the Americans of this, without mentioning the name of the Arab State concerned.)
2. That I again meet Tuhami in a fortnight.
3. That on a Begin–Sadat meeting, Begin was not prepared to make a commitment in advance that we would withdraw from all the occupied territories. In fact, however, Israel's position would be understood by the Egyptians when they read the document containing our peace proposals.

From Jerusalem I returned to my home in Zahala. The house was desolate. Before leaving for the United States, Rahel had emptied the fridge, turned off the electric boiler, and stripped the beds. Fortunately there was still gas, so I boiled some water, made myself a bowl of soup from a cube I found in the pantry, and drank it while listening to the one o'clock news bulletin on the radio. I then took a blanket, lay on the bare mattress and tried to sleep. I had had a long day, and at 6 p.m. I was to catch the plane for New York – not knowing that dramatic events were to supersede my further meeting with Tuhami in two weeks, as planned. The meeting did take place, again in secret and again in Morocco; but not for another two and a half months. By then, the pattern in the kaleidoscope of the Middle East had undergone an astonishing change.

CHAPTER FIVE

Preparatory Talks

The flight to New York this time, on 18 September, was direct and uneventful, with no evasive side-trips. Ostensibly, I was to attend the opening session of the UN General Assembly, customary for all Foreign Ministers. The main purpose, however, was to take part in what were called 'preparatory talks' for the Geneva Conference, and so I went on to Washington the morning after my arrival to meet first with Secretary Vance and his aides at the State Department, and then with President Carter at the White House.

The State Department meeting began at noon and continued through a working lunch, where special kosher food was served. Three of my aides were Orthodox Jews, and they enjoyed the meal. My own satisfaction stemmed from an appreciation of the solicitude of our hosts. The American group was much the same as the one we had met in Israel the previous month, with the addition of National Security Adviser Zbigniew Brzezinski, who joined us for lunch.

The furnishings of the Secretary of State's office had changed a good deal since I had last been there, when Kissinger was in office. Some of the abstract paintings had disappeared from the walls. When I had remarked on them, Kissinger had said that the medley of colours without shape represented the state of the world! Gone also were other objects which had reflected the personality of the occupant. I recalled Kissinger's amusement when I had looked round the room on my first visit. Watching me, he said jokingly: 'Nothing Anglo-Saxon about this office while I am here.' At the time, working closely with him were three men of Jewish, Italian and Lebanese origin, respectively – his personal assistant Peter Rodman, and Under-Secretaries of State Joseph Sisco and Philip Habib.

The Americans had done their homework well. They had studied every word and nuance in the peace plan that Begin had handed to Carter when they had met in July. Though they did not say so explicitly, it became clear from their remarks that after Vance's visit to Israel they had held a further round of talks with Arab representatives. Much of our meeting resolved itself into a kind of cross-examination to elicit our thoughts on the desired pattern of peace with our neighbours. But the Americans also brought up other subjects. The most significant was the possibility of an American guarantee. Vance said the United States would be prepared to underwrite a peace agreement when it was reached with all the Arab States. Since I failed to react, he repeated it several times, promising to formulate and transmit to us detailed proposals.

I considered an American guarantee for Israel's security to be a very valuable asset; but given in that context it had three grave failings. First, it was conditional on an agreement 'with all the Arab States', and I did not believe that Syria was ready to sign a treaty with us. Second, from what I knew, and from some of the things Vance said, the Arabs would demand that the guarantee be given jointly with the Soviet Union. The third and principal drawback was the intention behind the offer. Though it was not said in so many words, I had no doubt that the guarantee was to be given in exchange for the territories we held. It was the American purpose to get us to withdraw, and to cover the consequent risks to Israel's security by providing insurance through a guarantee.

My reply to Vance, therefore, was that there were various schools of thought on that subject, and my Government would consider the American proposal when it was received. It would have to be an American initiative. We would not request it. I added my personal view that I thought we – like the countries of Europe – needed a US guarantee only against Soviet aggression. We could manage with the Arabs ourselves.

The meeting was no more encouraging when we came to discuss the establishment of full diplomatic relations with the Arabs if and when we signed a peace treaty. Vance, and then Brzezinski, said the Arabs were not prepared to establish such relations with the signing of the treaty but only several years later. My reaction was quite sharp. I said the Arabs wanted Israel's withdrawal from the territories without an effective peace in return. President Carter had assured both Premiers Rabin and Begin that his intention was to help achieve absolute peace with absolute normalization, a package deal which would exchange territories for peace; yet now they came to us with a proposal which negated the words of their President to our Prime Minister. Vance clearly felt uncomfortable, and emphasized that what he had told us was the view held by all the Arabs, including President Sadat, and all he was trying to do was find out whether it was possible to bridge the gap between the two parties. He explained that Sadat had argued that Israel's withdrawal from Sinai would take time, and the Egyptians could not agree to an exchange of ambassadors so long as we remained on their soil. I did not accept this argument, and I repeated our position that full diplomatic relations had to be established one month after the signing of a peace treaty, together with steps towards the implementation of such other articles in the treaty as commercial relations and cultural agreements. As President Carter had said, peace had to rest on absolute normalization.

Border questions were taken country by country, starting with Egypt. Vance asked for details of the areas in Sinai where we wanted a reduction of Egyptian forces, areas we thought should be demilitarized, and whether there should be a buffer zone under UN control. He also sought our thinking on safeguards for freedom of Israeli shipping through the Straits of Tiran at Sharm e-Sheikh. The Americans, he said, would propose that reduction of forces and freedom of shipping should be supervised by the UN.

We went over to a large map hanging on the wall so that Vance could follow our proposals in answer to his questions. I said that in principle we preferred direct contact with the Egyptians – just as all other neighbour-countries maintained a peaceful common frontier without the interposition of the UN. What UN forces could do was supervise the implementation of the agreement. As to the borders themselves, I repeated our traditional stand. Israeli control of the western coastal strip of the Gulf of Eilat running from Sharm e-Sheikh in the south to Eilat in the north; and a widening of the area of our control to the northwest so that it included all our settlements in the approaches to Rafah. We needed, I told Vance, not only military forces but also a Jewish civilian population between the Gaza District and Egypt. Our proposed border would therefore run from El Arish in northern Sinai south-wards, past a point to the west of Eilat and on to Sharm e-Sheikh. The Americans again raised the question of UN personnel in the buffer zone, discounting the use of American forces because, if US troops were there, the Russians would insist on being there too. Vance finally said that the United States would produce her own peace proposal in an effort to bring the Arab and Israeli positions closer together.

We moved from Sinai to Syria, but spent little time on that discussion. It could only be hypothetical, I said, as President Assad would not make peace with us. In any case, we did not envisage pronounced changes in the current boundary line. The entire area of Golan was a comparatively narrow strip, and we had our farm villages there. Even in the arrangements for the Separa-tion of Forces Agreement following the Yom Kippur War, it had been impossible to establish a significant buffer zone, since, unlike Sinai, the Golan was populated. The Americans, too, showed little interest in a detailed consideration of the Golan, and I presumed they had found no encourage-ment from their contacts with Assad.

When we came to discuss the West Bank, Vance asked if we thought the legitimate representation of this territory could be a delegation comprising members of the Jordanian Government with the addition of West Bank mayors. I gave a positive reply, but observed that relations between the Government of Jordan and the PLO were tense, and the mayors would not join a Jordanian delegation without PLO approval; they feared for their lives. Brzezinski asked which of the mayors supported the PLO. All of them, I said, at least with their lips. Even the Mayor of Bethlehem, Elias Freij, who was a Christian Arab, would not dare say a word against the PLO.

The Americans then raised the question of sovereignty, and asked what we meant when we said there was to be no foreign sovereignty over the West Bank. It meant, I said, that it was not to be annexed by Jordan, nor would it be a Palestinian State. This, of course, did not disqualify Israeli sovereignty, but it was not our intention to apply it. At this stage, and for the immediate future, we were thinking of an administrative structure that would satisfy the essential interests of both sides. It was possible that unexpected changes would occur in the region and other prescriptions might then be available. But now, after ten years of negotiations with Jordan and ten years of living with the Arabs in the territories, I knew of no better solution.

Vance asked what kind of autonomy we were thinking of granting to the West Bank Arabs. I replied that we would not interfere in their lives, but autonomy could not be turned into Palestinian statehood. And what, he asked further, would we do if terror attacks were launched against us from Nablus or Gaza? In that event, I said, we would restore the previous situation: the Israel Army would return to the Arab cities and fight the terrorists. At all events, I added, I did not believe they would negotiate with us. After President Carter had said they had the right to their own homeland, and the Arab States had resolved that the PLO was the sole representative of the Palestinians, Jordan would prefer to remain on the sidelines, and the West Bank and Gaza mayors would not dare to appear as an independent delegation.

In the few minutes before we were to meet the President, Vance asked me to present Israel's view on Jerusalem. I replied briefly that there, too, there was no possibility of a division. Brzezinski said that the Arabs, too, were not proposing the erection of a dividing wall or barbed wire fence between the Arab and Israeli sections of the city. He therefore thought we should discuss not the map but the nature of the relations between the two sectors. If we were not going into the question of sovereignty, I said, but dealing with the day-to-day life of the two peoples in Jerusalem, the problem was simpler and, to my mind, could be resolved. I thought it was possible to settle matters pertaining to the Holy Places, transport, education, and elections to the municipal council. We all then left for the White House.

I had been there before, when Nixon was President. But this was my first visit since its new tenant had moved in and also my first meeting with President Carter and Vice-President Walter Mondale, who was with him. Our talk lasted almost an hour and was most unpleasant. At the session in the State Department, there were differences of view between the Secretary of State and myself, but the discussion was conducted in a calm and sober manner. Even when we turned down a proposal by Vance or his aides, we were not made to feel like the accused in a court of law facing the prosecuting attorney. President Carter, however, and even more so Mondale, launched charge after charge against Israel.

This took place at the private meeting between the President, the Vice-President and myself. On our arrival at the White House, Carter said he wanted a few words with me alone before starting the general discussion, and so Vance and his aides, together with my aides, adjourned to the conference room to wait for us, while Carter took Mondale and me to his study. Carter first asked me about a certain defence matter. My reply did not satisfy him and he said he would take it up with Premier Begin. He then turned to the subject of Israeli settlements in the occupied territories, speaking in language that was sharp both in content and tone, and making no effort to mask his anger. He said he had himself seen and heard one of our ministers say on television that we intended to settle hundreds of thousands on territory beyond our pre-June 1967 borders. He charged us with taking action and making statements that were liable to prevent the Palestinian Arabs from joining the peace talks. I replied that there never was and never could be a government in Israel that would fail to establish Israeli settlements in the territories. But the President continued with his accusations: 'You are more stubborn than the Arabs, and you put obstacles on the path to peace.'

I, too, was now angry. I told Carter that we did not accept the American opinion that our settlement was illegal, and Israel had never agreed to the Rogers Plan. (Rogers was Secretary of State under Nixon, and his plan called for Israel's withdrawal from virtually every part of all the administered territories, namely, a return to the pre-June 1967 borders except for 'insubstantial alterations'.) I added that the settlements in the Jordan Valley, the approaches to Rafah and on the Golan Heights had been established during the premierships of Levi Eshkol and Golda Meir, but it was not that which prevented peace. The Arabs had been refusing to reconcile themselves to Israel's existence for thirty years, even when we had lived within the pre-1967 boundaries.

The President then went over to the Palestinian question. Who, he asked me, would represent them? And how could we bring about the early convening of the Geneva Conference?

What I resented most was the part played by Vice-President Mondale, who at other times and on other occasions had been helpful. Now, however, whenever the President showed signs of calming down and holding an even-tempered dialogue, Mondale jumped in with fresh complaints which disrupted the talk. I was disgusted. I just let him say his piece and make his allegations, and when he wound down I remained silent. They both stared at me, but I said nothing. The President broke the lull by asking what I proposed. I said that the Government of Israel would not stop settlement in the territories, but, if he wished, I was prepared to suggest to Begin that the six additional settlements we planned to establish in the near future would be carried out within the framework of military camps. The settlers would be mobilized, or they could be considered civilians working for the army, and their families would be permitted to live with them in the camp. We had done that at Kiriat Arba, the suburb of Hebron, in the first stage of its establishment. The President reflected a few moments and then agreed. It was not what he had wished, he said, but it was at least a second best. I repeated that this was my personal suggestion, and I did not know if my Government would approve it.

We then proceeded to the conference room where the two groups, sitting opposite each other, awaited us. Carter opened with an introductory review, wearing his routine smile but leaving no doubt as to his mood. Those on my side of the table saw cold hostility in his blue eyes. The voice was quiet, but the language was strong, and at times his face was flushed with anger. He reported on our private conversation, missing not a single nuance of the 'I accuse' he had delivered to me against Israel. Indeed, he even elaborated on some of those points, charging that not only Prime Minister Begin but also I, the Foreign Minister, in the talk we had just had, had not thought fit to dissociate ourselves from the words of our Minister of Agriculture Arik Sharon. Israel was taking an obdurate line whereas the Arabs were flexible; Israel did not really want peace; our settlement was illegal; our deeds and the declarations of our Minister of Agriculture made it difficult to convene the Geneva Conference and impossible to fulfil the 'principal element' of Resolution 242 – Israeli withdrawal and peace.

My associates were astounded. After four wars and thirty years of Arab refusal to sit with us to discuss peace; their rejection of the Allon Plan (for a settlement with Jordan); their murder of King Abdullah (grandfather of Hussein) for daring to enter into negotiations with us; the three Noes of

Khartoum (where the Arab states vowed 'No peace with Israel, no negotia-tions with Israel, no recognition of Israel'); the Egyptian blockade of the Gulf of Eilat; their dismissal of the UN forces; their launching of the Yom Kippur War; the refusal of the PLO to respond to repeated American requests to stop their terrorism and recognize Israel. After all this, the Arabs were the 'flexible' ones who yearned for peace, and we were the rejectionists. Our calls for peace were 'insincere'.

I did not know whether it was to demonstrate our inflexibility, or really to get an informative answer, that the President then turned to me with a steely look and asked whether I insisted on Jordan's being the only Arab country with whom we would discuss the future of the West Bank. I said 'Yes': that was our position, and no other Arab State would have a say in the matter. And what, he asked further, was our view on the possibility of dividing the West Bank between us and Jordan? If Jordan were to make such a proposal, I said, we would give it honest consideration. In the last ten years, we had offered them the Allon Plan, which proposed a division of this nature, and Jordan had replied that it was 'totally unacceptable'.

There was no let-up from Carter. If the Arabs refused our programme of co-existence in the West Bank and Gaza, he asked, would we agree that after a few years – two, four or eight – a referendum should be held in those territories so the Arabs could themselves decide whether to be linked to Jordan or to Israel? I said I would oppose it, and I could tell him right away that the Arab answer would be for us to get out of the West Bank, so there was no need to wait two, four or eight years. We were not there to gain time. In that case, said Carter, how did I envisage a solution? My reply was that for the moment I did not know. I would recommend to my Prime Minister that the two parties should consider a permanent arrangement in another few years. One thing he should know immediately: in my view, if the West Bank were annexed to Jordan, it would lead to the destruction of the State of Israel. It would mean our return to the pre-1967 borders; the dismantling of our military installations on the mountain ridges; and the pull-back of our armed forces from the Jordan Valley. The territory would be ruled by the PLO, and would serve as a base for a devastating attack on Israel. I would not recommend this course to my Prime Minister.

The President moved on to procedural questions concerning the Geneva Conference. He repeated what, according to him, had been agreed between him and Begin: that at Geneva, Israel and Jordan would discuss the West Bank, and that Palestinians who were not known members of the PLO would be part of the Jordanian delegation. As for the subject of Palestinians who dwelt in other countries – namely, a solution of the refugee problem – that would be considered separately by multi-national delegations. At the opening phase of the Geneva Conference there would be a united Arab delegation.

At this point I broke in with the observation that as far as we knew this opening phase would be simply a ceremonial affair for the benefit of the photographers. Carter knitted his brows and said in a demonstratively flat tone: 'Not only photographers.' I did not react to this, but asked for the protocol of the meeting to record that it was agreed here that after the opening ceremony, the united Arab delegation would split up into its national delegations, and Israel would negotiate and sign a peace treaty with each Arab country separately. We would not discuss Sinai with Syria nor would we talk to the Egyptians about Lebanon.

The American group were of the opinion, apparently after their rounds of talks with Arab representatives, that when the future of the West Bank was being dealt with, the Arab States would insist that the Arab side would be represented by a united delegation, and not by Jordan alone. Carter asked if we would agree to postpone this matter, and decide on the composition of the Arab delegation that would discuss the West Bank only after we reached a peace agreement with the Arab States. I said I assumed that the Israeli Government would not object to a postponement. In any case, I added, we would be prepared to discuss the West Bank only with representatives of the Jordan Government and the Arab inhabitants of that territory.

Our next subject was security guarantees. Carter said that if the United States were to guarantee the peace, we would have to agree that this be done jointly with the Soviet Union. I had no desire to rely on hypothetical talk, so I said directly that I was in favour of guarantees but not in exchange for secure borders. If we were asked to remove our troops from the Golan and rely on guarantees, I would oppose it. But I would like to hear their concrete proposal: would the US give us the kind of guarantee she gave NATO? Carter replied that they had no firm position on this as yet.

If any of my associates thought the Americans had changed their approach to the question of borders, this meeting with Carter made them wiser and sadder. Vance, who presented the United States' position, reading occasionally from a text, informed us that the borders between Israel and her neighbours were to be identical with those of May 1967, with certain changes in the West Bank. Carter added that he had promised Begin, when the Prime Minister visited Washington, that he would not state in public that America called only for 'slight changes'. But we had to realize, he said, that the United States considered the West Bank and Gaza as 'occupied regions' and that Israel had to withdraw from them in accordance with Resolution 242 after agreement was reached between us and our neighbours on permanent boundaries. The United States also believed there should be a 'Palestinian entity', which should be linked to Jordan.

Mondale reverted to the subject of settlements and asked how many army camps were involved in my proposal. I said there had been talk of eight. Two had already been put up so only six remained; but I could not tell whether others might not be added later. Nor could I promise that the fact would not be published: such moves could not be kept secret; nor was it necessary; nor would we wish it. And I certainly could not promise what any minister might or might not say.

Carter, too, had no wish to abandon the subject. The American position that settlement was illegal was known to us, he said, and what worried him at the moment was the way in which we were handling the problem, and the public declarations we were making. If Sadat and Hussein wanted peace, our statements made it difficult for them, statements such as 'no foreign sovereignty' and 'this territory is part of the historic land of Israel'. Our Minister of Agriculture had talked on television of hundreds of settlements and a million settlers. This was not what our Prime Minister had told him. He, Carter, had told us openly that he had doubts about Israel's desire for peace. His doubts were prompted by these words and deeds.

The meeting came to a close; but apparently the President did not want it to end on a hard note, as expressed by his tough final remarks. He therefore called out, as we rose to leave, in a voice that he clearly wanted everyone to hear, that he harboured great friendship for Premier Begin and that he was a strong leader.

As we left the White House, Vance cornered me for a brief chat, primarily, it transpired, to emphasize three points: the Americans would like to convene the Geneva Conference before December; they were ready to give serious guarantees if a peace agreement were reached; and he would like to continue the talks we had begun that morning. On guarantees, I said the United States should give us concrete proposals. On continuing the talks, we arranged to meet again a week later, on 26 September, when we would both be in New York.

It was soon apparent that the Americans had sensed my discontent over the President's approach to the nature of an Arab-Israel peace, and my resentment at his complaints against Israel. The very next morning, White House Chief of Staff Hamilton Jordan telephoned the Israeli Ambassador in Washington to say that the President was very pleased with his meeting with me and thought the talks were good and helpful. The Ambassador told him I was back in New York and he would pass the message on to me there. A few hours later Hamilton Jordan again telephoned the embassy to ask what I thought of my talk with the President. He had received news from New York that I was not happy with the White House meeting; and the story on it which appeared in the *Washington Post* was also pessimistic. A few days later Hamilton Jordan rang our Ambassador and asked to see him urgently. He had heard that I was about to address a number of gatherings of various Jewish communities in the United States where I would no doubt speak of the differences between us and the American Government.

This was not guesswork on the part of the White House official. In my meetings with correspondents and Jewish leaders, I had seen no reason to conceal my disappointment. It was also true that I was scheduled to address Jewish meetings in several cities. They were to be fund-raising meetings for the United Jewish Appeal and the State of Israel Bonds; but there was no doubt that in my speeches I would criticize the American position on peace in the Middle East. I, of course, was not alone in this venture of publicizing one's views. Leaks from the White House and the State Department kept the media well engaged in transmitting American charges against us. I was glad at least to be away from Washington, away from the ugly atmosphere that had enveloped our talks.

The ambience was more congenial when they were resumed the following week in New York with Secretary Vance and his aides, first on 26 September and again four days later. But in substance, the talks were much as they had been in Washington. The Americans wanted to have their cake and eat it – trying to squeeze maximum concessions from us while committing them-selves to nothing.

They began by reopening the question of settlements, which I thought we had covered in my talk with Carter. They now informed me 'in the name of the President' that the US stand had not changed: they were opposed to settlement even within the framework of military camps. I was astonished, and said I hoped they were not denying what their President had told me. The army camps idea was not all he had wanted, but he said it was 'at least a second best', helpful, and could be lived with. Yes, they replied, but the President had also made clear that they were opposed to settlement in the occupied territories in any form whatsoever. All I could say to this was that we would do better to abandon the special arrangement I had proposed and continue our settlement activity without recourse to camps.

The pattern recurred when we discussed security guarantees, which the Americans had been waving like a carrot before our noses. What exactly were they prepared to do? Something like their commitment to NATO, they replied. I asked for a concrete and detailed proposal, but it was not forth-coming. Vance said he had talked to the President, but they had not yet reached a definite conclusion.

On 29 September the American delegation handed us two documents. One was a 'Working Paper' dealing with the Geneva Conference. The other was the draft of a joint declaration to be issued by the United States and the Soviet Union on Middle East policy. The two delegations met the following day and we were asked for our reaction. I told Vance that our Prime Minister had spoken to the US Ambassador in Israel and expressed our objection to any such two-power declaration, and specifically to the contents of this one.

Nor was the working paper on Geneva acceptable to us. It was a complete departure from what had been agreed at our White House meeting. We had gone out of our way to approach the US position, I said, and thought we had reached an agreed formula. My Government had approved our recommen-dation and even published the fact. And now they, the Americans, were reversing themselves. In the new working paper, they were again proposing a united Arab delegation, and again wanting to combine the three problems – the Palestinians, the West Bank and the refugees – under a single negotiating heading. Furthermore, they were maintaining that the negotiations between Israel and each of her neighbours would be conducted by sub-committees, but the final decision would lie with the 'plenary', namely, the united Arab delegation! This was an unwelcome document, and I was empowered by my Prime Minister to reject it.

It seemed obvious to me that there was a direct link between the new working paper and the US–Soviet declaration, particularly after Vance gave me details of the Soviet stand on a peace agreement. The Russians agreed that there should be full normalization of relations between Israel and the Arabs, but only on the basis of an Israeli withdrawal to the May 1967 lines. A Palestinian State was to be established, and the Arab countries were to appear at Geneva as a united delegation. The Russians also supported the Syrian view that the negotiations were to be conducted within the framework of functional and not territorial committees, so that one Israel–Arab com-mittee, for example, would deal with the nature of the peace, another the frontiers, yet another the Palestinians.

I asked Vance why they needed a joint declaration at all. To reach a co-ordinated policy on the Middle East with the Russians, he said.

Vance told me that Egypt was the exception among the Arab States. Her representatives had said they were opposed to a united Arab delegation, and were prepared to start negotiations with us even before the Geneva Confer-ence. He felt the Egyptians were sincerely anxious to make peace with us.

I asked Vance about Jordan, but got no clear answer. All I could extract from him was that she would not oppose the inclusion of the Palestinians in a united Arab delegation, but on no account would she agree to their being part of her own delegation. The Jordanian delegation would consist only of Jordanians.

The Americans were clearly uncomfortable over their back tracking. They seemed to be wriggling, and the causes were obvious. They knew how anxious we were to arrive at agreed positions with them, and so they used the tactic of getting us to make step-by-step concessions by trying to give us the impression that if only we would move a little further towards them, all our differences would be resolved. Moreover, they were searching for formulae that would be acceptable to the Russians as well as the Arabs. Thus, whatever was agreed between us would not be final unless it were approved by the other parties. All this I understood. But what annoyed me was their show of innocence, and their repeated excuse that they had wrongly interpreted what we had said, and we had misunderstood their intentions.

There were also moments of tension with my own Government. I thought it my task, within the framework of the Government's policy directives, to seek formulae and compromises that would also be acceptable to the Arabs and the United States. In doing so, I would make clear to the Americans that the proposals I recommended to my Government might not be accepted. Begin preferred that I secure prior governmental approval before putting them to the Americans. This was an issue that needed to be settled immediately, come what may. I told the Prime Minister that for the procedure he favoured he could use a courier dashing back and forth between America and Israel with proposals and replies. Both Begin and I spoke with restraint, but we both knew that this was a question of principle and it required a clear-cut decision. Our exchange ended with the Prime Minister's withdrawing his suggestion and giving me full support in conducting the negotiations.

A message from the State Department informed me that the President would like to see me again, and it was arranged that we would meet in New York on 4 October. I got in touch with Jerusalem, told them of the projected meeting, and suggested the terms of our own working paper which should be submitted to Vance before the meeting. Begin approved, offering changes in the wording of certain sections. I also asked him about the settlement situation. He said all was proceeding in accordance with the agreed policy. The settlers were working in military camps as civilian employees of the army, and six settlements were planned for the near future, as I had told Carter at our talk in Washington.

The meeting with Carter began shortly before 7 in the evening. With him were Vance, Brzezinski, Atherton and Quandt. I was accompanied by Simcha Dinitz, our Ambassador in Washington, and by three members of my Jerusalem staff. They were Meir Rosenne, the sagacious legal adviser to the Foreign Ministry (now our Ambassador in Paris); Eliakim Rubinstein, a young lawyer, talented and energetic, who was in the legal department of the Defence Ministry when I was the Minister and who joined me in the Foreign Ministry as my personal assistant and head of my bureau; and Naftali Lavie, who had also come over from the Ministry of Defence where he had served as the able and experienced press officer.

I had been told beforehand that the meeting with the President would be brief, as he was giving a dinner for European Foreign Ministers who were in New York for the UN Assembly. But it lasted until 1.30 a.m., Carter leaving during the dinner break to keep his engagement, and rejoining us thereafter. The main subject we were to discuss was the Geneva Conference.

President Carter can be congenial and easy to talk to. He listens attentively, formulates his ideas with clarity, and expects the same from his interlocutor, even though he may not like what he hears. His informal behaviour also puts one at ease. When he is tired, he just throws off his shoes, draws his legs up on the armchair, and hugs his knees. He has a keen sense of humour, can take a biting remark, and give as good as he gets.

I had learned enough from my first talk with him to decide this time to give him no pretext for claiming that I was not being clear. The first topic he raised was the US–Soviet declaration. It had many good points, and he failed to understand why we were so angry. I assumed he was aware of the fact that not only the Israeli Government but American Jewry and many members of Congress had been extremely critical, charging that the declaration gave renewed strength to Russian influence in the Middle East – when Egypt had gone to such lengths to weaken it.

I was reluctant to be drawn into a detailed debate on this subject: I preferred to use the time for the Geneva Conference. I therefore suggested that our legal adviser, Meir Rosenne, submit a memorandum setting forth our objections. However, the prime point that interested me was whether Israel could go to Geneva on the basis of Resolutions 242 and 338, with the accompanying announcement that she did not accept the two-power declaration. Or did America and Russia regard their declaration as the basis for the Geneva Conference?

Before replying, the President sought to make us realize how serious it would be for Israel if a public argument were to develop between us over that conference. Israel would be isolated, with world opinion against her. She would be particularly hurt by the public display of America's lack of support.

I did not underrate the gravity of his words, nor of the difficulties we would face in a crisis with the United States. But I stood by my question, and added that Israel would not go to Geneva on the basis of the joint declaration. I wanted to know whether we could reject it and still attend the conference.

Vance intervened at this point to give a positive reply. The basis for the Geneva Conference was Resolutions 242 and 338. 'What you say of the declaration is your own affair. Our agreement with the Soviet Union is binding only on us.'

I cannot say that I breathed more freely. A joint American–Russian policy would have a powerful impact, especially if it were supported by the European, Arab and Third World countries. But at least I had an answer: our objection to the declaration was no bar to our taking part in the Geneva parley.

The Americans had stated frequently that they would not support the establishment of a Palestinian State. Nevertheless I thought it proper to leave no doubt in the President's mind that Israel was utterly opposed to it, even in a federal framework with Jordan. Our aim, I told him, was to reach an agreed arrangement with the Palestinians on a pattern of co-existence, but we had certain vital interests in the West Bank and Gaza District which we could not give up. We would never return to a situation which left the populated part of the State of Israel squeezed into an eight-mile-wide coastal strip without an early-warning system in the West Bank and a military presence along the River Jordan. As a man, I said to the President, I did not think I was a coward; but as a Jew I feared for my people. We had suffered too many catastrophes in our history for us to ignore the possibility of their recurrence in the future. We could not afford to be lulled by the comforting but illusory thought that 'it can't happen to us'. Moreover, the security aspect was not our only consideration. We regarded the West Bank – biblical Judea and Samaria – as part of our homeland. We were not strangers there, and we could not give up our right to settle and acquire land in those areas.

Carter asked if we would consider a partition of those territories between Israel and Jordan. I said we would be prepared to discuss it, but I did not think it was what the Arabs wanted. The Allon Plan had been taken up with Jordan for some ten years, and the response was always a firm negative. However, if Jordan proposed it, we would give it serious study.

Since we were all being frank, and holding a gloves-off talk, I asked the President if we could be certain that the United States would not exert pressure upon us over the Palestinian issue, regardless of the Arab position.

Carter did not relish this question, but neither did he shirk an answer. He had no thought, he said, of exercising such pressure, but he did not wish us to force him that evening, in that room, to give us an undertaking not to do so. He would not commit himself to applying no pressure over Jerusalem, Sharm e-Sheikh, the Golan Heights, or the Palestinian question in general.

This was hardly reassuring, so I reminded him of his declaration that he would not saddle us with an imposed solution in our conflict with the Arabs.

That was true, Carter replied, and he gave us his 'word of honour' that he would abide by that promise. As for the establishment of a Palestinian State, he added, apart from Saudi Arabia and Syria, not one of our Arab neighbours had suggested it to him; and he personally took care to use the term 'entity' and not 'State'.

I wanted to pass on to the next topic, but Carter still had something to say about the Palestinians. He wanted no 'horse-trading', he said, but the stalemate over Palestinian representation at Geneva had to be broken. We, the Israelis, made things difficult both for the Americans and the Arabs by not allowing any Palestinian to participate in those deliberations. That was the hardest thing for them, the Americans, to explain. 'I have wasted dozens of hours on this question alone,' he said, 'and my time is of great importance to my people.' He believed Israel was far too rigid on this matter, and made it impossible for a Geneva Conference to be held.

Carter's tone matched his aggressive words. I had heard it said, I told him bluntly, that he, the President of the United States, believed we were an obstacle to peace. Was that true? Carter said it was: we had encumbered almost every issue with difficulties, and he gave several disingenuous examples. We were insisting that the practical negotiations at Geneva should be conducted with representatives of each Arab country separately, and not with a united Arab delegation. He failed to understand why. What difference did it make to us? We had explained the crucial difference several times, but that did not stop his continued questioning. We had done the same on the PLO question, yet he now cited, as an example of our stubbornness, our objection to the PLO's participation in the Geneva Conference. Why? he asked. The fact was, he said, that the obstacle to peace that caused him the gravest concern was Israel, and perhaps Syria. Egypt and Jordan showed greater flexibility. He ended with the hope that our attitude had now changed, that the difficulties would be surmounted, and we could all advance towards the Geneva Conference.

I saw little point in a long and detailed rebuttal. He knew that no one wanted peace more than Israel, but I thought he should know exactly the positions we took on the issues he had mentioned. One of them was the settlement of the refugees, and I said we were not prepared to discuss it at Geneva. The object of that conference was to reach peace agreements, and the refugee problem was outside its scope. As for the West Bank and Gaza, we were ready to negotiate with Jordan and Egypt, as well as with the Palestinians living there, provided they were included in the Jordanian delegation. We would not negotiate with the PLO.

But Begin had told him, said Carter, that he agreed to PLO participation if they were not well-known leaders. To lighten the mood, I observed that if these unknowns attended Geneva, they would quickly become very well known indeed!

The President went off to his dinner at 8 o'clock, and we resumed an hour and a half later. Carter now asked me whether within the framework of a peace treaty I would be prepared to accept an Israeli withdrawal to the May 1967 lines. He added, before I could reply: 'You once said you had been against the capture of Golan. Have you changed your mind?'

I said the clock could not be turned back. What we needed to do now was to visualize the overall map of Israel and determine the delineation of our boundaries on all the fronts. As a principle, we took the position that we would not return to the old lines, nor remove the civilian settlements, nor abolish the military installations we had established in the territories.

Carter asked if that meant no withdrawal whatsoever anywhere. I said that would be putting it too strongly. For my own part, I would go a long way to meet Egypt if its Government wanted peace. As for the West Bank, I thought it possible to reach an arrangement whereby we would not annex the area, but nor would it be under foreign sovereignty. We would remain there, maintain our military installations, and live together with the local Arabs.

Carter made no comment, though it was evident that he held to his views as I did to mine. Later in the meeting he said he believed that Arabs would show some elasticity over Sinai and the West Bank, but not over Golan.

The talk with the President lasted until midnight. We spent another two hours with Vance and his aides drafting an agreed working paper and a joint communiqué to the press. The texts of both were cabled to Israel for approval.

Our joint working paper, headed 'Suggestions for the Resumption of the Geneva Peace Conference', was brief, consisting of some half a dozen sentences, each one carefully phrased. It read:

1. The Arab parties will be represented by a unified Arab delegation, which will include Palestinian Arabs. After the opening sessions, the conference will split into working groups.

2. The working groups for the negotiation and conclusion of peace treaties will be formed as follows: Egypt–Israel; Jordan–Israel; Syria–Israel; Lebanon–Israel. (Lebanon could join the conference when it so requested.)
3. The West Bank and Gaza issues will be discussed in a working group to consist of Israel, Jordan, Egypt and the Palestinian Arabs.
4. The solution of the problem of the Arab refugees and of the Jewish refugees (who fled the Arab countries) will be discussed in accordance with terms to be agreed upon.
5. The agreed basis for the negotiations at the conference ... are UN Security Council Resolutions 242 and 338.

We had told the Americans that our Government might reject the document in whole or in part; and, indeed, a cable arrived from the Prime Minister next morning with two reservations. One was particularly annoying. He thought that in Article 1, which spoke of 'a unified Arab delegation', I had not ensured the exclusion of the PLO, when that was precisely what I had done. Not only was there no mention of the PLO anywhere, but in other ways, too, we had devised, together with the Americans, a suitable manner of dealing with this vexed question. Moreover, Begin well knew that he had himself told Carter he agreed to the participation of 'not known PLO members', and would not 'examine the credentials' of Palestinians in the Jordanian delegation. I considered such formulae a sham, and thought we had done well to keep them out of the working paper.

Begin's second reservation touched on a matter of principle. It referred to Article 3 which included 'the Palestinian Arabs' in the working group discussing West Bank issues. It was clear that there was no talk of their being a party to negotiations for a peace agreement nor candidates for statehood. It was true, however, that this was the first time we were recognizing them as legitimate partners in negotiating the future of the West Bank and Gaza. Up to then, the successive Governments of Israel had insisted on the participation of the Palestinian Arabs only as members of a Jordanian delegation. I had other views. If we rejected foreign rule in the West Bank, and sought an agreed means of living together with its inhabitants, we needed to involve them in talks on this subject. I knew that Israeli opinion was divided, and thought it proper for the Government to determine its stand on this important issue. After an exchange of telephone calls and cables, the Prime Minister told me that the text of the working paper I had recommended would be discussed by the Government immediately upon my return to Jerusalem, which would be on 11 October, soon after my address to the UN General Assembly.

I regarded the working paper and its appendices as a considerable achievement. Of course it was not yet an operational plan for Geneva. The Americans would still have to try to convince the Arabs to accept its guiding principles, and I thought the chances of that were slim. No one could yet tell whether or not there would be a resumption of the Geneva Conference. But the objective of prime importance was to secure a co-ordinated stand on this difficult issue with Washington, and we had done that. Therein lay the value of the working paper.

I gave my speech to the United Nations Assembly on Monday afternoon, 10 October, and promptly left for the airport, arriving in Israel after a long night flight at 9.30 in the morning. I drove straight to Jerusalem to see the Prime Minister, and we immediately took up the points in the working paper on which he had reservations, among them his concern over a possible PLO presence at Geneva. I added reassuring details, and he seemed satisfied that PLO members could not be included in the Arab delegation against our will. As for his hesitations about involving local Palestinian representatives in a discussion on the future of the West Bank and Gaza, I had nothing new to tell him. I simply repeated my arguments in support of their participation, but the Prime Minister was non-committal. He listened, made comments, but gave no indication of his stand.

Thus, when the Cabinet met, I could not be certain what the decision would be. But after my report and the detailed deliberations that followed, the Government's approval, which had been withheld when I was still in New York, was formally given to the working paper. The decision was favourable because that was what the Prime Minister had wanted: he had dropped his reservations and the ministers had acquiesced. (Though I was well satisfied with this result, I could not help thinking that in earlier Governments in which I had served, even the one under the forceful Ben Gurion, the ministers were less meek. When they disagreed with the Prime Minister, they spoke out openly and voted against him.)

I briefed the Knesset Foreign Affairs and Defence Committee next day on the background to our agreement with the Americans on the working paper. There was the usual criticism of the Government in this all-party forum, though this time it came not so much from the Labour Opposition as from the more extreme members of Begin's own party. However, this was not a decision-making body, and its views did not commit the Government. The main campaign arena was the Knesset plenum, which was to hold a special session the following day.

It had been called by the Labour Party. The House was in recess at the time, and members had been summoned from vacation to discuss, ostensibly, the political effects of the joint US–Soviet declaration. The central topic, however, was the working paper.

The opening speaker was Leader of the Opposition Shimon Peres, who gave a sorry performance. It is, of course, the purpose – and the right – of the Opposition to discomfit the Government. But his speech was full of pathos, and marked by a blithe indifference to reality – which was unlike him. He argued that the Government was using the negotiations as a substitute for peace rather than the means of attaining peace. He also claimed that we had given way to the American proposal for a PLO presence in Geneva, and held that the united Arab delegation would in fact become an operative group and not simply a ceremonial body.

Swept by the waves of his eloquence, Peres then declared it well-nigh scandalous for us to have agreed that 'Palestinian Arabs who were not known as members of the PLO' could be included in the united Arab delegation, and that we would not 'examine their credentials'. This may not have been a deliberate distortion, but his listeners may well have inferred that Peres was quoting from the working paper. This implication was strengthened when he went on to say that the practical interpretation that would be given to our agreement and our concessions was the readiness on our part to discuss with the Arabs the establishment of a Palestinian State! He ended with the warning that we might be closer to the Geneva Conference but not to peace. Indeed, we had brought ourselves nearer to a military confrontation with our neighbours.

I replied on behalf of the Government. I have known Peres for many years – we had been long-time colleagues – and I was astonished and saddened by his speech. What was particularly disappointing was the fact that only the previous day, as a member of the Foreign Affairs and Defence Committee, he had heard my detailed account of the moves that had brought about the agreed text of the working paper with the Americans, and thus knew that his charges were baseless.

However, I spent only a short time disposing of these allegations, preferring to use the occasion to stress the key importance of our sitting with the Palestinian Arabs of the West Bank and Gaza to talk about the pattern of living together. I made clear that I was not proposing that we discuss with them the prevention of Palestinian statehood: we would do that without their agreement. Nor would we discuss with them Israel's right to settle and maintain a military presence in these territories: Judea and Samaria were part of our ancient homeland, the cradle of our nation, and never again would we be cut off from them. But since we were not annexing the West Bank and Gaza, and nor would they be under any foreign sovereignty, we should certainly talk to the Palestinian inhabitants about co-existence.

The Labour Party took a different approach, clinging to its traditional stand that Israel should hold talks only with Jordan, and the representation of West Bank and Gaza Arabs should therefore be merged with a Jordanian delegation. The fact that the Government of Jordan firmly opposed their inclusion, and the King insisted that he was not the appointed patron of these Palestinians, left Peres and his friends unimpressed. For them, apparently, Jordan was presumptuous in assuming that she was a sovereign kingdom, and that she, and not Israel, had the right to decide on the composition of her delegation.

The Knesset defeated the Opposition resolution by 41 votes to 28. All in all, though I regretted the Labour Party's objection to Israel's talking to the Palestinian Arabs of the West Bank face to face, I was pleased that the subject had been aired in the Knesset, and that the working paper had thereby received not only Cabinet but also parliamentary approval.

This had been a special, though not very edifying, session of the Knesset. No one could know then that the next time Israel's parliament was to be called into special session would be five weeks later, the occasion one of the most dramatic in its three-decade history.

CHAPTER SIX

Sadat in Jerusalem

President Sadat, addressing Egypt's parliament on 9 November 1977, included a sentence he had uttered in other speeches, expressing his readiness to travel to the ends of the earth if that would help prevent a single Egyptian son from being killed or wounded in battle. This time, however, departing from his prepared text and emphasizing each word, he added that Israel would be surprised to hear that he was ready to go to her parliament - the Knesset itself - to parley with them.

He repeated this to members of a US Congressional delegation who had arrived in Cairo after visiting Israel. In Jerusalem they had been told by Prime Minister Begin that he was ready to meet President Sadat, and they now asked Sadat for his response. He said he was willing to go to Israel for a few days to address the Knesset and talk to its members about establishing a true peace between Israel and the Arab countries.

Israel did not rush in with an official reply. It was not clear to the Government whether Sadat's statement was one of operational intent - a clear acceptance of Israel's long-standing appeal for direct negotiations - or simply an exercise in propaganda. Begin's first public reaction was a general call to the Egyptian people to make peace. He added that Sadat could go to the Geneva Conference and present his views there, just as we could. Only four days later, speaking at a reception to a French delegation in Tel Aviv's Hilton Hotel, did Begin announce that he 'extends, on behalf of the Israeli Government, an official invitation to the President of Egypt, Anwar Sadat, to come to Jerusalem to conduct talks for a permanent peace between Israel and Egypt'.

Begin repeated the invitation two days later, again in a speech to an overseas delegation. This time, however, he said he was prepared to transmit it formally to Sadat through the good offices of the United States embassies in Tel Aviv and Cairo. He added that, for his part, if President Sadat were to invite him to Cairo he would willingly accept.

That same evening, 15 November, an official invitation went to Cairo, through diplomatic channels, proposing that Sadat come to Jerusalem the following week.

Pondering over Sadat's true intentions in the days following his Cairo declaration, Begin finally shed all doubt and scepticism, and wholeheartedly favoured the visit. He realized its value as a first step in the march to peace, and as an act of historic importance. There was also the impact of the dramatic atmosphere that heightened in intensity day by day. But no thorough deliberations were conducted in preparation for Sadat's arrival. This may have been because Begin had long held fixed traditional positions and defined formulae on all subjects at issue between us and the Arabs. They simply needed resharpening for the forthcoming dialogue.

I was far more restrained in my enthusiasm. Like the Prime Minister in the first few days, I felt that the purpose of Sadat's visit needed to be examined most carefully. But even when this had been done, not all the shadows vanished. True, ever since the Yom Kippur War I had judged that Sadat was interested in peace, and now, too, I believed that his projected visit to Jerusalem was in line with this purpose. But the question was what would Sadat expect from us in exchange? My mind was not eased by the sound of the voices that reached us from Cairo. The Egyptians seemed to be anticipating an unprecedented gesture on our part, a daring show of extreme generosity – nothing less than an Israeli commitment to withdraw from all the territories gained in the 1967 Six Day War. Nor could we find any cause for celebration in Sadat's trip to Damascus to co-ordinate positions with Syria's President Assad. Of course, knowing the Arabs, I recognized that the Egyptian press had to present a tough line as a defence against the attacks on Egypt by the media of the other Arab countries. Still, one could hardly ignore what was being said and written in Sadat's name.

The official Egyptian radio, for example, declared that Egypt remained firmly committed to the strategic aims of the Arab world, and that the purpose of Sadat's visit to Jerusalem was 'to unmask the true face of Israel, who presents herself as a lover of peace'. In a cabled message to a symposium in Tel Aviv organized by a monthly periodical critical of the Israeli Government, Sadat wrote, two days before his visit, that one had to recognize 'the unshakeable right of the Palestinian nation to a homeland of its own'. In his talk with the US Congressional delegation in Cairo, Sadat demanded that the PLO be represented at the Geneva Conference, and that the negotiations would bring about the establishment of a Palestinian State. Cairo's authoritative newspaper *Al-Ahram* wrote that Sadat's proposed visit was conditional upon an advance commitment by Israel to evacuate all the conquered Arab territories, and to recognize the rights of the Palestinians, including statehood. The newspaper *Al-Akhbar* declared that Israel had finally to understand that the purpose of the Geneva Conference was not to negotiate over co-existence between Israel and the Palestinians but over the establishment of a Palestinian State and Israel's withdrawal from all the captured territories.

I recalled the blustering words of Tuhami at our meeting in Morocco, that 'Sadat will not shake Begin's hand before Israel promises to withdraw from all the territories'. I was pleased that Sadat had backed down from this position, and that he would be coming to Jerusalem unaccompanied by any preconditions. However, while judging it of great importance, I awaited his visit with no little concern. I knew how it would open – with celebratory streamers and bunting, and a flourish of trumpets. But how would it end?

Sadat arrived at Ben Gurion airport at 8.30 in the evening of Saturday, 19 November 1977, shortly after the end of the Jewish Sabbath, and was received with the panoply of protocol, complete with red carpet, searchlights, salvo, flags, national anthems, and guard of honour. After an exchange of greetings, he shook hands with those in the front rank of invited guests, chatted briefly with a few of us, and drove to Jerusalem with our President, Ephraim Katzir.

The ceremony was impressive. But what moved all who were present, and all who were glued to the television screens, was the very fact of an Egyptian President arriving in an Egyptian civilian aircraft and landing at Israel's international airport as the guest of the Israeli Government, with Israeli troops at the salute, his party of aides and correspondents mingling with their Israeli counterparts, and all bursting with emotion. It was a great occasion.

We drove up to Jerusalem in a long convoy. With me in the car was Butros Ghali, Minister of State for Foreign Affairs, a lean man of sallow complexion and serious mien. It was our first meeting, and he looked rather tense; but I came to learn that there was always a tenseness about him, even when he smiled. In the drive to Jerusalem's King David Hotel, we spent little time on polite exchanges – he asked me about my archaeological interest, and told me of his own collection of Hellenistic antiquities. We then plunged into the issues uppermost in our minds.

Ghali spoke grimly of the angry reactions to Sadat's peace initiative by the other Arab leaders, who claimed it had torpedoed the united front the Arabs had hoped to present at the Geneva Conference. He stressed that Egypt had to avoid at all costs entering into a separate peace with us, and so any arrangement that was arrived at had to include the Palestinians and Jordan.

I told him I was aware of the opposition to Sadat's moves by the Arab world, and understood Egypt's problem. But to the best of my knowledge, there was no chance of bringing Jordan and the Palestinians to the conference table. Therefore Egypt had to be ready to sign a peace treaty with us even if she were not joined by others.

Ghali was noticeably upset. He had believed that Sadat's visit would break the 'psychological barrier', that Israel would be kind enough to retire behind the 1967 borders, and the Palestinians and Jordan would join the peace agreement. He had evidently interpreted what I had said not as my estimate of the situation but as my desired goal. 'I am very sorry', he remarked, 'that this is your approach to the problem.' Despite his displeasure, I saw no point in blurring the sharp lines of reality. I, too, like Ghali and Sadat, would have liked to secure a peace settlement not only with Egypt but with all our neighbours. However, it was clear to me that the gap between Ghali and myself was mainly over his concept of the price Israel had to pay for peace – total withdrawal and the establishment of a Palestinian State.

We also touched on the PLO in our talk. I suggested to him that it would be well if Sadat did not demand that Israel negotiate with that organization. If he did, he would receive a vigorous rejection. Ghali promised to tell this to his President, and, indeed, when Sadat addressed the Knesset next day, he made no mention of the PLO.

This was Ghali's first drive over the stretch of road from the airport to Jerusalem. But since it was dark, and there was little he could see, I gave him a running commentary on the countryside through which we were travelling. The airport we had just left was in the coastal plain, the Sharon of the Bible, and along it ran the route of the ancient Way of the Sea which was under the control of one or other of the great powers in ages past, Egypt and Assyria. From the Sharon, travelling eastwards, we had entered the biblical Shephelah, the strip between the coast and the Judean foothills, which had been settled largely by the Canaanites and, later, the Philistines. When we reached the Gate to the Valley – Sha'ar ha'gai in Hebrew, Bab el-wad in Arabic – I told him that from here we started the climb up the Judean hills to Jerusalem. These hills were part of the north–south range which had held the population centres of Israel in the days of antiquity, and this was the spinal column of the Land of Israel, lying between the Mediterranean and the River Jordan. Jerusalem, whose lights we could now see blinking in the distance, was built upon the ridge, and from there the road split into three – eastwards to the Jordan Valley and the Dead Sea, southwards to Hebron and Beersheba, and northwards to Nablus and the Galilee.

We entered the brightly lit streets of Jerusalem, decorated with flags and banners of welcome, and drove past cheering crowds who had come in their throngs to greet the visitors despite the cold and the lateness of the hour. Most of them were young people, their faces expressing genuine joy. When we arrived at the King David Hotel, we found the foyer thick with guests and correspondents, and it was with some difficulty that we made our way through to the elevator. I saw Ghali to his room and bade him goodnight.

The first meeting with Sadat in which I took part was at a working lunch the following day. We were six: Sadat had with him Mustapha Khalil, who was then Secretary of the ruling Arab Socialist Unity Party (and would later be Premier and Foreign Minister), and Butros Ghali. Accompanying Begin were Professor Yigael Yadin, Deputy Prime Minister, and myself. Begin invited Sadat to open the discussion. Sadat agreed, and related that he had been to the Kremlin four times, and on each occasion his Russian hosts had told him it was the function of the guest to be the first to speak. He soon managed rather elegantly to pass the ball back to us. 'You already know all I have to say, for I have expressed in public my views on the conditions for an agreement.' Yadin tried to press him, and asked what else he had to tell us in addition to what he had announced publicly. Mustapha Khalil stepped in and said we had to understand that they did not wish the impression to be created that Egypt was conducting direct negotiations with us. This remark was addressed to Begin who, at the beginning of the lunch, had suggested installing a Cairo-Jerusalem 'hot line', similar to the one between the United States and the Soviet Union. Khalil also urged us to raise no proposals which might suggest an Egyptian intention to sign a separate peace. Begin then took over with some general observations. It was high time we made peace. The problems to be solved were numerous and complex. We should therefore establish a procedure and mechanism for holding discussions. Sadat seemed disappointed. He did not want procedure but substance. Working papers did not interest him, nor did he think that 'appropriate preparations', suggested by Begin, were necessary.

Sadat's words were clear enough in spirit, but were not marshalled to convey precise meaning. What exactly, in practical terms, was he suggesting? I asked whether he wished to discuss substantive issues, such as the Palestinian problem, the Golan Heights, an agreement with Jordan, there and then, during his current visit. His answer was a firm positive. He had come to Jerusalem for that very purpose. In that case, I persisted, did he not want some procedural system, such as the appointment of a joint body, so that the talks could continue? No, he said abruptly. Such a body was unnecessary. Substance was what had to be discussed, and he wanted to know from us what we were prepared to offer and what we were not prepared to offer.

The President of Egypt was angry, and my own fuse was also getting rather short. I said brusquely that if his object was to discuss basic issues, then the programme of his visit left no time for it. It was taken up entirely with ceremonial and public functions. At 6.45 that morning he had gone to pray at the Mosque of el-Aksa – his visit coincided with the Moslem Festival of the Sacrifice. After prayers he had stayed to talk with the worshippers, who had greeted him with cries of 'With soul and blood we shall redeem the Mosque of el-Aksa!' At 11 he visited the Yad Va'Shem Holocaust Memorial. At 12 we had met for lunch, and when that ended, he would have to get ready for the main event of the day: his address to the Knesset. The evening, too, was busy. Begin was giving a festive dinner in his honour. At 10 next morning he would be meeting representatives of our parliamentary parties. At noon he would be giving a joint press conference with Begin. At 2 he would take his leave of President Katzir, and at 3 he would emplane for Cairo. When did he think it would be possible to hold serious discussions and reach agreement on such weighty issues?

Sadat softened. In that case, he said, we should at least start practical talks now, and continue them after his return to Egypt. The important thing was for us to go to the Geneva Conference with an agreed programme.

But who would be the parties preparing this 'agreed programme'? I asked him. The Syrians? The Jordanians? The Palestinians? The United States? Again he lost patience, and again he gave no clear answer. 'I don't care who they are, or who comes to the conference. Whoever wants to can come. Whoever doesn't want to can stay at home, and we'll carry on our deliberations without him.' Vague words. If indeed there were detailed prior discussions which led to agreement on all issues, what need was there for the Geneva Conference? Was it simply to set the formal seal on an agreement that would already have been reached, or was it to negotiate with those Arab leaders who refused to take part in the preliminary discussions?

The working lunch ended without any practical decisions being taken; but what Sadat sought to attain by his visit was now evident. He wanted to get a clear reaction from us to his peace plan: he would present this plan to our Knesset that afternoon, and he believed the Knesset would be persuaded by his words and accept his proposals.

Well before four o'clock on that Sunday afternoon, 20 November 1977, the crowded Knesset had an air of high expectancy. The public galleries, too, were full, and my wife Rahel found a seat in the row reserved for foreign diplomats. When the President of Egypt entered, accompanied by the President of Israel, everyone rose and greeted the visitor with prolonged applause. The Knesset in its time had known days of varied fortune in national affairs in war and peace, days of tragedy and of triumph, of mourning and of exultation. But never had there been a day like this. The Speaker of the Knesset rapped his gavel, welcomed Sadat, and invited him to deliver his address. He was to be followed by Prime Minister Begin and Leader of the Opposition Shimon Peres.

Sadat opened with the traditional Moslem blessing, followed it with a flow of words in favour of peace and opposition to war, and said he had come to the Knesset so that together we could build a new life founded on peace. After this preamble, he stressed the need to be frank and say clearly what was in our minds. 'I decided to go to Israel', he said, 'because I wished to present the complete facts as they are to the people of Israel.'

We had not received a copy of his text in advance, so while he spoke I tried not only to absorb what he was saying but also to grasp his intentions. When he went on to explain what he meant by 'complete facts', he defined the peace to be established between us and the Arabs as 'a just peace based on respect for the resolutions of the United Nations'. (I asked him what exactly he had meant by that when I sat next to him at dinner in the evening. He replied quite openly that the United Nations Charter did not demand that its member nations sign peace treaties and establish diplomatic relations with each other. A 'just peace', according to the UN, meant that differences between nations should be resolved through diplomatic means and not through war. That, and that alone, was what Egypt was prepared to undertake in her future relations with Israel. 'No more war' – simply the commitment not to embark on military action, and nothing beyond that.)

Continuing his address in the Knesset, Sadat went on to list his Noes, itemizing the things he and Egypt would not do. He would not sign a separate peace with Israel. He would make no interim agreement. 'Our land is not up for bargaining.' Neither he nor any other Arab had the right or the will to give up an inch of Arab land, or even to argue or bargain about it. Israel had to live within her borders, and she would receive all the guarantees needed to ensure that she would not be attacked by her Arab neighbours. 'Therefore,' he said, 'I have come to tell you that we insist on your total withdrawal from all the territories conquered by Israel in 1967, including Arab Jerusalem.' To make sure we understood, he repeated that sentence, and added: 'The heart of the struggle is the Palestinian problem, and you must recognize the right of the Palestinians to their own State and their own entity. That is the first step along the only path leading to peace.'

Sadat concluded with a restatement of the principles he said should underlie a peace agreement to be reached at the Geneva Conference: an end to the occupation of Arab lands; the right of the Palestinians to an independent entity and fulfilment of their other basic rights; the right of all countries in the region to live in peace within their borders, with suitable guarantees; the obligation of these countries to maintain relations with each other in accordance with the UN Charter, namely, to resolve conflict not through force of arms but by peaceful means; and an end to the existing state of war in the area.

It was a good speech, and it was listened to with close attention. True, it contained a good deal of rhetoric, and was sprinkled with quotations from the Bible and the Koran to evoke the vision of a supreme moral message. But this did not obscure the operative parts of the address. Sadat's demands for Israeli concessions on boundaries, Jerusalem and a Palestinian State were uttered with emphatic clarity.

This appearance before Israel's parliament was the central political event of his visit. Yet while his initiative, and his presence in Israel's capital, will long be remembered, his speech will not. Future historians looking through the archives will examine the text, compare it with what subsequently happened, and quickly discern those parts that were realized and those that remained mere words on paper, soon forgotten.

Sadat's delivery was not very distinguished, no doubt because he was speaking in English and not in his native Arabic. He was verbose, groped frequently for the right enunciation, stumbled over phrases. Yet he enthralled his listeners. The force of his personality dimmed his oratorical limitations. He radiated sincerity, and was at one with his audience, as though speaking personally to each individual from the heart.

Even after hearing his extreme demands, I judged that there was a chance of coming to an understanding with him. I felt he honestly wanted to end the successive series of wars with Israel, and this desire would bring him closer to our positions. We would need to sit with him face to face and explain what Israel would be prepared to do and what she was unable to do.

When the applause died down, it was Begin's turn at the rostrum. His speech was much shorter and more fluent, though it, too, was not lacking in rhetoric and declamation on the boons of peace, interspersed with biblical quotations. Yet I did not think his speech, either, would be writ large in the chronicles of history, though it must be said to Begin's credit that, in the substantive part of it, he made his position abundantly clear *vis-à-vis* Sadat's demands.

The President of Egypt, he said, knew before coming to Jerusalem that Israel's views on permanent boundaries differed from those of Egypt, and he urged Sadat not to rule out any subject with the claim that it was not negotiable. The approach of the Israeli Government was that everything was negotiable, and no party should submit preconditions. Our eyes would be open and our ears attentive to any proposal.

He ignored the Palestinian issue completely. He concentrated on Jerusalem, observing that since it was reunited in 1967 all creeds had free access to their Holy Places. 'We can guarantee to the Moslem and Christian worlds', he said, 'that this free access will be safeguarded for ever!' The assumption was that Israel had no intention of giving up control over the whole of Jerusalem, though he did not say so specifically. Nor did he point to the fact that Jerusalem was the capital of Israel.

On the procedural aspect, Begin expressed Israel's readiness to take part in the Geneva Conference with all the Arab States that wished to come. The negotiations should be held on the basis of UN Security Council Resolutions 242 and 338. The peace had to be a complete peace, and the first clause had to be a declaration cancelling the state of belligerency. If President Sadat wished to hold prior talks with Israel, Israel was ready to do so. We could begin that very day, he said, turning to Sadat, or the following day, and continue them in Cairo or any other place.

Begin was followed by Shimon Peres, who spoke for the Opposition. It was a good speech, but the best of speeches on such occasions from the Opposition benches can have no practical significance.

During the addresses, there was an air of expectancy in the Chamber, as though some miracle was about to happen – the leaders of Israel and Egypt might produce some redeeming formula, shake hands and announce that peace had been established. No miracle occurred. Each speaker delivered his address and sat down. The Knesset Speaker declared the special session closed, the distinguished guests departed, and the audience dispersed, leaving behind them an empty hall – as empty as their hearts.

Thirty of us reassembled for the Prime Minister's dinner at 8 o'clock, fifteen from the Egyptian party and fifteen of us. Ezer Weizman, full of fun and banter, was the only one who tried to introduce a spirit of liveliness into the proceedings. Sadat sat glum, absorbed in his thoughts, pecking at his food, uttering not a word. Begin was on one side of him, I on the other. After the first course, eaten in silence, I asked him about his visit. He said he was very disappointed, particularly by Begin's speech, and he proposed to say so at the joint press conference they would be having next day. We had turned down all his peace proposals, he declared. That was not true, I said: surely he did not expect Begin to say 'Aye aye, Sir' to everything he, Sadat, had demanded. Egypt and Israel held different views, and what Begin had suggested was negotiations without prior conditions, that everything was negotiable. Indeed, Begin had not even excluded the subject of Jerusalem.

Would there, I asked, be a continuation of the talks? Sadat said there would, referring to his arrangement with Begin the previous night that Tuhami and I would continue to meet in Morocco, or, perhaps as a gesture to Ceausescu, in Romania. As for Begin's mention of possibly going to Cairo to deliver a return address to its Egyptian parliament, Sadat said he could not agree to this as long as we continued to occupy Sinai, 'which is Egyptian soil'. 'I am ready', he added, 'to invite Begin to my house in Ismailia, and to bring there the members of parliament so that Begin can speak to them.'

'I'm sure you don't intend to allow your peace initiative to wane,' I said to Sadat. 'The way to advance is to continue the talks, and, believe me, you won't be sorry.' Sadat listened but offered no reaction.

At the joint press conference next day, an agreed statement by Sadat and Begin was read to the correspondents. It said that the Government of Israel proposed that the dialogue between the two countries should continue, and this would pave the way for negotiations leading to the signing of a peace treaty in Geneva with all the neighbouring Arab States. The statement did not say that Egypt agreed to a continuation of the talks, but it was to be understood that Sadat had not rejected the proposal.

Cairo's newspaper *Al-Ahram* had published an article that morning, written by its diplomatic correspondent who was with Sadat in Jerusalem, stating that Sadat had played his part. It was now up to Israel to play hers, by withdrawing from all the occupied territories and enabling the establishment of a Palestinian State. This Egyptian demand was to be expected. But the key point in the Egyptian stand was expressed by Sadat when he landed in Cairo on his return from Jerusalem. He announced that in the coming week he would prepare the second stage of the preliminaries for the Geneva Conference. (The first stage had been his visit to Jerusalem.) He would call a preparatory meeting, to which all the Arab States – and the PLO – would be invited, and the PLO, said Sadat, should also take part in the Geneva Conference itself.

The *Al-Ahram* article and Sadat's announcement were intended for export, primarily to the Arab world. They did not wholly reflect the conclusions reached by Sadat and his delegation before leaving Jerusalem. Ghali told me about them when we drove to the airport. He said the question of whether the visit had been a success or a failure depended on what happened next. The visit had caused something of an earthquake. A building had toppled, and we had now to consider what was to be erected in its place. The first need, he said, was to continue the talks – but in private, not through parliamentary speeches. The second was to recognize that the prime problem was the Palestinians.

I had a feeling of *déjà vu* – regurgitating our differences in the talk we had had two days earlier on our drive to Jerusalem. I suggested to Ghali that we talk, instead, of the relations we hoped to establish between our two countries; but he declined. We had first to determine the framework of a comprehensive arrangement, he said, to include all the Arab States and the Palestinians.

I tried to explain why his approach would lead inevitably to deadlock:

You don't want to be the first Arab State to make an agreement with us, and you don't want a separate agreement, but we can't discuss an agreement with Syria without the Syrians, nor can we solve the problem of the Palestinians without their representatives. Joint deliberations with all the Arab representatives are possible only in Geneva, but you Egyptians want to hold a kind of 'mini-Geneva' – your 'preparatory meeting' – before the Geneva Conference. But you've heard the reactions of your Arab colleagues to Sadat's peace initiative. Radio Damascus reported this morning that Sadat had embraced Begin and Dayan, 'the two greatest terrorists of the century'. Do you still think you are authorized to make an agreement with us on behalf of the Syrians? If not, then the only thing we can discuss about Geneva is procedure, but Sadat does not want to do that. He wants to deal only with substantive matters.

Ghali smiled. 'You know,' he said, 'I have not even read the working paper you prepared with the United States. Sadat had dismissed it as unimportant. The chief thing, he said, was his visit to Jerusalem. That would launch a new era.'

We had a few words on the problem of Jerusalem which, like that of Egypt, Syria and the Palestinians, was a central issue. I told Ghali that in considering the future of Jerusalem, we would do well to begin not with sovereignty but with the status of the Holy Places. To my surprise, Ghali remarked that we should look ahead and try to come up with a new concept as an alternative to sovereignty. I asked him whether he could persuade the conservative Saudis that sovereignty, in so far as it concerned Jerusalem, was outmoded. Ghali reflected for a few moments and then said quietly that, alas, I was right: it was not possible to conduct a sophisticated symposium with the Saudi Arabians as one could at a university.

I went back to my original thesis. If, I said, we wanted to progress and achieve practical results, we had to deal with matters on which the Egyptians were authorized to decide and to act. Ghali picked on the Gaza District, and said that Sadat wanted it to be given independence. I was amazed. Surely, I said, he was not serious. Gaza was cut off from the West Bank. It had no industry and no market for its farm produce. Forty thousand Gazans found work in Israel, and half the inhabitants were refugees. Did they want to make an independent State out of that territory and that population? Unfortunately,

I told Ghali, he and his people talked about Jerusalem, Gaza and the West Bank without knowing the realities of those places.

As we neared the airport, Ghali returned to the topic with which he had started, saying that to make a success of Sadat's visit, we had to continue our joint consultations with a view to reaching agreement on the points at issue. I told him that was precisely what Prime Minister Begin had urged in his speech. 'We are wholeheartedly in favour of continued consultations,' I said, 'and ready to meet at any time and any place – even at the North Pole.'

What had really prompted Sadat to take the daring step of going to Jerusalem? That was a question I had long wanted to ask the man himself. I could not do so during his visit – there was neither the time nor the opportunity nor the appropriate circumstances. I had also desisted on the several occasions on which I had seen him afterwards, at Camp David, in Egypt, and again in Israel – even when we were alone. The mood had to be right if I were to receive the frank answer I hoped for. This occurred a year and a half later, at a talk we had in Ismailia on 4 June 1979, after the peace treaty between his country and mine had been signed.

The Ismailia meeting had not been scheduled, and for me, at least, it was unexpected. I had come to Cairo to discuss certain matters relating to the implementation of the treaty with Mustapha Khalil and Butros Ghali. But when I landed at Cairo airport Ghali informed me that the President wished to see me, and a helicopter was waiting to take me straight to Sadat's residence at Ismailia, on the bank of the Suez Canal.

After an hour's flight we landed near the President's residence, and were taken to the broad terrace which looks out over the Canal. The President was engaged at the time with a delegation of notables from one of the Egyptian parliamentary constituencies – it was a day or so before the elections – but he appeared after about twenty minutes, greeted me warmly, and led me to a table and chairs that had been set up on the lawn facing the water. He was joined by his Vice-President, Hosni Mubarak, and Ghali.

Sadat sought to give our talk an air of informality, and indeed we were all in a relaxed mood. 'Do you know this place?' he asked with a smile. 'Yes,' I replied, 'but from the other side of the Canal. I spent a good many hours there.' We did not go on with this line of small talk. Neither of us wished to get immersed in past wars. We were now involved with peace, and the President kept stressing that he wanted to see the smooth fulfilment of the treaty. He promised he would carry out all the commitments and obligations he had undertaken, whether orally or in writing. Mubarak and Ghali tried to tone down some of his expressions, but Sadat brushed them aside, and continued in his forceful vein.

The opportunity to put my question presented itself when we were speaking about the problems Prime Minister Begin was having inside his Herut Party. Sadat said he had no doubt that Begin would prevail over his adversaries, as he was a determined and courageous personality. At first, said Sadat, he had been sceptical about Begin's willingness to conduct peace negotiations with Egypt; but during Sadat's official visit to Romania, President Nicolae Ceausescu had told him that Begin was a strong man. 'I knew', Sadat added, 'that the Egyptian people trust me, and the problem I faced was not the Egyptians but the Arab States. But Begin I did not know at all. So I asked Ceausescu, and now I know he was right. Begin is indeed a courageous man.'

This was my opening. I said to Sadat that his own visit to Jerusalem was of the highest importance, and without it there would have been no peace treaty. 'What made you come?'

Far from trying to duck the question, Sadat seemed to delight in talking about it. 'You know, Moshe, when I met Ceausescu, I put to him two questions: Is Begin strong enough to take daring decisions? And is he sincere? The Romanian President gave positive replies to both. He told me he had had a six-hour talk with Begin, and came to the conclusion that he was both strong and sincere.'

'And when did you first get the idea of a Jerusalem visit?' I asked. He replied:

When I was on my way to visit the Shah of Iran. It came to me suddenly as I was flying over Turkey *en route* to Teheran. I was searching for something that would produce shock waves, positive ones. The first idea that came into my mind was something else. This was to approach the five permanent members of the UN Security Council, the representatives of the big powers who have the right of veto, and suggest that they go to Jerusalem. I tell you frankly, I reckoned that since our 'cousins', the Israelis, are always stressing their security problem, big-power representatives sitting and deliberating for twenty-four hours could surely come up with a solution. After that, we, Egypt and Israel, could carry on ourselves.

From Iran, as you know, Moshe, I went on to Saudi Arabia, and from there, on the flight from Riadh to Cairo, I changed my mind. It occurred to me that the five big powers might not achieve what I expected from them, and their failure would aggravate the situation. I therefore decided that I would go myself to Israel. Later, as you may remember, the Saudis were angry that I had not told them, at the time, of my intended visit. They were not justified, for I took the decision to go to Jerusalem only after I had left Saudi Arabia, and while I was with them the thought had not yet entered my mind.

The principal reason for my decision was the one I have told you. I said to myself:

Israel has security problems, and she is sheltering behind them, and demanding direct face-to-face negotiations. Very well, I will go myself, meet directly and alone – I and Israel.

'What of my talks in Morocco with Hassan Tuhami?' I asked Sadat. 'Were they of any value, and did he give you an encouraging report?' Sadat said the talks were valuable and Tuhami's report had been positive. Tuhami had told him it was possible to come to certain terms with us. Sadat then added:

As a matter of fact, I sent Tuhami to meet you for quite another reason. At the time, preparations were under way for the Geneva Conference, and it was Tuhami's task to ensure that you and we, Egypt and Israel, would reach some kind of agreement before the conference convened so that it would not end in failure. The purpose of your talks with Tuhami was not to arrange a meeting between me and Begin. And my meeting with Begin, too, had another purpose – to sit face to face with Israel. You will remember that the United States was anxious to convene the Geneva Conference, and I wanted the Arabs to appear in separate delegations. President Assad of Syria was insisting that all the Arabs should be represented in a single united delegation. President Carter urged me to accept Assad's proposal and, since the Americans pressed vigorously, I was driven to comply: there would be a united Arab delegation. But after I had agreed, Syria announced her out-and-out opposition to the Geneva Conference!

I said to Sadat that I thought Syria did not wish to make peace with us. I told him of the long talk I had had with President Carter when the Geneva Conference was first being mooted, and I had argued that United States' policy would bring the Soviet Union back to the Middle East (since Russia was to be co-convenor with America). Not only Israel, I had told Carter, but a certain Arab State would also not be happy with such a conference. As far as I knew, I had said, President Sadat of Egypt had worked hard to get rid of the Russians, and here was he, Carter, bringing them back. Why was he doing this? Carter had replied that they had to co-operate with the Russians in order to solve the Arab–Israel conflict. I had not been persuaded by Carter's arguments, and – turning to Sadat – I added: 'I privately hoped that you, President Sadat, would feel the same way.'

Sadat listened to me without interruption, pulling at his pipe with long puffs, and said, when I had finished: 'I agree with you. I also remember how the peace process began. The first step was our Separation of Forces agreement.'

I told Sadat that long before that agreement, I had suggested to our then Prime Minister, Golda Meir, that Israel should retire unilaterally to a line about twenty miles from the Suez Canal. I believed that if we did this, Egypt would renew Canal operations for international shipping, and I had expressed the view to my colleagues that the Canal open to shipping was a sounder guarantee of peace than the Bar-Lev line.

Sadat was familiar with the episode. 'I know, Moshe, I know,' he said. 'It was a *chef d'œuvre*, a real *chef d'œuvre*. I know that the Lady [Golda Meir] did not want it.' To this I added that, to my regret, I was also unable to persuade the army commanders that a fully functioning Suez Canal was a better defence line than a system of fortifications.

As we rose at the end of our hour-long talk, Sadat said he had asked to see me that day as he was busy the next day, addressing the army in the morning and having to go to his home village immediately afterwards to cast his vote in the parliamentary elections. We parted as we had met, with a handshake. The Israeli Sadat was most fond of was Ezer Weizman. He always hugged and kissed him on both cheeks in the Middle Eastern manner. With Begin, too, there had developed a warm friendship, and they would hug when they met. With me, the relationship was correct, and no more than that. His coolness started with his first visit to Jerusalem, after Butros Ghali had reported to him on his talk with me. It will be recalled that I had told Ghali at the very outset that I did not think Jordan and the Palestinians would join the peace talks, and that if Egypt wanted an agreement with us she would have to sign a separate peace treaty. Ghali had gathered from this that a separate peace treaty was what I was after, and had passed his misconception on to his President.

Sadat's Jerusalem visit was also the subject of informal chats I had with the Americans during the subsequent Camp David negotiations. According to them, the main reason for the Sadat decision was that he was fed up with his Arab associates, and particularly incensed by the stubborn refusal of Syria and Jordan to take part in the Geneva Conference. He thought the key was in Washington, and the United States had the power to force its will on Israel, Saudi Arabia and Jordan, coercing them into making the required concessions to achieve an agreement.

Sadat, they said, had not consulted with the Americans before going to Jerusalem. Moreover, his announcement to the Egyptian parliament of his readiness to go and address the Knesset had not been included in the written text of his speech. It had been a spontaneous declaration, and had surprised all his listeners. Indeed, the stunned American Ambassador to Cairo had thought fit to telephone Sadat and tell him that if he was not certain that he would really be visiting Jerusalem, it would be prudent to prepare an immediate retraction. Sadat had been deeply hurt by the Ambassador's words, and had replied angrily: 'Do you think I would have said such a thing if I had no intention of fulfilling it?'

My American informants said that Sadat was very close to his people and sensed their general mood. He knew that Egypt was tired of war and yearned for peace - not the peace of surrender but a true peace that would put an end to her conflict with Israel. He well understood that a joint stand by all the Arab countries on the conditions of peace would inevitably be extreme and impractical. An Arab consensus would of necessity be based on the lowest common denominator. Thus, if he wanted peace, he had to be ready to go it alone, and hope that the other Arab States would follow.

Sadat put no trust in the Russians, and did not think they were interested in peace in the Middle East. He was convinced that for Egypt to reach an agreement with Israel, the Soviet Union had to be neutralized, and should certainly not be brought into the negotiations.

I was also told that at times Sadat had been unhappy about United States' policy. He had been disappointed with Kissinger, who had argued in 1974 that trying to secure a full peace was impractical: it was necessary to follow a policy of one step at a time. Sadat had believed it was possible, and the attempt should be made, to achieve a complete peace in a single move.

The Americans I talked to were of the opinion that the character of Sadat, no less than his reasoning and his calculation, was a factor in his decision-making. He was very independent, and he stuck to his chosen path with great determination, even when his top advisers and those closest to him in the highest echelons differed from him. He took no account of the views of other Arab leaders. He never forgot that he was the President of Egypt, which boasted a civilization going back five thousand years, while the other Arab States, even those who were rich in oil or equipped with the latest Soviet weapons, could not hope to match her in culture and political understanding.

CHAPTER SEVEN

Meeting in Marrakesh

I had left Morocco in mid September expecting to return a fortnight later for a further secret session with Tuhami. But developments overtook expectations, culminating in Sadat's dramatic visit to Jerusalem in November, which laid the foundations for a peace treaty between Egypt and Israel, and had a greater impact than any other event on the political pattern of the Middle East.

The gesture itself, the very presence of Sadat in Jerusalem, was a powerful political act, though he held no thorough discussions during his stay. He and Begin had only one basic talk, at which no protocol was taken, where the two leaders agreed to three principles: No more war between the two countries; the formal restoration of sovereignty over the Sinai peninsula to Egypt; and the demilitarization of most of Sinai, with limited Egyptian forces to be stationed only in the area adjoining the Suez Canal, including the Mitla and Gidi Passes.

Shortly after his return to Egypt, Sadat decided to convene a 'peace conference' in Cairo, and invited representatives of the Arab States, the PLO, the United States, the United Nations and Israel. It was not quite clear what the agenda or the level of the participants would be at this conference, but it seemed unlikely to prove an effective forum for practical negotiations towards a peace treaty.

A few days later came Sadat's request that I meet Tuhami once again in Morocco. (His request, and our reply, were transmitted through the good offices of the United States embassies in Cairo and Tel Aviv.) It might be imagined that if Sadat could come openly to Jerusalem, there would be no need thereafter for Israeli and Egyptian officials to meet secretly in distant places. But if that was what Sadat wanted, we were ready to comply; and perhaps something fruitful might emerge. It would, after all, be the first opportunity since the Sadat visit for the two parties to work out the broad content of a peace agreement. So I left on 2 December 1977 for another meeting with Tuhami in Morocco.

My flight this time was not through Europe but direct, much of it at low altitude, just above the surface of the Mediterranean, to avoid detection on hostile radar screens. I slept on a field cot in the plane throughout the six-and-a-half-hour journey, knowing from previous experience that I had a long night ahead. When we entered Morocco's air space, we were greeted by a Mystère plane which led us to an abandoned military airfield not far from Marrakesh, where we landed at 10 p.m.

The meeting was to be held in the royal palace at Marrakesh, a handsome building in the oriental style close to the walls of the old city. We were ushered into a palatial apartment in one of the guest wings, sitting-room, dining-room and bedrooms lavishly appointed, and the usual array of bowls of fruit and dishes of sweetmeats to tempt the most jaded palate. I spotted a sixteenth-century sculpture of Buddha in a niche in one of the walls, and wondered what it was doing there.

The King arrived at 11 p.m. The visitors – Tuhami and I, and our aides – rose, and the Moroccans kissed his hand. At first we sat together in the large guest hall, as tarbushed waiters served us mint tea and Turkish coffee, and the King gave us an introductory talk. It consisted largely of an appeal to Israel to find ways of satisfying the nationalist ambitions of the Palestinians. We then adjourned to the dining-room. It was now well after midnight, and I was becoming rather impatient to get on with the job for which we had come. But dish followed exotic dish until 3.30 a.m., hardly the hour in which to engage in serious political talk. We therefore decided to meet again at 11 a.m., and I promised Tuhami that I would set down on paper Israel's ideas on a basis for a peace treaty between our two countries, and have the document ready for discussion when we met.

At 7.30 in the morning I was at a desk writing the position paper. I had had a session with Prime Minister Begin before my departure, and we had gone over the principles which would guide me in these negotiations. I wrote in Hebrew, and my two aides produced an English translation. Tuhami arrived at 11.15, and we handed him the document. Since it was handwritten, and not too legible, we read it to him and he followed it from his copy, underlining certain points and putting question-marks against others. We were soon joined by King Hassan. This time there was a focus to the discussions – my document.

Before dealing with it, I told them that Premier Begin was preparing a plan on the subject of the Palestinians, and when it was completed and approved by the Cabinet, he would present it to President Sadat. In the meantime, however, I could tell them that it envisaged the introduction of far-reaching changes in the present pattern in the West Bank and the Gaza District, changes which would enable the Palestinian Arabs to enjoy autonomy and self-administration. The plan would not include the establishment of an independent Palestinian State in those areas, nor the withdrawal of Israel's civilian population or military forces. As for Jerusalem, we considered that to be a separate issue, and we believed that a practical solution to the problem could be reached to the satisfaction of all the parties, Arabs, Christians and Jews.

My own document made clear that the ideas therein were based on the assumption that 'a full peace treaty between Egypt and Israel' was to be established which would bring about a complete normalization in the relationship between the two States. By normalcy we meant the inclusion of such items as diplomatic and cultural relations, freedom of passage, mutual trade and tourism. Further assumptions underlying our approach were that the treaty would be concluded quickly, in about two or three months, and that it would not be conditional upon the conclusion of peace treaties with us by other Arab States. Achieving peace agreements with these countries – Jordan, Syria and Lebanon – would, of course, be desirable; but failure to do so should not be used to veto an Egypt-Israel treaty.

I told Tuhami and the King that the ideas I was presenting had not yet been brought before the Cabinet for approval; but the object of our meeting, as agreed upon with Premier Begin, was to discover the Egyptian response to them. If it were positive, the ideas would be formulated in a concrete proposal, and if they were approved by our Cabinet, we could enter immediately into practical discussions with the Egyptian Government. If, however, Egypt rejected them in principle, they were to be considered null and void, and to have no formal status. Israel would then need to re-evaluate her position.

The ideas developed in the document were based on two commitments made by President Sadat to Premier Begin during their Jerusalem talk: if Israel withdrew from Sinai, Sadat would declare the Sharm e-Sheikh Straits an international waterway; and he was ready for the whole of Sinai east of the Mitla and Gidi Passes to be demilitarized.

The document proposed alternative methods to ensure that the area remained demilitarized. The preferred one was supervision by mixed Egyptian-Israeli patrols. The second was the stationing of United Nations forces in the eastern strip of Sinai, roughly between the international boundary and the Ras Mohammad–El Arish line. In either case, Israeli civilian settlements were to remain. If the second alternative were chosen, then UN forces alone would control the eastern area, which would be barred to Egyptian and Israeli units. Thus, all Israeli military forces would be withdrawn from Sinai, except for special cases which required individual solutions, such as the status of the military airfield close to Eilat.

Among other points dealt with in the document were the future of the port and airfield at Sharm e-Sheikh and the military airfield east of El Arish. They were to be turned into civilian installations, administered by Israeli civilians under UN supervision, and opened to the ships and aircraft of all nations.

Israeli civilian settlements in Sinai were to be allowed police defence units, a mobile police patrol force, and defensive weapons. Such weapons might include armoured cars, anti-tank and anti-aircraft guns and minefields, but not planes, tanks or field artillery.

Egyptian police forces would be allowed in Bedouin and other Arab centres in the area under UN control. Israelis would be entitled to enter this UN area freely, and Egyptians from El Arish and Sinai would also have free entry not only to the UN controlled area but also to Israel. The agreement of both parties would be required to change the status of the area.

When the King and Tuhami had read and reread the paper, they put their questions and gave their reactions. What was strangely evident was their embarrassment. Not only the King but Tuhami, too, displayed a singular lack of the confidence that had characterized their posture at previous meetings. It was clear that they were much affected by the angry reactions of the Arab States to Sadat's visit to Israel, and also of internal developments in Egypt, such as the demonstrative resignation of Foreign Minister Ismail Fahmi. Even to operative questions, like the purpose of the Cairo Peace Conference, which was due to take place eleven days later, Tuhami could give no straightforward answers. He would apologize, and explain that he had been away from Cairo for several days and was not familiar with the latest developments. However, he thought we should continue to meet in Morocco for secret discussions. He begged us not to inform the Americans of our talks until we had settled all our differences. The point that most troubled Tuhami and the King was the prospect of our wanting a separate peace. They felt we could make progress in these Israel-Egypt talks only if we held similar talks with the other Arab States.

I, for my part, remained persistent. I kept asking Tuhami whether Egypt was prepared to make peace with us even if the other Arab States failed to follow suit. I cited Sadat's invitation to the Arab States to attend a peace conference in Cairo, and their response: it was turned down by Syria, Jordan and the PLO. What happened next? I asked. Tuhami replied that we would have to await developments. If the Arab States held firm to their refusal to join the peace process, he thought the level of participants at the Cairo Conference could be lowered, and Egypt-Israel talks could continue at a high level, but in secret, and not in Cairo. We would be better able to judge what to do when the positions of the Soviet Union and the Arab States were clarified. In the present situation, a meeting between Begin and Sadat could not be contemplated.

I tried to settle at least some of the issues which affected Egypt and Israel alone. I suggested, for example, that the method of supervising the demilitarization of Sinai should be the first alternative in my document, namely, joint Egyptian–Israeli patrols. Tuhami said he had discussed this with Sadat and it was not possible. This was also true of our proposals for the Israeli settlements in Sinai. Tuhami said they would all have to be withdrawn beyond the international frontier as it existed during the British Mandatory period. 'We insist on their evacuation.' It was possible, he added, to consider only the question of compensation for the houses they had built. 'The President and the people of Egypt will not agree to a single Israeli settlement or soldier remaining in Sinai.' It was idle to waste time on that subject, for there would never be a true peace between us 'as long as Israelis remain on our soil'.

Tuhami made the same point about Sharm e-Sheikh. It was true that Sadat had agreed to the presence there of UN forces; but that was only to ensure freedom of shipping through the Gulf. They would not be there to replace the Egyptians as rulers. The guiding principle was: withdrawal of all the Israelis; compensation for the evacuees; and UN supervision of the fulfilment of the treaty. Tuhami said that not even changes in the international border would be contemplated. 'You are gaining a great deal by the very fact that we would be recognizing your international frontier. You do not possess a single frontier which is recognized as an international border.' At all events, he concluded, the Sinai territory west of the international frontier would fly the Egyptian flag: not a UN flag, an Egyptian flag.

I told Tuhami that I had noted his words and would transmit them to my Prime Minister, but he should know that in my opinion Israel would not agree to his terms. His approach would not be acceptable to us as a basis for a peace arrangement.

After our discussion on the paper I had given him, Tuhami drew out his own document. It was in Arabic and, like mine, was handwritten, so he, too, read it aloud, stating the Egyptian position. When I asked him to let me have it, just as I had given him mine, he said he could not do so as it was a personal document which he had received from President Sadat.

It contained four principal points. The first insisted that the agreement we reached would need to include a resolution of the conflict with all the other Arab States, and therefore it was not to be presented as an exclusively bilateral agreement. The parts dealing with peace arrangements between Egypt and Israel would be more detailed, of course, while those concerned with the other Arab States would be set forth in general terms. These 'general terms' should include the guarantee of two principles: the return by Israel of conquered territory, and the establishment of an independent status for the Palestinians either through a Palestinian State or in some other way.

The second point touched on the kind of security guarantees that should be given to Israel – in Sinai and on the fronts with Israel's other neighbours. Egypt proposed that we rely on international or American forces. (Israel had told Sadat in Jerusalem that she wanted an Egypt-Israel solution.) Whatever was decided, the arrangement had to offer security to both parties, Egypt as well as Israel. Freedom of passage through the Sharm e-Sheikh entrance to the Gulf of Eilat should be included in this arrangement. Egypt also wanted details of the security provisions we would wish to see introduced for the West Bank, the Gaza District and the Golan Heights. Her readiness to reach a settlement with us on these subjects should demonstrate that Egypt was not interested in war, and that the issues on which agreement was required concerned not only borders but the overall problem of security – measures which would outlaw further wars.

On Sinai and the Egypt-Israel boundary, Egypt considered it essential to hold detailed discussions and reach a written agreement on 'every square yard'. On other areas, as indicated, general guidelines would suffice. However, care should be taken to ensure that our agreement should not appear as a bilateral accord, so that the Egyptians could retain the leverage to press for a comprehensive arrangement with all the Arab States.

Finally, Tuhami's document asked for Israel's expectations and proposals on co-operation with Egypt, open or secret. For example, the previous evening I had suggested that the Egyptians should attach one of their diplomats to the American embassy in Israel. Interestingly enough, said Tuhami, there was a similar proposal in his own document – that Israel attach one of its men to the US embassy in Cairo.

The talks ended towards dusk, and we could leave Marrakesh without exciting the interest of the curious. Before departing, I had a few words with the King in private, and delivered a message from my Prime Minister: Begin would like to meet him. The King responded without hesitation: he would be delighted to host the Prime Minister of Israel at any time, and would regard it as a great honour. I thanked him and promised to transmit his reply to Begin, but I doubted that the visit would indeed take place. The immediacy and graciousness of the royal reply seemed a polite substitute for the practical ingredient.

I bade him farewell, and he now kissed me on both cheeks. (The previous evening, on my arrival, he had simply shaken my hand!) I then took leave of Tuhami and his aides. A small plane flew us to the airfield where our own aircraft awaited us, and the sight from the air – it was just light enough to see – was reminiscent of the typical scenes in films with a North African setting: long-robed peasants on their way home from the fields, walking towards the high stone walls that encircled the old city; and olive groves covering the edge of the plain at the foot of the hills. Inside our aircraft we found packets of bonbons for my grandchildren and a royal feast for us and the crew. We reached the coast and turned east to Israel.

Reflecting on the day's talks, I was unhappy about the lack of clarity on Egypt's position. I had the impression that the status of Tuhami was obscure, and that his presentation of himself as the man closest to Sadat, whose words we could take as coming directly from his President, was not in fact the case. His reluctance to finalize matters, or to make a commitment on any issue, suggested to me that he had no authority to initiate ideas but only to speak and to listen – and sometimes not even that. For example, he himself raised the question of the future of the Golan Heights. Yet when I started to answer and suggest the principles of a solution, he promptly drew back and begged me not to include it in our discussions, lest the Syrians get to hear of it and castigate Egypt for interfering in what was not her concern. I also had an unhappy feeling about Sadat himself, in so far as what Tuhami and King Hassan told me reflected his policy. I did not think he would retreat from the course of peace on which he had embarked, but I suspected that he did not quite know how to advance. He knew what he wanted but not how to achieve it. I reached the conviction that unless the Americans could be involved and threw their weight behind the negotiations, the wheels of peace would remain at a standstill.

CHAPTER EIGHT

The First Steps

Two weeks after the visit of Sadat to Jerusalem, Secretary Vance went to see him in Cairo, and then came on to Jerusalem for talks with us. He arrived on 10 December with his senior aides who were dealing with the Israeli–Egypt negotiations – Habib, Saunders and Atherton – and was joined by Ambassador Lewis at the conference table in the Prime Minister's Office. Participating on our side were Premier Begin, Deputy Prime Minister Yadin, Defence Minister Ezer Weizman and myself. All were in buoyant mood, conscious that we were embarked on the road to peace.

The Americans gave us happy impressions of their Cairo visit and were optimistic about the prospects of the negotiations. Sadat believed it was possible to conclude a bilateral peace agreement with Israel, they said, but only on condition that it would be within a wider framework, otherwise he would lose the support of the Arab States. He was therefore anxious to arrive at an agreed formula with us on a declaration that could serve as the basis for peace negotiations with the Arab States. This was also his approach to the Palestinian problem. Sadat felt that the way to handle that question was through a 'declaration of principles', which could be formulated in general terms, but which would give him the necessary defence against domestic and external criticism, and enable him to conduct practical negotiations with us for a peace treaty.

I sensed that the Americans were about to complete the report on their Egyptian talks without intending to say anything about Sadat's reaction to the proposals I had put to Tuhami in Marrakesh a week earlier. These proposals, it will be recalled, were contained in the document I had given Tuhami, and dealt with arrangements in Sinai following an Israeli withdrawal. I had told Tuhami that if Egypt's response was positive, we could start practical negotiations immediately. I now debated in my mind whether to ask the Americans about Sadat's response. If it were negative, perhaps it was better not to ask. I decided to risk it, and framed the question as though I knew they had discussed the matter with Sadat.

There were a few moments of embarrassed silence. And then one of them said, choosing his words very carefully, that they had received the impression in their talk with Sadat that he accepted our proposal as a beginning to the negotiations, in the course of which we would need to consider it in detail. I was much relieved – and stole a glance at the protocol writer to see that it was being recorded in full.

So there was indeed room for optimism. On the Palestinian issue, Sadat would have been unable, even if he had wanted, to negotiate a settlement. That was a matter only for the Palestinians and the Jordanian Government, and it was understandable, therefore, that the President of Egypt would be satisfied with a declaration of principles. This was not true of Sinai. There, the two parties would need to reach a detailed and binding agreement, and if, as the Americans had said, Egypt regarded our proposals as a suitable basis for an arrangement, then there was a good chance that we would conclude a peace treaty.

The meeting ended, the visitors left greatly encouraged, and so did I – too much so, perhaps.

The next step – hardly a step, as the foot moved without advancing – was taken four days later, with the opening on 14 December of what was called the Cairo Preparatory Conference.

It was conceived by President Sadat in a euphoric moment upon his return to Egypt from his Jerusalem visit. People throughout the world, including his own citizens, hailed his daring move with uninhibited enthusiasm, and this prodigious success may have led him to lose sight of reality. He thought the other Arab States would follow in his wake, and that Israel, within the framework of an overall peace settlement, would agree to withdraw to the pre-June 1967 borders.

He accordingly invited the Arab States, Israel, the United States and the United Nations to meet in Cairo in order to prepare for the Geneva Conference. Their objective, in the words of Sadat, would be 'to achieve a comprehensive arrangement for permanent peace in the region'. He thought at first of making it a top-level conference, but the responses were such that he considered it wise to reduce the level of representation, and hope to follow it later with a further conference at the Foreign Ministers' level.

The Cairo Conference proved a total failure. Not a single other Arab State accepted the invitation. Only four delegations sat round the conference table, those from Egypt, Israel, the United States and the UN. The dialogue between Egypt and Israel was sterile. The Israeli delegates brought with them the model formula for a peace treaty that could have been signed by any two friendly countries anywhere in the world who had always lived in peace without need of a treaty. It did not address itself to any of the urgent issues that needed to be resolved between our countries which had been at war and which were now making peace with each other. It made no mention of borders, buffer zones, demilitarized areas, freedom of shipping, the Palestinian problem, nor of civilian Israeli settlements in Sinai. The Egyptians on their part submitted a list of principles which, they insisted, should serve as the basis for peace. These included the principle of Israeli withdrawal from all territories gained in June 1967, and the restoration of the national rights of the Palestinians with the guarantee of self-determination and independent statehood. There was also the affirmation that Egypt adhered to the decision of the Rabat summit meeting, and that the PLO was the sole representative of the Palestinians. The Israeli delegation flatly rejected these principles, and the Egyptians, of course, showed no surprise. Both sides knew they were only going through the motions of conferring, and the game they were playing was like a dialogue between two deaf people who could not yet lip-read.

Israel's representatives were Eliyahu Ben-Elissar, Director-General of the Prime Minister's Office, Meir Rosenne of the Foreign Ministry, and Major-General Avraham Tamir of the Defence Ministry. They and their Egyptian counterparts produced the appropriate smiles in public, and spoke of the atmosphere of goodwill and mutual understanding that pervaded the sessions. In fact, no agreement was reached on a single issue, not even on such procedural matters as who should be chairman and what items should appear on the agenda.

While this was happening – or failing to happen – in Cairo, two other events were stealing the world headlines. One was the Tripoli Conference of Arab States united in their vehement opposition to Israel–Egypt negotiations. These rejectionist States, headed by Syria and Iraq vigorously aided by the PLO, declared an economic and diplomatic boycott of Egypt. That made news. The other event which had more bearing on the peace process than anything coming out of the Cairo Conference was Begin's visit to Washington.

Yet despite its failure, the Cairo parley had one side-effect that was to prove positive in the long run. People in both Egypt and Israel began to accept and become accustomed to the fact that their representatives met each other face to face, and talked together as friends; that Israelis could walk freely through the streets of Cairo and Egyptians do the same in Jerusalem; and that correspondents from both countries covered the news together in each other's capitals, helped each other, exchanged views as colleagues. If the Cairo Conference produced nothing else, it contributed much to the promotion of friendly Egyptian–Israeli relations; and meetings between the nationals of both countries with interests in other areas, social, economic and academic, soon acquired the stamp of normalcy.

Begin had sought a meeting with President Carter in order to present Israel's plans for a peace agreement with Egypt and an autonomy arrangement for the Palestinian Arabs. He left for Washington the day the Cairo Preparatory Conference opened, and met with Carter on 16 December.

Before leaving, he held consultations with the ministerial security committee on the principles underlying the two plans he was to explain to the President, and the two documents, with certain amendments, were approved.

The prime motive behind Begin's initiative in proposing autonomy for the Palestinians in the territories was undoubtedly the genuine desire to achieve a suitable *modus vivendi* with the Arabs. The way he saw it, such an arrangement would give the Palestinian Arabs their own self-chosen administration.

Another possible reason was the success of Egyptian propaganda. Ever since Sadat's visit to Jerusalem, we had been urged unceasingly by friends and enemies alike to make some grand gesture to the Arabs after Egypt had done so much to end the state of war. Sadat had come to Jerusalem, broken the 'psychological barrier' of hatred, thereby isolating Egypt in the Arab world, and what were we doing in return? Where were Israel's concessions?

Thus, Begin's autonomy plan and his trip to Washington were intended in some way to balance Sadat's 'peace initiative'. Moreover, the Prime Minister was also empowered to tell the President that Israel was determined 'to solve the problem of the Palestinian Arabs in Samaria, Judea and the Gaza District'.

Begin's party comprised, as before, his close associates. But this time he also took with him Aharon Barak, who was then the Attorney-General (now a Justice of our Supreme Court). To have this brilliant jurist, who was also a man of wide interests, high intelligence and broad horizons, in the delegation was an undoubted boon for Israel.

Washington was already familiar with the broad lines of Israel's peace proposals with Egypt. Secretary Vance had received a copy of the document I had given Tuhami in Morocco, and had also heard the Prime Minister's account of his Jerusalem talk with Sadat on this subject. But the autonomy plan was new to the Americans. Carter and his aides listened to it with great interest, and saw it as a constructive and far-reaching step on Israel's part. Although it contained several points on which they differed, the President and his group heartily congratulated Begin on his courageous political approach.

Begin emerged from the White House well satisfied. It was unfortunate, however, that he hastened to make known Carter's more positive responses to the autonomy plan. Administration reaction quickly followed. Washington's official spokesmen stressed that this plan was an Israeli proposal, and it was for Israel and the Arabs to deliberate and decide on it.

The next move in the peace process came five days after Begin's return from Washington. On the morning of 25 December, an El Al plane took off from Israel's international airport with the Prime Minister, the Defence Minister and myself aboard, for a summit meeting with Egypt's President. We landed at the Abu-Suweir air base outside Ismailia (which we had severely damaged during the Six Day War) forty minutes later, to be greeted by Sadat and his ministers.

This was to be the most important step, since Sadat's Jerusalem visit, to determine the basis of our peace agreement. Begin was in high spirits. At last, he had gained his goal of direct face-to-face negotiations, without intermediaries, and under no foreign patronage. The documents he had brought with him, the Israel–Egypt peace plan and the Palestinian autonomy plan, had been well and carefully formulated, and had received the blessings of the United States President and Britain's Prime Minister (whom Begin had seen in a stopover in London *en route* back from Washington).

Not only Begin but the entire world seemed to consider the Ismailia summit meeting an historic event. Hundreds of press and television correspondents had come from far and wide to cover it. There were a hundred pressmen from Israel alone, headed by all the newspaper editors.

The town of Ismailia had a festive air, with banners and bunting and arches of honour at the main crossroads, and Egyptian flags fluttering from the rooftops above the specially swept streets. Yet I was troubled in spirit. It began with our arrival at the airport. When Sadat came to Israel he was received with the full panoply of accustomed protocol. Though I have already indicated my own attitude to pomp and ceremony, there are occasions when they carry political implications – and certainly so when they are absent. Our reception at the Ismailia airport was marked by studied casualness – no guard of honour, no Israeli flags, no national anthems. Even in the city itself, the streamers at the crossroads and giant posters in the streets bore slogans praising 'Sadat, bringer of peace'. There was no mention of Begin, and not a single welcoming sign. The only warmth came from the rays of a wintry sun.

Before beginning our talks, we attended a brief ceremony at which Muhammad Ibrahim Kamel was formally appointed Egypt's Foreign Minister, replacing Ismail Fahmi who had opposed Sadat's peace moves and resigned. Kamel, the Egyptian Ambassador to Germany, happened to be in

Cairo at the time to prepare for the visit of Chancellor Helmut Schmidt, and Sadat tapped him to succeed Fahmi. As he stood waiting to take the oath of office, he looked as though the new appointment had come to him like a bolt from the blue – and about as welcome. He did not want the job, but he lacked the courage to refuse Sadat.

From this ceremony we adjourned to the conference room, while Sadat took Begin into a study for a private half-hour talk. When they emerged to join us, Begin looked very pleased, while Sadat's expression was impenetrable. On the Egyptian side of the conference table, Sadat was flanked by Vice-President Hosni Mubarak, Prime Minister Mamduk Salem, Kamel, and Minister of War General Abd-el-Ghani Gamassi. Among those on our side, apart from the ministers, was Aharon Barak.

The great moment had come. Sadat cleared his throat and uttered appropriate words of greeting, and Begin replied in equally felicitous terms. Both leaders expressed the desires of their people for peace, and noted that the eyes of the world were upon us that day. Nor was the attachment to ancient heritage forgotten: both managed to draw Moses the Lawgiver into the Ismailia event. Sadat crossed the Red Sea with him, and Begin the wilderness of Sinai. At that point I stopped listening, and conjured up the giant figure of Moses: Moses the stammerer, who fled to the desert after he had struck down an Egyptian overseer who was beating a Hebrew bondsman; Moses who was frequently vilified by the very people he was trying to save; Moses who in his anger broke the Tablets of the Law; Moses who brought the Children of Israel out of bondage to freedom, yet who is not mentioned in the Passover Hagaddah; Moses who had borne such heavy burdens on his wilderness trek to the Promised Land, and had reached the threshold, only to be denied entry; Moses, the greatest of our leaders, buried in an anonymous grave.

Sadat made no mention in his opening address of the joint committees he and Begin had agreed to establish during their private talk before the start of our session. He may have wanted to consult with his advisers before announcing it in that wide forum. Begin clearly understood their significance: whatever the outcome of the current talks, the committees would ensure continued negotiations. He therefore reported to both delegations on the agreement he had just reached with Egypt's President. 'We have decided to establish two joint working committees,' he said, 'one for political and civil affairs, the other for military affairs. This is the start of the success of these talks!'

It was not only the start, it was also the end. On no other item was there agreement. Begin put forward Israel's peace proposals, and Sadat said they were not acceptable. Egypt, he said, would present counter-proposals, which would be based on the Rabat resolutions. And out came the familiar prescription: Israel's total withdrawal; Palestinian self-determination; no separate peace.

The Egyptians proposed that we draft a joint declaration of principles on the Palestinian question. We sat together for hours, but came to no agreement. We also found the gap very wide between our respective positions on an Egypt–Israel peace treaty. Egypt's representatives stood firm in their refusal to allow a single Israeli to remain in Sinai, neither civilian nor soldier. The most they would agree to was the presence of UN forces at Sharm e-Sheikh, but only subject to Egyptian sovereignty, and only to supervise freedom of passage through the Gulf.

The only optimistic note was provided by the sincere wish of both leaders, Begin and Sadat, to avoid a deadlock – not to throw up their hands and say the talks had failed, but to agree to continue them. This was important. It meant, for me, that Sadat truly wished to reach a peace agreement, and was seeking ways to overcome the obstacles. At the same time, however, I was deeply concerned about the price Egypt was determined to exact from us – total evacuation from Sinai; a commitment to withdraw completely from the West Bank and Golan; the rise of a Palestinian State. I sensed that there was deep feeling behind these words: they were not mere lip-service. And I suspected that Israel would indeed be faced by the grim alternative of having to make heavy concessions or achieving no peace treaty with Egypt.

At the guest-house during a conference break, I looked out from an upper window at the east bank of the Suez Canal. A few bulldozers were at work near the water, but beyond them nothing stirred. I gazed at the endless undulation of dune after dune stretching away to the horizon, and memory took me back there, back to my beloved Sinai, serene, timeless, with its vast, golden sandscape in the north, its hard granite mountains in the south. But I had never felt quite the same way about its western strip, abutting on the Canal. That area had worried me. The Bar-Lev line had posed as many problems as solutions. I had been less anxious when the artillery line had been established some ten miles to the east of it. How much blood, tension and effort had saturated our hold on the Canal!

No one can tell whether without that hold, and all it took to maintain it, Egypt would ever have been brought to the peace table. Or perhaps the reverse was true. It is at least conceivable that if Golda Meir had accepted my proposal in May 1971 to move our forces away from the Canal eastwards to the Mitla and Gidi Passes, we might have reached an arrangement with Egypt, and prevented the Yom Kippur War.

It was not, however, the unravelling of political conundrums that was uppermost in my thoughts as I gazed through the window of Sadat's guest-house. Surging into my mind came the recollection of the wars we had fought there, the inferno of the battlefield with exploding shells and rockets and mines, and burning tanks and half-tracks, and beneath the smoke the killed and the wounded.

I was being called to return to the conference table. I left the window, but the vision beyond it did not leave me.

The Ismailia summit meeting ended next day. The correspondents reported failure and disapointment: 'The mountain has given birth to a mouse.' We could not even draft an agreed communiqué, so two separate statements were given at the press conference. One read: 'The position of Egypt is that a Palestinian State should be established in the West Bank and Gaza Strip.' The other: 'The Israeli position is that the Palestinian Arabs residing in Judea, Samaria and the Gaza District should enjoy self-rule.'

On 28 December, a day after our return, the Knesset held a political debate. The Prime Minister reported on his talks in Washington and London, and on the meeting with Sadat in Ismailia. He explained the autonomy plan, reading out the full text (see Appendix 4); and he outlined the principles underlying our proposals for peace with Egypt. These covered demilitarization, civilian settlements, military withdrawal in stages, and freedom of navigation.

On demilitarization, Egyptian forces were not to move beyond the Mitla-Gidi line, and the strip of territory between that line and the Canal was to continue to be subject to the existing Reduction of Forces Agreement reached after the Yom Kippur War.

Israeli civilian settlements were to remain, and to be under Israeli administration and jurisdiction. Israeli forces would be responsible for their defence.

There was to be a transitional period of several years during which Israeli forces would fall back to a line in central Sinai, and maintain their air bases and early warning installations until their final withdrawal to the international frontier.

Freedom of shipping through the Straits of Tiran would be ensured and supervised, either by a UN force, or by joint Egypt-Israel units. If by a UN force, it could not be removed except by agreement of the two parties and a unanimous Security Council decision. The Straits of Tiran and the Gulf of Eilat to which it gives entry should be recognized by the two countries, in a special declaration, as an international waterway open to all vessels under all flags.

After hours of debate following the Prime Minister's speech, the Government's autonomy plan and guiding principles for an Egypt-Israel peace agreement were approved by a majority of 64 to 8, with 40 abstentions. The large number of abstainers came from the Labour benches. Opposition leader Shimon Peres said his party would not vote against the Government motion, but neither would it support it. 'We have removed the party whip on this motion', he explained, 'and given our members freedom to vote as they wish.'

The fact was that the Labour Party found itself in a dilemma and felt helpless. Its members did not wish to appear to be putting obstacles in the path of peace, but at the same time, as an Opposition, they felt it their task to castigate whatever the Government did. They thus took the easy way out, acting like a bewildered ostrich on a matter of vital importance to the future of Israel.

I was not present at the Knesset debate, for I was out of the country that day. I had returned from Ismailia the previous day, and left an hour later on a flying visit to Teheran for a further meeting with the Shah. He had told our diplomatic representative that he would like to see me to get a first-hand report on Sadat's visit to Jerusalem and my views on the prospects of peace.

Again, I reached Teheran late at night and met the Shah next morning. My first question to him was whether he would agree to an official announcement of my arrival. Since Sadat, the leading Arab ruler, had come openly to Israel, there was surely no reason for secrecy about my having come to report to him on the subsequent peace moves.

The Shah turned it down flat. He could not afford to make such news public. He also rejected my proposal to raise our diplomatic missions to the status of official embassies flying their respective flags. Even in the present situation, said the Shah, when the ties between our two countries were not official, he faced grave difficulties. The Palestinians and supporters of the PLO exercised considerable influence over the Islamic leaders in Iran. 'The problem of my country', he explained, 'is the religious fanaticism among the masses of the people who are uneducated. If it were not for that, Iran would today be as advanced as a European country, and not subject to the influence of the religious leaders who prevent progress and development.' He spoke in the same vein about the problem of Jerusalem. He did not share the position of the Saudi Arabians who viewed the issues of Palestine and the State of Israel through Moslem religious spectacles, and whose sole problem of concern was Arab control of the Holy Places in Jerusalem sacred to Islam.

His lack of courage over Iranian–Israeli relations did not hinder the Shah from offering some bold advice for the President of Egypt. Sadat, he said, should ignore the Arab rejectionist States and others who opposed his peace efforts, abandon his aspiration to be the leader of the Arab world, and press forward wholeheartedly with the implementation of the peace agreement with Israel, otherwise he would lose his standing and his leadership even in Egypt. Sadat's visit to Jerusalem was a step from which there was no turning back. As for the Palestinians, they should not be given even the fringe of a State. If Israel agreed to give the Palestinians any kind of independence, she would be establishing with her own hands a base for anti-Israel terrorism and destruction.

The Shah spent most of the time expounding on his favourite subject: the global struggle between America and Russia. The Soviets, he said, were making creeping advances towards Algeria, Libya, Ethiopia and Yemen. Their leaders, with the active help of Fidel Castro, were outmanoeuvring the United States. He related with pride that when he had last been in America, he spoke about this at length with President Carter and had found in him a readiness to listen, but also an ignorance of what was happening in the Middle East. He hoped Carter would decide soon to dissociate himself from the Russians and embark on an independent policy towards our region.

He ended with the warning that Russia did not favour peace in the Middle East, and would do all in her power to sabotage it. It was to this end that she was arming Iraq and Syria. Israel would do well to take into account that these countries, at the initiative and with the backing of Soviet Russia, would again make war on Israel.

I returned to the guest-house and reported the talk to our diplomatic representative. He told me that the standing of the Shah – this was December 1977 – was steadily weakening, and one could not say how long he could continue, with the help of the army, to keep his throne.

We lunched with several heads of the Iranian administration, exchanged views on developments in the region, and discussed matters pertaining to Iran's supply of oil to Israel. After lunch, I had a few hours to spare before flying home, and I thought the time would be well spent visiting dealers in antiquities. But there was the possibility that I might be recognized, despite the wide-brimmed hat and dark glasses. However, our representative, knowing my weakness, said there was one place he could take me to without risk – the home of a discreet Jewish dealer.

He had a wide collection of artefacts, but the cheap ones did not interest me, and those that did were beyond my pocket. I was particularly attracted by a three-thousand-year-old pottery vessel, of an enchanting shape and with a delicate rim. It was still encrusted with thick layers of stone dust which had accumulated over the centuries, but when much of this had been washed off, the vessel was seen to be decorated with three gazelles, two facing each other and the third couchant, with its head turned towards the rear. The animals were red, and stood out against the light grey of the vessel. I thought of how much brighter they would look when I got the vessel home and gave it a thorough cleaning with a special solution. But I could hardly match the competition – the numerous Americans in Teheran at the time, with an interest in antiquities and no shortage of dollars. So I left for the airport with a different memento from Iran – a bag of pistachio nuts.

CHAPTER NINE

The Short Life of the Political Committee

Prime Minister Begin had proposed at the Ismailia summit meeting that the two joint Egypt–Israel committees, the political and the military, should start work the following week. But President Sadat said that was too soon, and the date set for them to convene was three weeks later. The venue was to be Jerusalem.

Begin had returned from Ismailia 'a happy man', as he put it; but it was soon evident that nothing had transpired there to make anyone happy. The Egyptian and Israeli positions had been poles apart, and tension grew as the meeting moved to its close. As soon as it was over, the Egyptian press launched a verbal assault that knew no bounds. Personal insults were hurled at Begin. 'He should be pleased', wrote the newspapers, 'that he managed to leave Ismailia unharmed.' He had behaved at the summit meeting 'like Shylock'.

Sadat himself gave an interview to the Egyptian weekly *October*, in which he bitterly attacked Israel. The Egyptian President said he had lost all hope of being able to reach an agreement with Israel on the foundations of peace. Israel was no less a 'rejectionist State' than Syria. She had sown the wind, and she would therefore reap the whirlwind. He, by his visit to Jerusalem, had given Israel everything – the prospect of peace, security, and legitimate status in the region – and he had received nothing in return. He had risked not only his political future but also his life, but he had believed that by so doing he had put an end to the Arab-Israeli conflict; yet here was Israel refusing to agree to the peace principles he had proposed.

These principles called for Israel's return of Sinai to Egypt, the West Bank to Jordan and the Golan to Syria, and endorsed the Palestinians' right to statehood. Sadat said that if Israel agreed to this, it would give her normal relations with her neighbours, as well as Arab recognition. Put simply, he added, Israel had to choose between the two alternatives: territories or peace. There was no middle road.

The Egyptians aired additional complaints. Premier Begin, Defence

Minister Ezer Weizman and I had made 'stubborn declarations'. Agricultural Minister Arik Sharon had prepared the ground for increased settlement in Sinai. By such deeds and words, Israel was undermining the position of Egypt, and particularly its President, in the Arab world.

The United States Government, noting the growing estrangement between Egypt and Israel, decided on a dramatic intervention. President Carter flew to Aswan on 4 January 1978 to see Sadat. After lengthy talks, he emerged with a statement that peace between Israel and Egypt should bring about a normalization of relations; that Israel had to withdraw from territories she had conquered in the 1967 war; and that the legitimate rights of the Palestinians should be recognized, and they should be enabled to take part in the determination of their future.

This Aswan Declaration by the President of the United States was received with satisfaction by Egypt, misgivings by Israel, and contempt by the Arab rejectionist countries and the PLO. The apprehension in Israel was that, although it did not specifically say so, the statement might be interpreted as support for the establishment of a Palestinian State.

I was well aware of the difficulties posed for us by the Carter declaration, but I also recognized its constructive side. It differed from UN Resolution 242 in that it merged three basic premises: Israel's withdrawal from territories conquered in 1967, as stated in UN Resolutions 242 and 338; in exchange, full normalization of relations between the Arab countries and Israel, and not simply an end to the state of belligerency; and the linkage of the Palestinians with the peace agreement.

US Secretary of State Cyrus Vance was also drawn in to help the negotiations. He responded to the request of both sides and agreed to come to Jerusalem and take part in the sessions of the Political Committee. He promptly found himself in deep water. Even before leaving Washington and before the parties could convene, he became heavily involved in the immediate problem of the committee's agenda. The Egyptians insisted that its first item should be the ending of 'Israel's conquest of Arab territories' captured in 1967. They also wanted to include the 'solution to the Palestine problem on the basis of the Palestinian right to self-determination'.

We did not agree, and what followed was a repetition of the very debate which had led to failure at Ismailia. The Egyptians demanded that we accept in advance both the obligation to withdraw from the occupied territories, and, by implication, the right of the Palestinians to establish an independent State. We refused.

The American embassies in Israel and Egypt worked hard as message centres, serving as the communications link for signals between the Governments in Jerusalem and Cairo, but to little avail. Each side turned down the proposals of the other.

Vance, in Washington, finally cut through with the suggestion, which both parties accepted, that the agenda consist of three items for discussion: a declaration of intent which would govern the negotiations for a comprehensive peace agreement in the Middle East; guidelines for the negotiations over Judea, Samaria and the Gaza District; and the basis for peace treaties between Israel and her neighbours in accordance with the principles of UN Security Council Resolution 242. This, of course, merely deferred consideration of the controversial issues without settling them. The first item simply gave a neutral designation for Israeli withdrawal, and the second did the same for the Palestinian problem.

The Egyptian delegation arrived in Israel on 15 January 1978, headed by Foreign Minister Muhammad Ibrahim Kamel. Secretary Vance and his aides followed next day.

The fate of this Political Committee matched that of the summit talks at Ismailia. It achieved nothing. But its end was more dramatic. It had opened quietly enough with a morning session on 17 January, but on the following night the Egyptian delegation received a sudden order from Sadat to pack their bags and return home. President Carter's appeals on the telephone to Sadat proved fruitless. At 3 o'clock in the morning I accompanied the Egyptians to the airport and they flew back to Cairo. On the following day I was again at the airport – to see off Vance who was returning to Washington. After my farewells to our guests I could not say, as Begin had said after Ismailia, that I was 'a happy man'. But neither was I a surprised man.

The Egyptian delegation was made up of career diplomats: Kamel himself; Minister of State Butros Ghali; Egypt's Ambassador to the UN Abd el Majid; and the senior Foreign Ministry official Osama al-Baz. These men did not belong to the inner leadership group of Egypt, nor did they favour Sadat's peace initiative. This was already evident at Ismailia, when they tried to curb Sadat and prevent him from taking any step that might bring him closer to us. They were attuned through personal friendship with the thinking of the diplomatic corps of all the Arab States; and to the Arab world, Sadat was a traitor. Kamel and his friends therefore did their utmost to prove they were faithful to their brothers and had no intention of making any concessions to Israel. This they managed to do without any difficulty. For one thing, Sadat, too, thought Israel should accept all his demands after he had made his historic Jerusalem gesture. For another, the President of Egypt did not concern himself with the paperwork, and gave his aides a free hand in drafting and presentation.

There was thus no foundation for Begin's assumption that the obstructions encountered at Ismailia could be cleared in the Political Committee. The lower the rank of the participants, the greater was their rigidity. The way to overcome obstacles was to move the discussions from the bottom to the top level, not the reverse.

The Political Committee had run into trouble within minutes of its opening, faced with the first item on the agenda, the 'declaration of intentions'. Here, the Egyptians again demanded Israel's specific commitment to withdraw from Sinai, Golan, the West Bank and Gaza, and recognition of the Palestinian right to self-determination. Israel's formula on withdrawal was more general, using the words of Resolution 242 which stated that Israel would withdraw 'from territories occupied in the recent conflict' – the 1967 war. (In that UN Resolution the opponents of Israel had tried to get the word 'the' inserted before 'territories', which would have meant giving up every inch, with no border rectification whatsoever. This was rejected by the UN Security Council, and the resolution that was adopted stated that withdrawal was to be 'from territories', not 'from the territories'.) On the Palestinian problem, Israel proposed that it be solved by the settlement of the refugees and the granting of administrative autonomy to the Arab inhabitants of Judea, Samaria and the Gaza District.

When it became clear that we were unable to bridge the gap, we again approached the Americans to suggest a compromise formula. Vance and his aides produced draft after draft, and each time one and sometimes both of the parties pronounced it unacceptable. The fifth American draft was handed to us after Kamel had already announced that the Egyptian delegation was leaving. There was thus no point in discussing it, and I still do not know what the Egyptians thought of it. But there is no reason to suppose that this draft had better chances of acceptance than the others.

The head of our own drafting team was Aharon Barak, and I did not envy him. Negotiations with Begin were neither easier nor more pleasant than negotiating with the Americans or the Egyptians. There were occasional differences of opinion and tense moments between Begin and myself; but it was the Egyptians, not Begin, who were responsible for the failure of the negotiations. In Jerusalem, Cairo, Ismailia and now at the Political Committee, the Egyptians did not conduct negotiations. They issued ultimatums. They clung permanently to a three-part formula: that Egypt had contributed her part to peace by the daring visit of Sadat to Jerusalem; that Israel had to return to the pre-June 1967 borders; and that the Palestinians had the right to independent statehood.

I confess to finding the behaviour of the Egyptians rather arrogant and moralistic, and this was evident both in the content and style of their speech. It was noticeable at the very outset, as soon as the delegation arrived at our Ben Gurion airport. I greeted Foreign Minister Kamel when he came off the plane, escorted him to the microphones, made brief remarks of welcome coupled with hopes for the success of the committee's work, and then made way for him to respond. I expected him to follow suit, with the polite generalities customary on such occasions. Instead, he drew a paper from his pocket and read out a long political declaration reiterating Egypt's position and her demands on Israel. Egypt, he said, had already proved her devotion to true peace. Sadat's 'historic visit' to Jerusalem had opened a new era, but Israel had to recognize the basic facts that peace was not compatible with territorial occupation, and peace was not possible when there was a denial of the national right of the Palestinian people to self-determination.

I remained silent. The airport welcoming platform was not the place for his speech, but that was not sufficient reason for me to match his behaviour. I kept my reply for the following morning at a joint press conference held before the opening session of the committee. In reply to a hostile question, I said that it was better that this peace initiative should slip through our fingers than that Israel's security be snatched from our hands. The agenda of this committee was not designed to seal mouths, and there was nothing to stop the Egyptians from presenting their controversial proposals for a peace agreement. But Israel would not negotiate with a pistol at her temple.

However, what brought the Political Committee to an abrupt end was – on the face of it – the speech of Premier Begin at the festive dinner held in honour of our visitors. An hour or so earlier, at 6.30 p.m., Begin had invited Egyptian delegation head Kamel for a talk, and it was agreed, at Begin's initiative, that both sides should cease making political declarations. But when Begin rose to speak at the end of the meal, his address was political, detailing those conditions which Israel could not accept – the redivision of Jerusalem, the establishment of a Palestinian State, and a return to the pre-June 1967 borders.

There were more than a hundred invited guests – Israeli ministers, judges, members of parliament, Opposition leaders, newspaper editors, as well as correspondents from the world press, including the Egyptian media. In his flow of eloquence, Begin unwittingly offended Kamel by calling him 'young man', little realizing that to an Arab ear this term sounded derisive.

When it was his turn to speak, Kamel, hurt and embarrassed, instead of reading his prepared address, simply said that the place for discussing the subjects raised by the Prime Minister was the committee and not there. He then sat down and did not even raise his glass to toast the President of Israel.

A few hours later, after he had been in touch with Cairo and the delegation had packed their bags, I accompanied Kamel to the airport, and he told me that President Sadat had been particularly offended by Begin's words. This was due not to what Begin had said in his speech, but to the fact that he had made such a speech, in direct breach of the agreement made only three hours before, which Kamel had reported to Sadat and received presidential approval. Kamel himself, according to what he told me, had been so upset by what had happened at the dinner that though he had tried to get a little sleep, he could not close his eyes. 'I waited', he said, 'until the head of my Bureau woke up, and got a cigarette from him. Only after a smoke did I manage to doze for a couple of hours.'

The official reason for the sudden recall of the Egyptian delegation was given by Egypt's Minister of Information in a statement broadcast over Cairo Radio. 'Sadat ordered Kamel's immediate return to Cairo', he explained, 'when it became clear from statements made by Begin and Dayan that Israel's purpose is to secure partial solutions which cannot bring about a comprehensive, just and lasting peace in the Middle East.' The statement went on to say that Sadat had taken this critical decision in order to break the vicious circle in the negotiations, and to avoid their diversion to a discussion of marginal subjects. Egypt's approach had been clear and sincere from the very start. She had hoped that the Israeli side would accept the Egyptian proposals which alone guaranteed an unshakable peace. No other way was acceptable after the courageous peace initiative of President Sadat. Egypt had announced her basic position, insisting that Israel withdraw from all the Arab territories she had conquered in June 1967, including Jerusalem, and that the Palestinians be granted their legitimate rights. Israeli policy preferred a peace imposed by force of arms over a peace that sprang from the Arab conviction that peace was advantageous. The narrowness of Israel's territory and its proximity to Arab lands were not features that were special to Israel, and could not be used to justify the tension she engendered in the region with the plea of defence requirements against the danger of destruction. Egypt had undergone and withstood many trials in her long history. She had not gone in for deceitful manoeuvres, and this had not been the purpose of the initiative by her courageous President and leader. His purpose had been to prevent bloodshed. Egypt desired peace for the Middle East and for the world, and had done all she could to this end. The security of the region, and a just, comprehensive and honourable peace, would continue to be Egypt's aims.

CHAPTER TEN

No Ease in Washington

Following Carter's meeting with Sadat at Aswan, which led to the convening of the ill-fated Political Committee a week later, the Egyptian President was invited to Washington, and he arrived there at the beginning of February 1978. If anyone in Jerusalem expected Sadat to be roundly rebuked by the Americans for having dynamited the Political Committee, he was in for a disappointment. Sadat took America by storm, conquering the hearts of the people. In his television appearances and in his meetings with Congressional committees, he managed to impress his viewers and listeners with his sincerity and convince them of the validity of his political arguments.

He seemed to have done the same in his discussions with President Carter. The two Presidents and their aides isolated themselves for five days at Camp David, and when Sadat left for home on the 8th of February, Carter issued a statement of principles governing American policy in the dispute between Israel and the Arab States. He repeated his declaration at Aswan, and then went further. Contrary to the Israeli position, Carter's statement said that Resolution 242 covered *all* the fronts, thus requiring Israel to withdraw from the West Bank. Similarly, he said that no just and lasting peace was possible without a solution to the Palestine problem. And on the subject of Israeli settlement, 'President Carter reaffirmed the traditional position of the United States' that Israeli settlements in the occupied territories were contrary to international law, and represented an obstacle to peace. The establishment of further settlements hampered efforts to achieve a peace treaty.

Two days later, Secretary of State Cyrus Vance called a press conference and condemned the Israeli settlements in Sinai in extremely sharp language. President Carter, too, continued the propaganda campaign. He invited leaders of the Jewish community in the United States to a personal briefing on the US Government's stand. He told them that the Sinai settlements should be dismantled, and went on to say that the Israeli Government was more obdurate than the Arabs. For example, he said, Syria, Saudi Arabia, Jordan and

Egypt agreed that a Palestinian State was not to be established. King Hussein of Jordan was ready to join the peace talks if there was agreement on a declaration of principles. Moreover, said Carter, Sadat and Hussein agreed to slight border changes within the framework of Resolution 242. Israel was the obstacle.

Many of the Jewish leaders present were impressed by Carter's words, and some expressed support for his policy. One even said that American Jews should put pressure on Israel to get her to be more flexible. Carter had no reason to be disappointed with this meeting.

The news from the United States of Sadat's success in his public appearances, followed by the official statements of Carter and Vance, and, in particular, reports of Carter's meeting with the Jewish leaders, provoked widespread anger in Israel. The Israeli Government felt gravely injured by the unjust accusations levelled against her by one who maintained that he was an honest broker and even claimed a special friendship with Israel. On 13 February the Cabinet, after a review of the situation, issued a statement expressing 'regret and protest' at the words of Secretary Vance in his press conference on 10 February 1978. Vance had told the correspondents that, as regards the settlements in Sinai, 'we have said that we believe that all these settlements are contrary to international law and for this reason they should not exist'. To this, the Israeli Government's statement asserted that

the last part of that sentence is in direct contradiction to what the President of the United States told the Prime Minister on the 16th and 17th of December 1977 after the Prime Minister had presented to the President Israel's peace plan. ... That entire plan was favourably received. The Israeli Government insists that the Israeli settlement projects are compatible with international law, and were always, and remain, both lawful and essential ...

Concerning the West Bank territories of Judea and Samaria, Vance had said they should become 'a homeland for the Palestinians that should be linked with Jordan'. The Israeli statement said there could be no doubt that this plan would in fact lead inevitably to the establishment of a Palestine State ruled by the terrorist organizations. Moreover, under such a plan, densely populated parts of Israel would be squeezed into a narrow corridor only a few miles wide between the new State and the sea. 'No political aim of any kind can move Israel to place almost her entire civilian population within firing range of the enemy, and her very existence in direct danger,' said the statement.

It concluded with 'the hope that the Government of the United States will again weigh her position in the light of the positive talks between the Presi-

Moshe Dayan with President Sadat in Jerusalem.

Premier Begin visits Dayan in hospital after his cancer operation.

With President Ne Win in Burma.

With the Prime Minister of Singapore.

With the King of Nepal.

Moshe and Rahel Dayan are received by the King and Queen of Thailand.

King Hassan of Morocco whom Dayan met on three secret visits.

Above right: US Secretary of
State Cyrus Vance at Dayan's
home in Zahala, near Tel Aviv.

Far right: US Vice-President
Walter Mondale with Dayan in
Washington.

Former Secretary of State Henry Kissinger and Dayan before one of their Washington meetings.

President Sadat with Dayan during the Camp David negotiations.

The Israeli delegation at Camp David: Clockwise: Dayan, Ezer Weizman, Simcha Dinitz, General Avraham Tamir, Professor Aharon Barak, Meir Rosenne, Kadishman, Pattir and Poran of the Prime Minister's Office, and Premier Begin.

With President Carter at the White House.

dent and the Prime Minister in December 1977 in connection with Israel's peace plan'.

This exchange of declarations did not contribute to the creation of a suitable atmosphere in which to continue the peace process. Whatever the position taken by Washington, however, she had to recognize that without Israel's agreement, the conflict would not be resolved. Throughout the thirty-year existence of Israel, tough words from Washington had not brought Israel to her knees and had not achieved their purpose. From Ben Gurion to Begin, no Prime Minister had been prepared to accept American–Arab dictates. This was true not only of Israel's leaders: the people of Israel also reacted sharply and negatively when they believed that Washington had behaved unreasonably.

It so happened that on 8 February, the day Sadat left the United States, I arrived in New York for a series of lectures on Israel's policy which had been scheduled months earlier. I was immediately made to feel the cold wind in the wake of the 'Sadat festival'. The Israeli Government had been placed in the dock both by the American press and by some of the Jewish leaders. We were charged with inflexibility, and lack of understanding for the 'delicate' position of Sadat, who had acted 'above and beyond' what was expected for the cause of peace. More specifically, we were taken to task for pursuing a mistaken settlement policy. In the midst of all this came news from Israel of the Shiloh episode. A group from Gush Imunim had installed themselves at Shiloh, a few miles north of Jerusalem in the West Bank territory of Samaria. It had been given out in official circles that they had gone to undertake an archaeological excavation of this ancient site, which had been an Israelite religious centre in the time of Joshua and the Judges. But the Gush Imunim members declared in television interviews that this was merely an excuse, and it was their purpose and intention to establish a permanent settlement on the site.

My first meeting with Jewish leaders was under the auspices of a group known as the Presidents' Club, comprising heads of the major Jewish institutions in the United States. After my opening remarks, questions were flung at me from all quarters, most of them critical and provocative. They were not the kind that sought information, beginning with a 'what', but the sort that came at me with an arrowhead 'why' – why had we done this, and why had we not done that? The question asked with most heat was why settlements were being established in Judea and Samaria. Were we not thereby 'sabotaging Zionism'?

Opposite me in the crowded hall sat well-meaning fellow Jews, supporters of Israel (though I found some of them slightly patronizing). I myself happen not to be a votary of Gush Imunim; but the hostile moralizing tone from this group of American sons of my people was more than I could take. As I looked at them, my mind's eye went beyond them to a very different group, the pioneer settlers of a few decades ago: the men and women who had created kibbutz Deganiah out of the marshes bordering the Sea of Galilee; who had founded kibbutz Ein Harod in the swamp of the Valley of Jezreel, Hanita in the stony hills near the Lebanese border, brought life to the coastal region of Emek Hefer. I saw the stout links in the settlement chain from the 'wall and watchtower' villages established in the dangerous 1930s, to the proud outpost settlements of the Israel Army's 'Fighting and Pioneer Youth' corps; the kibbutzim and moshavim that rose in the Golan Heights and the Jordan Valley after the 1967 war; and the resettlement of the Etzion group of settlements in Judea which had been seized by Jordan's Arab Legion in 1948. I stared straight back at one American questioner who had talked of the 'sabotage' of Zionism by the Gush Imunim settlers, and told him that with all my differences of opinion with Gush Imunim, I saw them as dedicated pioneers, and I preferred them to the 'Zionists' who dwelt comfortably in the United States.

I cannot glory in the thought that I won the hearts of my listeners that day. I was also attacked by a few Israeli newspapers whose New York correspondents had been present. 'How', they asked, 'could Dayan dare to speak in this way to the Jews of America? Does he think he can gain their sympathy and support that way?'

I did my best in the United States to explain our situation and our actions, addressing meetings from coast to coast, notably in New York, Los Angeles, Chicago and Miami. I also appeared on the television networks and met with newspaper editors. At each town I came to, I spoke, was questioned, and gave answers; but I made no converts.

I had scheduled no political talks on this visit, simply setting aside the last day for a flight to Washington to pay a courtesy call on the Secretary of State, and from there I would be flying back to New York and on to Israel. However, a day after my arrival in the United States, Assistant Secretary of State Alfred Atherton came to see me in New York, to tell me, he said, about Sadat's visit to the US and his talks with the administration. He also hinted that when I came to Washington, President Carter expected to see me. I replied that, of course, I would be happy to accept an invitation from the President, but I had to emphasize that I was not requesting one, and that there was nothing special I wished to discuss either with Carter or Vance.

Atherton promised to transmit my reply to his superiors. My tone may have been severe, but I thought it proper to make my attitude clear. In the anti-Israel mood which I sensed all around me, I did not want it thought that I had asked to see the President. In her present situation, Israel had nothing to propose. If the other parties, Egypt and the United States, wished to continue the peace negotiations, they would have to turn to us.

I arrived in Washington, as originally planned, on 16 February, the last day of my American stay. I had talks in the morning at the State Department with the Secretary and his aides, which went on through lunch, and in the afternoon at the White House, followed by a meeting with a Congressional committee.

The meeting with the President was to have lasted twenty minutes. It went on for close to an hour. With the President were Vance, Brzezinski and Atherton. I had with me our Ambassador to Washington. Carter first wished to talk to me privately, and he asked whether I could join Prime Minister Begin on his visit to Washington, which was to take place soon. I said that if Begin asked me to accompany him, I would do so. What else was I expected to say to the President of the United States?

In our general talk, with the aides present, the central item was getting King Hussein to join the peace talks. They said Sadat had come to the United States a disappointed man. He had hoped that after his visit to Jerusalem, Israel would agree to return to the pre-1967 borders, and here they were with the Israelis going back to their old methods and being evasive. He could not continue in such a situation, and he was wondering whether or not to cease his talks with Israel. At the very most he could go on with them for another few weeks, but even that only on condition that Hussein would join him. The Egyptians were therefore insisting that the West Bank should be included in the declaration of intentions. Sadat had no doubts that if this were done, Hussein would join the peace talks.

I asked the Americans if this was also their view. Vance said he was not sure: Hussein had lately become more rigid. At all events, the United States' position was that the declaration of intentions had to include Israel's agreement to withdraw from the West Bank. The President emphasized that throughout the years the several Governments of Israel had said that Resolution 242, which spoke of Israel's withdrawal from occupied territories, covered all the fronts, including the West Bank.

I wished to state clearly and with full responsibility, I replied, that this was not the view of the existing Government of Israel. Israel had no wish to rule the Palestinian Arabs, but she was not prepared to see her military forces and civilian Jewish settlements forced to evacuate the West Bank and the Gaza Strip. For this reason we were also not ready to state in the declaration of intentions that Resolution 242 applied to all the fronts. As for Hussein, I said, I did not think he would join the talks. He did not regard himself as qualified to speak in the name of the Palestinian Arabs or to give up the rights of the refugees to return to 'their land and their homes', namely, to Israel. Israel would gladly welcome Hussein's participation in the peace talks, but not on the basis of advance commitments. Begin, I added, had told Sadat that we were prepared to consider any proposal that he wished to put to us. The Arab proposals could include the demand that we withdraw from the West Bank. But what they wanted from us was a prior undertaking that we would do so. This we refused. We went further, and stated explicitly that we would reject this proposal.

The discussions with the President and his aides were not fruitful. Carter said that we remained divided, and we would need to continue our deliberations on the subject. Atherton would be leaving for the Middle East the following week and would shuttle between Cairo and Jerusalem in an effort to secure an agreement on the declaration of intentions.

Before we parted, the President summed up the main points. He thought that Begin and Sadat should show greater flexibility so that they could reach an understanding. He felt we would be able to achieve a peace treaty with Egypt. As for the West Bank and Gaza, an agreement should be reached covering the next five years. Such an agreement would be in the spirit of Begin's proposal, namely, autonomy for the Palestinian Arabs. At the end of five years, well, we would see. In his view, the Palestinian Arabs should then be free to choose one of three options: to be linked to Jordan; to be linked to Israel; or to continue with the autonomy regime.

Though the talk this time was calm, I was left in no doubt as to which way the wind blew. No wonder Sadat had said, on leaving the United States, that he was not encouraged when he arrived in Washington, but greatly heartened when he left.

President Carter's invitation to Sadat, and the Egyptian leader's triumphant visit to the United States, were followed by a matching invitation to Israel's Prime Minister. Begin was to leave for Washington early in March, but unforeseen events obliged him to postpone his departure.

At 2.30 p.m. on 11 March 1978, two rubber dinghies with eleven PLO terrorists landed on the lonely stretch of coast near kibbutz Ma-agan Michael, some sixteen miles south of Haifa. The only person on the beach at the time was an American photographer, Gail Rubin, who specialized in nature photography, with particular interest in bird life – there is a bird sanctuary close to the kibbutz. The terrorists murdered her, proceeded to the main Haifa–Tel Aviv coastal road, shot up a bus travelling to Haifa, and injured several passengers. The bus was brought to a halt, and the terrorists ordered the driver to turn back and drive towards Tel Aviv. On the journey south, the terrorists fired at passing cars. After a few miles, they stopped, held up another bus at gun-point, and forced its passengers to enter the first bus. By now, the police had been alerted and they set up barriers, but the terrorists broke through them and continued towards Tel Aviv. The police then mounted a heavy road-block at a crossroads a few miles from the city, and when the bus approached, they fired at its tyres. The terrorists returned the fire and also began shooting some of the passengers. Two of the passengers managed to snatch the weapon of one of the terrorists and killed three of them. At the end of the shoot-out, nine terrorists were dead and the remaining two were captured. The toll of the passengers and those in passing cars who had been attacked *en route* was heavy: thirty-five dead and seventy-one wounded. Among the dead were one soldier and one policeman. All the rest were civilians: men, women and children.

From the surviving two terrorists it was learned that they belonged to the PLO and had set out on their murderous mission from the southern Lebanese port of Tyre. Three days later, on 14 March, the Israeli Army went into action. In a five-day operation called 'Operation Litani' – Litani is the river which divides southern from northern Lebanon – Israeli troops combed the entire stretch of southern Lebanon between Israel's northern border and the river to wipe out PLO bases. There were some two thousand terrorists in this area, based in villages, olive groves and in the mountains, and equipped with artillery, anti-tank guns, armoured cars and the usual small arms. Israel sent in a combined infantry and armoured force, with air support.

When the Israeli units crossed the border, most of the terrorists fled to the north. Of those who stayed, some three hundred were killed and several hundred wounded. Israeli casualties were sixteen killed and one hundred wounded. At the end of the operation, Israeli troops returned to Israel and were replaced by UN forces and the Christian militias commanded by a Lebanese army officer, Major Haddad, a member of the Christian Arab community which had also been the target of PLO attacks.

The coastal road massacre was one of the gravest terrorist incidents suffered by Israel and it shocked the country. The high number of civilian casualties was itself abominable; but the way the terrorists behaved towards the people inside the bus was particularly revolting. They bound the hands of their victims and then shot them in cold blood, murdering men and women alike, and even babies clinging to their parents for protection. I was sorry that not all the terrorists had been killed in the engagement.

This was not the first terrorist action, nor would it be the last, committed by the Palestinian 'freedom fighters'. Since the establishment of the State –

and before that, too – the murder of Jewish civilians by Arab bands has been a feature of our lives. In recent years, there were the killings in Kiriat Shmoneh in Upper Galilee; the brutal assassination of the children in the Galilean village school of Ma'alot near the Lebanese border; the murders at Tel Aviv's Savoy Hotel; the massacre at Ben Gurion airport; the exploding of booby-trapped cars in the city market-place and bombs in Jerusalem's cinemas and university; the mining of railway tracks and rural paths; the hijacking of aircraft. The common denominator in all these actions was their foul and cowardly character, and the exultation of the terrorists as they proudly acknowledged their responsibility.

History knows how to distinguish between such groups, disguised as combatants, mouthing high-minded slogans, and true revolutionaries, prepared to sacrifice themselves for a cause, who have become the symbol of heroism. Samson went to his death with the cry 'Let me die with the Philistines', as he pulled asunder the pillars of the pagan temple; Elazar, brother of Judah the Maccabee, sought to turn the tide of battle as he thrust his sword into the belly of the lead elephant in the enemy's 'armoured' unit, and was crushed when the beast fell. In our own day, courageous partisan commandos pitted themselves against the mighty hosts of Hitler. Soldiers were one thing, terrorists who killed civilians were another.

The Litani operation in reaction to the coastal-road murders was necessary for our nation's defence. But as a military action, it was not one of our more brilliant engagements. Only those terrorists who remained to fight suffered casualties. The others managed to run away in time. Israeli units advanced systematically, their path cleared by artillery bombardment and air support. This system is sound when the aim is to seize ground, but not when the object is to trap terrorists. True, great quantities of terrorist arms were captured; but it also meant destruction in their village bases, and thousands of peaceful citizens, with whom we had to try to live as good neighbours, fled in fear of war. The picture of long straggling lines of families, with their old and their young, leaving their homes and plodding northwards to find a place of refuge, scarred our good name.

Begin's visit to Washington was finally set for 21 March, and it lasted two days. This time, the Prime Minister was accompanied not only by his bureau staff but also by Aharon Barak, our Attorney-General, Meir Rosenne, legal Adviser to the Foreign Ministry, Eliakim Rubinstein, head of my bureau, and myself. In the United States we were joined by our Ambassador and Minister in Washington, Simcha Dinitz and Hanan Bar-On, and by the Head of the Defence Ministry's mission in the US, Yosef Czechanower. The American delegation at the talks included, apart from the President, Vice-President Walter Mondale, Secretary of State Vance, National Security Adviser Zbigniew Brzezinski and their aides.

Two developments had clouded the meeting even before it began: our Operation Litani, and Carter's open support of Sadat in his claims against Israel. They were given expression in the brief ceremony welcoming Begin. The President, after a formal greeting, said that Sadat's visit to Jerusalem had stirred the hopes of the world, but now the days of splendour had given way to gloom. (It was not difficult to grasp who was being held responsible for this change.) And when he went on to condemn the criminal terrorist attack on innocent civilians in Israel, he immediately added his regret at the loss of Arab lives and the flight of tens of thousands from the battle zones.

Begin did not ignore the critical words interwoven in Carter's remarks when he came to respond. He reminded the President that the mood at their December meeting had been cordial, sincere and frank, and this was also the case at his talks with Sadat in Jerusalem and Ismailia. He hoped for a renewal of this spirit.

The first business meeting at the White House began at 10.30 in the morning. Carter opened by deploring once again the murder of the bus passengers, and said the purpose of the terrorists had been to harm the Israel–Egypt peace negotiations. He then reviewed the steps taken so far in those negotiations and asked the Prime Minister what he thought were the prospects for continuing the process.

Begin gave a detailed reply. He, too, emphasized his point at the welcoming ceremony that the spirit of the early meetings had been excellent, and he hoped it could be recaptured. Sadat had called him 'my friend' at Ismailia, and they had almost reached an agreement. But things now were not the same. The obstacle to progress was Egypt's demand for Israel's prior commitment to a total withdrawal and the acceptance of Palestinian statehood.

Carter listened with undisguised impatience to Begin's detailed arguments. Nor was he interested in talk of 'the good old days'. He wanted to know what next. When Begin finished, the President said that what Begin had reported of Sadat's stand was not correct. Sadat did not demand an Israeli withdrawal from the West Bank to the pre-1967 lines. He was definitely prepared to accept an alteration in that border. Nor was Sadat demanding a Palestinian State. The reason for the deadlock in the negotiations was the lack of agreement on the 'Declaration of Intentions'. Israel, he said, wanted the declaration to be 'based on all the principles of Resolution 242'. The Egyptians demanded that it be 'based on the implementation of all the principles'. The

United States was trying to produce a compromise, and suggested 'implementation of the principles'. 'As God is my judge,' said Carter, 'I don't know the difference between these various formulae.' The Americans were looking for semantic compromises, and in so doing were expending considerable efforts in beating the wind, without point or need. The practical problems that needed to be tackled were Israeli and Arab demands concerning the West Bank; safeguards for Israel's security; and a solution for the Palestinians.

The core of the question as seen by the President was whether Israel regarded Resolution 242 as applying to the West Bank, namely, whether Israel was prepared to withdraw from this front. He turned to Begin and asked him squarely: Did the article in Resolution 242 relating to withdrawal also include the West Bank?

A direct question required a direct answer, and the first to offer one was Attorney-General Aharon Barak. Resolution 242, he said, covered all the territories, including the West Bank and the Gaza District. The plan of self-government for the Arab inhabitants of Judea, Samaria and Gaza (autonomy) was compatible with 242, including its article on withdrawal, and that was Israel's proposal as to the method whereby this Resolution was to be fulfilled.

I followed Barak, explaining that our proposal to abolish the military government stated that the Israel Army would withdraw from, and cease to govern, the Arab population. That, in our view, was a fit and proper accomplishment of what was called for in Resolution 242 as regards the withdrawal of Israeli forces. If the Egyptians had another proposal, they should put it on the table and we would discuss it. 'You,' I told them, 'the United States and Egypt, want the Declaration of Principles to state specifically, in connection with our withdrawal, the words "from all three fronts" [Egyptian, Syrian, Jordanian].' But those words, I said, did not appear in Resolution 242 and we objected to their addition.

I was followed by Begin, who reminded Carter that when they had met in July, the Americans had suggested five points as the basis for the negotiations. One was 'withdrawal from all the fronts', and Begin had not agreed to that.

The President could not claim that we had failed to make our stand clear on the demand for our withdrawal from the whole of the administered territories. We had opposed it. We had said we were prepared to redeploy our forces, to move them from centres of dense Arab settlement to the border region and other locations; but these would still be within the boundaries of the West Bank and the Gaza Strip.

Another point where we had differences was the future of the Palestinian

Arabs. Carter wanted us to agree that at the end of the five-year transitional period they could decide to join the Kingdom of Jordan: he was speaking in territorial terms. We, on the other hand, were thinking in terms of the individuals. We were prepared to allow any Palestinian, who so wanted, to opt for Jordanian citizenship, but on the condition that this would not mean turning the West Bank into a part of the Jordanian State.

In reply to Brzezinski's argument that the Arabs had the right to decide their own future, I said I agreed. But I did not agree that they had the right to decide *our* future. The annexation of the West Bank to the Kingdom of Jordan would be of profound significance not only for the future of Nablus residents but also for the future and security of the State of Israel.

Begin suggested that the question of what would happen after five years be left open and made subject to the decision of the joint committee of both parties. Carter objected, on the grounds that it meant leaving in our hands the right to veto an Arab decision if they wished to be linked to Jordan.

It was now 12.45, time for the session to end. Once again, the President did not hide his disappointment over our stand. 'You want', he said, 'to maintain your political control over the West Bank and the Gaza District even after the five-year transitional period.' He had hoped we would be ready to exchange our political control for security arrangements – the right to keep armed Israeli forces on the West Bank for the defence of Israel. This would have improved the prospects for peace. Now, because of the stand we had taken, that chance would be lost.

We met again with the President the next morning, 22 March, with the same composition of the delegations. Carter reported that after the dinner he had given the previous evening in honour of the Prime Minister and his wife, he had had the opportunity of a private talk with Begin, and they had clarified matters which had engaged the attention and efforts of both Governments for several months. The full details of this talk were not known to me, for there had been no time before the session started for Begin to give me more than a brief outline of what had transpired. He told me he had explained our position to Carter and hoped Carter understood it.

The President went on to say that this was Prime Minister Begin's third visit to Washington. He had previously been full of hope; he now despaired of any progress towards the attainment of peace between Israel and Egypt. He would be appearing that afternoon before the Congressional Committee for International Relations, and next day he was meeting with the Senate Foreign Relations Committee. It was his wish to present to these committees the respective stands of Egypt, Israel and the United States. The United States' position was not to demand total Israeli withdrawal from the West

Bank. Israel, he said, should hold a number of advanced military posts in that territory. There should also be certain changes in that border. The West Bank should not become a radical Palestinian State. During the five-year transitional period Israel should not establish new settlements nor even broaden existing ones.

He assumed that the United States would be able to issue a clear declaration that Israel was not obliged to carry out a total withdrawal from the West Bank, and that a Palestinian State should not be established. He believed that such a declaration would be acceptable to Sadat. But he understood that even after this declaration we held to the position that Israel would not give up her settlements in Sinai, nor her political control of the West Bank and Gaza, even though we would be retaining advanced military posts there. Nor were we willing to give the Palestinian Arabs the right to choose, after a five-year period, between three options: to be linked to Jordan; to Israel; or to continue the *status quo*. If we persisted in maintaining this position, the President concluded, he saw no prospect of advancing towards a peace agreement.

Though Carter spoke in a dull monotone, there was fury in his cold blue eyes, and his glance was dagger-sharp. His portrayal of our position was basically correct, but it could not have been expressed in a more hostile form.

His remarks were followed by an oppressive silence. Begin sat stunned, his face drawn and ashen. After a few moments, he told the President that his presentation of Israel's position was wholly negative, whereas that position was very positive. We were wholly committed to negotiate a peace treaty and to reach a comprehensive settlement. We wanted direct negotiations with the Arab Governments. We accepted Resolution 242 as a negotiating basis with all our neighbours: this called for the establishment of recognized and secure borders. It did not demand withdrawal from all the borders, nor did it indicate that the withdrawal had to be absolute. Begin then repeated the details of the Israel-Egypt peace plan we had presented, as well as our proposal for autonomy and self-government for the Arabs of the West Bank and Gaza. On the question of sovereignty in the West Bank, Begin said we had agreed that this should remain open since there were differing demands from both parties. As for Sinai, we had informed Carter that we would not establish new settlements there.

His words seemed to hang in space, unabsorbed, evoking no interest from the delegation ranged against us. Judgment had already been given. Carter was determined to blame Israel, above all Begin, for the failure of the peace agreement, an agreement, as far as Carter was concerned, which had been within reach thanks to the broad horizons and farsightedness of President Sadat of Egypt!

Begin urged the President to present our position before the Congressional committees in a positive way. Carter said he would, but his word was belied by his cold demeanour.

When Begin had finished speaking, he leaned back in his chair and closed his eyes, weakened physically by the psychological effort. I asked his permission to add to his remarks. Addressing the President directly, I said that if our plan for the West Bank and Gaza were accepted, it would free the Palestinian Arabs from Israel Army supervision and from Israel's political control. We did not want the Arabs to control the Israeli settlements in Judea, Samaria and Gaza; but nor did we wish to rule over the Arabs. It would be easier for us if they administered their own affairs.

Public security in the territories, I said, was more problematic. If an Arab town were to serve as a base for terrorist actions against us, our armed forces would have the right to enter that town and fight the terror. We could not ignore the situation in the Middle East, nor forget what was happening in Lebanon, or what had happened before 1967 in Gaza when it was under Egyptian control. Terrorists who called themselves *fedayeen* left the Gaza Strip night after night and entered Israel to sabotage, lay mines, and murder our families in the Negev. If we took no action, who would defend our citizens?

As for the rights of the Palestinian Arabs to determine their future, the question was how it was to be done. We objected to the suggested referendum, but there was another way. No one was preventing them from deciding whether to become Jordanians, or Israelis, or to retain their current status. For that, they did not need to wait five years: they could make their choice the moment the autonomy plan came into operation.

We had no objection to inhabitants of the West Bank and Gaza maintaining links with Jordan. But it was important to know that there was no work in the Gaza Strip for all of its 400,000 inhabitants, half of them listed as refugees. In my view, they themselves would not wish to give up their jobs in Israel, or stop selling us their produce. This was also true of the Arabs in Judea and Samaria: they, too, found work and markets in Israel. Thus, it would be best to watch developments during the five years of transition, and examine the impact of day-to-day experience upon the inhabitants' wishes with whom to maintain links, Jordan or Israel. Our own interest in the West Bank and Gaza was limited to our civilian settlements and our right to a military presence. We had no interest in the military or political control of the Arabs.

I ended on a personal note. 'I listened to your words', I said to the President, 'and the picture you painted was dark indeed. But to my mind the prospects for peace, compared to the past, are not so bad today.'

Whether the President was really impressed by what I had said, or whether he was just being polite, he did say that he saw possibilities, from the way I had presented the Israeli approach, to frame a formula that Sadat, too, would find reasonable. If Israel worked towards a solution of the Palestinian problem, the Arabs should have the right to participate. What I had said about there being no Israeli army camps in the centres of Arab population offered a positive opening for an agreement. Also helpful, said Carter, was my assurance that we had no wish to exercise political control over the Arabs.

Barak then read and explained our proposal for the Declaration of Principles, and the President and the Secretary of State suggested that Barak and I should stay over another day or two in Washington in an effort to reach an agreed formula on it with the Americans. Begin made no response to this, but simply urged Carter once again to put our position to the Congressional committees in a positive light, and Carter repeated his promise to do so. The meeting ended with Vance arranging to meet me after lunch to see if we could come up with an agreed text to the Declaration.

The most important event that afternoon, however, would be the President's appearance before the first of the committees. What would he say, and how would he say it? We were very apprehensive. And we soon felt we had good cause to be. Shortly after we left the White House, the information apparatus of the State Department and the White House went into high gear. Our position was presented adversely, with Israel shown as obdurate and recalcitrant, rejecting proposals that could bring about peace. The American press tended to follow the US Government view, and even Israel's friends in the House and the Senate, Jews and non-Jews, supported the President in his praise of Sadat and criticism of Israel. Relations between Carter and Begin were very strained.

I met Vance after lunch and we went over drafts of the Declaration of Principles, but made no progress. The core of our differences was the Palestine problem.

I telephoned Begin to ask if he wished me to accept the President's suggestion to stay over in Washington and continue the attempts to reach an agreed formula. Begin was against it, and so I told him I would leave that night for Israel. He himself was remaining in Washington for meetings with members of Congress and the press, and for television appearances. We said *Shalom* to each other and I flew to New York, and from there the same night to Israel.

The talks with Carter and his aides were very difficult, but they were not without openings for continued review and progress. Two were particularly important. The first was the American agreement to interpret the Israeli withdrawal clause in Resolution 242 not as the total evacuation of the Israel Army from the West Bank but only their retirement from the centres of Arab population, and redeployment in posts along the River Jordan, the ridges and elsewhere in the territories. The second concerned the Palestinians. The Americans did not turn down our proposed formula that the Arabs in the occupied territories would participate in the determination of their future within the framework of the discussions to be held between Egypt, Jordan and Israel. The United States is a superpower, but for the attainment of peace between us and the Arabs, our agreement is required. It was up to us to ensure that neither our armed forces nor our settlements would be removed from the West Bank, and that the territory would not come under foreign rule.

I was back in Washington a month later, on 26 April. I had left it in March with US accusations ringing in my ears, but it soon became clear to the Americans that repeated charges of Israeli intransigence were hardly the ideal way to make progress. In the meantime, Defence Minister Ezer Weizman accompanied by Aharon Barak had had talks with Sadat in Egypt, but though these were interesting and instructive, they made no headway. There was thus no avoiding a return at least to the form of tripartite consultations in which the Americans conducted talks with us and talks with the Egyptians. Washington accordingly sent Atherton to Cairo to see Sadat, and asked me to come to the United States upon Atherton's return. I took with me Aharon Barak, Meir Rosenne and Eli Rubinstein.

At an airport press conference before my departure, I said I would try to concentrate our discussions on practical proposals rather than on new formulae and paper declarations. Israel had put forward such practical proposals on peace with Egypt and autonomy for the Palestinians. The Egyptians had said they were unacceptable, and they would present counter-suggestions; but they had not yet done so. We were being pressed to agree to a Declaration of Principles, but that was merely a generalized verbal formula, to my mind of secondary importance. The essential question was what Egypt was proposing as a basis for a practical agreement and not as a basis for the text of yet another paper.

Atherton had got back to Washington the day before my arrival, and our talks at the State Department opened with his report of the meeting with Sadat. Egypt's President had told him that as time passed without any progress, his position in the Arab world was becoming more grave. Sadat also said that he could not enter into practical negotiations over Sinai before reaching an agreement with us on the Palestinian issue. If King Hussein and the Palestinians maintained their refusal to take part in the negotiations, Sadat would himself be prepared to discuss the future of the West Bank and Gaza without them. He agreed that certain Israeli forces could remain in the West Bank, and he also agreed to minor frontier changes. He demanded self-determination for the Palestinians, but he regarded the West Bank and Gaza as being linked to Jordan and not as constituting an independent State. In any event – and this was the important point for Israel – they would remain Arab territory. Israel, Sadat added, should now announce that she agreed to withdraw from the West Bank and Gaza, allowing, as he had indicated, for slight border rectification and the stationing of limited Israeli units in the evacuated territory.

The Americans did not say it in so many words, but it was evident that they supported Sadat's position, and that was the pattern in our two-day discussions at the State Department. There was much talk and argument, with each side trying to convince the other, but to little effect. The Americans represented Egypt's views, without the authority to change or concede anything, so they kept pressing Egyptian demands upon us; but when we queried them or sought to find some middle ground we were faced by a blank wall. The second party to the negotiations was far away – in Cairo. The American role was to ask not 'what', but 'how' – not what an agreement on the Palestinian issue should be, but how to get us to accept their stand. True, the Americans were not a direct party to this issue, but they had made up their minds and had a clear point of view on the matter, a view identical with that of the Egyptians.

Our difficulty was that we could expect no brighter results in negotiating directly with the Arabs than we could through American mediation. That had become apparent in the face-to-face meetings we had had with the Egyptians; how much more so would it be with the extremist Arab States and the Palestinians.

At our first session, after Atherton had given his report, Barak told of the meeting he and Ezer Weizman had had with Sadat and General Gamassi. I then presented Israel's position. If Egypt, I said, insisted on our undertaking that after a five-year transition period Judea, Samaria and the Gaza District would become sovereign Arab territory, there would be no agreement, not even if it were to include local border changes and any kind of security arrangement. If we wished to advance the peace process, we should therefore stop busying ourselves with declarations of principles or with what was to happen in five years' time. We had made a concrete proposal. The Egyptians said they would do the same. Where was it? Let them state what kind of regime they proposed for the West Bank during the transition period. The only encouraging thing I had heard that day was Egypt's readiness to negotiate with us on the Palestinian issue even without the reluctant Jordanians and Palestinians.

The fruitful course, I urged, was to concern ourselves with arrangements in the territories during the coming five years, which would prepare the ground for a permanent system thereafter. It was pointless to try to reach a final agreement now on post-transition arrangements. If such agreement were possible, there would be no need to wait five years.

Moreover, if we managed to achieve a peace treaty with Egypt and establish normal relations between our two countries, this would have a favourable impact on an arrangement with the Palestinian Arabs. Certain measures could be taken right away, some by Israel on her own, others with Egypt. For example, Israel could abolish her military government in the territories without the agreement of the Palestinian Arabs. And Israel together with Egypt could do much else on this Palestinian issue without the Palestinians and the Arab States.

On Israel's security, there was room for productive discussion on the nature of the Israeli army's function in the West Bank and Gaza. But the Egyptians should know that we would agree to no arrangement which would empower the residents of Judea and Samaria to tell us at the end of the five-year period to leave. We had just been compelled to enter Lebanon to deal with the terrorists who were attacking our civilians from Lebanese bases. We were determined to prevent such a situation from arising in the West Bank and Gaza. Our military presence there would not be temporary.

Nor was the proposal acceptable to me that our troops in these territories would be confined to closed camps. It would be their function to carry out reconnaissance patrols. And even when not on duty they would have the right to enter and leave the territories freely, not in order to interfere in the lives of the Arab residents but simply because Jews were not strangers to that stretch of land. It was inconceivable that Arabs from Nablus and Gaza should have unlimited entry into Israel while our people should be forbidden to visit Gaza and Nablus.

I then took up the question of Israeli settlements in the administered territories. The Americans well knew our position on this subject, I said. We held that Jews were entitled to acquire land and establish settlements there. If the Egyptians were opposed to that, we should sit down together to discuss it directly and frankly, and not avoid it.

As for the sovereignty of the West Bank and Gaza, I said this problem should be left open throughout the transition period, during which they would be under neither Israeli nor Arab sovereignty. At the end of that period, each side should have the right to raise it. We all knew, I said, that any attempt to decide it now would end in deadlock. We should therefore wait five years. By that time, the inhabitants of the territories would have been living under a new regime of Arab self-rule, new realities would have been created, and then, if the parties so wished, the question could be reconsidered.

Turning to Vance, I said I thought the Americans had accepted our autonomy plan as a basis for transitional administration. Vance replied that this was, on the whole, true, but the plan required material changes. He then asked if we intended that the Arab Administrative Council would have authority only over the Arab residents or also over the Israeli settlements. I said only over the Arabs. The Israelis would remain within the jurisdiction of the State of Israel.

The Americans then raised questions about the responsibility for internal security, migration and legislation under our autonomy plan, and Barak, Rosenne and I replied. But I kept stressing that we, the Egyptians, and the Americans should sit together and discuss the practical implementation of the plan instead of wrangling interminably about a declaration of principles. Migration was a good example of the inapplicability of a generalized principle. If some of the 1967 refugees wished to return to their families and found work on their farms, we would be ready to discuss it. But if, for example, the term 'migration' were to cover the transfer of refugee camps from Lebanon to the West Bank, we would not consider it. One had to solve the problem of the two hundred thousand refugees in the Gaza District and not add refugee camps from outside. These were practical matters which had to be solved by realistic measures, not by abstract principles.

The Americans again came back to the question of sovereignty after five years, insisting, despite all I had said on this point, that the decision on what the status would be at the end of the transition period had to be taken now. Otherwise, they said, there could be no progress in the negotiations. It seemed so illogical to me that I thought there must be a hidden motive. I told the Secretary of State that Sadat surely knew there was no prospect of an Israeli commitment to withdraw from the West Bank and Gaza after five years.

Vance asked me directly what I proposed instead. I replied that I had already made that clear: agree to discuss the question then, not now. Vance continued to press. Could we state categorically that a decision would be taken on the question of sovereignty in five years' time? I said that if the matter was not only to be discussed but also decided, we would have to know how it would be decided, through what machinery, and whether each side would have the right of veto. But since I did not think we could reach agreement now on the decision-making method for so vital a matter, all one could say now was that after five years, if either party so wished, the matter would be discussed. Vance did not give up, but was forced to disclose the motive: he said Sadat insisted on knowing now what the status would be at the end of the transition period. I told Vance that what Sadat wanted was not to know, but to determine, what the end would be. He wanted all the administered territories to be under Arab sovereignty, and to that we would not agree.

I thought we had finished that discussion, which had taken up much of the first day. But Vance telephoned in the morning to say he wished to concentrate our deliberations the following day on the post-transition status of the territories. And that was what we did, ending with the American demand for answers to two questions: Was Israel prepared to give an undertaking that the sovereignty issue would be decided after five years? And if so, how would the decision be taken?

I promised to transmit the question to my Government. But I had to tell them frankly that I did not take kindly to their questioning methods. They asked; I answered. They repeated the question; I explained. Then they asked again. This was not questioning for information. This was interrogation, as though we were in the dock, while Sadat was freed of the need to answer since he was with the interrogators. I said this system had to stop. The Egyptians should submit their proposals. We had already submitted ours. They should be put on the table, discussed, and we would see whether we could or could not come to an agreement.

Premier Begin came to the United States two days after we ended our talks in Washington, to attend a mass rally marking the thirtieth anniversary of the State of Israel. The American Government did not overlook his arrival – nor the occasion. President Carter gave him a splendid reception, to which he invited a thousand rabbis from all over the United States. Working sessions were also arranged for Begin with the President and the Secretary of State.

We had flown to New York to meet the Prime Minister when he arrived, reported to him on our talks, and consulted together on the meetings he would be having with Carter and Vance. I told Begin that the main question he would be asked would be the status of the territories after five years. He showed no inclination to go into the subject in any depth or take any decision. He said that when asked, he would simply say it needed to be brought before the Government, and the US administration would get the answer in a few weeks. I left him to his rally, the reception and his Washington meetings, and caught the next plane to Israel.

On my first day back in Israel I drove to Nahalal to visit my son Ehud (Udi) and his family, and to see his farm. This had once been my home, but when I found that first my military and later my ministerial duties left me no time to keep up the farm, I asked the co-operative village to admit Udi to membership of the moshav and I handed it all over to him, house, farm and everything.

Rahel was with me. As we approached the village, I said I wished to go first to the cemetery. It happened also to be the thirtieth anniversary of the death of my brother Zohar, who was killed in the battle for Ramat Yochanan during our War of Liberation on the eve of the establishment of the State. His son Uzi was born shortly afterwards, and the resemblance between the two is remarkable. Zorik, as we called my brother, was killed by a bullet in the head when he stormed the enemy lines at the head of his unit. He was twenty-two at the time and a Company Commander. Uzi was now serving in the regular army as commander of a crack unit.

In the years immediately following Zorik's death, I paid an annual visit to his grave; but then I stopped. My parents had died, and later my sister, so that I had less cause to visit Nahalal, and fewer opportunities to be near the cemetery. Whenever I am nagged by conscience for not visiting the family graves more often, I take consolation in the fact that one day I will be lying next to them.

The cemetery on the hillock is well tended, and the view is enchanting, especially in the spring. The Valley of Jezreel is spread out below in all its multi-coloured glory, with its green wheat fields, the golden barley that ripens early, the orchards of plums and peaches with their white and pink blossom, and the red-tiled roofs of the cottages in the kibbutzim and moshavim scattered from one end of the valley to the other.

I told Rahel about my family as we stopped at each grave: grandfather and grandmother, who had come to Israel from Zhukov in Russia; two uncles, one of whom was drowned at sea; an aunt, who died while giving birth to her daughter; Avner, a cousin, who met his death in a fighter plane; my brother, my sister, and my parents.

Rahel had met my mother when she was dying of cancer. When the doctors announced that there was no hope, I brought Rahel to her bedside. Rahel and I were not yet married, but I did not have to explain anything to mother. 'It's good that you have come,' she said. 'I've been wanting to see you.' She took hold of her hand and looked long at her with kind and gentle eyes.

We left the cemetery and walked about on the hill. Coming towards us was an Arab lad with a herd of cows. We greeted each other and I asked his name.

'Ali,' he replied.

'Ali what?' I asked. 'Whose son are you?'

'Ali, son of Yonas,' he replied.

'Yonas son of whom?'

'Yonas son of Mahmad el Hussein, of the Arab el Mazrib tribe.'

His grandfather's name was familiar. I had known him in my youth. I introduced myself.

'Are you Moshe Dayan, the military commander?' he asked.

I said I was he, but that now I was old and no longer in the army. I was a Cabinet Minister.

I had started to speak Hebrew, but switched to Arabic when I noticed he had difficulty with the language. I asked him about members of his tribe whom I had known. Several were dead, and the others were no longer living in tents in nearby Wadi Hawakir. They had moved to El Batuf, the hill north of the highway and had built themselves stone houses. They also had a school and a shop in their village.

'What does your father do?' I asked.

'He is a merchant. He buys from the villagers their olive crop while it is still on the trees, and then hires labourers to pick them, and he sells them on the market. In a good year, when the crop is big, he earns well; in a poor year, the crop is small, but then the price of the olives is high.'

'And does your father make money?'

Ali hesitated for a moment, and then said, 'Thank God we have food. We have no complaints.'

'And in your houses,' I went on, 'do you live like the peasants, cook on a tabun and use manure for fuel? Have you stopped burning forest trees for your fires?'

Ali looked at me as though he did not know what I was talking about. 'We cook on gas stoves, like the Jews.' But then he added, 'We also chop trees from the forest wood to heat the home and prepare coffee. When guests call, they sit outside near an open fire.'

I never did like the smell from the tabuns in the Arab villages. They used sun-dried cow and donkey manure as fuel for cooking. This manure kept the fires burning long, but its smoke was wafted far and wide - together with its stench. The Bedouin fires were quite different, emitting the pleasing odours of the dried twigs of oak and terebinth, as the thick bluish smoke rose from the thresholds of the tents. In summer, the smoke kept the mosquitoes away, and in winter beckoned the wayfarer overtaken by nightfall to come and warm himself.

I asked Ali if he went to school. 'Not always,' he replied. 'Sometimes I look after my father's herd.' As he said it, a red heifer started wandering off on its own, and Ali began throwing stones at it, accompanying the action with ripe curses in Arabic. He stopped only long enough to answer my farewell salutation. 'May God grant you peace,' he said, showing a well-bred familiarity with his culture of greetings. As Rahel and I turned to leave, he resumed his cursing, and at that, too, he was an expert.

We sat on a rock and looked out over the Jezreel Valley, and my thoughts again went back to the early days of Nahalal, to the tents and the primitive huts which were the homes of that time, to the travel by wagon, the ploughing by mule-teams. Mother was then young and beautiful, her hair tied back in a bun – except on Sabbath eve when she would release it for shampooing, and her thick locks would flow over her shoulders. There was never a grey strand to her dying day.

We returned to the car and went on to Nahalal. I recalled, as we drove, that I was to report to the Cabinet on my talks in Washington, which now seemed remote, unreal. This, and all that lay around me, was reality, and here was the true Declaration of Principles – the Valley of Jezreel, with its flourishing farm settlements, its orchards and fields and woods, recovered out of the swamp by the toil of wonderful people, both the dead and those who came after them.

The Americans continued to be preoccupied with the status of the territories after the transition period, urging upon us the commitment that the question of sovereignty would then be 'definitely resolved'. Begin had informed the President and Secretary of State in Washington shortly after my departure, as he told me he would, that the Israeli Government would consider their questions and give a reply. Before we had a chance to do so, US Ambassador Lewis called on me and handed me on behalf of Secretary Vance the text of the kind of reply they thought we should give. I asked the Ambassador if he would also be kind enough to tell me where I was to sign! The United States was assuredly a superpower upon whom we greatly depended, but this was going a bit too far. I promised the Ambassador that I would pass on their proposal to the Prime Minister, but I, for one, would recommend that we should not accept their text.

To my mind, the Americans were asking the wrong question and also seeking the wrong reply. The matter at issue was whether or not we could create a suitable *modus vivendi* with the Arabs in the territories during the transition period. The moment it was announced that the decision on sovereignty would be taken in another five years, a transition period would become pointless. For instead of those five years providing an opportunity for the undisturbed development of a pattern of normal relationships and co-operation between the two peoples, they would be marked by constant struggle over the prospective sovereignty decision.

The Government reply was handed to the Americans on 18 June, following its approval at a Cabinet session that morning. It was based largely on a memorandum I had sent to the Prime Minister, with amendments introduced during consultations with other ministers. After stressing how vital it was to continue the peace-making process, it set out two points: the Government of Israel agreed that five years after the application of Administrative Autonomy in Judea, Samaria and the Gaza District, the nature of future relations between the parties would be considered and agreed upon at the suggestion of any of the parties; and in order to reach an agreement, the parties would negotiate between themselves – but also participating in those negotiations would be representatives of the residents of the territories as elected in accordance with the Administrative Autonomy.

The reaction of the Americans came quickly. This was not the reply they either liked or had expected. What they wanted was an express agreement on our part to a process that would bring about Arab sovereignty over Judea, Samaria and the Gaza District after five years.

That was how matters stood until the middle of the next month, when a new initiative attempted to get the negotiations moving again.

CHAPTER ELEVEN

Leeds Castle

We had had no direct talks with the Egyptians since January 1978, when Foreign Minister Muhammad Ibrahim Kamel, who was in Jerusalem for the inaugural session of the joint Political Committee, was abruptly ordered by Sadat to break off the discussions and return to Cairo. During the next six months, American representatives had shuttled back and forth between Washington, Cairo and Jerusalem, conducting intensive talks in all three capitals in a fruitless effort to formulate a Declaration of Principles acceptable to both us and Egypt. My own view, which had been stated repeatedly to Secretary of State Cyrus Vance, was that the only way to advance the peace negotiations was to abandon the search for a formula on principles and get down to tackling the substantive peace proposals.

The Egypt–Israel–US conference that opened at Leeds Castle in England on 18 July 1978 was convened at the initiative of the Americans for precisely this purpose. Heading the four-man Egyptian delegation, which included senior Foreign Ministry official Osama al-Baz, was Foreign Minister Kamel. I headed the Israeli delegation which included Barak and Rosenne. And Vance led the US delegation, the largest of all. Among those accompanying him were Atherton, Saunders, the US Ambassadors to Israel and Egypt, and State Department spokesman Hodding Carter. It had been agreed that the central subject of our deliberations would be the Palestine problem, and each side would present its proposals for a solution.

In the original arrangements, the conference was to have been held at the Churchill Hotel in London. But the British then felt that safeguarding the lives of the participants might prove difficult at a hotel in the heart of the capital, and they chose the quiet and isolated Leeds Castle instead.

I arrived at London's Heathrow airport, stepped down from the plane, and wondered for a moment whether I had inadvertently stumbled into an imminent battlefield. Armed British troops were arrayed on the roofs of the surrounding buildings; several tanks and armoured cars lined the runway;

and our delegation were led along a special path to the VIP room of the terminal. With all my respect for the Palestinian terrorists, I did not think they warranted such consideration. I often drive to Nablus, Gaza and Hebron, visiting antiquities stores as well as private homes. In most cases, news of my visit is known in advance, yet personal security arrangements are minimal. Here, in London, I thought it was all too much. But the British are British, and their intentions were kindly and laudable. So was their hospitality – we were promptly offered the ritual English tea and biscuits. There is something about British tradition that is very engaging. It has no substitute.

We were not taken into town but flown from the airport directly to the castle. I have had occasion in the past to visit ancient forts in France, but I had never stayed in one. Leeds Castle is very impressive, with its stone towers, its stout battlemented walls, and its spacious halls. Age has turned the ramparts and long-deserted embrasures a hoary grey colour, which gives them added solidity and dignity, and evokes the medieval picture of jousting knights displaying their skills before the admiring glances of their ladies.

The surrounding scenery is a poem of tranquillity – an endless stretch of lush meadows dotted with clumps of ancient trees with huge branches, forming the perfect model of 'the peaceful countryside'. And pervading the castle itself is a spirit of unruffled calm. I could not know what impact this might have on our discussions, but I was quite certain that the participants would walk on tiptoe, and no one would raise his voice above a whisper.

The Secretary of State and I were accompanied by our wives. Kamel came alone. I was glad, as always to see Gay Vance once again. She is wonderful company, and delights by her very presence. She once told me she had volunteered for nursing duty during the Second World War and had had the most agonizing experiences tending the wounded. She was now to be drawn into the complicated maladies of the Middle East.

Each delegation was given a wing to itself. When the keeper of the castle showed us to our rooms, I recalled that only a few months earlier I had seen a television film taken when a group of correspondents had been given a tour of this very castle. Watching the film, I had spotted in one of the rooms what looked to me like an ancient Egyptian bronze sculpture of a cat. I now asked my host about it. 'You are quite right,' said the keeper, and promptly led us back from our wing to what was to be our conference hall. There, on a pedestal, sat the life-size cat, a royal animal of impressive arrogance, its throat decked with a necklace, its lobes pierced for ear-rings. Like all the sculptured cats of early Egypt, it was depicted sitting on its haunches, its front paws outstretched, its ears upright, its head turned to the rear. I judged this elegant creature to have been fashioned in the fifth or sixth century BC. It had a hollow inside, and had undoubtedly contained the embalmed body of a sacred or palace household cat.

Despite its beauty, I felt that this Pharaonic animal was out of place. All around him, hanging on the walls, were the portraits of English noblemen and the typical paintings of hunting scenes and the English countryside. The bronze cat, his eyes half-closed, was sunk in his own world. Nor did he seem interested in the conference over which he would soon be presiding. The Israelis were of the Mosaic faith, the Egyptians now turned to Mecca, and the Christians were the followers of Jesus. What had they to do with him whose god, in his day, was the sun-god Ra? And how ephemeral were the pencils on the table and the pads of foolscap on which we would soon be scribbling, compared to the ancient papyri of his day, bearing timeless hieroglyphs drawn by the hand of an artist. I took the bronze animal in my hands, examined him from all sides, and carefully restored him to his pedestal. The look in his eyes was chill but living. I felt drawn to him but he paid me not the slightest attention.

The Leeds Castle Conference was of the highest importance, proving a milestone in the peace negotiations. It was also a difficult conference. Both its difficulty and its importance stemmed from the same source: this was the moment of truth. Shortly before, Austrian Chancellor Bruno Kreisky had published in Vienna his own Declaration of Principles as a basis for peace between Israel and Egypt. This Declaration was acceptable both to President Sadat, who was in Salzburg at the time, and to Israel's Labour Party, whose leader, Shimon Peres, had helped Kreisky in the drafting. (When Abba Eban claimed that the copyright was in fact his, it became known as the Eban–Kreisky Declaration.) Its publication was followed by two announcements which revealed its worthlessness. One was from Kreisky, who said it had been made deliberately vague so that both sides could read into it whatever they wished. The second, made simultaneously with the publication of the Kreisky Declaration, came from Egypt's Foreign Minister, who gave the official Egyptian interpretation. It called, he said, for the total Israeli withdrawal from Judea, Samaria and Gaza; security arrangements without the presence of Israeli troops; a return to the international borders on the Egyptian and Syrian fronts; recognition of the rights of the Palestinians to self-determination. (Abba Eban and Shimon Peres, of course, gave a completely contradictory interpretation.)

At no time was the subject of a Declaration of Principles raised at Leeds Castle. The item that *was* presented for our consideration – officially for the first time since the beginning of the peace talks – was a detailed six-point proposal by the Egyptians for settling the future of the administered territories. It had been handed to us two weeks before the conference by the US Ambassador to Israel, Sam Lewis, and was headed 'Proposal Relative to Withdrawal from the West Bank and Gaza and Security Arrangements'. This title gave a clear indication of its contents.

It opened with the general statement that a solution of 'the Palestinian question' was essential to peace in the Middle East, and had to be based on 'the legitimate rights of the Palestinian people'. Consideration should be given to 'the legitimate security concerns of all the parties'.

To ensure the orderly transfer of authority, it proposed a transitional period of five years at the end of which 'the Palestinian people will be able to determine their own future'. Talks would take place 'between Egypt, Jordan, Israel and representatives of the Palestinian people, with the participation of the UN', with a view to agreeing upon details of the transitional regime, 'timetable for the Israeli withdrawal', mutual security arrangements 'during and following the transitional period', and the means of implementing the 'relevant UN resolutions on the Palestinian refugees'.

Point 4 stated that 'Israel shall withdraw from the West Bank (including Jerusalem) and the Gaza Strip, occupied since June 1967'. And it added that 'The Israeli withdrawal applies to the settlements established in the occupied territories'.

It then called for the abolition of the Israeli military government in these territories 'at the outset of the transitional period'. With Israel's departure, supervision over the administration of the West Bank would become the responsibility of Jordan, while Egypt would have that responsibility in the Gaza Strip. Jordan and Egypt would work 'in co-operation with freely elected representatives of the Palestinian people who shall exercise direct authority over the administration of the West Bank and Gaza'. The UN would 'supervise and facilitate the Israeli withdrawal and the restoration of Arab authority'.

Though Egypt's Foreign Minister Kamel headed his delegation, the principal Egyptian spokesman was al-Baz, an incisive, knowledgeable, Harvard-educated jurist. Slight of stature, thin, sallow-complexioned, he tried to avoid the social side of such gatherings as much as possible. At dinner he would sit silent, and only peck at his food. But at the conference table he came to life. His strength lay in the sharpness of his tongue, his expert familiarity with every subject under discussion, the clarity of his formulation, and his cutting replies in argument, which at times verged on the offensive. I could not tell whether or not he was genuinely committed to securing a peace agreement.

What was apparent, however, was that he bore no love for Israelis, and made no effort to hide his distaste at having to sit with us. If popularity had been the subject of our meeting at Leeds Castle, we need not have come.

There were three plenary sessions with the participation of all three delegations. The first two were held on the first day, 18 July 1978, and one on the next. Secretary Vance opened the conference, observing that the agenda consisted of two proposals, an Egyptian and an Israeli one, concerning the West Bank and Gaza. He noted that there were several points on which both sides were agreed: a transitional period of five years; abolition of the Israeli military government; an administration to be elected by the inhabitants of the West Bank and Gaza; the need for security arrangements during and following the transitional period; Jordan to be a party to the negotiations, and to bear responsibility for certain functions in the administration of the West Bank; and, above all, the common agreement that there be not only an end to acts of hostility but also the establishment of a genuine peace, including the normalization of relations between the parties. Of course, Vance added, there were areas of disagreement, but there was no need to go into details. They would find expression during the course of the discussions, and he, Vance, hoped they would be resolved.

He ended his remarks by asking me to clarify the Israeli proposal on autonomy. I did so, briefly, and stressed that it was not a take-it-or-leave-it ultimatum. If the Egyptians wished to offer changes, we were ready to discuss them. Aharon Barak followed, and expanded on some of the articles in our proposal.

The response of the Egyptian Foreign Minister was that we had left too many items open, and subject to negotiation. He thought they should be decided upon then and there. He was particularly opposed to the point in our proposal calling for the decision on sovereignty to be considered after five years. On that matter, he said, the United States had submitted clear and specific questions to Israel, but Israel's replies had thrown no light on the subject, and in fact they were evasive.

It was al-Baz who presented the Egyptian position. The Palestinian issue, he said, was the central problem, and unless it were solved there would be no resolution of the Arab-Israel conflict. Even if it were ignored, it would erupt again and again, like a temporary sleeping volcano. Israel's autonomy proposal was inadequate, and rested on foundations that were not acceptable to the Palestinian people. Any arrangement of this matter required their agreement. For them, autonomy was not enough. The Palestinians wanted self-determination. Moreover, he went on, what was needed was a comprehensive solution to the conflict. The Egyptians would not sign a separate treaty with us concerning Sinai. Solving the Palestinian problem had to be an integral part of a comprehensive arrangement. The principles of such an arrangement should apply also to the Syrian front, namely, Israel's obligation and commitment to withdraw entirely from the Golan Heights. Egypt's proposal, therefore, was based on two complementary elements: Israel's withdrawal from the territories she had conquered; and appropriate security arrangements to compensate Israel for the territories she was returning. Al-Baz then listed six security devices which, in Egypt's view, should satisfy our defence needs: demilitarized zones; limited forces zones; presence of UN forces; sophisticated early-warning stations; freedom of shipping through the Gulf of Eilat; and the normalization of relations.

Despite our basic differences, the morning session proceeded in a constructive spirit. There was frankness on both sides, and amiable intermingling during the coffee break. Kamel was the first to speak when the session resumed. He said it was possible to solve everything there, at that very conference table. All that was required was for the Israelis to undertake to withdraw. The rest were subsidiary problems which would be easy to settle. I asked him if he had read the interview Saddam Hussein (who was then Vice-President and is now President of Iraq) had given that very week to the magazine *Newsweek*. In it Saddam said that even if peace were established between Egypt and Israel, there would be another war, and the Israelis would be thrown into the sea and the land would become a Palestinian State. 'The decision you suggest we take in five minutes', I told Kamel, 'disregards the facts, and ignores the political and military realities, and the attitude of the Arab world around us. For you such matters may be of little concern, but for us they pose the question of our very survival.' Kamel replied that we should listen to the 'Voice of Cairo' and not to the words from Baghdad. It seemed that for him the problem was simply deciding which knob to turn on the radio.

I decided this was the time to get a clear answer from the Egyptians on two matters. The first was on our proposal for a peace arrangement with them. I asked if they accepted it as a basis for a settlement. If they rejected it, we would shelve it and they could regard it as cancelled. I put this to them with the knowledge of Prime Minister Begin. I had suggested it to him during our pre-conference consultation, and he had agreed. The Egyptians were embarrassed and did not hasten to respond. Indeed, Kamel asked for an adjournment so that his delegation could consider my question. When they returned, he said that his instructions for the conference covered only the Palestinian problem and they could give me no answer on the subject I had raised.

The second matter concerned the West Bank. Were they prepared, I asked them, to discuss its division in a territorial compromise along the lines of what had been termed the Allon Plan? On that, Kamel said, he could say right away, with complete authority, that the answer was a definite negative. They would countenance no division of the West Bank. Israel had to withdraw from all the territories she had conquered, including East Jerusalem. The only thing they were prepared to consider was the rectification of certain distortions. If, for example, the pre-1967 war border ran through and divided a village or its lands, they might agree to change the line of the frontier so as to reunite the village. But even such changes would need to be made on a reciprocal basis, with something given for whatever was gained. On no account was it to result in the enlargement of Israel's territory.

The Egyptians suggested that their proposed plan for the settlement of the Palestinian question be carried out in three stages. The first was Israel's acceptance of the plan. This was to be decided upon at once, at Leeds Castle, and within one month Egypt, Jordan and Israel were to determine the necessary arrangements for its implementation. Thereafter, and again within a period not exceeding one month, the second stage was to be inaugurated at the start of the transitional period, with Israel's withdrawal. The third stage was to be marked by the entry into the West Bank and Gaza of UN troops in place of the departing Israelis, and the Palestinian elections in these territories to establish their institutions.

The Egyptian proposals were concerned not only with the Palestinian refugees from the 1967 war, but also with those who had fled the country during the war of 1948, most of whom had gone to Lebanon, Jordan and other Arab countries, as well as to Gaza and the West Bank.

(A few hours after Israel's proclamation of statehood on 14 May 1948, five neighbouring Arab countries, Egypt, Syria, Jordan, Lebanon and Iraq, with contingents from Saudi Arabia, Libya and the Yemen, invaded the new State, and Israel had to fight her war of liberation. The Arabs were defeated, and half a million Palestinian Arabs who had left their homes during the fighting became refugees. Many had fled from the dangers of battle. But many, particularly those in Haifa, had left at the direction of their Arab leaders, in order to leave the Arab armies with a single target, the Jews, and hoped to return after the war to occupy the homes and property of the 'defeated' Jews. When their expectations of an Arab victory were dashed, they were stranded in the Arab countries and Arab-held areas of Palestine where they had found refuge. Instead of becoming assimilated in these territories, they were kept as refugees in special camps, and remain so to this day. Their Arab hosts did not lift a finger to help them. Their status as refugees was perpetuated by the United Nations Works and Relief Organization [UNWRA].)

The Egyptian delegation at Leeds Castle now called upon Israel to implement successive UN resolutions concerning these 1948 refugees. This meant giving them the choice of returning to their original homes or receiving compensation for the property they had left behind. 'Why', asked Kamel, 'do you not wish to implement these resolutions?' The practical implications of such a course, I replied, were best exemplified by what PLO leader Yasser Arafat said in his speech to the UN General Assembly on 13 November 1974. Arafat demanded an Arab–Israel State which would extend from the Mediterranean to the River Jordan (namely, covering the existing territory of Israel together with the West Bank and Gaza). He stressed that that State would have an Arab majority. 'Which means', I said to Kamel, 'the end of the Jewish State, the only Jewish State in the world, as against the many Arab States. Do you really imagine we would lend our hand to such a purpose?'

Kamel then proposed that we discuss the security arrangements, such as the entry of UN forces, which would make possible our withdrawal from the territories. I said there was no point to such discussion since we were not prepared to rely for our security on foreign troops, whoever they might be. Only Israel's soldiers deployed along the River Jordan and at key points on the West Bank and Gaza District could guarantee our safety.

The gap between the Egyptian and Israeli positions was wide, clearly reflecting their divergent aims. The Egyptians, with the help of the US delegation, proposed arrangements which would ultimately lead to our withdrawal from the territories and the granting of Palestinian self-determination, either statehood or annexation to Jordan. We for our part insisted that we were not foreigners in these territories, and we wanted an arrangement based on peaceful co-existence, but neither our settlers nor our troops would be withdrawn from Judea, Samaria and the Gaza District.

Between plenary sessions, the Americans held separate consultations with the Egyptians and with us to try to narrow the gap on the complicated issues of security arrangements in exchange for our territorial withdrawal, and Palestinian self-determination. In their talks with us, the Americans went very far on the question of our security. They asked me if inviting Israel to become a member of NATO would satisfy us. I replied that I personally would welcome it, but not as a substitute for our military presence in the West Bank and Gaza. 'Do we understand from what you say', they asked, in an effort to get to the heart of our thinking, 'that there exists no means of security which you would accept in exchange for pulling back your military forces to the pre-1967 borders?' I nodded agreement. That, indeed, was my view.

The talks with the Americans were held not by the entire delegations but by the ministerial heads, each accompanied by a single aide. Vance came with Ambassador Lewis and I had with me Aharon Barak. At their conclusion, and after consultation with the members of my delegation, I wrote a brief memorandum for Vance in which I formulated my position on what I considered to be the three main issues. After stating that this was my 'personal opinion' and was being given on 'my personal responsibility only', I wrote:

1. A proposal for a peace treaty which would be based upon the withdrawal of Israel to the pre-1967 demarcation lines (with minor modifications) and the establishment of Arab sovereignty over the areas will not be acceptable to Israel even if such a proposal is accompanied by a promise for security arrangements. Israel's opposition to any such arrangement stems from reasons of principle (national) as well as from practical and security considerations.
2. Should a proposal for a peace treaty based upon a concrete territorial compromise be submitted, Israel, in accordance with previous statements, would be ready to consider it.
3. If the Israel peace proposal (Self Rule) is accepted, Israel will be prepared, as provided for in two sections of the proposal, to discuss after five years the question of sovereignty (or permanent status) of the areas. Although these provisions do not call for a decision on the subject, it is the personal view of the Foreign Minister that an agreement on this question is possible.

As the Leeds Castle Conference ended, Vance suggested, and all parties agreed, that he visit the Middle East a fortnight later in order to continue the discussions.

I gave a full report of the conference to the Cabinet upon my return to Israel. Before doing so I met privately with Prime Minister Begin. He had already received and read the stenographic record of all that had been said at our talks and I simply added my personal impressions. Begin was pleased that I had put the direct question to the Egyptians about the Allon Plan. But then came a revival of the old disagreement I thought we had settled after my Washington talks: he was not pleased with my three-point memorandum, saying I should have asked his consent before giving it to Vance. I told the Prime Minister that what I had said and written reflected, to the best of my understanding, the Government's position, but I would not take it amiss, nor would it be improper, if he or the Government revoked it. I would accept their verdict and inform Vance accordingly. At all events, I added, I did not think I could conduct negotiations without being permitted to put forward ideas and suggest proposals, while stressing that they represented my personal views to which my Government might not agree. This was a well-trodden subject on which Begin and I held firm and differing opinions. I was not prepared to behave otherwise, and Begin knew it. The practical option open to him if he insisted on my accepting his approach was to get himself another Foreign Minister.

To my astonishment, when we moved into the Cabinet room for the Government meeting, Begin proposed not only that the Cabinet endorse my memorandum to Vance but also that it be brought before the Knesset for approval. I thereupon urged that there be a thorough clarification of Article 2 in my memorandum, which referred to our readiness to consider a territorial compromise should the Arabs submit such a proposal. I said I would certainly be asked about it in the Knesset and I-wanted the Cabinet to be clear about what it was they were endorsing. (The point here was that the Opposition Labour Party favoured such a compromise, whereas Begin's own party, Herut, was adamantly against any territorial division of the West Bank. And I had told Vance, and written in the memorandum, as my personal view, that should the Egyptians propose 'a concrete territorial compromise', we would be ready to consider it.) The difference in Hebrew between 'should' and 'if' is wider than it is in English and the phrase 'Should a proposal ...' could be interpreted as conforming to the Herut Party line on territorial division. I, on the other hand, wanted it understood that 'if' the Arabs were to make such a proposal, it would receive our serious consideration. Was the Cabinet prepared to approve that?

Begin, with great reluctance, said he was, but he still asked me to be careful to use the Hebrew word for 'should', as in the memorandum, and not 'if'. It was possible that he agreed because he was certain the Arabs would never make such a proposal. I was satisfied with the result, and saw in it a double importance. It would present to our public the realistic political situation; and it would take the wind out of the sails of the Opposition, who were always insisting that there was a way to achieve peace with the Arabs – by territorial compromise – but the Government was refusing to take it.

The Knesset held its political debate on 24 July and I delivered a report on the Leeds Castle Conference. I read out the memorandum, as a Government decision, and made clear that the word 'should' meant our readiness to consider a proposal for a territorial compromise if it should be made in the future. I myself did not think the Arabs would make such a proposal. I told the Knesset that the Egyptian Foreign Minister had rejected any possibility of dividing the West Bank between Israel and the Arabs. The Egyptian delegation at Leeds Castle had put as a condition for peace Israel's total withdrawal from all occupied Arab lands.

A lengthy debate followed my review, and ended with an Opposition motion declaring that the Government was conducting peace negotiations with Egypt in a manner which would lead to a political impasse; and that there was a chance of securing agreement on a declaration of principles based on the Vienna Document – the celebrated Peres–Eban–Kreisky Declaration referred to earlier. The Opposition motion was defeated and the Government position approved by a vote of 64 to 32. The memorandum which I had given to Vance at Leeds Castle became an official document representing Israel's position.

CHAPTER TWELVE

Camp David

The three delegations left Leeds Castle expecting to resume their talks two weeks later when Secretary Vance was to visit the Middle East. But these talks were not held. The Americans had made all the preparations for such a meeting, which was to take place at the US monitoring station of Um Hashiba in the Sinai desert, but at the last minute the Egyptians backed out. The reason they gave to the Americans was that as long as Israel was not prepared to commit herself in advance to a total withdrawal from the administered territories, there was no point to such a meeting.

The Americans did not give up. Vance came in early August 1978 to try to break the deadlock and find some way of continuing the peace negotiations. His first stop was Israel, after which he would go to Cairo, and from there back to Washington, leaving his aides to visit other Arab capitals.

He met Prime Minister Begin the day he arrived, accompanied by Atherton, Saunders and Lewis, among others. The Israeli group consisted of all the members of the ministerial Defence Committee as well as the entire senior staff of Begin's bureau. The Americans, not to be outnumbered, were compelled to mobilize several staff personnel from their embassy in Tel Aviv who had never before taken part in such high-level meetings.

The talks opened at 10 in the morning in the Prime Minister's Office with effusive greetings by Begin. In the name of the Government of Israel and in the name of the people of Israel, he said, he wished to tell Secretary Vance how much he was honoured and loved as one who worked for peace and who was a friend of Israel. Vance looked somewhat embarrassed at the profusion of flattering words, but did not follow suit when his turn came. He simply thanked the Prime Minister for his 'kind welcome' and plunged immediately into the purpose of his visit. He had come, he said, on behalf of President Carter to renew the peace momentum.

We concentrated on three subjects: the negotiations with Egypt; the situation in Lebanon; and America–Israel matters, notably arms supplies. The morning session was of little interest, being taken up mostly with ministerial speeches. The afternoon session, with fewer participants, was more promising. However, the most important item came up at neither of those two sessions, but at a private meeting between the Prime Minister and the Secretary of State, at which Vance told Begin that President Carter wished to invite him to a summit meeting at Camp David together with President Sadat. It was hoped he would accept. If he did, Vance would leave next day for Cairo and put the proposal to Sadat. If Sadat agreed, it was Carter's wish to hold the meeting early the following month, by which time the Moslem fast of Ramadan, which had started that week, would be over.

Begin accepted the invitation, and promised not to publish the news prematurely. It was arranged that William Quandt, a staff member of the US National Security Council who had joined Vance on this mission, would return from Cairo to report to us on the outcome of the meeting with Sadat.

Two hours before the morning session with Vance, I had a political talk with one of the principal Palestinian Arab leaders in the West Bank, Anwar al-Hatib. The meeting had been arranged some time before we knew of Vance's projected visit, and I had no wish to postpone it. Al-Hatib, an impeccably dressed, young-looking man in his sixties, was the son-in-law of Sheikh Muhammad Ali Jabari, head of the most distinguished family in the Hebron region, and had filled a succession of high posts from 1948 to 1967 when the West Bank and East Jerusalem were under Jordanian rule. He had been Mayor of the Arab part of Jerusalem, Secretary of the Supreme Moslem Council, member of the Jordanian parliament, Jordanian Ambassador to Egypt, and was Governor of the Jerusalem District when the West Bank and the Arab sector of Jerusalem fell to the Israel Army in the Six Day War of June 1967. Although he supported the establishment of a Palestinian State, he was very close to King Hussein.

We met at 8 in the morning – which left enough time for the ten o'clock session with Vance – in a private room of West Jerusalem's Plaza Hotel. Because of the Ramadan fast, we did not even have the traditional cup of coffee, but this did not affect our talk, which was frank and businesslike.

This was not the first time we had met, and I was able to get quickly to the subject I wished to discuss by opening with the politely amusing Arabic greeting: *'Min be'ad le'al-slam.'* The literal translation is 'After greetings of peace', and is an expression used by Arabs when they are pressed for time and wish to skip the formal, long-winded, ceremonious salutations.

I then asked him what were the chances that the Palestinian Arabs and the Kingdom of Jordan might join the autonomy talks. His personal view, he answered, was that our proposal should not be rejected outright, and this was what he was telling his colleagues. Given the choice between the existing situation and autonomy, he preferred autonomy. As for holding official talks with us, he thought they should wait another few months when the outcome of Sadat's initiative became clearer. For the present, it was better for both the Palestinians and Jordanians 'to sit this one out'. In the meantime, however, one might hold 'private talks' to clarify the nature of the autonomy and what it would develop into. On the possibility of 'private talks' – he was careful not to say 'secret talks', though that was what he meant – al-Hatib said he wished to consult with some of his associates in the West Bank and the Government people in Jordan.

He then spoke of the Israel–Egypt negotiations. He and his friends, he said, did not trust Sadat, and in their judgment Israel and Egypt would fail to reach a peace agreement. Nor did they place much hope in the Americans. Washington would not exert real pressure on Israel, and would not compel us to withdraw from the territories.

I put to al-Hatib my concept of the nature of autonomy, stressing that decisions on its permanent structure, including the question of sovereignty, would be made only at the end of a five-year transitional period. This he already knew, and he said there were certain problems which required immediate consideration, and unless there could be an agreed solution, normal relations between our two peoples would not be possible. There was the problem of settlement, for example, with the Jews 'trying to edge the Arabs out of the West Bank and crowding it with Jewish centres of population'. He also insisted that the Arabs who had fled the West Bank during the 1967 war should be allowed to return to their villages. He judged their number to be about 100,000. There were other questions that were easier to settle, but they, too, needed to be dealt with expeditiously, such as facilitating free trade between the Arabs in the territories and the Arab world, and the opening of Arab banks in Judea, Samaria and the Gaza District.

I told al-Hatib I saw no reason not to discuss the matters he had raised, nor others he had not mentioned, such as Holy Places in Jerusalem, and relations between the inhabitants of the West Bank and Jordan. And I, too, would be frank. On the subject of Jewish settlement, I did not think we would fetter ourselves with limitations. We did not establish settlements at the expense or in the place of Arab inhabitants, but alongside them. Could he cite a single case of Arabs having to leave their village, or suffer the slightest damage to their source of livelihood, as a result of the rise of a nearby Jewish settlement? On the contrary, our settlement brought with it new sources of employment, development and economic growth. I was not unaware, I told him, of Arab opposition to our presence; but this was political, a reaction to the fact that we regarded the West Bank and the Gaza District as parts of our birthplace, of our homeland, in which we could live as of right and not on sufferance. After all, I added, the establishment of twenty settlements in the West Bank meant a total of four or five thousand persons, and there was he, Anwar al-Hatib, objecting to them for 'crowding' and 'edging out' the existing inhabitants, while urging us to agree to the addition of another hundred thousand Arabs! These were matters which should be discussed, with each side listening to the other, but viewing the different aspects realistically and with a sense of proportion.

Al-Hatib went back to his opening remark. The autonomy plan should be examined. Perhaps the Arabs should accept it as the first step towards the realization of their desire for a Palestinian State. They might well have future regrets if they now rejected our proposal. At all events, for the moment it was premature to give an answer. He would need to consult with the Arab leaders in the West Bank, in Jordan and in Lebanon, and they would also need to see what happened between Egypt and Israel.

When he rose to leave, I asked him to send my regards to his father-in-law, 'a wise man', I told him, 'who cares for his people'. General Avraham Orli, co-ordinator of our affairs in the administered territories, who was with me, accompanied our guest to the door. As he reached it, al-Hatib turned to me and said, perhaps partly to himself, that if we sat at the negotiating table we could probably reach an agreement, but he did not believe we would, at least not in his lifetime. 'Do you want war?' I asked sharply. 'Heaven forbid,' he replied, not without anxiety.

I was not sorry that our talk had ended on a somewhat harsh note, without a smile or sympathetic word. It was not only the content but also the tone of our talk that he would be transmitting to King Hussein.

A few hours later, during the break between the morning and afternoon sessions with the Americans, I had a luncheon talk with Vance, and we discussed ways to advance the negotiations, and how to involve the Palestinian Arabs and the Kingdom of Jordan. I told Vance what al-Hatib had said about the mood of the Palestinians, and added my judgment on the stand King Hussein was likely to take.

Vance and his party left next day for Cairo, and a happy Quandt returned two days later, on 9 August, and met Prime Minister Begin and me. Vance's talk with Sadat had gone very well, he said. Sadat was full of self-confidence and wanted to move as quickly as possible towards a peace agreement. He accepted President Carter's invitation to Camp David with enthusiasm and without setting preconditions. Quandt said that Sadat and Vance had talked privately, without their aides being present. They were all there at first – Tuhami was among the Egyptian group – but that was only for the benefit of the photographers. When the cameras had stopped whirring, Sadat took Vance out onto the terrace, and none of the others was invited to join them.

The date for the Camp David summit meeting was arranged for the following month. It was to open on 5 September 1978. Each country was to send a nine-man delegation. Sadat urged that the Egyptian and Israeli delegation heads, he and Begin, should be empowered not only to discuss but also to take on-the-spot decisions in the name of their Governments, and so each should bring with him his trusted advisers.

Begin seemed well satisfied with Quandt's report and with the prospect of the summit. He promised Quandt he would let him know in good time whom he would be bringing, but he could give him one name right away: he would be accompanied by his wife, Aliza. (Sadat's wife Jihan would be staying behind.)

The crisis which Vance had come to settle was over – at least on the surface. Instead of the meeting in Sinai's Um Hashiba monitoring station at the Foreign Minister level, there would be a summit meeting in the United States at the level of heads of government: Carter, Sadat, Begin. There had been no demand for a prior Israeli commitment to total withdrawal and Palestinian self-determination – the very conditions on which Sadat had earlier insisted, and which had led to the deadlock. It was my private feeling that Sadat's agreement to the summit meeting had been given on the basis of America's assurance that at Camp David the US would back him on those demands.

The Camp David summit meeting lasted thirteen days, starting on 5 September 1978 and ending on 17 September. It proved the decisive, most difficult and least pleasant stage in the Egypt–Israel peace negotiations. The differences between the stands taken by Carter, Sadat and Begin were abundant, wide and basic, and all three parties had to resolve agonizing psychological and ideological crises in order to reach an agreed arrangement. It meant abandoning long-held traditional viewpoints and outlooks and taking up new positions.

The deliberations were marked by sharp and often bitter argument between us and the Egyptians, and even more so with the Americans. To my regret, even the discussions within our own Israeli delegation were not always tranquil. There were times when only by clenching teeth and fists could I stop myself from exploding. No one disputed Begin's right, as Prime Minister and head of our delegation, to be the final and authorized arbiter of Israel's position on all matters under review. But none of us was disposed to accept, as though they were the Sinai Tablets, those of his views which seemed to us extreme and unreasonable. We were not always at odds, and indeed, on most issues we held identical opinions. But on those occasions when I disagreed with him and questioned his proposals, he got angry, and would dismiss any suggestion that did not appeal to him as likely to cause inestimable harm to Israel.

We could not change the Prime Minister's character nor the style of his speech. But it must be said to the credit of the delegation members that none of them failed to make his ideas known even when they were distasteful to Begin. At one session, when some of our colleagues expressed critical views and the Prime Minister kept cutting them off with harsh retorts, I asked for the floor. I said such behaviour was a form of pressure which prevented the participants from presenting a different view. Begin said he was surprised by my words, but his behaviour changed.

I regarded the Israeli delegation to Camp David as a team with a mission of tremendous responsibility for the welfare of their nation in one of its most critical hours. They were committed to the supreme effort of reaching an understanding with a superpower, and with the most important of the Arab States, while exercising the utmost care to safeguard the future interests of Israel. To inspire the team, create the appropriate atmosphere in which they could work productively, united in friendship and mutual trust, with each member listening to his comrades with patience and open-mindedness – this was the function of the head of the delegation. Only he could do it.

The Big Three, Carter, Sadat and Begin, were housed in neighbouring cabins in a wing to themselves, some distance from the rest of the delegation members. Each cabin had its name. Mine was called 'Red Oak', and it had two bedrooms, a living-room and a large terrace. I slept in one of the bedrooms and the other was shared by Aharon Barak and Meir Rosenne. Eli Rubinstein, my personal assistant and head of my bureau, and the youngest member of the team, slept at first in the living-room, but soon shifted his bed into the room of Barak and Rosenne so that we could use the living-room for work and consultations.

Camp David is without doubt a charming retreat, set in the heart of forested mountains, far from the tumult of the city and remote from the disturbances of daily life. And if tranquillity were not enough, there are amenities for the energetic – tennis courts and swimming pool – and billiard hall and cinema for those less keen on exercise. It also boasts a superb kitchen, staffed by Filipinos of high professional standing. For me, their works of art were patties and ices. Anyone who came to Camp David to lose weight was making a grave mistake. Incidentally, special arrangements were made to provide kosher food to those delegation members requiring it.

The scenery at Camp David is spectacular, yet it is not my favourite landscape. The thick trees, the abundant greenery of shrub and bush, the golden-brown carpet of fallen leaves that covered the ground, failed to move me as does the wild and primitive desert. I love the wilderness, with its broad expanses stretching away to infinity, the occasional cluster of slender date-palms with roots burrowing underground in search of water, and the small lizards lazing on the sand, eyes closed, soaking up the sun.

What I liked most about Camp David was its utter lack of formality. There was no protocol to the table-seating in the dining-room, to the manner of speech, or to dress. We each received a blue wind-jacket marked 'Camp David' in letters of gold, and were told that we could dress as we pleased. President Carter wore a pair of faded blue jeans, Vance had on an over-sized sweater, and the other Americans were equally casual. The Egyptians were more formal. Sadat may not have worn a tie, but the rest of his attire was impeccable, and others in his delegation were equally careful to wear clothes of studied elegance.

Since I was neither a President nor an American, I possessed no jeans. Instead I donned what I usually wear in the garden of my home, a pair of khaki slacks, and rarely had to open the suitcase which my wife Rahel had carefull packed. The khaki did not exactly go with the blue of the anorak, but that was one of the few Camp David problems I could safely ignore.

There were no regular working hours. Most of our meetings with the Americans took place at night, and at times went on to the early hours of the morning. Each meeting ended with a few issues still to be clarified, and then it was mostly the legal advisers who had to continue sitting 'just a little longer' to formulate our conclusions. They did the best they could; but it transpired on occasions that the root of the problem was political and not juridical, and I would then have to get out of my pyjamas and into slacks and wind-jacket to deal with it.

President Carter was indefatigable. Apart from the long hours of consulta-tion with his aides and hard bargaining with the other delegations, he spent much time preparing himself for such meetings by trying to master every detail of the subjects under negotiation. It was not enough for him, for example, to hear about Sinai and the West Bank. He wanted all the details of their terrain, and he would study the maps and listen to explanations, while taking notes in legible longhand of the points he considered of particular importance. Such concentration for hours at a time was tiring, but he would never break off until he was satisfied that he had all the relevant facts.

One evening, at the end of a session between the American and Israeli delegations, he asked me to walk with him back to his cabin. It was after midnight, and we sat on the terrace so as not to disturb his wife Rosalyn and his daughter Amy. We talked till 4 in the morning. I knew that my answers to his questions – and his requests – did not satisfy him, but I hoped that at least I had presented a clear and reasoned account of Israel's position. Before I left, the President asked me to wait a moment while he went into the house to get something for me. He soon came out with a packet of peanuts in his hand. In his State of Georgia, he said, the peanuts, unshelled, were left soaking in salt water, and that was what gave them their special taste. He hoped I would like them ...

Carter's relations with Begin were correct; with Sadat they were much warmer. However, there was no doubt that the President of the United States made a supreme effort to bring the two leaders of Egypt and Israel closer together and to get them to reach a mutual understanding and agreement. As regards the members of our delegation, Carter had particular respect for Aharon Barak. Whenever we reached a deadlock in the talks, he would suggest that Barak, alone or with others, come to see him to try to find a way to break it. Barak is gifted with high intelligence, ingenuity, and integrity. He was punctilious, in his drafting, about safeguarding Israel's position, and at the same time conceived formulae which were also acceptable to the other side.

Barak also got on very well with Rosalynn Carter, after an informal encounter under amusing circumstances. One night, after a joint delegation session, President Carter asked Barak to reformulate a certain memorandum and bring it to him no matter how late. Barak completed it at 1 a.m. and went to look for a telephone to notify the President. When he left the session hall, which was close to the Camp David cinema, he noticed a barefooted young lady sitting on the steps. Thinking she was one of the secretaries who had got tired of the film and gone out into the fresh air, he approached her and asked if she could help him get in touch with the President. 'Certainly,' she answered, 'follow me. There's an office with a telephone in a nearby hut.' Only after they had reached the office and switched on the light did he recognize his guide. He hastened to apologize, but Rosalynn cut him off with 'That's all right. You'd never have found it yourself in this jungle. And anyway I'd better connect you with the President myself. The telephonist would hesitate to ring him at this hour.'

Relations between the Egyptians and ourselves did not extend beyond the bounds of formality. The exception was the Ezer Weizman–President Sadat friendship. Sadat took a great liking to Ezer, and they met often. The practical benefits of their talks may not have been very great, but at least they were a crack in the wall that divided the two delegations. The fact of the matter was that the meeting at Camp David was not a summit meeting in the true meaning of the term. The leaders did not get closer to each other and found no common language. Indeed, the meetings between the three were the least productive. The solutions to the knotty problems, the progress in the negotiations, and subsequent agreements were achieved at other meetings, mainly in talks with members of the American delegation, headed by President Carter, who kept going back and forth between us and the Egyptians.

Despite the crowded workdays, the delegation members found time for relaxation and entertainment. The Americans snatched an occasional hour for tennis and the Israelis for billiards or the cinema. Begin might watch a film, and he would also play chess with Zbigniew Brzezinski, but this was very competitive, and the game proved less a form of peaceful relaxation than a battlefield confrontation, with each one trying desperately to defeat the other.

I myself made do with a daily walk round the perimeter road of the camp. The cinema holds no attractions for me, and tennis is beyond me. A single eye is useful for firing a rifle – where the two-eyed need to close one – but not for tennis, ping pong or football. It is difficult, with one eye, to gauge the precise direction of a ball that is coming straight at you. I have often been the subject of derision by my grandsons for failing to catch the balls they throw.

Actually, what I needed at Camp David was not entertainment or relaxation but the reverse – free time. I have always required many hours for reflection and thought. At home I am sometimes 'caught in the act', and Rahel asks me: 'Where has your mind been throughout the meal? You didn't utter a word.' I have to admit that I was engrossed in prosaic matters, no fanciful dreams, no private wishes, but simply thinking through the various sides of some political or defence problem which engaged my attention at the time. At Camp David, we were busy with one meeting after another, and when we had a free hour, the last thing I wanted was to sit in a cinema and watch the stirring adventures of a Wild West film. What I wanted was to use the time to try to think up some arrangement that might help meet the unsolved problems of the Middle East.

I came to enjoy this morning walk. The stiff uphill climbs left me short of breath at first; but I soon got used to them, and my feet would do their automatic marching at a military pace while my mind was free to roam at

will. In the forefront of my thoughts were the current issues of the negotiations. But thoughts cannot always be straitjacketed, and perhaps it was
because I was in the open air, and amid rural surroundings, that recollections
of my youth would break into my pondering. I would suddenly find myself
back in the fields of my village in the Valley of Jezreel at harvest time, when I
would help my parents gather in the maize and the sorghum.

At the end of the season my friends and I would go on long hikes through
Galilee, the Jordan Valley and the Negev desert, declaiming, as we swung
along, the verses of Israel's poet Shlonsky, suffused with the daring spirit of
revolt. Shlonsky was the inspiration of our young generation, and we learnt
him by heart. I wish he could be translated from the Hebrew, but only a
genius like him could transmit in another tongue the superb rhymes and
jovial rhythm in his light ballads, and the vivacity of his language, rich with
biblical symbolism, in his more profound works.

Now, as I walked alone along the road that wound between the trees and
bushes of the Camp David woods, something of those youthful days came
back to me. I was no longer a boy, and my voice was not lifted in song or
declamation. But the pace of the march and the tramp of boots again
brought a poem to my lips, as it did then. Now, however, it was not the
Shlonsky poems of revolt and of building something new in the ancient
wilderness that had suited the temper of the undeveloped Israel in the 1930s.
What came to mind now were the works of the poetess Rachel, who was a
pioneer member of the kibbutz on the shore of the Sea of Galilee, Deganiah,
where I was born. Her poetry is sentimental and intensely Zionist, almost to
the point of banality. Yet I was greatly taken with them as a youngster, and
they have been part of me ever since. With her biblical namesake in mind, the
matriarch Rachel, she wrote 'Her blood courses through my blood;/Her
voice in my voice sings;/Rachel . . .

Walking round Camp David, I thought of the arguments that awaited me
at the conference table, and the sophisticated formulae that would be submitted by the Egyptians and the Americans. There would be proposals that I
be allowed or forbidden to preserve Jerusalem as my capital, permitted or
barred from settling in Judea and Samaria where the Jews once lived – in the
hills of Hebron, in the biblical Valley of Dothan, at Shiloh and Tekoa. And
as I walked, the words of Rachel were with me throughout: 'Thus, with such
certainty/will I hold to my path;/for preserved in my limbs/are those
memories of old,/of old.'

Permitted or forbidden? It would take a lot more than Camp David, with
all my respect for its importance, to prevent us from preserving Jerusalem as
the capital of Israel. Whoever wished to do so would have to rewrite the

Bible, banish from the Jewish prayer book the age-old cry from exile 'Next Year in Jerusalem', and wipe out three thousand years of history from the chronicles of the Jewish people, throughout which period Jerusalem has been their beacon.

CHAPTER THIRTEEN

The Proposals

The first meeting of the Big Three, unaccompanied by other members of their delegations, was held in the afternoon of 6 September 1978 in Carter's cabin. It was there that the leaders decided that the Camp David objective should be to reach a Framework Agreement, which should contain the essential elements of an Egypt–Israel peace treaty. Carter may well have hoped that the climax of the conference would be the signing of the treaty itself. But, as Sadat pointed out, this would require agreement, and decisions, on the numerous important details to be incorporated in the treaty, and this would take time, 'perhaps three months'. It was therefore resolved to concentrate the summit negotiations on reaching agreement on the crucial issues over which Egypt and Israel were divided. Thereafter, working within the agreed framework and in accordance with the agreed guidelines, the delegations would tackle the operational details – over which the differences between the two countries would prove equally sharp.

That first tripartite meeting was taken up by a discussion of Sadat's proposal for a solution to the conflict, and when it ended, the Israeli delegation was summoned to Begin's cabin to hear his report. I did not know how other members felt, but I was rather apprehensive. Who knew what news Begin was about to bring us? This, after all, was the first time in thirty years of war that such a meeting had taken place, with the President of the United States, the President of Egypt and the Prime Minister of Israel closeted together to consider a peace treaty between the erstwhile foes. The Egyptian leader would not have confined himself to general principles, which were well known, but would have submitted practical proposals, and I wondered what they would be.

There was an air of expectancy in the room as we grouped ourselves round Begin, hastily finished our tea, impatient for him to start, while aides sat with pens poised ready to take down every word. He opened with a colourful description of the preliminaries – the small talk, how Sadat was dressed – and his expression then became grave as he got to the heart of the meeting. Sadat had brought with him an eleven-page document which he insisted on reading to Carter and Begin. It was totally negative, setting out an Egyptian position even more extreme than that presented at the Leeds Castle Conference. Begin thought Israel should reject it outright, and prepare a constructive counter-proposal.

He added that Sadat, in his explanatory comments, had said he was ready to sign an arrangement for the West Bank and Gaza District before reaching an agreement over Sinai, but not the reverse, namely, he would not sign a peace treaty before we settled the Palestine question. Begin reported that he himself had promptly responded by saying that he, too, was ready to finalize an arrangement on the Palestine issue before signing an Egypt–Israel peace treaty.

After a few further clarifications by Begin, we all studied the written text of Sadat's proposal. Entitled 'Framework for the Comprehensive Peace Settlement of the Middle East Problem', the document contained an eight-clause Preamble, and an opening Article which was a general statement declaring the determination of the parties to reach a comprehensive settlement on the basis of Security Council Resolutions 242 and 338 'in all their parts'. The operative clauses were contained in the second Article. They called for:

the withdrawal of Israel from 'the occupied territories' (whereas the vital 'the' was deliberately omitted from Resolution 242);
withdrawal from Sinai and Golan to the international boundaries between mandated Palestine and Egypt and Syria, respectively, and from the West Bank and the Gaza Strip to the 1949 demarcation lines;
Israeli withdrawal to commence immediately upon the signing of the peace treaties; removal of all Israeli settlements in the occupied territories;
establishment of demilitarized and limited armament zones and stationing of UN forces along the borders;
abolition of the Israeli military government, and the transfer of its authority to the Arabs of the West Bank and Gaza, with a five-year transitional period during which Jordan would supervise the administration of the West Bank and Egypt would do the same in the Gaza Strip, 'in co-operation with freely elected representatives of the Palestinian people who shall exercise direct authority over the administration ... simultaneously with the abolition of the Israeli military government'; and six months before the end of the five-year transitional period, 'the Palestinian people shall exercise their fundamental right to self-determination' and be enabled 'to establish their national entity';
Egypt and Jordan 'shall recommend that the entity be linked with Jordan as decided by their peoples';

Palestinian refugees and displaced persons 'shall be enabled to exercise the right to return or receive compensation';

'Israel shall withdraw from Jerusalem to the demarcation lines of the Armistice Agreement of 1949' – namely, Jerusalem to be redivided – and 'Arab sovereignty and administration shall be restored to the Arab sector';

Israel 'to pay full and prompt compensation for the damage which resulted from the operations of its armed forces against the civilian population and installations, as well as its exploitation of natural resources in occupied territories'.

After reading this document, no member of our delegation held any opinion other than that of Prime Minister Begin that the Egyptian proposal should be rejected outright. We should, in fact, demand that the Egyptians take it back, for, contrary to what I had expected, this was simply a restatement of Egypt's extreme position. It was not a practical basis on which we were prepared to conduct peace negotiations. Had we been ready to discuss those dogmatic demands, there would have been no need for a Camp David summit.

Although Begin agreed that we should not hasten to present Israel's reply to the Egyptian document, he worried over our probable need to embark on a public information campaign. If the Camp David talks were to collapse, it was essential to demonstrate that the Egyptians were to blame because of their stubborn, impractical and unjustified proposals. Barak, Rosenne and Dinitz were to prepare our response, but it would not be handed in immediately so as not to accord official status to the Egyptian document. When it was completed and approved by Premier Begin, it was filed away. The moment was not yet appropriate for its publication.

We broke up our meeting with Begin without being certain of the Egyptian intention. Was their proposal really submitted as material for negotiation, in the knowledge that they would have to climb down later and change most of its clauses? Or were they intending to make it public in order to show the Arab rejectionist States that Egypt had herself taken the very aggressive and extreme position they themselves held? Whatever they had in mind, they could be in no doubt, after our several talks with them, that their proposal had no chance of being accepted by us.

The Big Three met the following afternoon to hear Begin's presentation of Israel's position and his reply to Sadat's proposal. He took it clause by clause and explained why it was unacceptable. The implications of one of them, for example, meant the establishment of a Palestinian State, when both Sadat and Carter had frequently stated to us that they were opposed to it. Sadat replied that this was so, but such a State would be demilitarized; and it would not be independent, but linked to Jordan. He, Sadat, demanded indeed that this question would be determined in a referendum of the Palestinians, but it was possible to guarantee in advance that the voters would support the link with Jordan. Moreover, he added, if King Hussein were to be unwilling to sign a peace agreement between the West Bank and Israel, he, Sadat, would be ready to do so in the name of the Palestinians.

Most of the talk at that meeting was by Begin and Sadat, with Carter listening carefully to the arguments of both as they went from one subject to another – arrangements in Sinai, Israel's aid to the Christian fighters in Lebanon, the future of the West Bank and Gaza and the presence of Israeli forces in those territories, Israeli settlements, Sadat's demand for Arab sovereignty over East Jerusalem which meant the redivision of the city, the absence from the Egyptian proposal of the establishment of diplomatic relations between Israel and Egypt.

Begin had gone into that meeting angry over Sadat's Framework for Peace document, but he came out of it well pleased. 'We broke the ice,' he told us. If indeed there had been a thaw, it went unnoticed by Carter and Sadat, for that talk between Begin and Sadat was not only the first but also the last at Camp David.

The only constructive outcome was Carter's conclusion that it was up to the United States to put forward her own proposals. Carter realized that the gap between the Egyptian and Israeli leaders was very wide, the chance of their reaching an understanding extremely slim. They would need to moderate their positions, and this could be brought about only if America demanded it of them.

Sadat hurriedly published the 'Egyptian proposal' in the Egyptian press so that all the Arab countries would know that he had made not the slightest concession to Israel. He had adhered meticulously to the extremist Arab line. How, then, would he face the later charge that he had not stuck to his word? To that he would reply: 'I conceded nothing to the Israelis, not even an inch; but I responded to the plea of President Carter, our friend and ally, an ally whose help we both need and receive.'

Begin, of course, was also mindful of the American aspect. While arguing with Sadat, he took careful note of the remarks – and facial expression – of Carter to try to discern which points he supported and which he opposed. The US President did not intervene much, but he took copious notes of the issues in conflict. Towards the end of the meeting he read them out to Sadat and Begin and said he would prepare his own suggestions for their resolution. It was then possible to detect his pattern of thinking on some of the subjects. The most important, perhaps, was his observation to Begin that if he, Begin, would propose a Knesset motion to remove the Israeli settlements from Sinai, it would be carried. Begin disagreed with this judgment, but the idea itself never ceased to worry him.

The first draft of the United States proposal was presented to us on Sunday, 10 September. Begin, Weizman, Barak and I were invited to the conference room in the afternoon, and there we found President Carter, Vice-President Walter Mondale, Vance and Brzezinski. Carter read out the proposal, a seventeen-page document, clause by clause. Every so often, he would stop, at our request, and he and his aides would add oral explanations. When he had finished, Carter wanted us to begin a discussion of the proposal on the spot, but Begin refused. We had to give extremely careful study to the document and consult with each other before we could offer our comments. Carter, with demonstrative displeasure, was compelled to acquiesce, but he urged us to keep our consultations brief so that, in the light of our reply, he could enter into discussions with the Egyptians. Begin promised him our reply by 10 the next morning.

Before submitting their proposal, the Americans had put out feelers in several talks between members of their delegation and ours. Harold Brown, US Secretary of Defense, for example, had talked to our Defence Minister, wanting to know what we had in mind when we said we would be prepared to redeploy our forces in the West Bank and Gaza. Ezer had replied in general terms. Brown was not satisfied with that and wanted us to go into detail, but Ezer had refused.

Brzezinski said they wished to base their proposal on our autonomy plan, and he and Vance therefore wanted to know the practical implications of some of its clauses. What, for example, would be the guidelines covering the return of Palestinian Arabs from the Arab countries to Judea and Samaria? I replied that our plan did not refer to the refugees of the 1948 war, though if an international body were established to deal with the solution to their problem, Israel would be ready to join it. As for the refugees of the 1967 Six Day War, I said that during the fighting some 150,000 Arabs fled from the West Bank and Gaza. Since then, about 50,000 had returned, within the framework of our 'Family Reunion' scheme. And further applications under this scheme would be given favourable consideration if there were an economic basis for the absorption of the returnees. The fact was, however, that half the current population of the Gaza Strip were refugees, and they had to be settled before additional refugees returned to that strip of territory. The sources of employment on the West Bank were also limited, as witness the fact that tens of thousands of its inhabitants came to work in Israel and many others sought a livelihood in the wealthy Arab States.

The Americans said there were four major issues on which they did not see eye to eye with us. They wanted us to freeze settlement in the territories for five years, namely, to establish no new settlements, and not to add new members to existing villages. They wanted a categorical decision from us on the manner in which the sovereignty in Judea, Samaria and Gaza would be determined after five years. They wanted to know the source of authority in the territories, namely, whether it would be possible to abolish the autonomy and who would have the authority to do so. (In the American view, Israel should have no such authority.) And fourthly, an appropriate formula was required to ensure the implementation of the injunction in Resolution 242 concerning Israel's withdrawal from territories conquered in the 1967 war.

Neither these issues nor the respective positions of the various sides were new. The one over which there were the greatest differences was settlement, on which our position was final. I told them that we would accept no limitations on this matter. Moreover, the manner in which they presented this issue was incorrect. In the coming five years, I said, we would establish twenty additional settlements – villages was a more accurate word. (This was the figure I had received from our Minister of Agriculture.) Each village would be settled by fifty to one hundred families, so that the total number of additional Jewish families in the territories would be about fifteen hundred. This the Arabs opposed, yet at the same time they demanded that fifty to one hundred thousand Arabs be returned to the area, namely, ten to twenty times the number of Israeli settlers. Where, then, was 'Israeli hegemony through "colonization"' in the West Bank and Gaza? In Jerusalem, the Arab population had virtually doubled, from 65,000 to 120,000, during the very years since 1967 when it had come under Israeli sovereignty. It was not our intention to seize private Arab land, or use settlement to drive away the Arabs. Not a single Arab had been forced to leave because of our settlements. On the contrary, they had provided new sources of employment and income for the Arabs in the territories and had greatly improved their economy.

The lawyers in our delegation, Barak, Rosenne and Rubinstein, sat with the Americans to discuss the 'source of authority' in the West Bank and Gaza, and all tried to come up with a formula on the withdrawal of Israeli forces that would not be interpreted as requiring their total departure from the territories.

There was a growing conviction as the discussions continued that, if we were to reach a framework agreement, the only way out of the difficulty posed by the differences of opinion on these major issues was to ignore them – either by leaving them unmentioned in the agreement, or by devising vague formulae which each side could interpret in its own way. This would lead later to tough and vexatious bargaining, when the parties came to fill in the framework, but at least a primary agreement would have been achieved.

Dealing with the practical issues was our main purpose at Camp David. But there was also a problem of certain definitions and expressions which we, and Begin in particular, wanted excluded from the agreement. One, for example, was what was known as the Aswan Formula, which spoke of the 'constitutional rights' of the Palestinians and their 'right to determine their future'. Another was the obligation to fulfil UN Resolution 242 'in all its parts', namely, including its Preamble which held inadmissible the acquisition of territory by war. We were concerned that when it came to giving flesh to these formulae, we would be told that Israel was obliged to evacuate the whole of the West Bank and Gaza, and that the Palestinians had the right to establish their independent State.

In our meetings with the American delegation when neither President Carter nor Mondale was present, Vance took the chair. Defense Secretary Harold Brown spoke little, and occupied himself only with specifically military matters. This was not the case with Brzezinski, who took an active part in the discussion on all subjects. Although the Americans appeared to present a united stand, there was a marked difference in the manner of presentation between Vance and Brzezinski. Vance set forth his views with clarity and, though he was disinclined to make concessions, he listened attentively to our arguments, and when he was persuaded that they were just, he sought ways to narrow the gap. Not so Brzezinski. He was, of course, polite and articulate, but his remarks held the deliberate purpose of sharpening the divisions between us, as though he was trying to 'break' us. This was evident not only to us but also to Vance, and his displeasure was very noticeable. There may have been other reasons for the coolness between them, and it may not have been due to chance alone that at all the meetings at which both were present, they sat as far from each other as possible.

The presidential aides showed both respect and genuine affection for Carter. And his own attitude towards them – and at times to members of our own delegation – was one of companionship. Neither in word nor behaviour was he ever pretentious or supercilious. On the contrary, when any subject cropped up on which he was not well informed, he would say so, and without hesitation ask for a simple explanation.

The major shortcoming of the American delegation members, to my mind, was their superficial grasp of the Middle East, its peoples and their problems.

They had met and talked to the leaders of the countries in the region time and again; yet it seemed as though they accepted what they were told by these Presidents and Prime Ministers at their face value, without reservation, and without distinguishing between their words and reality. I also suspected that not all their ambassadors were able to understand the true situation in the countries to which they were accredited. The judgment of the United States Government of what was likely to happen in Iran or in Lebanon, and the probable reaction to Sadat's peace initiative by Saudi Arabia, Jordan and Morocco, failed to stand the test of time. Perhaps it was too much to expect from a superpower, involved as she was in the problems of the entire world from the USSR to Timbuktu, to acquire a more basic knowledge of the trends in each country which would enable her to perceive the ferment beneath the surface, and to make a true appreciation of what could and what could not be achieved. It may also be that the system whereby each US President, upon taking office, brings in his own fresh group of advisers, militates against the acquisition of specialist expertise in the problems of foreign affairs (though there have been some brilliant exceptions). Whatever the reasons, I confess that throughout the period in which I held public office and came into contact with American representatives who dealt with the Middle East, I often felt that in addition to their goodwill, sagacity and diligence, they could also have done with a more thorough knowledge of our region.

At consultations within our own delegation, we decided to treat the American proposal as a first draft. Carter had told us that after receiving our observations he would approach the Egyptians. This signified his intention to produce a new formula, after hearing both the Egyptian and our reactions, aimed at bridging the gap between us. We therefore avoided comment on details of formulation and concentrated on the basic issues.

On Sinai, we stressed that our readiness to withdraw to the international boundary was to be read in the context of the peace proposal we had submitted, namely, that the Israeli settlements and airfields in north-eastern and south-eastern Sinai would remain within our control.

As for the West Bank and Gaza, we emphasized that we were not to be obliged to withdraw from these territories. Here, we saw the source of danger in the reference in the Preamble to Resolution 242 on the inadmissibility of the acquisition of territory by war. We therefore resolved that this part of the Preamble was not to be included in the peace treaty.

On the subject of the Palestinians, we were determined to avoid a formula which might be interpreted as our agreeing to their right to self-determination and statehood. We proposed that the future of the Palestinian Arabs dwelling in the West Bank and Gaza would be determined at talks to be conducted between them, Egypt, Jordan and Israel.

Two other central issues were highly controversial: Israeli settlement in the territories, and the status of Jerusalem. But these subjects were not marked with special emphasis in the first draft of the American proposal, and so we, too, paid them little heed at this stage.

By and large, there were no basic differences between members of our Israeli delegation; yet our internal deliberations were not devoid of friction. The Prime Minister, when sticking firmly to his opinion, would often brand our opposing view as potentially harmful to the status of Israel. This kind of comment irritated me, and when he saw the reaction he forced himself to show greater tolerance, and despite the tension, the discussions would resume their orderly pattern. It must be said to his credit, however, that when we finally agreed on our approach, with Begin for the most part conceding, he did so without losing his sense of humour.

We handed our comments on their proposal to the Americans, they met with the Egyptians, and then they returned to us, this time with the peremptory demand that we agree to their proposed formula. The demand was made with a note of anger and exasperation, and it was accompanied by the warning to heed the effect on Israel's standing in the world if she were presented – as she would be – as the party responsible for blocking the peace agreement.

CHAPTER FOURTEEN

Touch-and-Go

After several days and nights of feverish and repetitive discussion, bargaining and drafting, cooped up in the high-pressure chamber of the Camp David Conference, our American hosts thought it might not be a bad idea to open some of the valves. The first unusual step towards this end was taken one evening when the three delegations, together with press correspondents and specially invited guests, were treated to a parade-ground display by the Marine unit in charge of security at the Camp.

I have a soft spot for the Marines. I had got to know some of them when I joined one of their jungle patrols during a visit I paid to Vietnam in 1966 (when I was out of the Government) to see the war at first hand. I found them excellent fighters, bold, courageous, dauntless in storming an enemy position, and handling their superior weapons with proficiency.

On the evening at Camp David, too, they fulfilled their tattoo functions with meticulous skill. A special viewing stand had been constructed for the guests, who were seated according to rank. In the front row sat the Big Three, behind them came us, the ministers, and behind us sat the advisers and aides. The Marines carried out their complicated marching with immaculate precision, and received the well-merited and enthusiastic applause of the onlookers. I, too, clapped my hands in appreciation of their accomplished performance, but somewhere within me I felt a certain distaste, even anger and humiliation, at this use of combat troops as marionettes, as though they were chocolate soldiers in some opera. From the very beginning of my army career I had resented drill, parades and march-pasts. The soldier's job is to fight, and one does not do battle - at least not today - in straight and regular ranks and with fixed rhythmic movements. Moreover, combat is not only the most dangerous venture in the life of man. It also demands, certainly in the heat of battle, a supreme physical and mental effort. With bombs, shells, mortars and rockets bursting all around, the commander has to concentrate on his task, perceive what is happening, judge the enemy's next move, exploit the terrain, give appropriate covering fire to the advancing troops while being ready to redeploy to meet an outflanking move, sharpen all his senses so as to make the correct response at the critical moment.

It is true that the fighting man is called a soldier and the men in an army wear uniform clothing, but battle demands of every man that he exert to the maximum his individual capability, and not that he move his legs and swing his arms like a robot at the press of a button.

As a youth in Nahalal when I was a platoon commander in the Haganah, the Jewish underground force during the British Mandatory administration, I received an infantry training manual one day from the Haganah High Command. It was a Hebrew translation of a British Army brochure called 'Right and Wrong', which gave illustrated examples, set side by side, of how to, and how not to, perform actions in the field. They ranged from crawling and running with a rifle to assaulting in platoon strength.

Not a single example suited the circumstances of a Haganah unit in Palestine having to confront bands of Arab attackers. I therefore prepared a training manual of my own, similar in format to the one I had received, but with examples of situations and actions taken from our combat experience at the time. I sent it to the top commander of the Haganah, Yaacov Dori (who later became Israel's first Chief of Staff), and he summoned me to GHQ to expand on my approach to military training. Some months later, the Haganah withdrew the old manual and distributed a new one, which incorporated most of my proposals.

Many years and battles have passed since then, but my views about soldiers and combat training have remained unchanged. And such were my thoughts as I watched the Marines' tattoo at Camp David on that night. The troops, with split-second timing, spun their rifles in the air in a double turn, and caught them as one man. It was a magnificent spectacle, but the proper place for it was not an army parade-ground but a circus, and performed not by soldiers but by jugglers and acrobats.

We were treated to another bout of relaxation on the following Sunday, 10 September, with a six-hour guided tour of the Gettysburg battlefield, close to Camp David. Here, too, as at the Marines' display, Carter, Sadat and Begin drove in a special car, followed by a bus with members of the three delegations, and after us a long convoy with hundreds of correspondents, guests, and guides.

This was not my first visit to Gettysburg, and I was already familiar with the course of the action which had resulted in the defeat of the Confederate forces under General Robert E. Lee. Yet there was something special about this particular visit which gave vivid reality to the three-day battle in July 1863 that proved the turning-point in the Civil War. What was special were the descriptions, stories and comments by President Carter. We were, of course, accompanied by a professional guide; but Carter, a Southerner from Georgia, could not contain his feelings as the guide gave his dry recital, and he injected his own observations on the moves of the rival Federal and Confederate troops. He did so with great emotion, and spoke with genuine warmth and praise for General Lee and his men. He seemed to know every hill and boulder which had served them as cover. And when he told the story of how the tattered, bedraggled and barefoot Southern fighters had an additional incentive to capture Gettysburg upon hearing that it had large stores of boots, he seemed to be talking about his own family.

I do not suppose that anyone who is not an American can understand what the Civil War means to them. It is probably not why or how or which side won this or that battle that gives the war so prominent a place in the consciousness of the Americans to this day. What they feel so deeply is a personal identification with the men, their brothers, who fought in that bitter and bloody struggle with courage, dedication and self-sacrifice. When Carter described how on the third day of the battle of Gettysburg General Lee's men were forced to retire to Virginia, and did so under cover of rain and darkness, he emphasized that this was not a retreat in orderly units. Out of the original 75,000 men, some 30,000 were casualties. They withdrew, defeated and disorganized, but, Carter added with pride, without panic, and unbroken in spirit.

From the beginning of the Camp David Conference Ezer Weizman had wanted Sadat and me to meet for a private talk. He knew that the President of Egypt had reservations about such a meeting and about me, suspecting that I would try to outdo him by getting peace and giving nothing in exchange.

Nevertheless, he finally acceded to Ezer's request and invited me to tea on Thursday, 14 September. Carter, who knew of the forthcoming meeting, asked me to come to see him, and suggested that I should not discuss with Sadat the issues on which we were in conflict. Such discussion, he said, would not be helpful. Indeed it would be harmful, for we would both entrench ourselves in our positions and this would only increase tension between our delegations. I promised the President that I would talk only of camels and date-palms.

Sadat received me with a polite smile; his manservant brought us small cups of the sweet and fragrant tea he is fond of; and when he left, Sadat plunged straight into the problems of the conference. It was about to end without an agreement. The main reason, he said, was our stubbornness over retaining our settlements in Sinai. 'The concept of building the city of Yamit

in the north-eastern corner of Sinai was yours, was it not?' he asked rhetori-
cally. 'What did you think, that we would resign ourselves to its existence?'

The camels and the date-palms vanished. 'The idea of creating Yamit was
mine,' I said.

But before going ahead with its construction we approached you and offered to hand
back to you the whole of Sinai within the framework of a peace treaty – and that idea,
too, was mine. What was your reply? No peace, no negotiations, no recognition of
Israel. What was taken by force, you said, would be recovered by force. That was the
resolution adopted by the Khartoum Conference at the initiative of Nasser. What did
you think we would do, sit with folded arms, while you announced that you were not
prepared to reconcile yourselves to Israel's existence, and that you wanted to take Sinai
back not peacefully but only through war?

The course of this dialogue was not to Sadat's liking. The smile disappeared,
and opposite me sat an angry and troubled man. His Foreign Minister, he
said, Muhammad Ibrahim Kamel, was anxious to follow his predecessor,
Fahmi, and resign. His adviser, al-Baz, was strongly opposed to a peace
treaty with Israel, was venomous in his outbursts among members of his
delegation, and strengthened their doubts. If there were no change in the
negotiations in his favour, he would have to return to Egypt and admit he
had failed. We were obliged, he said, to start a new chapter: withdraw from
the entire peninsula of Sinai and hand it over to Egyptian sovereignty. 'My
people,' he said,

will not agree to any foreign regime on our soil, neither to American forces in the
Sinai airfields, nor to your settlements, not even one, not even for a brief period. If
you want peace with us, the table must be cleared. We fought to get rid of the British,
and later we fought so that the Suez Canal should remain in our exclusive control. I am
now ready to make peace with you, a full and true peace, and ignore the opposition of
the Arab States, but you must take all your people out of Sinai, the troops and the
civilians, dismantle the military camps and remove the settlements.

I saw no point in arguing, just as I saw little point in taking up past issues –
the wars waged against us by Egypt while our heads of government were
offering her peace. There was no question that he was adamant about Sinai,
and if we were not prepared to withdraw, the Camp David Conference would
end without a peace agreement.

I told Sadat I would report on our meeting to Premier Begin, and rose to
leave. He accompanied me to the door and produced his polite smile as we
bade each other *Shalom* and *Salaam*. But any expectation that our talk
would narrow the gap between our respective positions, or, on the personal
level, bring us closer together, remained unfulfilled.

Time was running out. Carter and his party lost patience both with us and the Egyptians, and the President announced categorically that the conference had to end by Sunday, 17 September. I do not know what pressures he applied to Sadat; but to us he said that failure of the talks would be 'catastrophic' for relations between Israel and the United States. He would be obliged to report to Congress that Israel was not prepared to take the necessary steps to achieve peace. The focus of his anger was directed against Begin. 'Premier Begin's immediate response to anything we propose is No, No, No,' he said. 'Later, in your internal consultations, he softens his stand and agrees.' I contained myself, and refrained from asking the President how he knew what went on in the private talks of our delegation.

On 14 September we received from the Americans their second – and amended – proposal for an agreement. It was preceded by several talks between their people and ours. The question of our settlements in Sinai – whether or not they were to remain – was covered by an agreed formula: the Prime Minister would refer it to the Government and Knesset for their decision. Sadat for his part announced that only if Israel acceded to his demand that the settlements be abandoned would he be able to sign the agreement. On Jerusalem, the gap between the Israeli and Egyptian positions remained wide, and it was clear that we would need to hold further discussions on this thorny subject if and when agreement were reached on the other items.

The principal advocate for the Egyptians was Osama al-Baz. He and our own legal expert, Aharon Barak, were frequently summoned by Carter, and they would sit together for hours trying to reach agreed texts. The stubbornness and extremism of al-Baz often enraged Carter. According to Barak, even when the Americans suggested a formula that the Egyptians should have grasped with both hands, al-Baz refused to accept it. He kept insisting that not only the UN Security Council resolutions but also the UN resolutions on the right of the 1948 Palestinian refugees to return to Israel should be included in the agreement. He was not even prepared to accept the Aswan Formula – Carter's declaration at Aswan in January 1978 which was so favourable to the Egyptians – because he claimed it gave Israel the right to veto a Palestinian State. He wanted the agreement to state specifically that the Palestinians should be enabled to gain self-determination.

The new American proposal was far more acceptable to us than the initial one, yet it still contained several articles to which on no account could we agree.

Towards evening, Vance came to Begin's cabin to hear our reply. He found the Prime Minister very tense. The protracted discussions, arguments and bargaining had sapped his patience. He told the Secretary of State that he had to speak frankly in expressing his profound disappointment. After eight days of long, exhaustive and detailed clarifications, the Americans had presented us with a paper containing formulations which would lead inevitably to the establishment of a Palestinian State. In the course of our discussions, we had gone far in finally agreeing to expressions which we had previously rejected outright, expressions like 'legitimate rights', 'redeployment', 'specified locations'. We had done so in order to arrive at an Israel-Egypt agreement. And, indeed, on the principal subject of the Palestinians, we had reached an agreed formula with the Americans. And now the Americans were retreating from what they had approved. Israel could not accept this proposal of theirs.

Vance was very angry. This time, unlike his demeanour on earlier occasions, he failed to preserve his calm. He became red in the face, gesticulated with his hands, and raised his voice. Though Begin quoted only fragments of sentences, the Secretary of State well knew what they meant and to what they were linked – 'legitimate rights' to a Palestinian State, 'redeployment' to the withdrawal of Israeli forces and their containment in 'specific locations'.

'We tried', said Vance, 'to the best of our ability to get the parties to reach agreed texts. You, Begin, are right about a formula on which we both had agreed. We told you that in our judgment the Egyptians would accept it. We then discovered that our judgment was mistaken, and we had to abandon it. The Egyptians will not agree to it.'

Begin pursed his lips and was sunk in silence. Barak took the floor and went on to deal with other Articles in the American proposal which we found unacceptable. The additions introduced by the Americans about a referendum to be held among the inhabitants of the administered territories, and the establishment of a Palestinian Government, constituted a radical change from the Aswan Formula, a formula to which we had become reconciled only with great reluctance. The meaning of the new formula was the creation of a Palestinian State, and both Egypt and the United States knew that Israel would not agree to this. Moreover, President Carter had repeatedly declared in private and public that the United States was against it.

While Barak was speaking, the telephone rang. It was the President, asking for Vance to come and see him. The room fell silent. The mood of anger gave way to sadness and disappointment. In a calm and soft voice, Begin told Vance before he left that the Camp David Conference would apparently end not with an agreement but with an exchange of declarations by each side explaining why it could not accept the other's proposals. Vance replied that he was ready to return in the evening to meet with representatives of both the Egyptian and Israeli delegations to renew the search for a compromise. Begin agreed. Barak, Rosenne and Rubinstein accordingly repaired to the other room and started for the nth time to prepare a new text of our proposals.

Saturday, 16 September 1978, was a day of intense activity. Barak, Dinitz and I met with Mondale, Vance, Brzezinski and Samuel Lewis, to tell them about the changes we were prepared to introduce in order to reach an agreed position with them. We took up the contentious Article which dealt with the Palestinian issue. After comparing our proposed formula with theirs, I explained that in our view there should be a clear distinction between the principles which should serve as a negotiating basis for autonomy for the Arabs of the territories, and the basis for any future peace negotiations with Jordan which should have as its objective a peace treaty with that country. I said that in order to reach a compromise we were prepared to assume that in a peace agreement with Jordan, it would be possible to include parts of the agreement with the Palestinians, but these were two separate issues. Discussions with Jordan would be concerned with a peace agreement to be concluded between two States and would be based on Resolution 242, whereas autonomy did not apply to a State, and so there could be no mention of boundaries nor of Resolution 242.

Vance said the Americans held a different position, but it seemed to have been arrived at for practical considerations rather than reasons of principle. It was impossible, he said, to reach agreement with the Egyptians over autonomy if it applied only to people and not to boundaries. This was particularly true of the formula 'the final status of Judea, Samaria, and Gaza', on which we had already agreed.

Barak set forth our arguments, the main one being that if we were to accept the American position, it would mean our consent to laying the foundations of a Palestinian State. That was the practical interpretation of an agreement on boundaries, and therefore we could not accept it. A peace treaty, the determination of boundaries, the terms of Resolution 242, applied exclusively to an arrangement with a sovereign State, in this case the Kingdom of Jordan, and would be discussed five years after the start of autonomy.

Each side kept explaining its position, and then we pulled a rabbit out of the hat – the working paper which had been produced and agreed to by the Americans and ourselves in talks that had preceded Sadat's visit to Jerusalem. In that memorandum, there was a clear distinction between the peace treaties, which were to be concluded between us and the Arab States, and the issues that were to be discussed with the Arabs in the administered territories. Vance admitted that was indeed true, but that was in the context of the proposed Geneva Conference, and since then things had changed.

The talk was conducted in a constructive spirit, with an effort by both sides to reach agreement. They did in fact come closer to each other, but they did not arrive at an agreement. The principal achievement was the American recognition that we would accept no formula, however vague and tortuous, which might serve to buttress the demand for the establishment of a Palestinian State.

Though I did not mention it to my colleagues, I had the feeling that both the Americans and the Egyptians would eventually reconcile themselves to our stand. On the previous day, Friday, 15 September, Begin had met Carter, and afterwards Carter had requested a talk with me in private. This was not a formal meeting. Throughout the ten days that we had been together we had come to know one another. Friends told me he had said I had 'a creative mind'. Whatever he may have said or thought, he was certainly aware that what I had to say I said frankly, and, I hoped, clearly.

In his talk with me, Carter emphasized that this was the eleventh day of our negotiations, and only two days remained before the summit conference was to end. The gap between us and the Egyptians, he said, was not wide: could we not really come closer towards the Egyptians? Why not remove our settlements from Sinai? And could we not agree to a Jordanian flag over the Dome of the Rock in Jerusalem? After all it was a Moslem mosque, and we recognized it as such. Only three or four appropriate formulae, he said, could make the difference between the achievement of peace and the collapse of the conference in failure. Could not I, who was so much more familiar, as he put it, than anyone else at Camp David with the thinking of the Palestinians, discover some way out of the impasse?

I emerged from that meeting with the US President less despondent than when I had gone in. I had not expected to win him over; but when it became apparent that the problem was more one of words and formulae than of substance, there was a good chance of finding a solution, particularly when we were favoured by the legalistic brilliance of Barak and Rosenne.

The last day of the Camp David Conference, Sunday, 17 September 1978, was not only a day of packing bags but also of closing gaps. President Carter telephoned me in the morning to say he was going to Sadat to try to get his agreement to our demand that UN forces to be stationed at Sharm e-Sheikh could be told to leave only with the agreement of both parties, Egypt and Israel. (In 1967, President Nasser, alone, had ordered them to go, and they had gone.)

On the thorny issue of the removal of our settlements in Sinai, Begin had decided on a final formula. After a talk with Carter, he reported to us that he had told the President of his intention to ask the Knesset to vote on the following question: 'If Israel and Egypt reach agreement on all other issues, but the condition for signing a peace treaty is the removal of Israeli settlements in Sinai, does the Knesset approve or disapprove of their removal?' There would be a free ballot, with each member voting according to his conscience and not within the framework of party discipline. Although Begin did not ask me how I would vote, I thought it proper to tell him that in such a circumstance I would vote in favour of the removal of the settlements.

The third and last obstacle to be handled before we could reach agreement on a Framework for Peace was Jerusalem, the city where Jews and Arabs had succeeded in living together for the last ten years. Moslems, Christians and Jews had been living side by side since the 1967 Six Day War without barriers between them and without communal conflict.

The sharpest difference of view on this issue had arisen between the Americans and ourselves. I could not avoid the feeling that the motive underlying their opposition was not only Sadat's ultimatum but also their own approach. The United Nations, with the concurring vote of the United States, had demanded in 1949 that Jerusalem be internationalized because it was holy to three faiths. But the Americans were moved primarily by political considerations in refusing to recognize Jerusalem as the capital of Israel. Our highest State institutions – the Knesset, the Presidency, the Government – are housed in West Jerusalem, yet the United States to this day does not recognize Jerusalem as our capital. She held to this position even during the period from 1949 to 1967, when Israel's eastern boundary excluded the West Bank but included West Jerusalem, while East Jerusalem was under Arab control. During one of our tough and at times bitter arguments at Camp David, I told the Americans that in order to arrange for Jerusalem *not* to be our capital, it was not enough for the United Nations Security Council and Assembly to pass resolutions to that effect. They would also need to rewrite the Bible, and nullify three thousand years of our faith, our hopes, our yearnings and our prayers.

Begin also met Carter in the morning of that last day of the Camp David negotiations, and at one o'clock he informed us that he had reached agreement with the President on formulae for those issues which until then had remained unresolved. On Jerusalem, he said, the agreement would state only that it would remain 'undivided'. Begin appeared very pleased with himself: there was agreement on every formula, word for word!

We were all very happy. But an hour later we were again plunged into gloom. What happened was that during lunch in the refectory, Vice-President Mondale showed our Ambassador to Washington the draft of a letter President Carter was about to deliver to Sadat. In it Carter stated that the

United States considered East Jerusalem to be conquered territory. Dinitz told Mondale that Israel would not sign a document that included such a letter. Moreover, the agreement to be signed was an Israel–Egypt agreement – why, then, should it include a statement on the position taken by the United States? Was it an agreement between Israel and the United States? The heart of the matter was the meaning of the President's proposed letter, which was that Jerusalem should be redivided, with only the western part going to Israel and the eastern part, including the Hebrew University campus and the Hadassah Hospital on Mount Scopus, to Jordan. Up to then, the Americans had said they supported a united Jerusalem.

Mondale realized that the matter was very serious, and he said he would go immediately to Carter with our reaction. A half hour later we were called to a meeting in the billiard room. There we found the President, Mondale and Vance, while Barak, Dinitz and I represented the Israeli delegation, but it turned into an exchange between Carter and myself. The President said Sadat insisted on the letter as a condition of his signing our agreement. He, the President, feared that agreement would not be achieved unless Israel agreed in principle to evacuate East Jerusalem. He had promised Sadat that the agreement would include a statement of the United States' position on Jeru-salem, and he would not break his promise. 'Do you want to dictate to me', he asked with considerable anger, 'what to say in the name of the United States?'

I, too, was furious. I told the President that had we known that the Americans intended to announce their stand on the Jerusalem question, we would not have come to Camp David. There were other subjects on which we were divided, such as Israeli settlements in the administered territories, yet the agreement contained not even a hint of America's position on this issue. We wanted to reach a peace agreement with Egypt, and also, as far as possible, an understanding with the United States. But how could the Americans and the Egyptians argue that the Western (Wailing) Wall, the Hebrew University, the Hadassah Hospital, the Mount of Olives and Mount Scopus belonged to the Hashemite Kingdom of Jordan? Why was the Jewish Quarter in the Old City regarded as 'conquered territory', held by us in contravention of inter-national law? Simply because the Jordanian Arab Legion conquered it in 1948, destroyed its synagogues, killed or took captive the Jewish civilians who lived there? What was there holy about the military conquest by the Jordanian army in 1948, and profane about our victory in the 1967 war – a war which also started with Jordan's attack on Israel? We had no wish to control the places holy to Christianity and to Islam, and in that area I believed that an appropriate formula could be found. But the meaning of the

President's proposed letter to Sadat was that the whole of East Jerusalem was to come under Arab sovereignty.

Carter's reply was that he was not prepared to take back what he had promised Sadat, and our agreement with Egypt was to include a letter signed by him, President Carter, expressing America's position on Jerusalem, a position which had not changed since 1967.

Our meeting ended with the standard result: America's Vance and Israel's Barak would try to find an agreed formula. For good measure, Carter asked Barak to accompany him to his cabin so that they could have a talk before Barak's meeting with Vance. Barak did not seem surprised. During the harsh discussion, when it seemed that the issue of Jerusalem might torpedo the agreement, I noticed his furrowed brows as he jotted down various formulae in his notebook.

An hour later, at 3.45 p.m., Barak walked into our delegation room with a revised version of the American letter in his hand. In addition, he said, it had been proposed that both Begin and Sadat would also attach to the agreement their own letters in which each would present his country's position. Begin studied the new version of the American letter, read it out to us, and said: 'I accept it.'

Although the stand – and the action – of the Americans greatly angered me, I considered the attachment of letters stating the views on Jerusalem of Egypt, Israel and the United States as an expression of the reality with which we had to come to terms. It was the lesser of two evils, since the American and Egyptian letters were not of an operational character. They did not commit Israel to withdrawing from this territory. The practical question as to who would control Jerusalem would be discussed within the framework of the negotiations for a peace treaty with Jordan five years after the establishment of autonomy in the West Bank. Time would tell.

As Begin was about to draft the letter which would set out Israel's stand, Barak observed that the President was very rattled, and had said he could not work in the shadow of ultimatums from all sides. Begin thereupon telephoned Carter and told him, in friendly tones, that the proposal which Barak had brought him was acceptable. I did not hear Carter's response, but I could see the smile on Begin's face and his nods of approval. The Camp David Conference had come to an end.

At 11 o'clock that night, Sunday, 17 September 1978, in the East Room of the White House in Washington, Carter, Sadat and Begin signed 'The Framework for Peace in the Middle East' (see Appendix 1). It was not a peace agreement. The Framework Agreement was only the basis – the establishment of principles which would serve as the foundations for negotiations now to be conducted to conclude a peace treaty with Egypt and autonomy for the Arabs of Judea, Samaria and the Gaza District. Nor did the framework agreement have validity as yet: it was conditional on the approval of Israel's Knesset to the removal of Israeli settlements in Sinai, and upon the ratification of Egypt's parliament. In the meantime, Sadat continued to maintain that he would not sign a peace treaty with us if an agreement on autonomy were not reached before or simultaneously; but his position on this matter was greatly weakened. It was now clear that peace negotiations with Egypt would be conducted prior to discussions on the Palestinian issue.

The peace treaty between Egypt and Israel was to rest on four principles:

1. Total Israeli withdrawal from Sinai and recognition of Egyptian sovereignty over this territory.
2. Demilitarization of most of Sinai.
3. Supervision of the demilitarization by United Nations forces, and in particular the direct responsibility of these forces to ensure freedom of shipping through the Gulf of Eilat.
4. Full normalization in relations between Egypt and Israel.

Normalization was to go into effect after Israel's withdrawal from the western part of Sinai. This would leave two years in which Israel would still be in control of the area east of the line El Arish–Ras Mohammad, with its settlements, airfields and army camps. This eastern section of Sinai was not only closest to Israel's borders, but was also, from the military point of view, the most important for Israel's defence.

The evacuation of western Sinai would present a grave economic problem for Israel, for it meant the loss of oilfields which supplied some two million tons of oil a year, about a third of Israel's needs. It would be necessary to ensure that Egypt would at least sell us the oil produced by these wells, which we ourselves had drilled and which we now had to abandon.

The Camp David Conference was of great importance, for without the Framework Agreement Sadat was not prepared to negotiate a peace treaty. Principles had now been established, acceptable to both sides, governing peace with Egypt and an arrangement of the Palestinian problem. Thus, Camp David represented a breakthrough; but the fulfilment of its aims was still far off. A long and difficult journey lay ahead.

CHAPTER FIFTEEN

The Signing

We arrived in Washington from Camp David at the close of the conference at 8.30 on the Sunday evening for the signing ceremony at the White House, and discovered that various commentaries were already being aired on what had transpired during the previous thirteen days. As long as we were all penned in at the Camp, and with the final agreement undetermined until the last moment, there was almost no leak to the press. Now, with the 'quarantine' lifted, and the agreement sealed against additions or changes, sundry 'senior officials', 'official spokesmen' and even the heads of state themselves allowed their tongues free rein, and responded to the questions of the crowds of correspondents who flocked to their doors. Each one gave his own version of the Camp David 'bible', and the versions were at times totally different.

The most important issue on which the Americans and the Israelis were at loggerheads was the question of Israeli settlements in the administered territories. The American spokesmen claimed that for the next five years – during the transitional period – Israel would not establish new settlements in Judea, Samaria, the Gaza District and the Golan Heights, and would not strengthen the existing ones. Israel's representatives – Begin, Barak and myself – stated that there had indeed been such a demand during our negotiations, but we had rejected it. We had not agreed to cease strengthening existing settlements, and we had agreed to refrain from setting up additional ones only for the next three months, the period designated for negotiations on the peace treaty with Egypt.

The settlement issue had been raised several times at the Camp David discussions, as we have seen. But since it was evident that agreement on this issue would be very difficult to achieve, it was put off for further consideration until the final stage of the conference. On the evening of the penultimate day, Saturday, 16 September, Carter asked for a meeting in his cabin after dinner of a limited group to try to solve outstanding problems. On the American side there would be only Carter and Vance. Begin said he would be accompanied by Barak and myself.

The meeting lasted five hours, breaking up at 1.30 in the morning. This was the most basic and exhaustive discussion at Camp David. The previous twelve days represented an intensive course of study and comprehension of the divisions with all their nuances between the parties. All were now aware that the eleventh hour of the negotiations was upon us. The moment of decision had arrived; and it was given added drama by what had happened in the Egyptian delegation the previous evening: Foreign Minister Muhammad Ibrahim Kamel and the principal legal adviser Nabil al-Arabi had resigned. They had told President Sadat that they were unable to bear responsibility for his 'concessions to Israel'. Sadat had replied that when peace was achieved, they would realize they had erred; but if they felt as they did he would accept their resignations. Others, who were prepared to go along with his policy, would replace them.

Despite these words, however, one could not discount the impact on Sadat of disapproval by ministers who had been close to him. Moreover, this act by Foreign Minister Kamel had followed the similar action of his predecessor, Fahmi, who had resigned over the original peace initiative. And others who had remained, Tuhami, Butros Ghali and especially Osama al-Baz, had not hesitated to express their reservations about Sadat's moves, greatly down-grading the benefits to Egypt of a peace treaty. They did not trust our commitments, and they were disappointed in the Americans. They had ex-pected President Carter to compel us to return on all fronts to the pre-1967 borders. Their hopes had been dashed, and Egypt's isolation in the Arab world had become more marked. Even those countries on whose support Sadat had counted – Jordan, Saudi Arabia and Morocco – had dissociated themselves from his moves.

Not only in Egypt but in Israel, too, matters were not simple. Begin did not enjoy general support. Apart from the Opposition parties, there were also those in his own coalition and even in his own party who were vehemently against this readiness to compromise with the Egyptian and American positions.

The talk in Carter's cabin that night was like meeting in the middle of a creaking bridge, and trying to save it from collapse. I myself was convinced that the three parties sincerely wanted peace, and were prepared to go to the extreme limit of their capacity towards the positions of the others. This desire to end the Camp David Conference with an agreement was prompted no less by the wish of the participants, particularly the President of the United States, to register success, than by the urgent political need to bring the Arab-Israeli conflict to an end, or at least to lay the foundations for its solution.

Among the five of us sitting round the table were three legal experts,

Barak, Vance and Begin. Even the other two, Carter and myself, were not entirely new to the task of drafting and formulation. But the heart of the matter on that evening was not semantics. The problem we had to grapple with was substantive, and of supreme importance, and if we could reach agreement on that, the formula would pose no insuperable difficulties.

Carter chaired the meeting, and although all the participants spoke freely it was he who guided the course of the discussion. As was his wont, he put down in his notebook in clear handwriting the proposals and decisions, occasionally adding notes to himself in the margin.

It was not unpleasant to talk to Carter and Vance even when our views were widely divergent. At no time throughout our stay at Camp David did I doubt their sincerity. But there were times – and that evening was one of them – when I felt that neither the President nor the Secretary of State had sufficiently penetrated the core of the complex problems of the Middle East. They did not put themselves in the shoes – or rather the hearts – of either side. They knew what the Israeli and the Arab representatives were saying, but they did not always distinguish between what was being uttered for bargaining purposes and external consumption, and what was the profound expression of the spirit and the yearnings of a nation.

We disposed of some subsidiary items at the beginning of the meeting, and then moved on to the central topic – Israeli settlements in the administered territories. The talk was practical, but based on principle, and it seemed as though Carter understood the historical significance of Judea, Samaria and Gaza to Israel. He repeatedly stressed that the American approach was that every Jew had the right to buy land and to live in Judea, Samaria and Gaza, and that an Arab Government, whether Jordanian or Palestinian, was not entitled to pass a law preventing this. However, he added, from the immediate political standpoint, the establishment of settlements during the negotiations was an obstacle to their progress, and, in America's opinion, illegal in international law. The current Jewish settlement was intended, he said, to establish facts which would determine the future map, and this was being done while the subject was still under discussion. It was political action aimed at the eventual annexation of the West Bank and Gaza to the State of Israel. He therefore urged us not to set up new settlements and not to strengthen existing ones during the period of the negotiations.

Carter had said all this following his talks with Sadat, and as I listened to him and watched his expression, it seemed to me that he would not change his mind on this issue since he found himself up against an impenetrable Egyptian wall. He might also have been guided by the thought that he would do better for America if he diminished his commitments to Israel and felt freer to strengthen his links with the Arabs – even if this was not the best thing for Israel.

Begin, Barak and I explained, each in his own way, that the Americans had every right to consider the security, territory and boundaries of Israel from their own point of view; but we had to set forth our own view of these matters. Begin, in a style different from the terse speech of the Americans, said the establishment of a Palestinian State, or laying the foundations for one, would bring the administered territories under the control of the PLO, and thus under the influence of the Russians. They would then do all they could to liquidate the State of Israel. The Governments of Europe and the United States had not prevented Hitler's destruction of the Jews of Europe, and we were not prepared to rely on them to safeguard Israel's existence. The guarantee for our security was the presence of our army in Judea, Samaria and the Gaza District.

We wished to live in peace with the Arabs in the territories as equals; but we would not agree to foreign rule over these territories, whether it was the sovereignty of a Palestinian State or of Jordan. Even if it were formally Jordanian sovereignty, in practice Jordan would transfer the territories to Palestinian control. Any foreign rule would therefore mean the right of the extremist Arabs to destroy Israel. For this reason the PLO refused to accept UN Resolution 242 and recognize Israel's right to exist. This was an organization of murderers that should be uprooted. As for the President's request that settlement be stopped during the peace negotiations, he, Begin, would give it thought.

During this discussion, Barak concentrated on taking a record of the meeting, and only when Articles in agreements were being quoted and formulae considered did he lay down his pen to give the accurate text and interpretation.

When I spoke, I addressed myself to the charge that we were trying to maintain control of the territories through 'colonization'. It was without substance, as we had explained time and again to other members of the US delegation. I was sorry to have to repeat that some twenty villages were expected to be established in the West Bank and Gaza during the next five years, with some fifty families per village, giving a total of some five thousand persons. Far outnumbering this total was the high annual natural increase, running into scores of thousands, of the Arab population of the territories, which itself totalled a million and a quarter. In addition, the Arabs were asking us to permit some of those who had fled the West Bank in the 1967 war to return to their villages, and I was recommending to my Government that we allow twenty to thirty thousand of them to do so, subject to security and economic considerations. Where then was the danger that the territories would be 'swamped by Israelis'? By a mere five thousand additional Jewish villagers?

The sole path to co-existence of Arabs and Jews in the West Bank and Gaza, I concluded, was through their living side by side. That was the situation today. Israel's Beersheba lay with the Hebron hills on one side and the Gaza District on the other. Jerusalem lay between Hebron and Nablus. And, in addition, there were Kiriat Arba, the Etzion bloc of kibbutzim, and the Jewish villages in the Jordan Valley.

Not all the arguments justifying our settlement policy were repeated at this meeting. We said very little, for example, about our historical connection with the territories, and the sentimental attachment. Even the security importance of our settlement was barely mentioned. The Americans were very familiar with our position on this subject, and whenever it had come up for discussion they had heard detailed expositions on why our settlements along the Jordan Valley border and others on the mountain ridges were of high strategic value. They did not accept our explanation, and I saw no sign that they would change their stand. The fundamental policy of the United States on this issue had remained unchanged since 1967. They adhered to the Rogers Plan (conceived by Nixon's Secretary of State who preceded Kissinger), which called for Israel's withdrawal to her 1948 borders on all fronts, with civilian settlements as well as the Israel Army included in the withdrawal. Washington knew that every successive Israeli Government had rejected this plan, and Begin's Government was even more stubborn on this score than its predecessors, the Labour coalitions.

I myself viewed an Israeli military presence in the West Bank and Gaza District as inextricably bound up with settlement. I did not believe it was politically possible to maintain Israeli troops in these territories unless there were also an Israeli civilian population. I thought that several groups of Jewish villages should be established, with army units stationed in or near them. If the population of the territories were exclusively Arab, the role of the Israeli unit would appear to be that of an occupation force stationed among a resentful population, and Israel would be under constant pressure to remove it.

The Americans listened carefully but remained unmoved. Carter finally suggested an exchange of letters between him and Begin in which Begin would include the following commitment: 'After the signing of the Framework Agreement and during the negotiations, no new Israeli settlements will be established in the area, unless otherwise agreed. The issue of further Israeli settlements will be decided and agreed by the negotiating parties.'

It was now one o'clock in the morning, and it was time to end our talks. The question of further settlement was not clarified exhaustively that evening, and the following day we began to receive information that both the President and Vance were claiming that at our late-night meeting Begin had agreed to write the letter that Carter had requested. Begin claimed that all he had said to Carter's proposal was that he had to think it over and would give his answer the next day. (And, indeed, ten days later, after Begin's return to Israel, Barak's written record of that meeting was examined, and Begin's version was found to have been correct.) In the meantime, however, the ball had continued to roll. At 4 p.m. on Sunday, 17 September, four hours before we helicoptered out of Camp David on our way to Washington, Begin had handed the following letter to the President of the United States:

Dear Mr President,
I have the honour to inform you that during the agreed period of negotiations (three months) for the conclusion of the peace treaty, no new settlements will be established by the Government of Israel in Sinai, in the Gaza District, and in the area of Judea and Samaria.

The difference between Begin's letter and Carter's proposal was primarily that Begin was referring to the negotiations with Egypt, while the Americans had in mind the overall negotiations, including those with the Palestinians (whenever they might be launched).

Those last twenty-four hours had been heavy going, with moments when it was touch-and-go whether or not the entire Camp David exercise would end in an accord. It was understandable therefore that everyone was in good heart when we left for Washington at 8 p.m. on the Sunday so that the agreement reached at the last minute could be signed that same evening. But some of us were nagged by one item. It transpired that that morning, well before Begin had transmitted his letter to Carter, the President had seen Sadat and told him that Begin had accepted his proposal to freeze settlement 'during the negotiations'.

The crisis over this issue broke out forty-eight hours later. On 20 September, Saunders of the State Department got in touch with our Ambassador in Washington and informed him that in the opinion of the President and of Secretary Vance, Begin's letter did not conform to what had been agreed upon at the Camp David meeting on the night of Saturday, 16 September. According to their record, Begin had agreed to the formula that the President had proposed. Furthermore, Carter had notified Sadat the next morning of the text of the letter which, according to him, Begin had agreed to write on behalf of the Israeli Government. The Secretary and the President were absolutely convinced, said Saunders, that they were not in error, and he was therefore returning to Begin his letter of 17 September. Saunders explained that, on the substantive issue, it was not intended that the freezing of settlements or their expansion should be for the five-year transition period, but only until the inauguration of autonomy for the Arabs of the territories.

After the notes of Barak were deciphered – and none doubted his trustworthiness – it seemed that even the Americans would agree that what had happened was the product of a misunderstanding. Perhaps they simply had not listened properly to Begin's response at the 16 September meeting. Later, however, when the Americans, especially the President, stuck to their erroneous claim, I suspected that they were determined to use it as a lever against the settlement policy of Begin's Government. At a breakfast meeting with selected correspondents at the White House on 27 September, President Carter said that 'Begin's recollection' of his response to Carter's settlement proposal on 16 September 'that he would let me know [his reply] the following day . . . was not the recollection of us' – himself and Vance. The President continued:

There are two issues involved. One is whether Begin actually agreed, which I consider his having done. And the other is that Begin has insinuated that the West Bank settlement agreement was tied to the Sinai discussions with Egypt. We have never connected the two. My belief is that Begin did agree not to start any new settlements during the time the negotiations on the West Bank–Gaza self-government were being conducted, and that the status of the future settlements would be determined by the negotiators.

This statement by Carter was given wide publicity in all the American media, and undoubtedly cast grave doubt on the credibility of Israel's Prime Minister.

What Carter said next contained an additional clue to the promptings behind his harsh words against Begin and Israeli settlements. The President said:

There are three elements that no Arab leader would ignore, nor on which they would yield, including Sadat. One is Israeli withdrawal from the West Bank–Gaza Strip territory. Secondly, a return of eastern Jerusalem to Arab sovereignty [though he was careful to add 'possibly excluding the Hebrew University area, and probably excluding the Jewish Holy Places, particularly the Wailing Wall']. And the third one is a resolution of the Palestine question 'in all its aspects'. These three points are the ones that Jordan and Syria and Saudi Arabia and Egypt continue to emphasize. I don't think they will ever publicly or privately yield on those.

Incidentally, on 19 September, just two days after signing the Framework

Agreement, Sadat himself told a press conference that Israel had agreed to freeze new settlements 'for another three months'. Thus, on the time element, there was no difference between what Begin had promised in his letter to Carter, and what Sadat had understood from what Carter had told him of Begin's commitment. Both said that Israel had undertaken to cease settlement activity for three months. It is possible, of course, that Sadat believed the negotiations both for the peace treaty with Egypt and for autonomy would be completed within three months; but that was not the significant point. The key fact was that even the President of Egypt understood that Israel's commitment was for three months only; and, indeed, during the three months that followed, Israel refrained from starting new settlements in Judea, Samaria, the Gaza District and the Golan Heights.

If the world were run on the lines of a High Court of Justice, Israel would assuredly have been given the verdict on 'the affair of the Begin letter'. But the political truth was that there were basic differences between us and the United States on the future of the administered territories. America wanted us to withdraw to the boundary lines of 1948 – ignoring the history of all that had happened since then – and we were refusing to do so. The incident of the letter soon faded; but the difference of view on the subject of the settlements remained.

The signing ceremony of the Framework Agreement was held in the East Room of the White House. It was bleak and rainy outside, but the atmosphere inside was charged with emotion, for this was, indeed, a moving event: an agreement was about to be signed which was expected to bring peace between Israel and the greatest of the Arab countries. Spirits were high, and were given an added boost by the surprise of the success after the long suspense. From the first until the very last day at Camp David, the points on which we differed outweighed those on which we agreed, and the negotiations were accompanied by press commentaries which laid heavy odds on failure.

Members of the three delegations were seated in the front row. With us were leading members of the American administration and other VIPs. At precisely 11 p.m. the Big Three entered the hall to a great ovation and took their places on the dais, with Carter in the middle flanked by Sadat and Begin. Despite their visible fatigue, they were a happy and beaming trio.

All three addressed the gathering. Carter and Sadat spoke briefly, reading from a written text. Begin spoke extemporaneously, salting his speech with a good deal of humour.

I, too, regarded Camp David as an historic achievement of prime importance for Israel. True, this was but the start, the foundation stone; but I fervently believed that both Sadat and Begin not only wanted peace but were also ready to make many concessions to gain it. The Palestinian question was more complicated. Vance was scheduled to leave two days later for Jordan and Saudi Arabia to try to persuade King Hussein to join the peace talks and King Khaled to support the agreement. The Palestinians as well as the Jordan Government had expressed opposition to Sadat's moves and to the autonomy plan, and so the Palestinian subject had been dealt with in the Framework Agreement largely in general and obscure terms, lending itself to varied interpretations.

From the White House the Israeli delegation drove to the Hilton Hotel where the Israelis and leaders of the Washington Jewish community had gathered to toast Premier Begin. I drank a toast, then went to my room, sat in an armchair and reflected on all that had happened.

That evening was one of the most momentous of my life. I had travelled a long road from the battlefield to the peace table, from our 1948 War of Independence followed by my armistice talks with Jordan's King Abdullah, through the 1956 Sinai Campaign, the 1967 Six Day War, the 1973 Yom Kippur War, right up to Camp David. The toughest stretch of that journey had been the years since that fateful Yom Kippur until the White House ceremony I had just attended. We had just marked the achievement of the Framework Agreement, and I was glad to have had the privilege of being one of its architects.

I was tired, and the hour was late; yet I could not sleep. I longed to be home. Had I been there, I would have celebrated the event in the way I liked best – eating a snack in the kitchen with Rahel and afterwards reading to her the poems of Nathan Alterman. That night they would have been the 'noble' ones which deal with the chronicles of the House of Israel, poems about the long and weary road, paved with hardship, trekked by the Jewish nation, my nation, my people, dispersed, denigrated, oppressed, massacred, a people who had hung on desperately to life, almost with their fingernails, and survived.

The Jews had always faced a dual challenge, having to fight their oppressors, and to fight for the preservation of their singular identity. How poignantly was this expressed in Alterman's 'The Battle for Granada', a poem which portrays the remarkable Shmuel Ha'Nagid (Samuel the Governor), Hebrew poet, scholar, statesman, soldier, who nine hundred years ago was leader of Spanish Jewry and at the same time Chief Minister of State to the Berber King of Granada and commander of his army.

Alterman sets a battlefield scene where Samuel the Jewish general is being addressed by a Spanish commander. The Spaniard tells him, in this rough translation of Alterman's exquisite Hebrew: '. . . for apart from the military campaigns of Granada / you have another war / a war of your own / an unending war. / It is the war of your people / whose shepherd you are. / It is the war of your language / whose hosts you command. / It is the war of your son / whose teacher you are / to teach him the writing of antiquity . . .'

I was leaving for Israel the following morning and would report to the Government, as Begin was staying on in the United States for another few days. There would be a special session of the Knesset on his return, devoted to the Camp David accords. We would no doubt be severely criticized, with the arrows of the Labour Opposition barbed with 'the slovenly way' in which we had conducted the negotiations. It would be up to the elected parliamentary representatives of Israel to decide whether to approve or reject the proposal for the Framework Agreement for Peace. Whatever their decision, Heaven knew that at Camp David we had fought to the limit of our capacity what Alterman in his poem referred to as the unending war of the Jews.

CHAPTER SIXTEEN

The Home Front

Sadat returned home from Camp David to an enthusiastic welcome. The treatment given to our own delegation was hardly cordial. Among the Israeli public many were censorious and full of reservations. Barak complained that our critics had not bothered to give careful study to the text of the agreement. This was true even of the political scientists and constitutional lawyers, who based themselves on newspaper reports. Begin said that had he sought approval from his party, he would not have had a majority. There were also rumblings within the coalition's National Religious Party.

The critics pounced on our having agreed to total withdrawal from Sinai, including abandonment of our civilian settlements, rather than on Egypt's having agreed to make peace with us and establish normal relations. Though I was far from delighted by this cold reception, I was neither surprised nor put out. Criticism, whether responsible or frivolous, is a fact of democratic life.

The official discussions in Israel proceeded through four phases. The first was on 20 September, immediately on the return of Ezer Weizman and myself, when we gave a preliminary report to the Cabinet on the Camp David talks. The second took place four days later with the arrival of Begin, when the subject was given its basic review at another Cabinet meeting. It was then brought before the Knesset, debated at two sessions, and put to the vote.

The Cabinet meeting presided over by Begin lasted seven hours. The Prime Minister was authoritative and single-minded in his defence of the agreement, emphasizing its positive qualities, and mercilessly attacking those ministers who were doubtful or opposed. As a highly experienced parliamentarian, and every inch a political party man, he used skilful debating tactics and procedural techniques. He arranged for the Knesset debate to be held the following day, so there was no time to convene the parliamentary Foreign Affairs and Defence Committee. He also refused to hold discussions within his own party before the debate, customary when major policy decisions are to be taken. The other parties represented in the coalition insisted on such consultations, and so the religious party's ministers, for example, did not take part in the Cabinet vote as their faction had not yet met to decide on their position.

At the end of that Cabinet meeting, Begin put to the vote the proposal on which our delegation had agreed at Camp David, and it was carried by a large majority. Eleven ministers voted in favour, two against and one abstained. The religious party ministers announced they would recommend to their parliamentary faction that they support the Government's decision. They also asked me to attend the faction meeting so that I could explain the agreement to their party colleagues and answer questions.

The Cabinet decision authorized the Prime Minister to propose to the Knesset the adoption of the following resolution:

The Knesset approves the Camp David Accords that were signed by the Prime Minister at the White House on 17 September 1978. If, in the negotiations between Egypt and Israel towards the signing of a peace treaty, agreement is reached ... [and] finds expression in a written document, the Knesset authorizes the Government ... to evacuate the Israeli settlers from Sinai and resettle them anew.

The main official discussion of the Camp David agreement was, of course, the Knesset debate. It was carried over to a second session to enable Opposition parties to hold consultations after hearing the Prime Minister's opening statement, and to study all the documents of the agreement which were made available to them. The Government decision, supported by almost all the coalition ministers, paved the way for a favourable Knesset majority, and the results represented an impressive achievement for Begin. But the real achievement was his own approval of the agreement he had proposed.

The Knesset was in recess when we returned from Camp David, and had to be specially convened for the debate. It opened at 10 a.m. on Monday, 25 September 1978, with the entry of the President, and the customary rising to their feet of all the members. For those few minutes, the Chamber was respectful. And then came the disturbances, starting as soon as the Prime Minister made his way to the podium.

Knesset member Geulah Cohen, who belonged to the extreme wing of Begin's party and thought we had conceded too much to the Egyptians, called out on a point of order that she wished to submit an urgent procedural motion. The Speaker of the House, Yitzhak Shamir, told her that under the Knesset rules the motion had to be submitted in writing. The Prime Minister started to speak, but Geulah persisted in her demand; and in the shouting that followed it became clear that the motion she had in mind was for the

Prime Minister to resign. She was called to order three times, but continued with her disturbance. The Speaker thereupon adjourned the session for five minutes, and when we reconvened he called for a vote to expel Geulah Cohen from the Chamber. It was carried, and the offending member left. The Prime Minister then began, for the third time, to deliver his address.

'I bring to the Knesset,' he said, 'and through the Knesset to the nation, news of the establishment of peace between Israel and the strongest and largest of the Arab States, and also, eventually and inevitably, with all our neighbours.'

Begin's speech continued to be punctuated by catcalls and inter-party heckling even after Geulah Cohen's departure. It was possibly on that account that he cut short his opening address, which had been expected to run for more than an hour. But he would have his say when he wound up the debate.

The Prime Minister was followed by the Leader of the Opposition, Shimon Peres. He began, unexpectedly, by congratulating the Prime Minister and the Government on 'the difficult, awesome, but vital decision they had taken to secure peace at a price which had been thought impossible for this Government'.

The Opposition's support for the Camp David accords had been based on a decision by the Central Committee of the Labour Party at a meeting called to determine their position. Peres told the Knesset that at that meeting

a lady, no longer young, dressed in black, went up to the rostrum. She is one of the great women in the history of reborn Israel, a woman who has lost two sons in Israel's wars, a pioneer in all spheres in which she is active. She is Rebecca Guber, known in Israel as 'the mother of the sons'. At the rostrum, speaking without notes, she had said to our Labour Party members: 'Dear Friends, it is difficult for me to speak, nor had I intended to, for I have just risen from the seven days of mourning following the death of my dear husband. But I had no one to send in my place, for my sons left me no grandchildren. I therefore came myself to say to you that, astonishingly, peace beckons, the peace we have all yearned for. Can we allow this moment to slip away?'

Continuing his speech, Peres, as befitted an Opposition leader, moved from praise to sharp criticism both of the agreement and the way the negotiations were conducted. He charged us with paying the price of mistakes which could have been avoided. He called the Camp David accords worse than the Rogers Plan. We had given up a defensible border and had conceded the Sinai airfields, and he thought we could have done better on both these points. 'I say this', he added, 'after my talks with Sadat.' (Peres had met Sadat at a European meeting of the Socialist International.) The evacuation of our Sinai settlements, too, could have been avoided, according to Peres; and as for the autonomy, it would lead to the establishment of a Palestinian State, even if it were not called by that name.

After his sniping and moralizing, couched in language that suggested 'we know more' and 'we would have done it better', the Leader of the Opposition had perforce to explain why, then, he was supporting the Government's resolution. To do so, he extolled Sadat's initiative, and indicated that voting against the Government would be interpreted as spurning the outstretched Egyptian hand and questioning the value of the Camp David Conference. This would gravely damage the chances of peace, the standing of Israel, and our relations with the United States.

The Government laid copies of two documents before the Knesset members: 'Framework for Peace in the Middle East agreed upon at Camp David' and 'Framework for a Peace Treaty between Egypt and Israel'. The Knesset adjourned after the speech by Peres, to reassemble two days later.

The next session lasted five hours, ending with the Prime Minister's reply and the voting – by roll-call. It was a difficult question to resolve, and not only the Cabinet and the parties but each member of the Knesset had to struggle hard to make up his mind and announce publicly whether he was voting for or against the agreement. There was no escaping this moment of decision, and abstention would be an evasion of responsibility. No parliamentarian could argue that he was not involved, that he need not take sides.

All 120 members of the Knesset voted. The result was 84 in favour of the Government's action, 19 against, and 17 abstentions. One of those who abstained was Yehuda Ben Meir, head of the religious party faction in the Knesset. I could not help sending him a note with a one-word change in an old Talmudic quotation: 'By abstention shall the righteous live.'

The last person to take the floor before the winding-up speech by the Prime Minister was myself, and I was allowed to speak undisturbed. My opening point was that at Camp David we had not been under pressure from the United States, but under the very pressure each one of us was feeling now: having to decide between a dream and the price of its fulfilment, between peace with Egypt and the withdrawal from Sinai of our army and our civilians. We had never before had such a peace proposal, with the normalization of relations between the two countries as one of its specific terms.

One speaker in the debate had complained that we had come to the Knesset with a *fait accompli*. This was not correct. We had made it clear at Camp David that the agreement was subject to Knesset approval, and what we had brought was a recommended proposal. The Knesset could endorse it, and thereby turn it into the basis for negotiating a peace treaty with Egypt.

Or it could reject it, and another piece of paper would be added to the heap in the archives. It was for the Knesset to decide.

But if it decided on rejection, it would need to consider further – what next? What were the likely developments the next week, the next year, the next decade? Would the circumstances be more propitious later for a more favourable peace? Would we be better off if the Arab world were united? Would we find it more advantageous if America and Russia forged a common approach to the Middle East? Was King Hussein becoming more accommodating from year to year with his increasingly uncompromising declarations and his overtures to his more powerful brother-Arab rulers? Could anyone be sure that the regime in Egypt that followed Sadat would be any more willing to make peace with us than the one that had preceded him? And would we find it a blessing to continue military government in the territories for the next ten years, live in a state of war with our neighbours, face world criticism, remain dependent on the United States?

We had faced different situations in different periods, and I recalled what Prime Minister Ben Gurion had been prepared to do at the end of the 1948 War of Independence. He had been willing to sign a peace agreement with the borders as they were then – even though the Old City of Jerusalem was not in our hands – because that was all it had been possible to achieve at that time. But the Arabs had not been ready to agree to anything beyond the limit of an armistice agreement.

In 1967, when Levi Eshkol was Prime Minister of a national wall-to-wall Government, we had reached Suez, we had got to the River Jordan, and we had taken the Golan Heights. Did we not then propose peace agreements in which we would return Sinai, with special security arrangements for the freedom of shipping, and we would return the Golan Heights, with appropriate arrangements to ensure non-interference with the sources of the Jordan?

I neither criticized nor regretted the fact that after the Presidents of Egypt and Syria turned down our peace offer, we decided not to sit with folded arms and wait until they were forthcoming, but to establish settlements according to specific plans in Sinai, the Golan Heights, Judea and Samaria. To mark time was assuredly not the way to advance towards peace. But we repeatedly declared that it was not the location of our settlements that would determine our borders if we achieved peace, but that the borders would determine the location of our settlements.

We had come up with all sorts of plans, based on the best military and national considerations, and there were differing opinions. Some favoured the Allon Plan, others were against it. There were also differing views as to how deeply we should go into Sinai to establish settlements: should we create a permanent settlement in Nahal Sinai which is beyond El Arish, or should we limit ourselves to the Rafah approaches? No one sought unlimited settlement.

But there was one drawback to what we had been doing: we were arguing not with the Arabs but with ourselves. True, we tried to judge what we thought the Arabs would be prepared to accept, but we were still conducting an internal debate. Now, with Camp David, there was one blemish and one virtue. There was disappointment in the discovery that the reality did not match the dream. But there was advantage in that our encounter was with an Arab Government, and the reality was a concrete proposal for peace. What we now had to face up to was the reality as it emerged in dealing with the other party, and not the 'reality' we had conjured up when speaking to ourselves.

I reminded the Knesset that Egypt was not the only Arab State, nor the first, that had been prepared to hold peace talks with us. The Government of Jordan had also shown a readiness to do so in recent years. During both the Golda Meir and Yitzhak Rabin administrations there had been protracted negotiations with them, but no agreement had been reached.

This brought me incidentally to the charge made by some members that our conduct of the negotiations had been inept. I recalled that there had been no cries of ineptness at the previous Governments when they had failed to convince the Jordanian administration to accept such proposals of ours as, say, the Allon Plan. No one then said that if he had been entrusted with the negotiations he would have done it better, and would have succeeded in bringing the King round to our point of view. All that was said was that Jordan would not accept what we proposed, and we would not accept what Jordan proposed. This was due not to the lack of negotiating talent, but to the veritable chasm between our aims and desires and those of all the Arab Governments.

The United States had found itself in a similar situation at Camp David when trying to help Israel and Egypt to reach agreement. She had suggested at one point the establishment of an American air base in Sinai in place of one we were evacuating. The Egyptians turned it down, refusing not only us but also the Americans. We thought this could be the key to break the deadlock, as it could resolve some of our doubts; but Egypt rejected it time after time despite the personal pleas of President Carter to President Sadat. No one said, or thought, that this reflected ineptness on the part of Carter.

Returning to my main theme, I said there was no escaping the question we all had to ask ourselves: were we prepared to pay this price for peace? If not, how did we envisage the future – another Israel-Arab war followed by another agreement, with our sword at the throat of the attacker? Most of our agreements with the Arabs had been of that order. After the 1948, 1967 and 1973 wars, with our army victorious and still mobilized, and the Arabs in disarray, the agreements were the product of those conflicts. They were therefore cease-fire armistices, and separation of forces agreements, all with the purpose of stopping the war but not for the inauguration of peace. Now, for the first time, an agreement was being considered not under war pressure. Did we really wish to wait until we could negotiate another agreement that was to follow, and be the product of, war? Would the chances of its being more favourable be any better than the current ones?

Put starkly, we had now to decide whether we were prepared to move fourteen settlements and three airfields to within our former borders – after the conditions of full normalization and the establishment of diplomatic relations were met – in return for a true peace. Or did we regard such a withdrawal as too steep a price? If we were not prepared to pay it, did we have a better plan for our future?

I then added a personal note. The questions to myself were far more acute, for I had once gone on record as saying it was better to retain Sharm e-Sheikh without peace than to secure peace without Sharm e-Sheikh. What had changed since then? What I had said then fitted the circumstances of the time, for Nasser was the President of Egypt, and Sharm without peace was definitely to be preferred. But eight years had passed, and the situation, and the regime in Egypt, were different. Now I thought that peace without Sharm was preferable, on condition that we could guarantee freedom of shipping for Israel through the Gulf of Eilat.

I finally touched on those understandings and arrangements with the United States, linked to the Camp David accords, which ruled out any intention to consider statehood for the Palestinians. The joint US-Israel working paper of October 1977 had made it clear that peace agreements were to be negotiated and concluded between the sovereign countries of Israel and Egypt, Israel and Jordan, Israel and Syria and Israel and Lebanon, while matters associated with the West Bank and the Gaza District – not peace agreements – would be discussed with the Arab residents of those territories. This was also stipulated with great clarity in the agreement before the Knesset: our deliberations with the representatives of the local residents of the territories would not be concerned with a peace agreement. Such an agreement on the basis of Resolution 242 could be reached only with Jordan, while the Palestinians, if they wished, could be linked to the Jordanian delegation, but could not appear as a separate delegation to hold peace talks. Only with Jordan would we determine our eastern boundary, and only with Jordan – not with the Palestinians – would we sign a peace treaty, in accordance with Resolution 242. This was the formula signed by Premier Begin and President Sadat – and also, as a witness, by President Carter.

I drew attention further to the significant fact that the same document, with the three signatures of the heads of government, also recorded, for the first time, that during the three-year transitional period, Israeli forces would withdraw, but would then redeploy in the Gaza District, Judea and Samaria up to the River Jordan.

Most of the Knesset members who opposed the Government motion, or who abstained, came from Begin's own party and from the National Religious Party. In Israel, as in all countries, the parliamentary representatives did not always reflect the mood of the people. It was my conviction that Rebecca Guber, 'the mother of the sons', in her remarks to the Central Committee of the Labour Party, was the spokeswoman of the majority. This aged lady had devoted all her life to her people. She had arrived in Israel from Russia fifty-three years ago, had worked in the fields from dawn to dusk, together with her husband and sons, to build up their co-operative farm, and had befriended, guided and instructed the new immigrants. Her two sons fell in the 1948 War of Independence. The elder, Ephraim, was killed at the age of twenty in the battles in the south, two months before the proclamation of the State. His younger brother, Zvi, was also killed in the south, one month after the State was established. He was seventeen. Rebecca's husband died a few days before her appearance at the Central Committee. As Chief of Staff and later as Cabinet Minister, I had met her from time to time when she would ask to see me. She would point to areas in which the State institutions should do more, or better, than they were doing, and suggest ways in which the underprivileged could be helped. She never demanded anything for herself, and came with no personal complaints. She spoke quietly, with profound conviction, and with a courageous spirit. What she had said in favour of the peace agreement was dearer to me than anything else I had heard.

CHAPTER SEVENTEEN

Blair House

The Knesset decision approving Israel's evacuation of Sinai if a peace treaty were signed was transmitted to the United States and Egypt. President Carter sent a warm congratulatory message to Prime Minister Begin on his courage and wisdom in carrying through this historic resolution. Now, wrote the President, we had to start negotiations to bring about peace. Carter proposed that the talks be held in Washington, at Blair House, in October 1978. The United States would be represented by Secretary of State Cyrus Vance. The White House spokesman stressed that this time the aim was not to reach a general formula for ending the state of war between the two countries, but specifically to reach a peace treaty.

The State Department called our Ambassador in Washington with the urgent plea that during these peace talks, which in the meantime were being dubbed 'the Blair House Conference', there should be only one spokesman – American. They added that, of course, they were not setting a time limit, but they judged that it should not last more than two or three weeks. The conference would open at 12 noon on 12 October.

Both Egypt and Israel accepted Carter's proposal and announced the composition of their delegations. The list sent by Egypt contained the name of General Gamassi as the principal military representative. Two days later, however, Egypt notified the Americans that Gamassi would not be coming. In his place they were sending General Kamal Hassan Ali. It appeared that Sadat had decided during those forty-eight hours to drop Gamassi and appoint Ali as Defence Minister. The other members of the Egyptian delega- tion were Butros Ghali, Osama al-Baz, General Taha Magdub, Ambassador Gorbal, and Professor Arian, an expert in international law.

Israel's delegation included two ministers, Ezer Weizman and myself, as well as Meir Rosenne, and General Avraham Tamir of the Defence Ministry. We would be joined in Washington by Ambassador Dinitz and Minister Bar- On. A few days later. Aharon Barak was co-opted to the delegation at my request. I was to head the delegation.

The Knesset decision followed by the announcement of the forthcoming Blair House talks sent a wave of hopeful expectation throughout the country. Perhaps peace might really be achieved. I even received a warm letter from the very friend, Yehuda Tubin of kibbutz Bet Zera, who had excoriated me when I had joined the Begin Government. He now 'rehabilitated' me. 'This morning', he wrote,

it is my wish, if only through this note, to shake your hand and bless you. I know nothing more than the news I heard on the radio this morning, and your reaction. I also recall your face on the television screen at the White House signing ceremony, and I saw that you were very moved – as moved as you were last year when you paid your visit to the Bergen Belsen death camp in Germany. I know of your heartfelt wishes towards Judea and Samaria, and I can guess how much you contributed towards this stunning agreement.

In my reply, I wrote that there were still many obstacles on the road to peace, and there was no certainty that we would surmount them all. 'Let us hope we shall,' I said, adding that as long as it was given me to act, I would continue to do so, provided I would not be asked to abandon my views on the pattern of relations that should exist between us and the Arabs. 'The peace treaty, if gained, is of great importance; but more so are the national, organizational and human relations with the Arabs, with whom we must live. No peace treaty can last without a system which takes that into account.'

The Americans, for their part, did not make things easy for us. *En route* to Washington I was to stop over in New York to address the United Nations General Assembly, and the Americans entreated me not to say anything in my UN speech that might upset the Egyptians, as they found themselves in 'a difficult situation'. 'Please', they asked me, 'try not to embarrass them in front of the delegates from the Arab countries by being too friendly. And don't stress your appreciation of their readiness to make peace with you.'

Furthermore, in their public appearances, the United States representatives made a point of giving pro-Arab – and incorrect – interpretations of the Camp David framework agreement. In an official letter to Secretary Vance, I drew attention to the differences between what he had said in his speech to the UN Assembly and what had been agreed upon at Camp David. Not that I expected a change in Washington's behaviour, but I wished him to know that Israel did not consider 'how not to make it hard for Sadat' to be the principal concern of the peace exercise. We had enough problems of our own, and it would be well for the United States to recognize that Israel had reached the limit of her concessions.

We had left Israel for New York and the Washington negotiations on 5 October 1978, and next day we were handed 'for our information' the text of a questionnaire which King Hussein of Jordan had submitted to the United States Government. We already knew the content, for the questions had been broadcast·over Radio Amman, and I confess that when I heard them I imagined that the Americans would not deign to reply. Most of them were couched in provocative terms, rather like those of a prosecuting attorney and, as broadcast by Jordan, their propagandist character was much in evidence. The intention was clearly to justify Jordan's refusal to join the peace negotiations. The subjects on which unequivocal answers were demanded of the Americans included the status of Jerusalem, Israeli settlements, the withdrawal of Israeli forces, the return of the Palestinian refugees, and self-determination for the Palestinians.

The questions were cleverly designed to elicit public statements by the American Government as to where the US stood on key issues where Israeli–Arab views were poles apart. The aim was to get the Americans to commit themselves – in advance of the very negotiations whose purpose it was to bridge the gap – as to whether they sided with Israel or with the Arab States. This was why I imagined the Americans would not reply. I was wrong.

Three days after the opening of the Blair House talks on a peace treaty with Egypt, Saunders of the State Department told me that he was about to leave for Jordan and he wished to talk with us before he went. He arrived at the meeting with Atherton, and I had Ezer and Dinitz with me. Saunders said he was anxious to share with me his ideas on what to tell the Jordanians. He would like us to be on the same wave-length, and to explain that we were all interested in making an advance on the subject of the West Bank and the Palestinians. His discussion with King Hussein would be conducted on the basis of Jordan's questionnaire and America's replies.

I told him I had no idea what answers the United States proposed to offer, but I did not think that Jordan and the Palestinians would join the negotiations on the basis of the Camp David accords. Israel, on the other hand, wished, as agreed, to reach a peace treaty with Egypt, and only after that would she discuss the question of the West Bank and the Palestinians. To this, Saunders replied that he would let us have America's answers to Jordan's questionnaire, and added that he assumed not all of them would be to our liking.

As our talk progressed, it became increasingly clear that Saunders intended to make promises to the Jordanians on a number of items to which we were opposed and which were a departure from the Camp David accords. When I said this, the Americans replied that they would say nothing to Hussein that had not already been heard from the lips of US representatives in the past. I pointed out that the Camp David agreement had established a new and basic framework for the Palestinian question, which was different in many respects from what American spokesmen had said earlier. Now, with the ink of the President's signature hardly dry on the agreement, it seemed to be America's intention to ignore it. And they even wanted our agreement to do so!

It was a very unpleasant talk, and it ended in differences of view and a sense of grievance. I was angered not only by the position they had taken and their deliberate disregard of what was written in the Camp David accords, but particularly by their pretended innocence and their attempt to present views – which we had previously rejected outright – as though they had never heard of our objections and expected none now.

On 18 October Atherton handed us 'President Carter's replies to King Hussein'. To our dismay, our anxieties had not been unwarranted. The replies distorted what had been agreed upon at Camp David; were hostile to Israel's security needs, and to the position taken by every Israeli Government; and even contradicted President Carter's own declarations. Carter, for instance, had repeatedly told us, and stated publicly, that every Israeli had the right to acquire land and settle in the West Bank and the Gaza District without the right of any Arab authority to prevent it. He now appeared to backtrack. Indeed, in their efforts to find favour in Arab eyes, the drafters of the President's replies knew no bounds. There were lapses even when they 'quoted' their position on the Camp David agreement. They wrote, for example, that the Palestinians would be enabled to fulfil their 'legitimate aspirations', whereas the agreement used the more limiting term 'legitimate rights' – a limitation arrived at only after a great deal of discussion at Camp David.

To Jordan's question about the presence of Israeli forces in the West Bank and Gaza, the reply was that the United States would not oppose the stationing 'of limited numbers of Israeli security personnel in specifically designated areas' in this territory – 'if agreed to by the parties'. How magnanimous! As to the status of Israeli settlements that might remain in the administered territories after the five-year transitional period, the American assumption was that this 'would be a matter for discussion during the negotiations regarding the final status of the West Bank and Gaza'.

I made known to Saunders and Atherton what I thought of their document, and then transmitted it to Jerusalem for the Government to issue an appropriate reaction. I was sorry to see that the State Department still held to the belief that by its wayward behaviour it could capture Arab hearts. I was reminded of a meeting between Ben Gurion and Judah Magnes in the years before the establishment of the State of Israel. Magnes, who was President of the Hebrew University and very active in the cause of an Arab-

Jewish covenant of peace, said that if we could achieve such peace, we could then gain statehood. Ben Gurion's reply was that only after achieving statehood would we reach peace with the Arabs.

I had no doubt that Saunders would return from his visit to Jordan empty-handed. Hussein would not join the talks, and the American replies by President Carter would only add ammunition to the arsenal of the Arabs who objected to Israel's very existence.

Before the opening of the conference in Washington, I had had a busy time in New York, meeting Foreign Ministers who had also arrived for the UN Assembly, and preparing my address to it. My first talk, on the day of my arrival, was with the Iranian Foreign Minister. I called on him at his luxurious suite in the Waldorf Astoria, furnished in the Persian style. He did not hide his anxiety over what was happening in his country. The situation of the Shah, he said, was progressively deteriorating, and the influence of the Ayatollah Khomeini was on the increase. (Khomeini at the time was still in Paris.) It was the hope of the Iranian regime that the army would remain loyal to the Shah. Although he expressed his vigorous conviction that the Shah would emerge successfully from the crisis, the sadness in his face was a truer expression of a worried heart.

I saw Secretary Vance next day, for an hour's meeting at his hotel, and we talked mostly about the situation in the Lebanon. On the forthcoming Blair House Conference, we discussed only procedural matters. I told him that at this conference we wished first of all to consider the nature of the peace we sought to establish. It had to be a true peace, with normal neighbourly relations, diplomatic ties, economic and cultural agreements, and freedom of movement for tourists and travellers. Vance said this approach was acceptable to him and he would hand us the draft of a peace treaty which the Americans had prepared. Its first Article dealt with the very subject I had raised – the nature of peace.

I delivered my address to the UN General Assembly in the morning of 9 October. It was a short speech covering Israel's position on international issues, the problems of Jews in the Soviet Union, and the persecution of the Jewish community in Syria by the Government of that country. I touched on the Camp David accords only in general terms, going into detail on one item alone – Jerusalem. This was a matter which was bound to come up for discussion between the parties, and I was anxious to make clear Israel's position. I said:

Jerusalem, for us, is the eternal capital of Israel, and our only one. We have no other, and we never will, no matter whether others recognize it or refuse to recognize it as our capital. This eternal city is holy to three faiths, Jewish, Islamic and Christian; but the link between us and Jerusalem is not only religious. It is also national, the inspiration which has enabled us to preserve the Jewish identity and Jewish nationhood throughout all the centuries of our history, during the periods both of our sovereignty and of our long exile.

As usual at the annual gathering of the UN Assembly, the Arab delegations left the hall when the representative of Israel rose to speak. On this occasion, however, there was a change. As I took my place at the rostrum, while the other Arabs left, the delegations from Egypt and Bahrein remained to listen.

While I was speaking, an aide of UN Secretary-General Kurt Waldheim approached the Israeli delegation desk with the message that Waldheim would like to see me after my speech. When I got to his office, I found him with Under-Secretary-General Brian Urquhart. Our talk was brief. Waldheim said how pleased he was that under the Camp David agreement UN forces would be entrusted with the task of safeguarding the peace. That, after all, was the basic function of the United Nations Organization. I replied that we had no difference of opinion on the functions of the UN, but I reminded him, with regret, that in 1967 the UN and its forces at Sharm e-Sheikh had failed to fulfil their functions. They had abandoned both their mission and their posts, and had brought about war between Egypt and Israel. Waldheim quickly diverted the conversation to Lebanon, and we both agreed that the situation in that country was tragic. The problem would be solved only when a Lebanese Government and army emerged who were capable of exercising control over their country. At the moment, this was very far from the case. The forces in control there were Syria and the Palestinians, while the Lebanese were fighting each other, Christians versus Moslems – and there were even warring factions within each community.

There was no practical outcome to our talk, and I never did discover why Waldheim had called for it in the first place. But I was glad to have met Brian Urquhart, for whom I had a warm feeling and about whom I was curious ever since I heard of his strange experience during the Second World War. It appeared that towards the end of 1942, an air drop was contemplated in the operational planning for the capture of Tunis after the Allied landing in North Africa. Urquhart was then a young company commander in a British paratroop brigade that was to take part in the operation, and was carrying out training exercises on Salisbury Plain in Britain. On one training jump, Urquhart stood at the plane's exit to see that all his men were out, and then jumped himself. To his surprise, although he was the last man out, he rapidly overtook his men, who were floating gently towards the ground while he was plummeting. His parachute had failed to open completely, and he landed hard on a ploughed field, unconscious, bones broken – but alive. There may have been other freak cases of survival after such falls, but I have not heard of them. Urquhart's doctors thought it would take two years to put him together again, though he would remain a cripple. In fact, he returned to active service nine months later, and became chief intelligence officer on the staff of General Browning, commander of the British Army's Airborne Corps, which made the celebrated drop at Arnhem in Holland in September 1944.

I flew to Washington the following morning, the day before Yom Kippur, and, together with Ezer Weizman, met with President Carter for a preliminary talk on the Blair House Conference, which was due to open two days later, on 12 October. Carter had with him Vice-President Mondale, Secretary Vance, Brzezinski and Atherton. Carter spoke of the need to reach an arrangement quickly, before the start of the projected Baghdad Conference on 1 November. Not only this conference, he said, but other, unexpected, events were likely to present difficulties to President Sadat and diminish his readiness to make peace. I asked when Sadat would be prepared to establish diplomatic relations with us, and Carter judged it would be four to six weeks after we withdrew to the El Arish–Ras Mohammad line.

The first part of our talk dealt with military matters. Ezer said that we, too, wanted an early evacuation of western Sinai. But it was fraught with many difficulties, and building two new airfields in place of the ones we were abandoning would cost about two and a half billion dollars. Carter observed, with a smile that belied his serious intent, that he could not fathom how our Defence Minister had managed to oblige the United States to build two new airfields when he, Carter, had thought there would be only one. Vance confirmed that the talk throughout the negotiations had been about two airfields. I gathered from the President's words that the United States would indeed foot the bill.

After exchanging views on the UN force and the establishment of early-warning stations upon the withdrawal of Israeli troops from Sinai, Carter took up the Palestinian question. He thought we should refrain from setting up new settlements during the three months of negotiation on the future of the West Bank and the Gaza District. I replied that I would not propose to Premier Begin that he change one word of the letter he had handed to the President on this subject (on 17 September 1978) at Camp David (in which Begin had stressed that the three months' freeze referred specifically to the negotiations for the conclusion of the Egypt–Israel peace treaty, and not to the negotiations for autonomy in the West Bank and Gaza). This matter had been thoroughly threshed out on earlier occasions, and there was no point in considering it again in all its details. We moved on to the next item, which was Sadat's wish to link the Palestinian question to the peace treaty negotiations between Egypt and Israel. Carter told us we had to find some way of bringing the Palestinians to the negotiating table.

The experience at Camp David had made me familiar with the character of discussions with the US President and his aides, and I knew that it was best to respond in straightforward terms. I told the President that there was no shortcut to that. The more that America, Egypt and Israel continued to deal with their affairs the more the Palestinians would feel they were being patronized and would accordingly stiffen their objections. The way to bring them closer was to reach a peace agreement between Israel and Egypt. Once the Palestinian Arabs realized that we were determined to arrive at an agreement, they would in the end also join. Brzezinski and Vance argued in favour of linking the negotiations with Egypt to discussions on the West Bank and Gaza, for this, they said, would ease the problems for Sadat. He faced growing isolation in the Arab world, and he was being accused of betraying the wider interests of the Arab people and concerning himself only with the interests of Egypt. In a throw-away line, Carter mentioned that Sadat had invited him to visit Egypt and he had accepted, though the date had not yet been set. He said nothing about a possible visit to Israel.

No official decisions were taken at this meeting. It was an exchange of views. Nevertheless American intentions seemed clear. They would not raise the question of settlements in the next three months, since even our own formula called for the non-establishment of additional settlements during that period. They were most anxious for the Blair House Conference to end quickly – the President had mentioned two to three weeks. And if the Egyptian delegation sought to tie the Palestinian question to the Egypt-Israel peace negotiations, the United States would support her, but would not insist if it meant failure to reach a peace agreement.

It was 6 in the afternoon when we emerged from the White House, and the Yom Kippur eve services were almost upon us. We sent off our cars, and hastened on foot to the synagogue.

Next evening, at the end of Yom Kippur, I met with Butros Ghali. He and Kamal Hassan Ali, head of the Egyptian delegation, had gone over to Ezer's room for a chat, and Ghali now left to visit me – to pour his heart out on the difficulties facing the Egyptians, and to try to get me to recommend Israeli 'gestures' which would ease their lot. He and Ali had also seen Carter and they, too, had been urged by Carter to get the negotiations finished quickly. He, Ghali, had no objections to this, but solutions had to be found for two problems. One was Egypt's isolation in the Arab world, and here they were relying on the United States to persuade her allies, Saudi Arabia and Jordan, to support Sadat. The second problem was that of the Palestinians, and on this matter it was up to Israel to act. The 'gestures' he had in mind were the redeployment of our forces in the West Bank and Gaza District so that they were further away from Arab population centres; abolition of military government in the territories; and release of Arab prisoners (who had been sentenced for acts of terrorism).

I told Ghali I was not unaware of their problems, nor did I make light of Arab attacks on Sadat; but the purpose of the Blair House Conference was to attain an Egypt–Israel peace treaty, and not to solve the Palestinian problem. I at all events would not lend my hand to combining the two issues. Ghali did not hide his disappointment, and went back to Ezer's room.

The Blair House Conference opened officially the following morning with a brief ceremony at the White House. President Carter larded his blessings for the success of our negotiations with effusive praise of Sadat and Begin, and emphasized the obligation of the United States to continue the process for peace until it was attained. Kamal Ali responded for the Egyptian delegation, and I for the Israelis. Everyone applauded, the cameras clicked, the lights flashed, and the ceremony ended. We shook the President's hand, and went off to Blair House to begin work.

The opening session was a joint meeting of all three delegations. It would be followed, at Vance's suggestion, by two separate meetings, between the Americans and us, and the Americans and the Egyptians. A further joint session of the three delegations would wind up the day. This system would enable the United States representatives to clarify the stands of the two principal parties on the issues on which they were divided, try to bridge the gap, and devise formulae which both could accept. We and the Egyptians indicated that our acceptance of any formula would necessarily be provisional, as it required the approval of our Governments.

After the joint opening session, which was brief, we held our first meeting with the Americans. On the agenda was the draft peace treaty they had prepared, which they had handed to the Egyptians and to us the previous evening. We had given it careful study and decided to accept it as a basis for discussion. So had the Egyptians, both parties adding, of course, that they would suggest changes in those items to which they objected.

Now, sitting with the Americans, we went over the draft paragraph by paragraph, the principal speaker on our side being our Foreign Ministry legal adviser, Meir Rosenne. He told them which Articles were acceptable, and what amendments we required in the others. The Americans took note of our reservations and proposals. When some seemed to them to be too extreme, we made joint efforts to find formulae which would satisfy us and yet not arouse sharp objections from the Egyptians.

One of the principal items on which we sought amendment was the timing of the establishment of diplomatic relations: we wanted it to be simultaneous with our withdrawal to the El Arish–Ras Mohammad line. Another concerned the UN forces in Sinai. We wanted a clear definition of their nature, functions and authority, and a precise distinction between 'observers', who were to supervise the carrying out of the terms of the agreement relating to the size and weaponry of troops stationed in the various zones, and 'emergency forces', who were to control certain Sinai areas which we were evacuating. We also had reservations about referral to the International Court of Justice at The Hague of any differences between us and the Egyptians over the interpretation of the treaty. Finally, we wanted firmer commitments about freedom of shipping and aircraft through the Gulf of Eilat, oil supplies from the fields we were abandoning, and the continued operation of the American early-warning stations in Sinai.

At the end of the meeting, I had a private talk with Vance, at his request, in which he told me of Carter's proposed visit to the Middle East. He said the President would be pleased to visit Israel if and when he would be visiting Egypt. On the Blair House Conference, he said he was optimistic. Egypt's reactions to the American draft proposals were 'not bad'. With goodwill, it would be possible to overcome the differences between the two principal parties. I could only respond with a 'let's hope so', using a single expressive word in the most appropriate of the three spoken languages heard in Blair House at the time – the Arabic *Inshallah*.

We had a two-hour morning session with the Americans the next day, when they came up with a new draft. The Articles on which agreement had been reached appeared in their agreed text, while those which had not been resolved appeared in two versions, the Egyptian and the Israeli.

The Egyptians wanted the Israel–Egypt peace agreement linked to the Palestinian issue, and the preamble to the agreement to state that this was the first step in a comprehensive agreement. Rosenne objected to this, since it would mean that if there were no further step, the Egyptians could claim that our agreement had lost its validity. It now transpired, from what the Americans told us of their talks with the Egyptians, that the divisions between us were neither few nor narrow. The principal one was the repeated Egyptian attempts to tie the proposed peace treaty with an agreement on autonomy for the Palestinians, particularly in the Gaza District. I told Vance that the Egyptians should put an end to these efforts, for if they persisted we could pack our bags and return to Israel. We had not come to Washington to discuss the Palestinian problem. The purpose of the Blair House Conference was solely to secure a peace agreement between Israel and Egypt. We were discussing here the proposed frontier between our two countries, the frontier that, as agreed at Camp David, should be identical with the international boundary as it existed during the period of the British Mandate. The Gaza District lay on the Israeli side of that frontier, and therefore any discussion of that piece of territory belonged to the negotiations on autonomy.

At the close of this meeting, the prospects seemed far less rosy than they had the day before. Moreover, the Government in Jerusalem had not yet considered the American draft, nor our own suggestions. I told Vance it would be doing so at the next Cabinet meeting on the following Sunday, and I was not at all sure it would approve all the positions my delegation had taken. Vance understood. At Camp David, as well as on visits to Israel, he had become aware on occasion of the gap between the views of Premier Begin (and several ministers) and mine. 'I see', he said, 'that you will need to conduct double negotiations – with the Egyptians and with your own Government.'

I had no illusions about the problems I would have with both, and so I did not share the optimism of my colleagues at Blair House, who pointed out, after reading the first American draft, that most of its Articles were, in principle, acceptable to us. Nor did I think, as did Carter and members of my delegation, that we could complete the negotiations quickly. I had come to know the two men with a determining voice in the Egyptian delegation, al-Baz on the legal side and Butros Ghali on the political, and I judged that they would propose changes in the American draft which we would be unable to accept.

As for my own Government, I knew they would not ease my Blair House task. At Camp David, with Prime Minister Begin leading our delegation, ministers who were not happy with the way the negotiations were going did not, nevertheless, vote against the agreement, since they did not dare oppose Begin. But at Blair House, with Begin in Jerusalem, and myself heading the delegation in Washington, the ministerial trust was very limited. Most of them saw it as their duty to be on the watch lest I concede too much and 'sell out' Israel's interests. A few days after the opening of the conference, as the stream of directives from Jerusalem kept increasing in volume, I picked up the telephone for a straight talk with the Prime Minister. I first asked that Aharon Barak be sent to join our delegation so as to 'broaden our shoulders'. It was not a simple matter, for since Camp David, when he had been our Attorney-General, Barak had been appointed to the Supreme Court bench, and some of his fellow judges objected to his undertaking a mission with specific political elements. There were objections also from some of the senior members of our delegation, who believed the negotiations would be completed within days, and in any case there were no special problems that required the services of Barak. I told them they could air their objections directly to the Prime Minister but I would not withdraw my request.

The rest of my telephone talk with Begin was not pleasant. I was aware, I said, of the attitude of other ministers towards me, and I had also been told by some of them that they wished to take part in our conference. 'For my part,' I said, 'you can send any minister you wish to join the delegation, and the same holds true for anyone at the professional level. If, in addition to Barak, you deem it appropriate to strengthen the delegation with more personnel, by all means do so.'

Begin replied that he had no wish to send out more ministers. But he then came out with a revival of our old argument over a free or fettered negotiating hand: he asked that we confer with him on every clause in the American draft which we proposed to delete or change – and to do so before submitting our proposals to the US representatives. I was no more disposed to change my mind now than I had been on earlier occasions, and I told the Prime Minister this was simply not possible. It was inconceivable that in talks with President Carter or Secretary Vance we should sit tongue-tied, and have to keep rushing to a telephone before we could tell them whether we accepted or rejected their proposals, or suggest a compromise solution. In any case, I added, whatever agreement was reached at Blair House required the approval of the Government. However, I assured Begin that Meir Rosenne would be in direct touch with him to provide progress reports and receive directives. He and the Government would have the last word.

As against my insistence on freedom in the general negotiations, I told the Prime Minister that talks on the specific subjects of oil supplies and financial support should be handled by the experts and those with government responsibility in these areas. There was none on our delegation, and I therefore requested that representatives of our Ministries of Finance and Energy should be sent to Washington to try to get what they required. We would give them whatever help we could. Begin accepted my suggestion, and he also agreed to send Barak. He arrived on 18 October.

Thereafter, Barak joined Rosenne and Froike Poran (the Premier's military secretary, who was also on the delegation) as the links with Begin, keeping him informed about the proposals on 'every clause' in the American draft. Barak and Rosenne found the Prime Minister attentive on the whole to their explanations; and he in turn screened our delegation against the demands and complaints of our critics in the Government.

The American delegation also caused us problems. Vance left Washington two days after the opening of the conference on visits to South Africa and other countries, and his place was taken by Atherton, who lacked Vance's authority and strength. I did not know how he dealt with the Egyptian delegation, but when he came to us he looked for easy solutions, simply recommending that we accept the Egyptian proposals. There was also trouble over the map of our withdrawal which the Americans had prepared. For some reason they marked the El Arish–Ras Mohammad line east of our Naot-Sinai settlement, thereby including it in the area we were to evacuate in the first phase of our withdrawal and not, as agreed, in the second phase three years later. After some contentious argument the error was rectified, but our suspicions of American one-sidedness remained.

We continued our tripartite and bilateral talks, but made no progress. Both sides entrenched themselves in their positions. Gloom settled over the Blair House Conference rooms. Told of the deadlock, Carter declared his readiness, if we so wished, to involve himself in efforts to break it. We decided it would be helpful and asked him to receive our delegation for a talk.

The Egyptians, too, were troubled by the lack of progress. The Arabic press gave wide coverage to the Washington talks, and charged Egypt with surrendering to Israel. Butros Ghali approached us in the name of Sadat and requested permission for a high-level Egyptian delegation to visit the Gaza District, meet with the local inhabitants and secure their support for Egypt. We recommended to Prime Minister Begin that he accede to this request, which he did, and I thereupon informed Ghali. I found him visibly embarrassed. They had changed their minds and decided to abandon their plan. It transpired that they had made investigations and found that if their delegation appeared in Gaza, they would be greeted with hostile demonstrations and cries of 'Down with Sadat'.

We met Carter in the afternoon of 17 October in the conference room of the White House. With him were Mondale, Brzezinski, Atherton, Quandt and Jordan. I appeared with Ezer Weizman, and we were accompanied by Dinitz, Rosenne, and Rubinstein.

Carter asked for my opinion on the state of the negotiations. I told him that three basic obstacles were holding up the advance, and after dealing with them I would submit three requests to the United States. The first hurdle was the conflict between an Egypt-Israel peace treaty and Egypt's treaties with Arab States which obliged her to join them if they should go to war with

Israel. We wanted a clause in our agreement stating specifically that our peace treaty would have 'priority of obligations'.

Rosenne explained that Egypt had some fifty treaties with Arab States which called for hostile action against Israel under certain circumstances. We should really have demanded that she disengage herself from these treaties; but this was not possible for political reasons. We were therefore concerning ourselves only with the case of a possible conflict, and wanted our treaty to take priority. This now needed to be done because we were entering into an agreement with Egypt knowing full well that she was committed by other treaties. Carter asked Atherton what position Egypt was taking on this matter, and he said they wanted us to be satisfied with a general formula, which even the Americans considered insufficient. Rosenne explained further that in international law earlier treaties took priority over later ones. Thus, if our proposal were not accepted, our peace treaty would be null and void. Carter said he would be meeting the Egyptian delegation that evening and would try to take up this issue with them.

The second obstacle was Egypt's insistence on linking the peace treaty with the Palestinian question. I told Carter that we on our part wished to fulfil all our obligations under the Camp David framework agreement; but we were not prepared to make our peace treaty with Egypt part of another agreement. We wanted this treaty to stand on its own. We had agreed to the formula on this point proposed in the first American draft, and this had been approved by the Israeli Government; but the Egyptians had rejected it. They wanted stronger ties between the treaty and the Palestinian issue. This we could not accept, for it would mean that if no agreement were reached on the Palestinian question – even if the fault lay with the Arabs – the Egypt–Israel peace treaty would lose its validity. The Egyptians could claim that our treaty was conditional upon such an agreement. Carter said he was certain that it was not Sadat's intention to strew the peace path with bolders, but we had to understand his problems with the Arab world. However, he agreed to take up this matter, too, with the Egyptians that evening.

The third obstacle concerned the establishment of diplomatic relations and an exchange of ambassadors. The Egyptians had agreed that this would be done simultaneously with our withdrawal to the El Arish–Ras Mohammad line. They had now changed their minds and wanted the process to be 'gradual'. They wished to start with an exchange of *chargés d'affaires*, and in the course of time, perhaps when we had completed our evacuation of the whole of Sinai, to establish full diplomatic ties. This meant a postponement of three years. At the same time, they were asking us to hasten the pace of our withdrawal – beyond what had been agreed at Camp David – and

Premier Begin, President Carter, President Sadat and Moshe Dayan on a visit to Gettysburg during the Camp David talks. The man with the beard and hat next to Dayan is the local guide at the site. Between Sadat and the guide is US Ambassador to Israel Samuel Lewis. Mrs Begin is at extreme right.

The US and Israeli delegation heads at Camp David. Clockwise: President Carter, US Secretary Vance, National Security Adviser Zbigniew Brzezinski, Vice-President Mondale, (gentleman unknown), Dayan and Begin.

Egypt's Dr Hassan Tuhami (left) and Butros Ghali with Dayan at Camp David.

With Egypt's Prime Minister at the time, Mustapha Khalil.

The Egypt-Israel-US delegations at Washington's Blair House Conference.
Clockwise round the table from Dayan: Simcha Dinitz, US Assistant Secretary
Alfred Atherton, Secretary Cyrus Vance, Saunders, Butros Ghali, Egyptian Defence Minister
Kamal Hassan Ali (extreme bottom right with back to camera), (bottom middle,
back to camera, unknown), and Ezer Weizman.
Sadat, Carter and Begin at the White House after signing the Peace Treaty.

Egypt's Minister of State for Foreign Affairs in the Dayan garden.

Dayan with Egypt's Foreign Minister Muhammed Ibrahim Kamel.

Egyptian Defence Minister Kamal Hassan Ali greeted by Dayan at a party in the Dayan home.

Above: with Rahel in Burma.

Above right: Dayan at the podium in the Knesset, Israel's parliament.

Right: The backbencher.

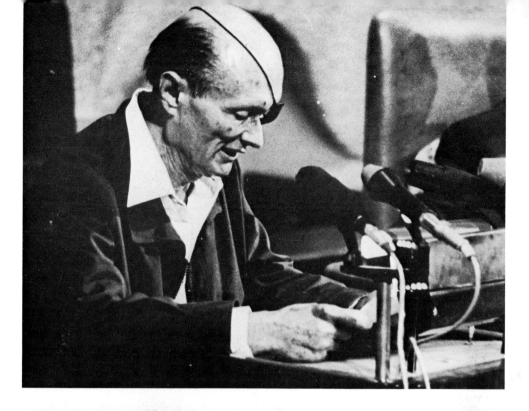

In the 'archaeological corner' of his garden.

hand them back El Arish six months after the signing of the treaty. Carter said that on this matter he agreed with us completely. He said he had talked about this to Sadat at Camp David, and the Egyptian President had agreed, albeit after much hesitation, to establish full diplomatic relations with Israel immediately upon the completion of the first phase of Israel's withdrawal.

In Vance's absence, Brzezinski took an active part in the talks, and his approach was highly tendentious. Here, in the presence of the President and with a written record being taken of all that was said, he tried by oblique and apparently innocent questioning to get us to commit ourselves to positions which we had consistently rejected. For example, we had refused to discuss the future of the administered territories since this was outside the scope of the Blair House Conference. However, when we had finished discussing the point about an exchange of ambassadors upon the completion of the first phase of our withdrawal from Sinai, Brzezinski promptly asked whether we would then allow the Arabs of Gaza free movement to El Arish, which would be on the Egyptian side of the line. I replied that as soon as normal relations were established between Israel and Egypt, there would be freedom of movement between the two countries, and therefore between Gaza and El Arish. Brzezinski did not appear happy at my having linked such freedom of movement with normalization.

Carter said he had noted down four points which required elucidation: UN forces; Sharm e-Sheikh (the Gulf of Eilat) as an international waterway; oil; and the review of the treaty after a certain period. I told him that we had not raised these matters since they were still under current discussion. On the oil question it was agreed to set up a committee of experts. As for UN forces, I said that if it were not found possible for the UN to assign such a body to carry out the duties of the 'international force' as required by the peace treaty, then it seemed to us that there were only two alternatives: either a United States force or a joint Israeli–Egyptian force. At all events, I added, we would not agree to evacuate Sinai if the territory from which we withdrew were controlled by Egyptian forces alone.

I reminded the President that I had a few requests which concerned America and Israel. The first was that the United States assume responsibility for there being no abrogation of the treaty we would sign with Egypt. We were concerned that Egypt, after our withdrawal from Sinai, might not honour her obligations. Rosenne then read out a proposal we had formulated. Carter smiled and said that in principle he had no objection to involving the United States in our treaty, but not necessarily in the terms of Rosenne's formula. His expression then became serious and he asked whether we would agree to his giving a similar undertaking in the event that we, the Israelis, should breach the treaty. I said we would agree. Brzezinski then jumped in with the observation that the United States would have to be the sole judge of what was considered a breach of the treaty. Carter asked us to present him with the exact text of our proposal. I was pleased to note that not only did he not recoil from the idea but, on the contrary, he regarded such involvement as being an American interest.

I finally broached the matter of United States' financial help for projects directly connected with our retirement from the Sinai peninsula. I told the President that we were now faced with enormous expenditures to transfer our armed forces and civilian settlements from Sinai into Israel proper. The military expenditure alone would be more than two and a half billion dollars. Defence Minister Ezer Weizman then gave details of the main projects: the establishment of new airfields; moving the installations of the land forces; creation of the infrastructure for the new deployment – roads, water, electricity, etc. We would be leaving behind for the Egyptians the infrastructure and some of the installations we had constructed in the course of more than ten years. Egypt would be receiving 'an ordered and well-organized Sinai', while we would have to move to the southern Negev and start from the beginning.

Carter said he was ready to have personnel from the Pentagon examine our requests, but he was unable to commit himself to bearing even the slightest portion of the burden of our expenses. 'We have given you all these years', he said, 'large sums of money, and now, with the approach of peace, we hoped we would be able to diminish the amounts.'

As long as we were discussing the military part of the expenditure, Carter maintained his composure. He promised nothing, but listened attentively to our explanation. However, when I again mentioned our request for financial aid in moving the fourteen civilian settlements, it was argued that America had long regarded these settlements as illegal and an obstacle to peace, and to ask them now to help pay for their removal was rather much. 'This has been the United States' position since 1967. You thought differently. I will not recommend to Congress that any help be extended to you for this. My heart would not be in such a request.'

The tension and hostility in the room was almost tangible, and I thought it appropriate to return to the problem we would face by giving up the offshore oil sources we had developed in the Gulf of Suez. I wanted the President of the United States to recognize how much we would be losing materially by signing the peace treaty, and how much Egypt would be gaining in revenues and resources. I told him that if the joint US–Israel committee of oil experts failed to agree on proposals which would guarantee fuel supplies to Israel after our withdrawal from western Sinai, we would have to return to him for his help. It was inconceivable that we should hand over the oilfields to Egypt without suitable arrangements to replace the supplies we would be losing. It was true, I added, that Butros Ghali had said Egypt would be prepared to sell us the oil from the fields we would be giving them, but the issue was complicated, and we would need more than the non-binding declaration of Ghali.

The meeting ended, and as we got up to leave Carter told me that in addition to meeting the Egyptian delegation that evening, he would also be telephoning both Sadat and Begin to underline the urgency of solving the problems that were still controversial.

The press was waiting as usual as we stepped out of the White House, and in reply to their questions I said we had hit some snags in our negotiations with Egypt, and in our talk with the President we had sought his help in overcoming them. Apparently Carter was not overpleased at my mention of snags and difficulties, and he took the opportunity of telling the press, before the arrival of the Egyptian delegation, that his meetings with us in the afternoon and with the Egyptians in the evening did not signal any special problems. It was simply his first opportunity of meeting the two delegations since the opening of the Blair House Conference, and he wished to hear what progress was being made on those issues which had not yet been resolved. The meetings that day, he said, were purely routine and nothing else. 'Everything has gone as well as can be expected.'

In his talks that night with the Egyptian delegation and, on the telephone, with Sadat and Begin, Carter found himself no closer to solving the controversial problems. But he did not give up, and two days later, on 19 October, he informed us that he would come to Blair House for a joint working lunch with the delegations. He arrived with Atherton and Brzezinski at 12.30. The Egyptians at the lunch were Ali, Ghali, al-Baz and Gorbal; our delegates were Ezer Weizman, Barak, Rosenne and myself.

The President opened by observing that if we failed to reach agreement, he would come up with his own proposals. He listed what he thought were the four issues which appeared intractable: Egypt's obligations under her earlier treaties; the timing for the establishment of diplomatic relations; the Israeli settlement of Naot-Sinai; and Egypt's need to show some achievement on the Palestinian question - the Egyptians had to demonstrate to the Arab world that they had not signed a separate peace. They thought, moreover, that if there was early movement towards the introduction of autonomy in Gaza, King Hussein would agree to join the peace talks.

I mentioned a fifth subject that should be discussed – the involvement of
UN forces in the implementation of the peace treaty. What would happen if
the Security Council failed to approve their despatch to Sinai? Carter replied
that he was aware of the importance of this question for Israel and he would
think of alternatives.

Both delegations then repeated the proposals each had presented to Carter
at their meetings with him two days earlier. To underline their point about
linkage, Ghali and al-Baz said that the leading articles in Cairo's newspapers
that morning had urged the importance of tying the Israel–Egypt peace
treaty to the satisfaction of Palestinian demands. Ghali then asked Atherton
if King Hussein, after receiving from Saunders the American replies to his
questionnaire, would now be joining the peace talks. But it was Gorbal,
Egypt's Ambassador to the United States, who answered his fellow Egyptian. No, Hussein would not be taking part. The King thanked the Americans for their replies, but he saw no basis that would enable him to join.
Gorbal then reported that he had invited the Arab Ambassadors to Washington for a talk, but the Jordanian Ambassador had refused to attend. In
order to move the Jordanians, he observed, they had to be given an induce-
ment. As he said this, both the Egyptians and the Americans looked at us
expectantly. I did not even smile at the sound of this old and worn record, the
repeated efforts to bribe the Arabs in Israeli coinage. I let them stare, and
said not a word.

But Carter kept at it, seeking a compromise. It would not be right, he said,
to separate the two absolutely. On the other hand, he added, 'Moshe is right
when he says that it is out of the question for the maintenance of the Israel–
Egypt treaty to be dependent upon the Palestinians or Jordan.' And he
concluded, therefore, that there had to be a political link while avoiding a
legal link between the two agreements. He also opposed Ghali's proposal
that autonomy should be established first in Gaza. He thought it would be a
mistake to separate Gaza from the West Bank, as it would produce complications for all the agreements, including the Camp David accords, and these
were sacred. If they were tampered with, all would be lost.

Carter said they had information that the Arabs, including the Jordanians
and the Saudis, would encourage the participation of representatives of the
West Bank and Gaza in autonomy talks. To make that possible, Israel would
have to declare publicly that political activity would be permitted for the
purpose of implementing the Camp David agreements. Carter asked us, the
Israelis, to agree to have the point of linkage written not in the body of the
agreement but in the preamble, and also to attach to the agreement an
exchange of letters between Sadat and Begin about ending the Israeli military

government in the territories. From Sadat, he would request the diplomatic exchange of ambassadors immediately on completion of the first phase of Israel's withdrawal from Sinai. On the question of the presence of UN forces, he would try to influence the Chinese and Russians to agree, but if he failed, the Americans would guarantee the despatch of an international force of one kind or another, from Canada or other friendly countries.

I asked the President if Sadat would be prepared to negotiate with us on autonomy even if King Hussein refused to join. Carter said he would.

After a two-hour discussion, Carter concluded with the warning that if we went on arguing about these controversial issues, 'national pride' would become involved and they would be even more difficult to resolve. We were close to agreement, he said, and with a joint effort it would be attained.

This working lunch with the President may not have solved all the problems but it undoubtedly advanced the parties towards their goal. At least we now felt that we were no longer bogged down.

After receiving in Jerusalem our report of the meetings with Carter, Premier Begin said the Government wished to hold deliberations with the participation of the Defence Minister and myself. We arranged to leave on Saturday night, 21 October, which would get us to Jerusalem in time for the regular weekly Sunday morning Cabinet meeting. We informed the Egyptians and Americans that we would be away for a few days. On Friday, the day before our departure, Carter invited Ezer and myself to meet him at 2.30 in the afternoon. We asked whether he could postpone it until the evening as Barak and Rosenne were out of Washington. Carter insisted on our meeting at 2.30 and said there could be a further meeting in the evening with their participation.

That Friday was a very busy day for all of us. Ezer met with Defense Secretary Harold Brown in the morning, and, as he reported, Brown had spoken with concern about the stories in the media that the cost of Israel's withdrawal from Sinai would run to between two and three billion dollars, and this was worrying his Government. Brown believed that Washington had already decided which projects the United States would pay for and which not. To this, Ezer had remarked that President Carter had already promised that America would finance the two new airfields Israel would have to establish in the Negev after abandoning those in Sinai. As for the other huge expenses – the infrastructure, the transfer of our ground forces and installations, and the other military needs – American experts were to visit Israel, carry out their investigations on the spot, make their estimates and submit their proposals. The Government's decision would follow. Ezer said Brown advised us, as a friend, to do nothing which might create the impression that our readiness to make peace was conditional on our receiving American financial help in exchange.

Brown undoubtedly meant well; but the additional economic burdens we would be assuming could not be ignored. On oil, a joint Egypt–Israel committee had finally been set up and was considering various proposals. Representing Israel were Joseph Vardi, Director-General of our Energy Ministry, and Zevi Dinstein, the economics minister at our embassy in Washington. But there was no headway in the crucial area of economic aid. This was being handled by our Ministry of Finance, and the Director-General, Amiram Sivan, had come specially to Washington. But he was kept hanging around, as the US Treasury officials refused to enter into discussions with him as they had received no presidential directive to do so. The grant of aid on the scale required to finance our withdrawal from Sinai could be decided only by the US President. This was a political matter, and before the Treasury experts could get down to work, it had to be dealt with at the highest level, by Begin directly with Carter. I might have spoken to Vance to prepare the ground, but since he was away, I telephoned the Prime Minister and suggested that he have a word with US Ambassador to Israel Samuel Lewis.

The meeting at the White House at 2.30 p.m. on that Friday was very businesslike. I arrived with Ezer, and the President had with him only Brzezinski. Carter explained that before we left for Israel the following night, he wished to ascertain what were the issues, large and small, on which we and the Egyptians still differed. It was his intention, he said, after talking to us, to talk to the Egyptians, and meet with us again in the evening, in an effort to reach an agreed draft which I could take with me to Jerusalem. If he succeeded, he would ask Begin and Sadat to approve it, and thus make possible the signing of the peace treaty. I enjoyed watching Carter in all his obdurate persistence. He was like a bulldog whose teeth were fastened on his victim.

I told him that in the military field, the problem of Egypt's missiles had not yet been resolved. The Egyptians wished to deploy ground-to-air missiles among their forces in Sinai; but these were not an organic part of the weaponry of infantry or armoured forces, and were thus contrary to the Camp David accords. On the political side, the most difficult question was still that of Egypt's prior commitments under earlier treaties. If the Syrians attacked us in the Golan Heights, they could claim they had done so in self-defence, and the Egyptians could go to their aid under their mutual defence pact. This would make our peace treaty with Egypt worthless. Brzezinski suggested several devious solutions, but I refused to deal with them. I said we would be asked about this in public, and we would need to give truthful, clear and convincing answers.

The unresolved issues I mentioned included the linkage between the peace treaty and the Palestinian question; the level and timing of the establishment of diplomatic relations; the boundary west of the Gaza Strip; and freedom of shipping for Israeli vessels through the Suez Canal. The President, as usual, took notes of all these points, and added his own comments in the margin. As we rose to leave, he said he hoped to be able to present us with a final proposal when we returned for our evening meeting.

At 9.30 p.m. we were back in the White House, this time with Ezer and myself having been joined by Barak, Rosenne and Dinitz. The President, too, had strengthened his group, which now included Herbert Hansell, Atherton, Quandt, Jordan and David Aaron.

We started off in a relaxed mood, with Carter giving us the good news first. He said Egypt agreed that our ships would be allowed through the Suez Canal immediately upon ratification of the peace treaty. Egypt also agreed that diplomatic relations would be established at the ambassadorial level. However, as against this, Carter said the Egyptians objected to our proposed formula giving our peace treaty 'priority of obligations'.

At this point Aharon Barak drew forth his trump card. He said this was a central legal question, and he and Rosenne had therefore made a special journey to New Haven, Connecticut, to consult with three Yale professors highly reputed in the field of international law – Eugene Rostow (who had been a former Under-Secretary of State for Political Affairs), M. S. McDougal and L. Lipson. After extensive and detailed deliberations, the American professors had proposed a formula which was virtually identical with ours. They held that the formula proposed in the American draft was inadequate.

President Carter was not only surprised, but also hurt and angered. And he became even more angry when I told him I could not recommend that my Government accept the proposal in the United States draft when it was invalidated by three most distinguished international lawyers. Were we suggesting, he asked, that he, the President, should quit the negotiations and that Israel would conduct them through legal experts?

Neither Barak, who was much esteemed by Carter, nor Rosenne was able to calm him down. The President remained stubborn and said he failed to understand why we attached so much importance to this issue. Barak and Rosenne carefully explained to him, as they had several times before, that we were signing a peace treaty with Egypt knowing that she had earlier signed commitments to join her Arab allies if they should fight us. Therefore it had to be clearly established that our treaty with Egypt took priority. Carter thereupon asked Hansell, the legal adviser to the State Department, to get in touch with Eugene Rostow.

In the meantime the discussions widened to include the controversial linking of the treaty with the Palestinian problem. Carter said we had known very well at Camp David that the two issues were linked. Barak argued that if linkage were included in the preamble, an antidote had to be introduced into the body of the treaty, to ensure that it would remain valid even if no agreement were reached with the Palestinians.

The tone and content now were a departure from businesslike deliberations. I told Carter that it was he himself who had termed the link between the Egyptian and Palestinian issues political and not legal. Here we were dealing with the legal aspect. But the President did not abandon his polemical style. 'Are you prepared to accept every statement I might make?' he asked. 'Not a single one before I hear it,' I replied. I had no taste for this kind of exchange, but there was no escaping it.

The discussions on priority and linkage were accompanied, on Carter's part, by some pretty harsh language. But we, on our part, could not retreat from our position on these vital issues, nor was there reason to. We might alter a particular phrase here or there, but not the content. When the President saw that we could not be moved and there was no point in continuing, he suggested that Hansell, Barak and Rosenne redraft the controversial clauses into a form acceptable to us. If that were done, he asked us, would we then be able to recommend to our Government that they approve the treaty? Barak and Rosenne replied in the affirmative, and I joined them. Next morning, said the President, he would be meeting with the Egyptians and he would try to persuade them. We would hear the results from Atherton.

By the time we broke up it was 11 p.m. We were all tired, and not in the happiest of moods. We left with polite salutations. The President wished us a pleasant journey and we thanked him for devoting so much time to our concerns.

At 8.30 next morning I was called to the telephone. It was the White House. The President wanted to tell me directly, not through Atherton, that at 7 that morning he had seen the Egyptian delegation. They had had a good meeting, and he had no doubt that agreement could be reached. He suggested that we sit with them immediately so that I would be able to take with me to Israel a draft treaty agreed to by all three delegations.

We met the Egyptians together with the Americans at 9.30, and five hours later reached agreed formulae for all the clauses. The corrected texts were sent to the State Department, and within the hour, at 3.30 in the afternoon, we received the new – and agreed – American draft, the seventh!

CHAPTER EIGHTEEN

Change of Mood

We left Washington for New York at the end of the Sabbath aboard an American Air Force plane, and at Kennedy airport we transferred to an El Al aircraft and took off for Israel. The racks held Israel's Friday newspapers, with their high-standard literary supplements, which are a feature even of the mass circulation papers. After reading some of the more interesting articles and the new poems, I turned to another regular feature of the Friday papers which was very familiar to me - the political commentaries. Most were critical of Government policy. Some were sober, presenting a reasoned point of view - though I did not share it - and written in unexceptionable language. Others, however, were full of captious criticism, the tone pseudo-philosophical, arrogant, and often malicious. They gave me a tired feeling. I was saddened by those fellow Israelis who weakened our hands by criticizing us for not acceding to the demands of radical Arab nationalists, just as I was by the preaching of some of my fellow Jews in the free countries. As I read the carping commentaries, they triggered the memory of the Galilee village of Ma'alot, and the faces of the children who were shot to death by Arab terrorists, sent on an operational mission by the Palestinian 'freedom movement'. I thrust the newspapers aside in a murky mood.

The stewardess came along to prepare the table for dinner, but I was no longer hungry. I asked instead for a blanket and pillow. She reappeared a few minutes later with a message from the captain offering me a bunk in the crew's rest cabin. I declined with thanks. If I had not felt so depressed, I might not have recalled my reservations about El Al captains. Almost all were former regulars in the Israel Air Force, and I had held them in great esteem. As Chief of Staff or Minister of Defence, when I had heard the debriefings on their return from aerial battle, I could have hugged them. They were superb. They were dedicated men, prepared to give their all for the State. Yet these same men, as soon as they changed their Air Force blue for the uniform of the national airline - though still in the reserves - seemed to have become different. Their professional union demanded from the young and needy State *de luxe* salaries for their commercial services. This took the edge off the warm feeling I had had for them when they were fighter pilots, and in the mood I was in I preferred not to accept the hospitality of their cabin. There was no hammock this time, and so I curled up on the floor behind the seats and closed my eyes.

Flooding into my mind came the vision of other groups of dedicated people I had known, who had carried over their youthful idealism into their later years, their spirit unchanged. These were the kibbutzniks and moshavniks who had pioneered the settlements of Deganiah in the Jordan Valley and Nahalal and Kfar Yehoshua and Ein Harod in the Valley of Jezreel. I pictured them now as they were when age had overtaken them – pioneers like Chaim Sturman, women like my mother, their faces creased and worn, but still plodding through the orchards of a revived Jezreel hip-high in mud in winter, or dehydrating in the new plantations near the Jordan in the burning summer sun. And I saw them at the end of a hard working day attending a general meeting or a long lecture on some serious subject – which they would never dream of missing, though weary unto death, lids drooping, trying to fight off the urgency of sleep.

The transition from this vision to biblical times was almost automatic. I thought of King Saul, who even after being crowned continued to plough his fields with his own hands, the tragic Saul whom the Prophet Samuel never stopped rebuking, while the King never stopped fighting Israel's enemies, right up to the last day of his life. And what a final day that was! He, who during his reign banned witchcraft and soothsayers, had gone secretly to the 'witch of Endor' the previous evening for a forecast of how the battle would go against the Philistines at Mount Gilboa on the morrow. And who should the witch conjure out of the depths to answer Saul's desperate question? None other than the ghost of Samuel, who now told Saul grimly, 'tomorrow you and your sons shall be with me': defeat in battle, death of the King and his sons. But also consolation – the fate that awaits us all. In the end, Saul would be joining Samuel. And what an end, the end of a leader of Israel who had begun life as a soldier fighting for his people, and ended it in the same way; a leader who between battles had worked his fields, and was buried beneath a tamarisk tree: death of a warrior-farmer.

The luxurious Madison Hotel, the State Department, the White House, the negotiations and the legal formulae – all vanished into the mists of the past. And the criticism inside the Government and the heckling in the Knesset which awaited me, also seemed unimportant. The fighters and pioneers of Israel had always overcome difficulties, in the past and in the present.

I got up from the floor, folded the blankets, went to shave, and returned to my seat next to Rahel. She, who knows what I need without my saying a word, asked the stewardess for strong coffee and croissants. 'In a little while', she said, her face lighting up, 'we'll be home.'

Ezer and I spent four days in Israel, and flew back to Washington on the morning of 26 October 1978. During those four days there were two Cabinet sessions, one meeting with the Foreign Affairs and Defence Committee of the Knesset, and one with the Knesset's Likud coalition faction.

We met the Prime Minister before the first Cabinet meeting, seeing him, as usual, in his home. Also, as usual, we were served tea. Begin, like my parents and others brought up in Russia or Poland, was a confirmed tea drinker, and I fancy that what he would most like to do is restore the samovar to its former place of honour in the home.

He had no need for any further reports of our Washington talks. He had received all the information, and he not only knew all the various formulae by heart but was also familiar with their evolution through all their incarnations. The question we had met to consider was 'What next?' I recommended advancing the date of our evacuation of western Sinai. If we did this, and the normalization of our relations with Egypt were to become operative when we retired to the El Arish–Ras Mohammad line, we would then have more time at our disposal before our total withdrawal from Sinai. This additional time was highly important to us, since this was the very period when it would be possible to gauge Egypt's behaviour. It was to our advantage, I said, to put the peaceful relations to the test while we were still in control of the eastern region of Sinai, the area which contained our military airfields and civilian settlements.

The Prime Minister said he had received a letter from Carter in which the President informed him that he had asked Sadat to accept our position on the missile batteries, the exclusion of the Naot-Sinai settlement from the area of our withdrawal, and the establishment of diplomatic relations within one month of our first-phase retirement. It was to be assumed that these issues would be settled with a favourable response from Sadat.

On the question of the status of Gaza, I told Begin that we had to be careful not to lose what we had gained – recognition of the international border as the boundary line between Israel and Egypt. (The Gaza District was on the Israeli side of the international boundary.) This was the first and only one of our borders which was recognized, if not by every country, at least by the United States and Egypt: the border running from the Mediterranean to Eilat. The future of the Gaza District was a separate question, and was not to be involved in the subject of the border. We had to find a formula, acceptable to both parties, that would include Gaza within the autonomy framework. The Egyptians had agreed that that border ran west of Gaza and was to be guarded by Israel Army forces, so that anyone wishing to cross the frontier into the Gaza District had to behave in accordance with the laws of the State of Israel. We should on no account depart from this formula.

On Israeli settlements, I proposed to the Prime Minister that we notify the US Secretary of State that the term of our agreement to freeze settlements had now expired, and it was our intention in the near future to add a few hundred families to existing settlements. The Americans would be angry, but they should know that we could not ignore the statement of Assistant Secretary of State Harold Saunders about the 'temporary nature' of the settlements. We would fulfil all the obligations to which we had committed ourselves at Camp David, but we would not go beyond them. I stressed, however, that settlement should not be accompanied by land expropriation and should not be established on private Arab property.

At the Cabinet meeting, and in the discussions with the Knesset groups, the Defence Minister and I gave our report, and we also presented the positions we had taken. In the deliberations that followed, sharp criticism, as expected, was directed against our delegation: we had conceded too much. The delegation's jurists, Barak and Rosenne, successfully rebutted most of the legal arguments, but several ministers and Knesset members said we should have gained more than we did.

The crucial question was whether the Government would approve or reject the agreement we had reached at Blair House – American draft No. 7. I warned my colleagues that unless they approved the agreement as it stood, in all its parts, Israel would be blamed for the failure to achieve peace. Begin understood this, and though he wanted certain changes, he threw his full weight behind approval. Of the sixteen ministers at the Cabinet meeting, fourteen voted for the resolution proposed by the Prime Minister, which stated:

The Government approves in principle the draft peace treaty between Israel and Egypt which was brought before it by the delegation to the peace talks in Washington. The Government approves the changes proposed by the Prime Minister to the draft peace treaty. The Government accordingly gave appropriate directives to the delegation, and authorized it to continue the negotiations for the signing of the peace treaty. . . . The final draft of the peace treaty with Egypt, with all its appendices, will be brought for approval before the Government and the Knesset.

Despite this favourable Government decision, I had no wish to ignore the critical mood I encountered both in the Cabinet and among the Likud faction in the Knesset, the mainstay of the coalition. I was particularly concerned about the autonomy plan for the inhabitants of the administered territories, and although there had been no formal deliberations on the handling of the negotiations and the implementation of the plan, I was anxious for the Prime Minister to know my views. I therefore wrote him a letter on the eve of my return to Washington, saying that I had wished to be the one who dealt with this matter, since I regarded the problem of living together with the Arabs, without abandoning our interests, as being of central importance. However, in the light of the strong criticism in the Cabinet and the Knesset coalition parties, I proposed that the Government should discuss and decide who was to be in charge of the autonomy negotiations. Should another minister be given the responsibility, the Foreign Ministry would, of course, send its representatives and extend its wholehearted co-operation, if requested. But I personally would take no part.

This was not, nor was it intended to be, a threatening letter to compel the Prime Minister to give me the appointment. There could be no threat anyway, since I was fairly certain that Begin himself did not wish me to head the negotiations on autonomy. Nor did I seek a more honoured status and function within the Government. I wrote this letter simply because I was convinced that we had a chance of moulding the nature of co-existence with the Arabs of the West Bank and Gaza only if we followed the policy which I espoused. I was not prepared to compromise on this issue, and I thought it right and proper to make my position clear to the Prime Minister. He could then decide whatever he thought best – with me or without me.

We reached Washington in the late afternoon, and awaiting us at the airport was Alfred Atherton. It was not only protocol that brought him. He wished to talk to us on an urgent matter, and as soon as Defence Minister Weizman and I entered his car, he handed us a copy of a letter Carter was sending to Premier Begin. Atherton said that our decision to extend our settlements had caused a storm in Washington. The President was absolutely furious, holding that it was contrary to the Camp David accords and severely harmed the peace talks. Carter said that our delegation had explained at Camp David that additional people had to be allowed to join the existing settlements only for humanitarian reasons – wives and children to rejoin husbands and fathers. Secretary Vance had published an official statement denouncing the Israeli decision.

I told Atherton that nothing of the kind had ever been said at Camp David, and he would do well to examine the transcript of our talks. Our principal argument – and I remembered that it was I who put it forward – was that it was impossible to maintain a settlement without a suitable number of members. It was inconceivable to provide such essential services as schooling, medical facilities, shopping, and guard duties for only a handful of people. As for the President's complaint, reported by Atherton, about the timing of our decision, I told him they should have thought of that when they sent Saunders to King Hussein to deliver America's replies to the royal questionnaire. Atherton then said that the President expected the Prime Minister's response to his letter to be an instruction to cease expanding the settlements. I said I was not authorized to speak on behalf of the Prime Minister, but in my judgment there was not the slightest chance that he would agree.

We went on to discuss the continuation of the negotiations, and Atherton said that Vance had returned to Washington and intended to devote most of his time to our talks. He would like to meet us next day, and to receive before that any proposed changes in the draft treaty we had brought from Israel. He had already been given the ones from Egypt.

All this was in the car from the airport to the hotel. Before leaving us, Atherton mentioned casually that he had heard that the Egyptian delegation had been recalled to Cairo for consultations. This surprised me, and I also detected from the tone and manner in which Atherton had tossed off the information that behind it lay a hint of pressure. I told him that before leaving Washington for Israel we had notified them of the date we would be returning. If the Egyptians were now planning to leave, there was no point in our remaining. We would return to Israel and get back to Washington when the Egyptians did so. We had not come just to twiddle our thumbs in the US capital. The Egyptians did not leave after all.

At 10.15 next morning, Ezer and I met Vance in his office at the State Department. The Secretary repeated what we had heard from Atherton and expressed his grave displeasure at our decision to expand the settlements. He was also displeased by what he called the personal attacks in Israel on Harold Saunders. To this I replied that it was not a personal matter, and we would make the same protest if the American replies to King Hussein had been announced by the Secretary himself. On the substance of Saunders' words, did the United States Government think we would accept them in silence? What had happened was that at the very moment when we were negotiating over the desired pattern of living together with the Arabs, the Americans declared that we would be withdrawing from the West Bank, Gaza and East Jerusalem, and that we would have to dismantle our settlements. We were talking of co-existence, and they, the Americans, of our evacuation from the territories. Did he himself, I asked Vance, think that the US announcements contributed to the achievement of an agreement between us and the Arabs on the basis of the autonomy plans? If they came out with such declarations, did they really expect us to do and say nothing?

The Defence Minister reinforced my words. Ezer told him of the mood in Israel, and said that if anyone, American or Arab, thought that our evacuation of Sinai was to be taken as a model for the other fronts, he was deluding himself. Neither from the West Bank and Gaza nor from the Golan Heights would we remove our settlements or fail to maintain a military presence.

We were to meet again that afternoon. Vance said he had hoped it would be a tripartite meeting, but the Egyptians had refused to attend, so it would be just us and the Americans.

I left the State Department sensing that there was a fundamental change in the atmosphere. Instead of holding constructive negotiations, we were again in the dock facing charges.

A telephone call from Prime Minister Begin introduced some brightness into the Washington gloom. He informed me with understandable emotion that he and Sadat had been awarded the Nobel Peace Prize. I offered him heartfelt congratulations both from myself and on behalf of the other members of the delegation. Begin asked me to transmit through the Egyptian delegation his felicitations to Sadat. This I declined. Ezer and I had asked to meet Ali and Ghali, but they had been evasive. Moreover, I did not want us to be put in the position of congratulating their President without receiving a reciprocal greeting to Begin.

On 28 October we met with the full US delegation, headed by Secretary Vance. (It was our Sabbath, so the Americans came to our hotel.) On the agenda were our proposed changes in the draft treaty, and Barak and Rosenne explained the legal aspects of our demands. The discussion on these legal points took up most of the meeting, and included various suggested formulae. It seemed that some of our proposals would be accepted, but these did not include the principal subjects: the link between the Israel–Egypt treaty and the Palestinian issue; and the contradiction between our treaty with Egypt and her commitments in treaties with other Arab States. On these two matters, not only did Vance disagree with our formulae, but he also stubbornly refused 'to open them anew'. According to him, any attempt to change what had been achieved after so much effort, and after the pressure exerted on the Egyptians by President Carter, would have the opposite effect. The Egyptians might even go back on what they had already agreed to.

We telephoned Begin and reported on the results of the talk. The Prime Minister suggested that I request a meeting with the President. I declined. There was no chance at the moment, I told him, of persuading Carter to accept our position. If we met, all he would do was criticize us severely for our decision to expand our settlements. If he, Begin, thought it important for us to approach Carter again on these subjects, I suggested that he had best do so himself in a personal letter.

As the Egyptians were keeping away from us, I gave instructions that no member of our delegation should get in touch with them. I judged that either the negotiations would come to a dead end or the Egyptians would approach us. And, indeed, on the following day, Ali, the head of the Egyptian delegation, asked to meet me. I said I would be happy to receive him, adding that I would be joined by Ezer. Ali said he would be accompanied by Butros Ghali.

We met at 6 on that Sunday evening and talked for two hours. This was one of the most difficult meetings we had had, but also one of the most important in clarifying the issues between us and the Egyptians.

The 'sulking game' played by the Americans and the Egyptians upon our return to Washington had been childish. To make peace with us, they had to talk to us. We might then reach, or fail to reach, agreement; but we would certainly not accept ultimatums. Even as a tactic, designed to soften us up, it was pointless. After all, it was not we but the Egyptians who wanted us out of Sinai, together with our settlements and our troops. If the negotiations broke down, we would be blamed for being inflexible; but we would remain in Sinai.

Vance recognized this from the outset, did his best to ignore the annoying problems created by an ill-advised manoeuvre, and concentrated on advancing the negotiations and resolving the differences between the parties. To my regret, however, not everything rested with him. In a moment of utter frankness, he told me that he was unable to reply to some of our queries because when he brought them to the President he could get no answers. Carter at the time was silent and impenetrable on matters affecting us, continuing to claim that he had been led astray on the settlement issue. The truth was that if the US President wanted clear and specific commitments from us, he should have demanded and tried to get them before the signing of the Camp David accords. Since he was then satisfied with the limited commitment Begin was prepared to give, he could not now blame us but only himself.

As for the evasive behaviour of Ali and Ghali, I presumed that they were simply following orders from Sadat. It was he who decided to ban, and he who decided to renew, their talks with us. When Sadat cancelled the 'quarantine' and Ali and Ghali came to my room, I remarked to Ghali that he must have been very busy indeed if he could not find ten minutes for a talk with me. Ghali responded with an artificial chuckle.

Though Ali was the head of the Egyptian mission, it was Ghali who was the chief spokesman, and that evening, too, it was he who opened the discussion. They were worried, he said, by the 'accidents' that occurred from time to time. He was referring to our decision to expand the settlements and our intention to move our Prime Minister's Office to East Jerusalem.

I said it was good that we were having this talk, for it was now incumbent upon us to clear the table and clarify to each other, openly and sincerely, where each of us stood. At Camp David, I reminded them, we had committed ourselves to freeze the establishment of new settlements for three months; but we never agreed to stop the strengthening of existing settlements. The Egyptians could be assured that what we promised not to do we would not do, and what we said we would do, we certainly would. If they thought there was any analogy between what we had agreed to in Sinai and what we might do in the West Bank and Gaza, they were making a basic error of judgment. We had no intention of abandoning these territories. We would not remove our settlements nor remain without a military presence there. This fact was the principle guiding our conduct in the peace negotiations. We were proposing autonomy for the Arab population in these territories, but this would be accompanied by a continued Israeli presence. We had no wish to rule the Arabs. The basis of our plan was co-existence, not evacuation. We could redeploy our troops, but we would not withdraw them to the 1967 borders. Our forces would be deployed along the River Jordan and mountain ridges in order to safeguard the security of Israel, and for our security we would not rely on the United States nor on the Egyptians.

As I spoke, I saw Ghali's expression getting more and more gloomy. Ali, on the other hand, did not seem shocked. Ghali repeated that Egypt wanted independence for the Palestinian Arabs; but even granting our opposing positions, did we not think that our decision on expanded settlements was ill-timed? To this I replied that the timing was determined by the statements of Saunders and the reaction to them in Jordan and Israel. Just as the Americans and they, the Egyptians, had their problems with the Arab world, so did we have internal problems with our Israeli public.

Ghali seized upon my mention of problems with the Arab world to lecture us on their gravity. He cited as an example Saudi Arabia's decision to slash the financial help she had promised Egypt for her acquisition of the F 15 warplanes. He was not amused when I remarked that I had read about the Saudi financial cut in the press a week before we had made our settlements decision.

Ali broke through this discussion by saying that we had to find a common tongue and avoid surprises, and there was a slight lowering of the tension. Ezer told of some of his talks with Sadat, and stressed that Egypt's President had never spoken of our having to leave the West Bank and Gaza District. On the contrary, Sadat had always explained that we had to find some way of living together with the Arabs in those territories. Ezer also reiterated Israel's intention to keep settlements and troops there permanently.

Since I was anxious in this talk to exhaust all aspects of the points at issue, I told the Egyptian ministers that we would not agree to grant Egypt a special status in the Gaza District. I reminded them that I had already made this clear at the Leeds Castle Conference. Ghali observed that their request at Leeds Castle had been a tactical move to bring Jordan to the conference table. Ali confirmed this.

We moved on to the subject of the Palestinians, and we were all of one mind that without the agreement and co-operation of the Arab residents of the West Bank and Gaza, there would be no autonomy.

Vance gave a dinner party in his home for the members of our delegation and some of his senior aides in the evening of 30 October. The object undoubtedly was to inject a little warmth into the chilly behaviour of the Americans since our return to Washington a few days earlier, and it was, indeed, a very pleasant evening. The Vances are perfect hosts, the gracious Gay, and the courteous - and hard-working - Cyrus, skilfully carving the roast turkey and handing to each his favourite portion. We talked very little business. Atherton told me that next day, at last, there would be a meeting of all three delegations. I advised Vance not to raise the question of Jerusalem nor to ask officially about the Prime Minister's intention to move his office to East Jerusalem, which in any case was not about to be implemented. If and when we decided to act, we would do so openly and not as thieves in the night. I reminded him that Begin was due in New York in another two days. Vance would be meeting him and could ask him directly.

Begin arrived on 1 November. He was on his way to Canada on an official visit and stopped over in New York for a couple of days. We received him at the airport and had consultations with him that evening and next morning before his meeting with Vance.

The Prime Minister said he proposed to take up with the Secretary two main subjects: economic aid; and the linkage between our treaty and Palestinian autonomy. Begin added that, in accordance with our Government's decision, he would insist on removing or changing the sentence in the preamble to the treaty which made the maintenance of peace with Egypt conditional upon our reaching an agreement with the Palestinians and the Government of Jordan.

He also told me of the new work-pattern of the Cabinet in reviewing the draft treaty. This, at first, had been entrusted to the ministerial defence committee. But when he saw that the other ministers were disgruntled, Begin decided that the entire Cabinet would consider and decide on the drafting of each clause.

The meeting with Vance took place in the Prime Minister's suite in the Regency Hotel. Vance came with Atherton and Saunders, and together with Begin were Ezer, Barak, Rosenne and myself.

All went well at the beginning. Begin presented the treaty changes we proposed and underpinned them with cogent argument. He also produced the draft of a joint letter on the autonomy discussions to be signed by him and Sadat. Though Vance had reservations about some of Begin's suggestions, good progress was made.

The difficulties started when we reached the principal points of controversy. Vance was adamant in rejecting Begin's demand to change the unfortunate sentence in the preamble to the treaty. The Prime Minister gave all the valid reasons behind our demand, but there was nothing new in that. Barak and Rosenne had done the same on earlier occasions with no less skill. The one point which Begin added, and which appeared apologetic, was that our Cabinet had taken a unanimous decision on the subject. Vance explained that he and the President rejected our proposal since there was no chance that Egypt would accept it, and if the United States exerted pressure on Sadat to give way, Sadat would in turn raise his own demands, and it would mean restarting the negotiations from scratch.

The big surprise came, however, during the discussion on economic aid. The Prime Minister asked not for a grant but a loan. 'We shall repay', he stressed, 'every penny that we receive! We shall make our annual payments without delay.'

Begin explained that Israel lacked the financial resources to erect all the installations required to replace those we would be leaving behind in Sinai. We would be in danger, he said, of achieving peace and going bankrupt. The sum involved was three billion eight hundred million dollars. This would include the cost of establishing two new air bases and transferring the farm settlements. He had spoken to our Finance Minister, and we were requesting this amount as a twenty-five-year loan at an interest of between two and four per cent. He knew, said Begin, that the request for help in transferring the settlements had angered the President. We did not want to move them; but unless we did we would have failed to reach a peace agreement with the Egyptians. He, Begin, had had to weigh up and decide between holding on to the settlements in Sinai and peace. He had chosen peace. He then said he

would like our Finance Minister, Simcha Ehrlich, to come to Washington the
following week to discuss the details of our request with Treasury Secretary
Blumenthal.

I was not the only one to be surprised by Begin's request for a loan rather
than a grant. Ezer said that the financing of the new air bases had already
been arranged.

Vance said that, of course, he could tell us nothing until he had first spoken
to the President, and the President would then have to speak to the leaders of
Congress. This could not be done in the next few days as Carter was busy
appearing on election platforms in support of Democratic Party candidates.
That very day, for example, he was in New York appearing with Koch who
was running for Mayor.

I asked Vance if we could at least say that he, Vance, had asked Israel's
Finance Minister to come to Washington soon to discuss the economic
aspect. Vance refused. He wished to say nothing on this subject until it had
been considered by the President and the Congressional leaders.

The meeting ended, and Begin and Vance went off to meet Carter. This
was a chapter in itself. On his arrival in New York the previous evening *en
route* to Canada, Begin had been asked by correspondents whether any
meeting had been scheduled with the President. No, said Begin. This was
reported in the media as a demonstrative snub by Carter to the Prime
Minister.

During our session with Vance next morning, the Secretary was called to
the telephone, and he took the call in another room. When he returned, he
told Begin that the President would like 'to shake his hand and say hello'.
Could Begin come at 1.30 to the home of Arthur Krim? (Krim, a wealthy
Jewish supporter of the Democratic Party, was hosting the President during
his electioneering visit to New York.) Begin accepted, observing that 'this
will put an end to talk of the snub'. And so the two met, shook hands, and
said hello.

Begin went on to Canada and we returned to Washington, to learn from
Atherton that the formula submitted by Begin on the offending sentence in
the preamble had been turned down flat. The Egyptians were resolutely
against any change. We also learned that Butros Ghali and al-Baz were going
to Cairo for consultations and would be returning in a few days. Awaiting us
was a cable from Israel informing us that the Government did not accept our
recommendation to advance our withdrawal to the El Arish line and hand
over the city to the Egyptians six months after the signing of the treaty. The
Government insisted on adhering to the timetable agreed upon at Camp

David whereby we would evacuate El Arish after nine months. Ezer decided on a flying visit to Jerusalem to discuss this further with the Government and the General Staff.

There was an outcry in Israel when press reports appeared that Premier Begin had asked for a loan and not a grant to cover the huge cost of our withdrawal from Sinai. Finance Minister Ehrlich asked us for urgent clarification, and I saw Vance on 4 November, two days after his meeting with Begin. I informed him that the Prime Minister wished to correct what he had said about the loan. We requested that the seven hundred million dollars required for the construction of the two air bases should be a grant and the rest a loan. Vance reacted sharply, saying that he had reported Israel's request to the President in Begin's very words. He had done the same at a press conference in reply to a question, stating that Israel had asked for a loan, not a grant.

The unfortunate meeting in New York, the negative response to changing the preamble, the American refusal to meet with our Finance Minister, and the handshake meeting of the President and Begin, were hardly calculated to raise our spirits.

When we resumed our talks in Washington, as there was little point in dealing with the demands which had been raised in New York with the Prime Minister, we moved on to two other subjects which still needed to be explored. These were the bilateral agreements between the United States and Israel; and the appendices to the treaty, which included both military and political provisions. There were four proposed agreements with the United States: reiteration of past US commitments to Israel; US involvement and responsibility in the implementation of our peace treaty with Egypt; America's responsibility to supply an alternative to the UN forces if these should not be forthcoming; and matters arising from our withdrawal from the Sinai oilfields.

Military affairs were dealt with on the American side by General Lawrence, while Vance, Atherton and legal adviser Hansell handled the other topics. On our side, these subjects were dealt with by the whole delegation, except for oil, which was handled separately by a team headed by our Energy Minister, Yitzhak Modai. The bilateral agreements and appendices, like the treaty itself, were reviewed in Israel by the entire Cabinet, which showered us with ideas, criticisms, approval and censure.

Butros Ghali returned from Cairo on 9 November. Vance had asked to meet him at 4.30 that afternoon, but Ghali said he was tired and would meet the Secretary the next day. The truth was that he wished to meet with us first. At 5 o'clock he and Ambassador Gorbal came to my room, and our meeting lasted three hours. With me were Ezer, who had been to Israel and back, and Rubinstein.

Ghali appeared more resolute and unequivocal than usual, due, no doubt, to his having just come from Cairo with clear instructions from Sadat. He did not hide the fact that the Baghdad Conference, which had ended four days earlier, had been a shock to the Egyptians, with its denunciatory resolutions against the Camp David accords and attacks on Egypt. Contrary to their hopes and to America's assumptions, Saudi Arabia and Jordan had joined their opponents. Even Mahmoud Riad, Secretary of the Arab League, himself an Egyptian and a former Foreign Minister, had voted in favour of transferring the Arab League secretariat from Cairo to Tunis. The conference had also resolved that if Egypt were to come to terms with Israel, she would be subjected to an economic and political boycott by all the Arab States. This was likely to cause Egypt grave harm. More than a million Egyptians had jobs in the Arab States, and if they were dismissed and returned to Egypt they would swell the unemployment rolls. There was also a more direct financial aspect: if the Arab States stopped their grants, and drew out their deposits from Egyptian banks, they could cause an economic crisis. All this was widely known by the Egyptian public, said Ghali, the topic of daily talk and press reports. Nevertheless, Sadat was firm in his intention to continue the peace process.

However, Ghali went on, in order to preserve his standing and prestige, Sadat had to show that he was not abandoning the pan-Arab aims and ideals, and it was for this reason that his principal demands concerned the Palestinians. It was up to Israel to follow in practice the principles on this issue which were determined at Camp David. Egypt had committed herself to a timetable whereby she would establish diplomatic relations with Israel and introduce normalization, whereas Israel had made no practical commitment on the subject of the Palestinians. Indeed, we were continuing with our settlement, and Prime Minister Begin in recent speeches in New York had declared that Greater Jerusalem would remain within Israel's sovereignty. The Prime Minister knew that there was a conflict of opinion over Jerusalem, so why should he bring up the subject now in his speeches? Our behaviour was causing Egypt embarrassment and putting her in an untenable position.

Ghali concluded with the information that he had been instructed in Cairo to insist on the inclusion in a joint Sadat-Begin letter of a specific timetable for the implementation of autonomy for the Palestinians. The timetable was to contain clauses covering the following four stages: within one month of their signing the peace treaty, Israel and Egypt were to start the autonomy negotiations; it was to be agreed in advance that elections to the Palestinian

Council (to replace the military government) were to be held five months after the signature of the peace treaty; one month later, the Israeli military government was to hand over its authority to the newly elected Council; thereafter, the Israel Army would carry out its redeployment in the West Bank and Gaza District.

Ghali added that even according to this proposed schedule it would take time before autonomy was established. Egypt therefore wished to return to the subject on which they had already talked to us at Camp David – that Israel make unilateral gestures of goodwill, and make them as quickly as possible so as to win over the Palestinian Arabs to the side of Egypt. Ghali went on to state specifically what these 'gestures' should be: removal of military government headquarters from the Arab towns; freedom of political activity in the administered territories; release of Arab prisoners (serving sentences for terrorist action); the return to the West Bank and Gaza District of two thousand Arabs who had fled during the 1967 war; and allowing a permanent Egyptian mission to be stationed in Gaza.

Ghali explained why elections to a Palestinian Council should be held not later than five months after the treaty signing: to show the Arab States that the Palestinians had gained self-government before Egypt had established normal and diplomatic relations with Israel.

That was the operative message that Ghali brought back from Cairo. But what I found of special interest was the picture that emerged of Egypt, a country beset by grave internal and external problems, increasingly isolated among the Arab countries as well as the nations of the Third World, and complaints against Israel's behaviour from Egyptian army commanders and supporters of Sadat's peace process. Ghali and Gorbal had another such complaint when Ezer reported to them that the Israeli Government had not endorsed his recommended gesture to hand over El Arish within six months – in advance of the date agreed upon at Camp David. They considered this 'a violation of the agreement'! Even at Camp David, they said, they had gathered that Israel would indeed shorten the term from nine to six months, and up to that very week, in all their talks with our military delegation, they had assumed that this would be done. True, they added, we had said that anything agreed on by our delegation in Washington had to be approved by our Government; but they never imagined that this would not be forthcoming.

Ezer and I told Ghali and Gorbal that Blair House was not the place to lodge their proposals and demands on the Palestinian issue. At this conference we were dealing, and authorized to deal, with the peace treaty between Egypt and Israel and not with the Palestinians. We would transmit Ghali's message to Jerusalem, but we were not the address for replies. Unofficially, however, I could tell them that Prime Minister Begin was ready to start the autonomy talks one month after the ratification of the peace treaty. Israel would not commit herself to hold elections to the Palestinian Council after five months. The point made by Ghali was the very one that deterred us: we were against making the implementation of the peace treaty with Egypt conditional on Palestinian autonomy. On the contrary, we wanted to see the fulfilment of the terms of the treaty, including the exchange of ambassadors and the economic and cultural agreements, before the implementation of autonomy. As for our military government's local headquarters in Arab towns, Ezer and I said we would recommend that they be removed as soon as possible from Gaza and Nablus; but this did not mean any diminution of military government authority. It was simply a technical change. On Ghali's request for a permanent Egyptian mission in Gaza, I reminded him that this had been proposed at Camp David and turned down by us. When diplomatic relations were established, Egypt could open a consulate in Gaza, just as we would be able to open one in Alexandria. His other requests, such as allowing the immediate return of two thousand refugees to the West Bank and Gaza District, also did not seem to me to be valid. There was an orderly process governing the return of refugees within the category of reuniting families, which included security checks of the applicants. This could not be waived. The process might be hastened but it could not be abolished.

I did not interrupt Ghali or Gorbal when they spoke; nor, when I had the floor, did I counter their arguments and demands by restating Israel's position. They had already heard that time and again, just as I had heard theirs, and I had no wish to score debating points. But I confess that while listening to them I wondered at their boldness. We were giving up the whole of Sinai, leaving our air bases and our settlements and the oilfields, and here they were asking us for 'unilateral gestures', as though such huge concessions on our part for peace were not gesture enough. We were being asked to release Arab prisoners who were in jail after due process for having committed murder and sabotage, when in any Arab country such men guilty of terrorist acts would have been summarily executed – prisoners who, if released, would be sent in again on terrorist missions. But I said none of these things to Ghali and Gorbal: they were known to them anyway. I was there not to parry arguments but to try to make peace.

The one positive element in Ghali's presentation was not in what he said but what he did not say. He did not propose reopening the discussion on the treaty or changes in any of its clauses. The general spirit in which he spoke was harsh, but I had the impression that this indeed stemmed from Egypt's difficulties and from their reluctance to enter into a separate peace with us. Peace – yes: I felt that their basic aim had not changed, and that Sadat wanted to make peace with us – but not a separate peace.

We flew to Toronto next day, 10 November, to report to the Prime Minister on our talk with Ghali. Energy Minister Modai was also with us to report on his oil negotiations. The Egyptians were refusing to grant us special rights. They took the position that with the establishment of normal relations, we could buy oil or bid for drilling rights like any other country.

Nor was there any good news to report to Begin on financial aid. All my efforts to get Vance to agree to Treasury Secretary Blumenthal's discussing our request proved fruitless. The Americans were not even prepared to let Blumenthal hear what we had to say without reacting. He was not authorized, said Vance, even to listen.

Ezer reported on his brief visit to Jerusalem, speaking with bitterness at the reception he got at the Cabinet meeting. Even before he had a chance to open his mouth, the Minister of Education had asked him, 'Well, what did you sell today?' This, said Weizman, was a Government hostile to its Washington delegation.

We left Begin to return to Blair House after arranging, at the suggestion of Vance, a further meeting between him and the Prime Minister. Vance and his aides would come to Kennedy airport when Begin made a stop over landing in New York on his flight back to Israel from Canada.

Butros Ghali handed Vance the instructions he had been given by Sadat on the subject of the Palestinians, and the White House foresaw a critical encounter with us. The Egyptian demands were extreme, and there was still no American response in the areas of oil and economic aid. It was in this atmosphere of imminent crisis that a 'senior official' in the White House (Jody Powell) gave a background briefing on 10 November in which he spoke of America's 'growing concern over the outcome of the talks' and impatience with 'the continued haggling over details'. He added that 'neither side is the villain of the piece'. But press commentators hastened to explain that these White House remarks were intended as a message to Israel, warning her not to hold up progress in the negotiations.

The next day, Atherton gave us the Egyptian delegation's proposals on autonomy, together with suggestions from the State Department. The Egyptians proposed that there should be a joint letter signed by Sadat and Begin setting out, among other things, the autonomy timetable as outlined by Ghali at our meeting two days earlier. This letter was to be attached to the peace treaty.

The difference between this proposal and the accompanying State Department suggestions was insignificant, except for the American submission that the timetable should be regarded as a goal – to offer a certain flexibility – rather than a fixed schedule. What irked me in the behaviour of the Americans was not only their virtually complete identification with the Egyptian demands but that they should have sent a copy of their suggestions to the Egyptian delegation. They must have known that doing this would make it very difficult to get the Egyptians to change their stand. Why should they be ready to compromise more than the Americans thought necessary?

Atherton also gave us the draft of a letter he wanted me to sign in which I would inform the Egyptians of the unilateral 'gestures' which Israel was to make immediately upon the signing of the peace treaty and before the start of the autonomy talks. This list, too, matched the list we had heard from Ghali, but at least this time the Americans had the good grace not to send a copy to the Egyptians. I told Atherton I would transmit copies to the Prime Minister, who was still in Canada, and to Jerusalem, but I added that to me they were not acceptable. I also thought it well to tell him what I thought of the technique adopted by the Americans in sending a copy of their suggestions to the Egyptians: it only made the achievement of an agreement that much harder. Atherton countered with a lollipop – Treasury Secretary Blumenthal would be ready to listen to what our Finance Minister Ehrlich had to say about economic aid!

When Israel's Cabinet received the report on the Egyptian and American proposals, the ministers were extremely angry. Some recommended that we break off the talks. The Cabinet statement at the end of the regular Sunday morning meeting on 12 November announced that the new Egyptian demands deviated from the Camp David accords and were unacceptable to Israel. The very submission of these demands made the negotiations more burdensome and added grave difficulties to the agreed path to peace.

After the talk with Atherton came a meeting with Vance. The mood was sombre, the difference of opinion wide. The Secretary said that the agreement which had been reached at Camp David was beginning to disintegrate. The instructions from both the Egyptian and Israeli Governments were becoming more and more harsh, and mutual suspicion was on the increase. He had had long talks with the Egyptian delegation, and it was clear to him that if Israel would not make a commitment to hand over El Arish within six months following the treaty signing, Sadat would cancel his agreement on normalization and the exchange of ambassadors. It was also the American view that Israel should agree to the autonomy timetable proposed by Egypt, as well as to the unilateral 'gestures' she requested.

I told Vance that I was not unmindful of the shock waves that rocked Sadat and his Government after the Baghdad Conference resolutions. But I would not recommend acceptance of their demands – neither the timetable nor the 'gestures'. He was asking us, I said, to agree to a permanent Egyptian mission in Gaza. What was the point in signing a peace treaty and determining the international boundary between us and Egypt if Egypt was to have, as she requested, a 'special function' on the Israeli side of that border? We had already heard the idea of a 'permanent mission' and a 'special function' at the Leeds Castle Conference. The Egyptians sought to replace us in the Gaza District. We would not agree to this.

Modai, who was with us, asked whether the United States could help us secure an agreement with Egypt on oil supplies. Vance shook his head. No, we would have to do that directly with the Egyptians. Ezer and I raised the matter of financial aid. I said that our Government could not take a decision on the treaty until we knew the nature and location of the substitutes for the military and civilian installations we would be leaving behind in Sinai, and the source of funding the transfer. To this Vance replied that the American public as well as both Houses of Congress took a poor view of our tying our readiness to sign a peace treaty to the receipt of American financial aid. At all events, he could give us no answer to that. The administration would need to study our request, and thereafter it would go through the customary constitutional process, which took time.

Thus, the meeting ended as it had begun, with differences of opinion and a mood of depression.

We had possibly only one more evening left, for Vance would be meeting Begin next day at Kennedy airport, and if the differences remained we would return to Israel. The Government would support Begin's stand, and the Blair House Conference would end in failure.

This was evidently also the judgment of the United States delegation. They had had lengthy deliberations with the Egyptians, with the President, and among themselves in a search for solutions, and they must have realized that it was now touch-and-go whether their reach could exceed their grasp. Thus, at 9.30 in the evening of that very day, 11 November, when we had already met earlier with Vance, we received a call asking us to come to the State Department. The building, which usually hummed with the comings and goings of diplomats, officials and correspondents, was silent and deserted. Apart from the guards, we did not see a soul. We were taken up to the office of the Secretary and found him with Atherton, Hansell and Sterner. We were also three – Barak, Rosenne, and myself.

Vance, who usually appears to the outside world as unemotional and unperturbed, and who speaks briefly and in practical terms, was different that night. He was reflective and noticeably full of anxiety. His opening words expressed his inner feelings. This, he said, was not a normal working session but the making of history. What we did or did not do that evening would be of decisive significance. If we failed to reach an understanding, we would be blamed by future generations. He, on his side, would do all he could to secure successful results.

I remained silent. I believed that he spoke with sincerity, but I wanted him to feel the full weight of the responsibility that rested with him. It was not only that the power of the United States was infinitely greater than ours, but that she now held the key to the solution of the deadlock for which she was largely to blame.

To everyone's surprise, the plea to rise above ourselves and try to view matters as they would be viewed by 'future generations' came from none other than our own jurists. It was Barak in particular who stressed this, saying that we would be neither understood nor forgiven if we failed to reach an agreement because of a few words in a clause here or there. Throughout the negotiations he, like Rosenne, had fought over every word and apostrophe, demanding a 'should' instead of a 'would', and 'ensure' rather than 'assure'. In any case, he now said, the peace treaty would be respected or violated as a result of political developments and not of this or that interpretation of the significance of a word.

The first proposal presented to us by Vance concerned the phases of our withdrawal from Sinai. He stressed that as against the Egyptian demand, his suggestion did not stipulate any timetable but established principles, and he did not know whether the Egyptians would accept it.

I said that the two remaining elements of importance associated with our Sinai withdrawal were the dates for leaving the oilfields and for handing over El Arish. Quite apart from the three hundred thousand dollars we would be gaining each day that we held on to the oilfields, we needed the oil. Vance, who in the past had shied away from the oil problem, now said he was ready to get involved. I thanked him, but refused to widen the discussion on this subject, as I lacked both the knowledge and the authority.

On El Arish, I said that my Government, as Vance already knew, was not prepared to commit itself to giving up this city within six months, but I would pass on his proposal that night both to Jerusalem and to the Prime Minister, so that he would get it before leaving Canada. I added that I personally supported Defence Minister Weizman's recommendation for an early evacuation, but the decision rested with the Government. Vance said he had spoken about this to the President twice that day, and Carter maintained with some vehemence that Sadat had agreed to establish diplomatic relations upon our evacuation of El Arish only on the basis of our promise at Camp David that this would be done within four to six months of the signing of the treaty.

We moved on to the subject of autonomy. Vance said that without a target date for the end of the autonomy negotiations, our current talks would fail. He was aware of our reasons for objecting to a six-month limit, and he was therefore willing to suggest to the Egyptians a target date of nine months. In making this point, Vance again spoke with great feeling about the judgment of history, and how our refusal to set a date for ending the autonomy talks would not be understood 'by our children'. It would appear to them that we were not anxious to make peace. Would nine months really not be enough for the negotiations? he asked me. And anyway, he added, his proposal was couched in flexible terms – a target date, denoting an estimated period, not a cut-off date.

The issue was complicated and the hour was late – nearly midnight. I told Vance that I tended to favour his flexible definition of a target date, but that the period should be one year after the ratification of the peace treaty. However, I said, he was sitting opposite three tired and exhausted men who anyway were not authorized to make the decision. This particular subject, from Begin's point of view, was more personal to him than any other, and it was he himself who would have to sign the joint letter with Sadat. It seemed to me, therefore, that he should discuss it with the Prime Minister when he met him in New York the following day.

Vance did not care for my suggested period of one year. If Israel and Egypt agreed to it, he said, he would not object. But if the Americans were to submit their own proposal, it would be nine months. Atherton then let the cat out of the bag. Sadat, he said, would not agree to the normalization of relations going into effect before the establishment of Palestinian autonomy. I told him that was precisely the reason I proposed one year, so that normalization would start operating three months before the end of the autonomy talks, and would not be dependent upon them.

We broke up at one o'clock in the morning, and returned to our hotel. Rosenne worked till 4 a.m. on cables to Begin and Jerusalem. We were anxious for the Prime Minister to have the report of the proposals and the discussion before he met Vance. Rosenne added a recommendation from the three of us that there should be a joint letter by Begin and Sadat on the autonomy negotiations giving a target date for their completion of one year after the ratification of the peace treaty, namely, three months after the start of normalized relations.

The time in Israel was now after 8 a.m., and I telephoned Rahel. She asked me how the talks were going but I preferred to talk about home. There was no special news in the morning papers, just that the reports on the Blair House Conference were pessimistic. She urged me to get some sleep, which I did, but not before I had gone into the kitchenette and polished off a bowl of cornflakes and cold milk. I had an unpleasant taste in the mouth – hunger was not the cause – and the kitchenette yielded the most refreshing moments of that long day.

CHAPTER NINETEEN

Crisis

With the morning came crisis – at America's initiative. Atherton telephoned me to say that the President did not approve the draft we had agreed on at our evening meeting on the autonomy talks. Carter insisted on the deletion of the sentence which stated that the autonomy negotiations were not to be dependent upon the implementation of the Egypt–Israel peace treaty.

I begged Atherton, in the spirit of Vance's appeal not to allow a few words to torpedo the treaty, to forbear from making such a demand. We had already cabled the draft to the Prime Minister. If the sentence were taken out, Begin would see, with justice, that it was Carter's purpose to make the peace treaty conditional upon an agreement with the Palestinians, and this at a moment when both King Hussein and the Palestinians rejected the Camp David accords outright and refused to have anything to do with them.

It was evident that there had been an attempt to persuade the President to go along with the agreed draft, and when that failed, Atherton had come to me – with a complaint. Why, he asked, had we sent the draft to Begin before they had had the chance of showing it to the President? The excuse was transparent. I reminded him that the draft proposal was theirs, and whether or not they consulted with the President before handing it to us was their affair. They were now simply going back on what they had suggested the previous evening.

The meeting at Kennedy airport that day, 12 November, started at 7 in the evening and lasted two and a half hours. We came from Washington in Vance's plane and Begin flew in from Canada. Vance was accompanied by Atherton and Saunders. Our side fielded a full team: Begin, Finance Minister Ehrlich, Energy Minister Modai, Defence Minister Weizman, Barak, Rosenne, Dinitz and myself.

It was a tense meeting from the start. Begin wanted first to deal with the financial aspect and for the Finance Minister to present the problem. Vance ignored this and opened with a review of the peace negotiations, listing those items on which agreement had been reached and those where there were still differences. His purpose was to show that most of the problems had been solved and completion of the treaty was within reach. The memoranda on America's obligations connected with the peace treaty had also been given their final formulation.

But Begin was not to be put off. He had almost been stoned in Israel, he told Vance, for requesting a loan instead of a grant. He had then corrected his error, but had not yet had Washington's reply. He had also telephoned President Carter from Canada. In Israel the peace accords were becoming less popular from day to day, with Israel having to give up so much, and then being saddled with enormous financial burdens for doing so. Our Finance Minister was to meet a high official in the US Treasury to discuss the problem, and at the last minute was told that he would not be allowed to raise it. Begin concluded by saying that he had to know before the next Cabinet meeting what the Americans could tell him on this urgent matter.

Vance replied that our request would go through the normal process of consideration, which would take considerable time. Begin persisted, wanting to know in general terms what would be the President's recommendation to Congress. Vance stuck to his script. They had to study the subject before reaching a conclusion. That was all Begin could tell his Government. With no other choice, and with undisguised dissatisfaction, Begin had to accept the outcome of this discussion: US Treasury Secretary Blumenthal would listen to what Israel Finance Minister Ehrlich had to say.

The dialogue did not improve when the principal characters proceeded to a discussion of the treaty. Begin asked what had happened to the changes Israel wanted introduced into some of the clauses. Vance said the Egyptians also wanted changes, and so the Americans had turned down all such proposals, otherwise everything that had been achieved would be undermined. Begin repeated his arguments and Vance did the same. Neither conceded to the other.

The last subject was the joint letter to be signed by Begin and Sadat, which we had redrafted the previous evening with a target date of one year for the autonomy talks. Vance said that Sadat's response would be known only a few days later, but he urged the Prime Minister to consent to the proposed draft. Begin refused, saying that if we took it upon ourselves to end the autonomy talks in twelve months, there was a danger that we might not be able to fulfil our promise. The discussion on this matter was not very pertinent or constructive. Begin was irritated at having all his proposals and requests turned down by the Americans, and Vance was limited by the President's instructions, both on financial aid and the target-date letter. It was decided to take a few minutes break.

When Begin left the room, Vance remarked bitterly that with each additional moment of talk we kept slipping backwards. Perhaps, he asked, they could hear what the Foreign Minister had to say? I replied that when the Prime Minister returned, and if he agreed, I would tell them what I thought.

When Begin came back ready to resume the dialogue, Vance came out openly with his request: perhaps the Foreign Minister would like to air his opinion? Begin, already angry and tense, reacted with icy reluctance: if he wishes, let him speak. The tone was not to be ignored, and so I turned to him and said in Hebrew that if I spoke, I would express my view openly: was that what he wanted? Begin replied also in Hebrew that it was not he who had asked me to speak. It was Vance who seemed to have taken over the running of the Israeli delegation. In that case, I said, I would remain silent.

The next subject taken up was oil, and our Energy Minister reported on Egypt's stubborn position. Here, too, we ended up in a cul-de-sac. Begin asked Vance if he had any suggestions as to how America could help, and Vance replied that he had none.

Thus, as Begin observed in Hebrew, summing up for our delegation the discussion on the two important items of aid and oil, we had received nothing. When he returned to Israel, he would summon the Cabinet and report on the situation.

Vance asked to return to the subject of the proposed joint Sadat-Begin letter. Begin now asked in a different tone whether I wished to express my opinion. This time I did. I then explained why I had thought the previous evening, and held the same view now, that we could accept the formula of the target date for ending the autonomy talks provided that it was set at twelve months from the ratification of the peace treaty. Begin did not agree, and I thought I knew what would happen when it came up at the Cabinet. The Prime Minister would reject it and the other ministers would go along with him.

At the end of the meeting, Begin flew off to Israel and we in the delegation returned to Washington, not to continue the Blair House Conference but to disband in orderly manner. We informed both Vance and the Egyptian delegation that we would be leaving for Israel the following night, 13 November. Ghali said he was also leaving – he had been called back to Cairo.

Late next afternoon I was packing my bags, giving a last glance round my suite at the Madison Hotel, and leaving without regret. Not that I had anything against the Madison; but this had been my home, working office and crowded conference room for almost a month, and I longed for the fresh air and quiet and pleasure of my garden in Zahala.

The delegation secretariat had space of its own, with a room for meetings, but in fact all the internal consultations and conferences were held in my sitting-room. We worked quite hard, meeting with the Americans or the Egyptians during the day and often late into the night, consulting with each other in the early morning, and being in touch with Jerusalem from midnight on. (Israel time was seven hours ahead.)

I am not fussy about tidiness, unlike Barak – it was not unusual to find him with a broom or a duster removing the slightest speck. But I could hardly abide the sitting-room after a meeting, the tables an anarchy of heaped ashtrays, cups with coffee dregs, biscuit crumbs, bits of paper, orange peel and skins and cores of other fruit.

In whatever time was left between meetings and paperwork, I was confined to the hotel. The museums were closed when I was free, and in any case I was familiar with the exhibits that interested me from my previous visits to Washington. The same was true of the theatre and cinema, though I am not a great fan of either screen or stage. What I needed most was to be alone, to think, without having to talk or listen.

And so, when there were no official dinners, I ate alone. It seemed odd, at first, with the other members of the delegation sitting together in the hotel restaurant and I sitting at a table on my own in a corner. But they got used to it and knew that there was no intention to slight them. Drink parties I shunned, and anyway alcohol was not allowed me after the recent emergence of an ulcer. Nevertheless, after a heavy day when I was tired of the subjects we had been grappling with *ad nauseam*, I would take a glass or two of sherry before dinner. I would pay for it next day – but that would be tomorrow.

At my bedside I had three Hebrew books, the Bible, the *Carta Bible Atlas* by Professors Yohanan Aharoni and Michael Avi-Yonah, and the *Collected Poems* of Nathan Alterman. The Atlas helped me to set the biblical chronicles in their geographical context. I am familiar with the Bible, as I am with the geography of Israel. But who knew, for example, exactly where 'the rock Etam' stood, where Samson took refuge when the men of Judah sought to hand him over to the Philistines? What were the boundaries of the Kingdoms of Saul and David, or the route followed by the Children of Israel from their Egyptian Exodus through Sinai, right up to their capture of Jericho? The locations proposed by Aharoni and Avi-Yonah may be questioned by other historians and archaeologists, but to me they seem reasonable. And with their directives, I can climb a hill or cross a valley and feel I am walking in the very footsteps of my forbears.

I love reading the Bible not only for the magic of its language, nor only for its written words, but also for the pictures that emerge between the lines, the patterns of living and of faith of the Israelites when they dwelt on their own soil and were involved with their neighbours. Samson, who fought the Philistines from his youth until his death, nevertheless always sought their company. He chose as his wife 'a woman from Timnath, of the daughters of the Philistines'. And when she was murdered by her own people and Samson avenged her death, he went 'to Gaza', the heart of enemy country, to spend time with a Philistine harlot. Later he fell in love with Delilah, a Philistine woman from the valley of Sorek, who delivered him into the hands of his foes. This was the man who began 'to save Israel' from the Philistines and who judged his people for twenty years. Why did he seek the society of his enemy neighbours? Was 'there never a woman among the daughters of thy brethren ... that thou goest to take a wife of the uncircumcised Philistines?' his parents chided him. Why was the moth attracted to the flame? Such was the man – and the Bible does not judge him errant.

With the return to Israel of Begin from Canada and our delegation from Washington, the Cabinet held lengthy deliberations before setting forth its position two weeks later. In the midst of these discussions, the Prime Minister received a ten-page message from Sadat, mostly complaining of Israel's stand during the Blair House negotiations, and reiterating certain demands which we had rejected in Washington. Among them was his insistence on a fixed timetable for implementing autonomy for the residents of the West Bank and Gaza. He also declared that the formula of Clause 6 in the peace treaty (which dealt with the problem of priority in the conflict of obligations) as agreed in Washington was not acceptable to him.

Our fellow ministers in the Cabinet were disappointed and embittered. The Prime Minister had come back empty-handed. He had been able to get nothing from his meeting with Vance and his telephone talks with President Carter. The treaty changes our Government had asked for had been turned down. No progress had been registered in the areas of economic aid and oil supplies. The Egyptians were putting up new demands, and there was now no certainty that the United States would maintain her reservations about them.

The Government finally summed up its position at the Cabinet meeting of 30 November 1978 in the following decision:

1. The Government of Israel is prepared to sign the peace treaty with Egypt, which was brought before them for consideration by the negotiating delegation, if the Egyptian delegation is willing to do so.
2. The latest Egyptian proposals are a deviation from the Camp David accords and are not acceptable to Israel.

3. When the peace treaty between Egypt and Israel is signed and ratified, Israel will be ready to start negotiations towards an agreement on the introduction of administrative autonomy in Judea and Samaria and Gaza, in accordance with what was stated in the Camp David accords.

The proposal to take this decision was mine. The Prime Minister supported it, but only after a great deal of worry. When one of the ministers asked why this proposal should be accepted, when it meant waiving our demands for changes in the treaty, Begin replied: 'To achieve peace.'

This Cabinet decision showed that it was Egypt and not Israel who was refusing to sign the agreement which was reached in Washington after so much effort and mutual concessions.

We also showed flexibility in the phrasing of the joint Begin–Sadat letter on autonomy. Begin announced that he rejected any formula which set a fixed timetable for the implementation of autonomy or a target date by which the negotiations were to be completed; but he would not be averse to signing a letter on this subject if its content and formulation were reasonable. He would accept, for example, instead of a twelve-month target date, the formula 'at an early date', without specifying a time.

I did not place much value on such variations of phraseology. The important aim for me was to hold fast to our basic positions, but to do so in a way that did not seal off further negotiations.

Washington was not resigned to the deadlock in the talks and sought to break it, showing in the process a good deal of sympathy for Sadat's problems and for the hardening of his position. Egypt's Vice-President Hosni Mubarak and Prime Minister Mustapha Khalil visited Washington, spoke to Carter and Vance, and drew a grim picture of what was happening in Egypt. They again underlined the effects of the Baghdad Conference: the shock given to the leaders of Egypt's administration, including Sadat, was of deep and far-reaching significance. The revolution in Iran also had its impact. There was a growing anti-American feeling in the countries of Islam, from Pakistan to Saudi Arabia and Morocco. Sadat's standing and his reliance on the United States were being put to the test.

Carter decided to send Vance to Egypt and Israel to try and get the two sides to resume negotiations. It was arranged with both countries that he would visit Egypt on 10 December and go on to Jerusalem two days later.

We held two meetings with Vance and his party on 13 December, the first with a limited forum, and later with all the members of the ministerial Defence Committee.

Vance's mission turned out to be an unfortunate one. Not only did it fail to shift the peace ship off the shoals but it almost shattered it. The 'compromise' proposals which Vance brought from Cairo were quite unreasonable, and the manner in which they were presented was both reprehensible and ineffectual. According to Vance, Sadat, like Israel, was ready to sign the peace treaty as it stood, without opening its clauses to renewed discussion and without change. But this was a transparent exercise in legerdemain. Sadat's agreement was given only after the Americans had agreed to attach to certain treaty clauses 'interpretative notes' and 'legal opinions' which annulled their value and changed their meaning. Sadat had also retracted his agreement to exchange ambassadors with Israel one month after our withdrawal to the Ras Moham-mad–El Arish line. At that stage, there would be only diplomatic recognition and the appointment of consuls and *chargés d'affaires*. The exchange of ambassadors would take place only upon the establishment of Palestinian autonomy.

The Secretary said these were indeed Egyptian proposals, but they were acceptable to the United States. Moreover, he and his aides had worked hard to get Sadat and his people to agree even to these formulae.

We could not avoid the feeling that the Americans had misled us, and were applying a double standard, one for the Egyptians and another for us. Washington had adamantly refused the Israeli Government's demand for two changes in the draft treaty, on the ground that changing a single stone might bring the whole peace edifice tumbling down. Yet now they were agreeing to Egypt's demand for more than two changes, in order to appease Sadat. Israel had agreed to approve the treaty as it stood, with all its clauses and appendices intact, only after a good deal of teeth-grinding reluctance. The Americans had now joined with Sadat to get round the most essential clauses on which they had already agreed, in a new attempt to link Israel–Egypt normalization to autonomy, and secure a special status for Egypt in the Gaza District.

The talks with Vance did not last long. When they ended, the Government issued the following statement on 15 December:

1. The Government of Israel is ready to sign without delay the peace treaty with its appendices as transmitted on 11 November 1978.... The absolute responsibility for the non-signing of the treaty rests with the Government of Egypt.
2. This week, in contacts between the two countries through the United States Secretary of State, Egypt presented Israel with the following new demands:

    a. An exchange of ambassadors to be conditional upon the introduction of Palestinian autonomy at least in the Gaza District.

    b. A fundamental change in Clause 4 of the treaty concerning a re-study and revision of the security arrangements in Sinai after five years.

    c. An interpretative letter on Clause 6 – the 'conflict of obligations' clause – which nullifies its significance.

    d. The setting of a fixed date, called the target date, for the implementation of autonomy in Judea, Samaria and Gaza.

3. These Egyptian demands deviate from the Camp David accords, or are not included therein, and fundamentally change the content of the above peace treaty. They are therefore not acceptable to Israel and are rejected.

4. The Government of Israel rejects America's stand on the Egyptian proposals and her exposition thereof.

5. The [proposed joint] letter on autonomy arrangements needs clarification and reformulation.

Vance returned to Washington, but while he was still in the aircraft *en route* he had harsh things to say about us. A 'senior official' in his party briefed the accompanying correspondents, and explained that it was the Government of Israel who prevented the signing of the peace treaty. He termed the Government's statement as unworthy of reply.

After Vance's departure, I suggested to Begin that we set up a working group for continued negotiations with Egypt – they would go on even though we would not be returning to Blair House. I proposed that this group be headed by the Minister of Justice, since the subjects that still remained to be clarified were of a definite legal character. Begin, after some consideration, turned it down. Those subjects, he said, were an integral part of the peace negotiations, and therefore I would continue to direct them. I could get the help of legal experts, and we – Begin and I – would continue to consult together.

The sharp attack on Israel by the Americans did not go well for them. It was not only the Jews of the United States who protested, but even the American press considered the Administration's criticism unjustified, and called it 'overkill'. Why was Israel obliged to endorse proposals which Vance and Sadat had concocted between them in Cairo, they asked. President Carter announced that he would publish a White Paper with documents proving that Israel was to blame; but after further reflection he decided not to do so. The material was unconvincing; and, more important, Washington recognized that attacking Israel had not advanced the peace process but damaged it. The only way out of the impasse was to renew the three-sided contact between Egypt, Israel and the United States.

Vance approached Sadat and Begin, and suggested a meeting in Europe, with his own participation, between Egyptian Prime Minister Mustapha Khalil and myself. Sadat and Begin agreed, and it was arranged that I would meet Khalil in Brussels on 23 December 1978. The purpose of the meeting, according to Vance, was to undertake a general examination of the ways in which we could proceed with the treaty negotiations. Vance suggested that news of the meeting be kept secret. Both sides agreed and, as usual, the 'secret' was leaked to the press within twenty-four hours.

I had already met Mustapha Khalil, but I had never had the opportunity of a thorough talk with him. I knew that he was close to Sadat, that he supported peace with Israel, was a member of Egypt's elite, and belonged to one of those highly educated and wealthy families from whom the holders of high office were drawn.

I combined the tripartite meeting with other engagements which required my presence in Brussels – attending the Common Market Council session, meeting with the German and Belgian Foreign Ministers and NATO Secretary-General Luns, as well as briefing Israel's Ambassadors in Europe. Vance was due to arrive in the afternoon of 22 December, but he then informed us that he would be arriving late. I had therefore planned to have a quiet dinner with Rahel in our room at the Hilton, but, to my surprise, Khalil telephoned inviting me to dine with him at the Hyatt House Hotel, where he was staying. I accepted willingly. We arranged that it would be a 'men only' dinner, and we would be six: Khalil, his brother, who was Egypt's Ambassador to Brussels, and Osama al-Baz; and I would be accompanied by Meir Rosenne and our Ambassador to Brussels, Yitzhak Minervi.

When we arrived at Hyatt House, we found ourselves awaited by our hosts and a crowd of correspondents and television crews. Khalil explained that this was a private dinner, and the objective was good food and informal conversation. Our working meeting would begin when Vance arrived.

The food was indeed good, and the talk frank. Khalil is a worldly man, charming, courteous, with an expression that is at once serious and friendly. He exuded self-confidence – even when he described the grave difficulties faced by Egypt. On the controversial questions, neither he nor al-Baz sought to blur the stand they took. It appeared, indeed, that they feared misunderstanding more than disagreement. At 11.15 p.m. Vance arrived, together with Saunders and Quandt, and we adjourned to the Secretary's suite. We found him exhausted. He had reached Brussels after a long and heavy day, and a night without sleep. We decided we would talk only until midnight, and continue in the morning.

Vance asked me to open, and I informed him that Israel's position had not changed since his visit to Jerusalem. After outlining the points at issue, I said we had come to Brussels at America's initiative, and would be happy to hear how the Egyptians regarded the possibility of advancing towards agreement. From what I had heard at the dinner table that evening, I feared that the gap between us was still wide.

Khalil said he did not wish to deal at the moment with clauses but with problems. Egypt's main anxiety was her isolation in the Arab world, and so the treaty had to be made more acceptable and attractive to the Arab States. These States might not join Egypt in such a treaty, but they would be able to support it or at least become reconciled to it.

We had already discussed this during dinner, and I now asked him if the practical meaning of what he had just said was that, in order to secure Arab support for Egypt, Israel had to undertake to withdraw from the West Bank, from East Jerusalem and the Golan, and also agree to Palestinian self-determination. Khalil affirmed that that was so. Vance was not surprised. From his talks in Cairo, he had learned that Khalil and al-Baz wished to change the very foundations of the treaty, but Sadat was preventing this.

Khalil again said that he did not wish to spend time on details but on substance. If we got to understand each other, it would be possible to find the appropriate legal formula for the solutions. The crux of the matter was that he wanted peace with Israel, but not Egypt's isolation.

It was now after midnight, and we had promised not to stay late. We would meet again at breakfast in the morning.

We were a formidable group round the breakfast table, with all the teams present. When it was over, Vance asked that only Khalil and I remain, so that we could speak with greater freedom, and without a stenographic record.

Vance, after a night's sleep, was his old self, vigorous, and alert to every nuance in expression and formulation. Khalil had organized his thoughts anew and was ready to present them. I ordered another black coffee and listened with close interest. Khalil was not too familiar with the details either of the text of the peace treaty or of the Palestinian issue. For him, the West Bank, East Jerusalem and the Gaza Strip were concepts rather than a physical reality. But he found this no drawback, for the core of his concern was Egypt and her relations with the other Arab States, and here he was on solid ground. He was bone of the bone and flesh of the flesh of the leadership in the Persian Gulf States, the Sudan and North Africa. He may not have been at

254   BREAKTHROUGH

one with their subjects, the peasants and the Bedouin, nor even with the professors and the young students; but he was of the same mould as those who determined policy, the royal households and the princes who held the reins of power and struggled to maintain that hold. Thus, on the question of commitments to other Arab States and priority in the conflict of obligations clause, Khalil argued that the United States and Israel should be urging Egypt to make alliances with the moderate Arab countries if she had not already done so. Only Egypt could rush to their help against the wave of radicalism and Khomeiniism that was sweeping the area - but not if Egypt were to be isolated and considered a stranger. Since Sadat's visit to Jerusalem, and the denunciation of Egypt as a traitor, Egyptian technicians working in the oil States were being replaced by Koreans and Pakistanis. This was a danger to the stability of their regimes, to Egypt and to the West - particularly the United States.

I told Khalil that he had to consider the significance of Egypt's alliances with the other Arab States also from Israel's point of view. Syria could attack the Golan Heights and claim that this was a defensive war. She could also argue that she had wished to retrieve her 'holy soil' - the phrase Sadat had used in Jerusalem - without a war, but that Israel had refused. What, then, would be Egypt's obligation in such a case? Khalil said Egypt would side with Syria, but would take no part in the war. Moreover, he added, no Arab State could embark on a war against Israel without Egypt, and so this danger was non-existent. I brought up other examples, such as terrorist action from PLO bases in Lebanon against our civilians. Israel had no alternative but to respond to such action by force, and Lebanon then charged us with invading her territory. What would be the practical impact of our peace treaty with Egypt in such an event? Khalil repeated that Egypt would join those who condemned Israel, but would not go to war. She would be active with the other Arab States in a diplomatic, but not a military, campaign.

When I emphasized those subjects on which we differed - East Jerusalem, the West Bank, a Palestinian State - Khalil began to recognize that his ideal solution was unrealistic: Egypt could not be part of the common front of our adversaries, and at the same time maintain peaceful relations with us. If, for example, we continued with our settlement of the West Bank, he said, then Egypt would not send an ambassador to Israel. To which I replied that if an exchange of ambassadors was to be conditional upon our stopping such settlement, we would not sign the peace treaty.

It was a sincere dialogue. To find the golden mean whereby Egypt could both remain in the Arab anti-Israel camp and yet sign a peace treaty with us seemed as impossible as trying to square the circle. But I had no feeling of despair. Policy does not follow the rules of geometry. Nations live side by side in peace, even when they have opposing interests. They compromise.

Vance took almost no part in this exchange. Only towards the end did he venture the observation that Israel's security interests and Egypt's pan-Arab interests were very real, and a solution had to be found. He did not think there was much point in convening a summit meeting for the moment. It would not be productive. It was better to continue the talks at the current level. Khalil's response was non-committal; and when the official statement on our meeting was being prepared, he took care to see it specified that the delegations would report to their Governments on the Brussels talks and the Governments would decide on the next steps. Thus, it was up to the Governments of Egypt and Israel to decide when and how the next talks were to take place – if they were to be renewed at all.

The Brussels meeting was interesting. Had it also been useful? I could not be sure.

Back in Jerusalem, I reported to the Cabinet, which devoted two sessions to the talks. There was a good deal of dissatisfaction among my fellow ministers. Some argued that we should never have agreed to the Brussels meeting, and their mistrust of me was apparent, even though it was not put into words. They evidently felt I might have promised concessions, or hinted at our readiness to grant them, and feared I would drag the Government into a course it did not wish to take. The one specific complaint they made was over something I had said at Ben Gurion airport on my return. Why, they asked me, had I said in answer to correspondents' questions that if both Governments displayed flexibility, I thought we would be able to reach agreement? I replied to my colleagues that I did not regard 'flexibility' as a disreputable word, and I preferred to strike a chord of hope rather than of despair. I had not despaired of the chance of peace.

The Prime Minister was at one with the hostile tone at these sessions, and when he came to sum up the Cabinet decisions and formulate the announcement, he was attentive to those ministers who demanded tough language. The decision in its final guise sounded like something that had emerged from the UN Security Council. It read:

1. The Government heard a report from the Foreign Minister on the Brussels talks.
2. The Cabinet reconfirms its resolution of 15 December 1978 in all its parts.
3. In accordance with this decision, and its previous announcements, the Government expresses its readiness to continue negotiations with Egypt to

   reach an agreed text of the letter concerning the autonomy arrangements
   without setting a target date, and a reclarification of Paragraph 4 of
   Article 4 of the peace treaty without determining in advance any mandatory date for a review of the security arrangements.
4. The Cabinet takes note of the letter of the Foreign Minister of 28 December 1978 to the Secretary of State of the United States, which rejects
   completely the American interpretation of Article 6 (on conflict of obligations). Israel will approach the United States Government with a view to
   ensuring a single and unequivocal meaning to this Article of the peace
   treaty.

   During one of the Cabinet sessions, the Prime Minister received a message
from President Carter. Begin studied it and then read it out to us. I took
special note of the operative part. The President expressed the hope that now,
after the Brussels meeting, it would be possible to renew the negotiations
between Israel and Egypt. Begin would need to reply, and he could not very
well say he was unwilling to continue the talks. After all, the objective was
not to mollify a few irate ministers but to sign a peace treaty with the
Egyptians.
   On 17 January 1979, Alfred Atherton and Herbert Hansell arrived in
Jerusalem to try to clear up the problems with three clauses in the proposed
peace treaty contained in Article 6 (paragraphs 2 and 5) and Article 4 (4). The
Egyptians had asked for changes, and had suggested attaching to these
Articles 'interpretative notes' and 'legal opinions' by the United States
Government. Article 6 (2 and 5) dealt with the conflict of obligations between our peace treaty and Egypt's prior alliances with Arab States. Article 4
(4) was concerned with the right of each side to review the security arrangements laid down in the peace treaty. In the 'interpretative notes' to Article 6,
the Americans had stated that it did not prevent Egypt from coming to the
aid of a country with which she had a mutual defence treaty or a collective
security agreement if such a country should come under armed attack. The
Israeli Government had rejected these Egyptian–American proposals when
Vance had come to Jerusalem on 13 December after spending two days in
Cairo; and now Atherton and Hansell were here to try to find a solution
acceptable to all parties.
   It was decided that the consultations would be conducted at the level of
officials, though at Begin's suggestion the Government authorized him and
myself to guide our representatives during the talks. The Israeli team was
chaired by Eliyahu Ben-Elissar, Director-General of the Prime Minister's
Office, and included Meir Rosenne, Yitzhak Zamir (who had succeeded

Barak as Attorney-General) and Professor Ruth Lapidot, of the Hebrew University's Law Faculty.

The problem for us was that the State Department had already given its legal opinion. Thus, when we came to sign the peace treaty, we would be doing so with the knowledge of the American interpretation, and this would signify our agreement. The way to overcome this obstacle was for the Americans to add an interpretation to their original interpretation which would set our minds at rest.

The discussions and bargaining between the two teams lasted a week, into which were crowded sixteen day and night sessions, and the Americans came up with ten drafts before producing the redeeming text. This was in the form of an agreed letter which Secretary Vance would send us. It would not replace but be an addition to the interpretative notes the State Department had sent to the Egyptians.

Israel's reservations about the American interpretation of Article 6 sprang from the difficulty of determining when and whether a country was the attacker or the attacked. After every war the question had been asked: Who fired the first shot? With us there were two additional and special problems, one arising out of 'conquered territories' and the other out of 'reprisal actions' against terrorists. Syria and Jordan would claim that our occupation of the West Bank and the Golan Heights was an act of aggression, so that if they attacked us it would be a defensive war, and Egypt could go to their help. As for our reprisal actions against terrorist bases in adjacent Arab lands, these countries could argue that the entry of our forces constituted an armed invasion.

To meet these problems it was agreed that Vance's letter to us should state that the Israel–Arab conflict was to be resolved through peaceful means, and the United States held that neither side had the right to use, or threaten to use, military means to do so. In accordance with this principle, Egypt would be neither obliged nor entitled to extend help to her allies if they used military force against Israel because of Israel's presence in the territories captured in 1967. The determining sentence on this subject would state that Israel's presence in these territories did not constitute a military attack or an act of aggression which justified military action against her.

On reprisal operations, the letter was to state that military action taken by Israel for self-defence – including actions such as those against terrorist attacks – could not be regarded as an aggressive step or an armed attack, and therefore could not justify military help against Israel.

There was argument not only over the content but also over the terminology. Begin did not wish our presence in the territories to be termed occupation. The Americans said this was their view and they were not prepared to change it. The agreed compromise formula was: 'Israel's presence in the territories is not agression.'

All was well until Atherton and Hansell arrived in Cairo, and the Egyptians heard the interpretation now given to the original American 'interpretative notes'. They were furious. They told the Americans they were granting legitimacy to Israel's occupation of conquered territory. They preferred to do without the 'interpretative notes' they had been given, if only to cancel the interpretation given to us. Atherton returned to Jerusalem to report on Egypt's reaction.

The Egyptians had also rejected our proposal on Article 4 (4). We had agreed to this clause on the right of each side to request a review of the security arrangements in Sinai, but on the condition, of course, that any change in these arrangements could be effected only with the agreement of both parties. I had no doubt that our proposal also met the wishes of the Egyptians, but in their angry mood they turned that down too.

The Prime Minister and I reported on the negative response from Cairo at our next Cabinet meeting, and the Government issued a statement regretting this, but reaffirming Israel's readiness to continue negotiations. I wondered what would be the status of the two sets of interpretations that the Americans had produced. After all, both Egypt and Israel had copies. Two months later Hansell gave us the answer: neither set of interpretations had gained final agreement, and so both had been abandoned, and had no status.

Atherton's mission had failed. But apart from returning to Jerusalem with hopeless replies from Cairo, Atherton also brought the notification that Egypt considered the talks should be resumed, and suggested they be held at the ministerial level. Actually, even if Atherton and Hansell had been successful in settling the stubborn clauses, there were other issues of importance that still remained unresolved, such as the Sadat–Begin letter on autonomy, diplomatic relations, and oil supplies. If peace were to be attained, further negotiations were inescapable.

CHAPTER TWENTY

Camp David II

The Americans responded quickly to Egypt's proposal for a renewal of the talks at the ministerial level. President Carter wrote to Begin and Sadat urging that they be held in the United States, and without delay – in his letter to Begin of 2 February 1979 he suggested that they start on 21 February. He would place Camp David at our disposal so that the negotiations could proceed without the pressure and fanfare of the media. Heading the talks would be Prime Minister Mustapha Khalil for Egypt, Secretary Vance for the US and myself for Israel. Carter thought it likely that Khalil and I might need to return to our countries after a few days to consult with our Governments.

Coincident with the arrival of Carter's letter, US Ambassador to Israel Samuel Lewis called to give me further details. The US administration this time would initiate proposals for resolving the conflicting issues. The President was moved by a sense of urgency. He felt that time was running out, and an energetic push was required to secure the peace treaty. It was possible that following this new Camp David Conference he would call for a summit meeting.

The Government met to consider the President's invitation. There was no doubt that we had to accept it, but several ministers expressed the fear that decisions might be taken without the knowledge of the Government. Begin and I assured them that any proposal made by our delegation would be conditional upon the Government's approval. But now they raised another point. I had reported that the United States was preparing its own proposals, and ministers suggested that these be brought before the Cabinet for discussion before the Camp David meeting. But the Americans refused. They were still working on them, they said, and would not have them ready before the eve of the conference. In any case, they added, they were aware that the Israeli delegation would not be able to give a categorical response on the spot and would need to refer back to Jerusalem.

The Camp David II Conference turned out to be cold, short and sterile. It started on the night of 20 February and ended four days later, on Saturday night, 24 February.

The arrangements were excellent, the weather less so. The ground was covered by thick snow, and to get from one's cabin to the communal dining hall meant negotiating a narrow icy path. Because of the altitude, the Camp was enveloped in a thick mist most of the night and much of the day, and when the sun broke through for a few moments – both in the conference discussions and outside – it was wintry and distant.

As an opener Atherton met with our delegation on the evening of our arrival while Saunders met with the Egyptians, Khalil, Butros Ghali, al-Baz and their aides. The principal members of my delegation were three legal experts, Zamir, Rosenne and Yehuda Blum, as well as Ben-Ellissar, Director-General of the Prime Minister's Office, and Froike Poran, the Premier's military secretary.

At our meeting, Atherton, referring to notes dictated by Vance, explained America's approach to this conference. In the light of what was happening in the Middle East – the Khomeini revolution in Iran, and the spirit that had prevailed at the Baghdad Conference – this might be our last opportunity to achieve an Israel-Egypt peace. It was their hope that we could now complete what had begun there, at Camp David, the previous September. A peace treaty reached with the participation of the United States could be an important factor in securing the foundations of stability in the region. At this conference, the Americans expected us to propose a package solution to the issues that were still outstanding. The President was also ready to call a summit meeting if he thought it helpful.

Vance and I met next morning. He had just come from a talk with Khalil, and his first question to me was the extent of my authority. Khalil had told him that he had been authorized by Sadat to decide on and finalize all the subjects we would be discussing. I said I had no such authority. I would discuss the various proposals and even make suggestions of my own; but the decisions would be made only in Jerusalem. Vance was not surprised. If we made good progress in our talks, they would be followed by a Carter-Sadat-Begin meeting to conclude the process. Vance suggested as work procedures that the three of us, he, Khalil and I, should meet for discussions on the basic principles, and the delegations – chiefly the jurists – would devise the formal texts for our positions.

I asked him about the American proposals. Vance said they regarded the treaty as standing on its own, and its implementation was not to be conditional upon the obligations of any other treaty or subject. However, one could not disregard the treaty ties existing between Egypt and the Arab

States, nor the political link between the peace treaty and the grant of self-rule for the Arabs of the territories, nor yet the consideration of our treaty as the first step towards a comprehensive peace with the other Arab countries. As to the joint letter on autonomy, both the Americans and the Egyptians were willing to change the wording – substituting 'goal' for 'target date' – but not the content.

The tripartite meeting in the afternoon began with a long speech by Khalil on the situation in the region. The main problem was the undermining of its stability, the principal cause was the wave of Islamic fanaticism that was sweeping the area. Against this background, he said, Egypt should not at this time be forging an alliance with Israel. Rather she should strengthen her ties with the Arab States and prevent an Egypt–Israel peace treaty from becoming a wedge that split the Arab world. Countries like Sudan and Oman, who supported Sadat, had notified Egypt that they would cut their ties with her if she signed such a treaty. And the Egyptian public was also much influenced by the mood in these States. Khalil said that he himself, against the view of Sadat, had been compelled after a five-hour debate in Egypt's parliament to send a congratulatory message to Khomeini. The thrust of his argument now was that Egypt could not sign a separate peace with Israel. The treaty had to be linked to the grant of self-government to the Palestinians. Despite all the difficulties, he was an ardent supporter of peace, and believed it could be gained. Camp David had been a tremendous achievement, and he, Khalil, wanted to see its accords put into effect.

When it was my turn, instead of engaging in argument on his judgment of the situation, I asked him what practical things needed to be done in order to reach agreement on the treaty. Khalil's response was that if I wanted to discuss practical matters, he wished to know whether I had the authority to make compromises and decisions. He himself possessed such authority; but he had learned from the Israeli press that I was not authorized to finalize anything. If that was the case, he said, there was no point in his wasting his time sitting with us, for even if we reached agreement it would have no validity. Moreover, he added, he was obliged to tell me frankly that he doubted whether Israel really wanted peace, and as evidence he pointed to our 'bombastic announcements about settlements', and our 'heavy-handed behaviour' towards the Arabs in the territories.

I acknowledged that I had no authority to make decisions but only to clarify, suggest and make recommendations to my Government. My proposals were sometimes accepted, sometimes not. If he thought meeting with me was a waste of time, we could all go home. We had not misled anyone. Both the Americans and the Egyptians well knew the exact nature of my delegation's authority. Indeed, President Carter had written about it in his letter to Begin, saying that because of it, Khalil and I after a few days of discussion would need to return to our respective countries to report to our Governments, for it was they who would decide.

As for what Khalil had said about our not really wanting peace, if this were indeed so, I said, we would never have agreed to withdraw from Sinai and evacuate our settlements there. I was very familiar with the strategic value of Sinai, and it was not easy for us to agree to give it up. As to what he had said about our 'heavy hand' in the territories, he had to bear in mind that every two or three days there was terrorist sabotage in our cities. We were not prepared to accept the kind of co-existence where one party laid mines and set off explosive charges, and the other party simply sent out ambulances to pick up the victims. We would not tolerate that sort of situation. When two Imams (Moslem ministers of religion) prepared explosive devices in their village of Abu-Dis which were then planted as booby-traps in Jerusalem, we blew up their houses. And we would continue to do this until terrorism was stopped. If Khalil wished to discuss this subject, he would do well to begin with the murder of our women and children by terrorists operating from bases in the territories.

The talk continued in this tone, with harsh exchanges. Khalil raised the familiar suggestion that we make a start with autonomy in the Gaza District if the Arabs of the West Bank refused to take part in the elections. I said this matter had never been discussed by my Government, but I was prepared to recommend it on condition that Egypt would not then seek to represent King Hussein in negotiations about the West Bank. If and when autonomy was established in Gaza, and if and when Jordan was ready to negotiate over autonomy in the West Bank, we would do so with her, not with Egypt.

Khalil did not accept this, and insisted on Egypt's authority also to represent Jordan about the West Bank, and to establish self-government there after its establishment in Gaza. Furthermore, Egypt had to be given the right to send Egyptian police into the Gaza District. This was not stated in the Camp David agreement, but it should be agreed to now. I turned it down, and asked him about oil supplies. Khalil said Egypt would be prepared to discuss this with us only after agreement was reached on the peace treaty – but not as a precondition, and not as part of the treaty.

In addition to such three-cornered meetings, there were also alternate meetings between the Americans and the Egyptians and the Americans and us. After each round, the Americans would present us with a new version of the celebrated joint letter on autonomy and the 'agreed minutes' – the minutes of those portions of the talks dealing with points on which we appeared to have agreed. The gap, instead of being narrowed, widened. Each party tried to get the Americans to introduce the changes it wanted into their proposals. The legal experts in our delegation scrutinized with extraordinary diligence every change in word or term that was proposed. We also suffered no dearth of comments from Jerusalem. Never, of course, were we ordered to moderate our stand; and on no subject was there a suggestion of how we could come closer to the Egyptian position.

There was little value in continuing the talks. It seemed to me at times that Khalil was making a conscious effort to torpedo the negotiations and prevent the conclusion of a peace treaty. This was particularly apparent when we discussed the exchange of ambassadors. Khalil was insistent that Egypt would not commit herself to such an exchange. He was referring not only to the timing – it would not occur even if we advanced our evacuation of El Arish. Nor was it linked to the inauguration of autonomy. Under the Camp David accords, he said, Egypt was committed to establishing diplomatic relations, and this she would do. But she did not accept the injunction that this had to be at the ambassadorial level. The commitment had been agreed upon at our Blair House meetings, and appeared in Appendix III of the treaty; but Khalil said this agreement was only a draft. It had not yet been signed, and was therefore not an obligation. I asked Vance whether the ambassadorial exchange had not appeared in Carter's letter to Begin, but he answered that that letter, too, was a draft proposal. I turned to Khalil and said he surely knew where his argument was leading him. We, too, could hold up our departure from the oilfields, called for in the first phase of our withdrawal, and the whole treaty would be eroded.

There was similar lack of progress on bilateral matters between us and the Americans, though the fault this time was largely with us. Before leaving Israel, we had been asked to clarify the overall problems in this area. But when, from Camp David, we asked Jerusalem for the list of arms we were requesting so that we could transmit it to Vance, we were told this would be handled by our Defence Minister directly with Secretary Harold Brown. The same went for our request for financial aid: our Finance Ministry would be in touch with its counterpart in Washington.

The one remaining bilateral item we could raise with the administration was the Memorandum of Agreement between us and the US, which I considered of great importance. Vance's reaction suggested that the US administration, too, tended to favour such an agreement with us – and also, perhaps, with Egypt. Our delegation prepared an outline for such a memorandum, cabled it to Jerusalem, and received approval to transmit it to Vance. It dealt with six points, one of which covered the functions which the United States would be prepared to assume in order to ensure that there was no breach of the peace treaty. I expanded on this and the other items in the outline in a private talk I had later with Vance. He promised to have the subject studied by his people and he would then discuss it with the President. I received the impression that this seed had not been sown in vain.

Though I considered that my complaints against Khalil and to a large degree also against the Americans were justified, I was as mindful as they were of the very worrying developments in the region. I recognized that Egypt's position had become more extreme not only because Sadat's advisers had gained the upper hand, but also because of what was happening in the Arab world. Khalil's explanation of these events had a realistic basis. My meetings in the palace of the King of Morocco seemed to belong to a distant era, as did Sadat's visit to Jerusalem.

I was apprehensive about our situation in the Middle East and our standing in the world, faced as we were by the increasing power of the Arab oil States and the religious nationalism that was sweeping the Islamic countries. The peace treaty with Egypt was the lone exception to this trend, and the time for securing it was liable to pass. Would we have the stamina and the wisdom both to safeguard our vital interests and to reach an agreement?

I had intended returning to Israel on Saturday night, 24 February, but Vance informed me that the President wished to speak to Khalil and to me before we left Washington, and the meeting was set for Sunday afternoon. I wanted our Ambassador to be with me, and Khalil brought the Egyptian Ambassador as well as Butros Ghali. But as we were about to enter the President's office, the Ambassadors and Ghali were stopped, and only four of us went in - Khalil, Vance, Brzezinski and myself.

Carter opened, as Vance and Atherton had done, by emphasizing the need to complete the negotiations quickly. He, as President of the United States, had to determine America's policy in the Middle East, and he proposed to do that within the next ten days. During that time, he also wished to solve the problems that were still outstanding between Egypt and Israel. The treaty, he said, was within our grasp. The controversial items were marginal, and we should all be impelled by a sense of urgency.

The occasional smile with which he tempered his words was thin and fleeting, never extending beyond lips and teeth. His expression was grave, his look harsh. When he had ended his preamble, he asked Khalil how he would sum up this meeting of Camp David II. The Egyptian Prime Minister said progress had been made, and that he, like the President, felt that time pressed and we needed to hasten the conclusion of the negotiations. Saudi Arabia was calling for another Arab summit conference in addition to the one at Baghdad. Egypt could not possibly afford to be isolated in the Arab world. It was essential, therefore, to move on quickly to the decisive phase of the process – the signing of the peace treaty.

Carter then turned to me for my estimate. I told him that far from achieving any progress whatsoever, we had in fact slipped back. The treaty was based on full withdrawal in exchange for full normalization of relations. The Egyptians now wanted total territorial withdrawal on our part but only partial normalization on their part. They had reneged on their agreement to exchange ambassadors, and . . . Carter stopped me at this point, saying that my recapitulation of this event was inaccurate. It was Israel who had rescinded her agreement to evacuate El Arish in advance of the committed date, and Egypt had reacted by dropping the ambassadorial exchange. At all events, he added, if all the other questions were settled, he hoped he would get Sadat's agreement to settle this one, too, and establish diplomatic relations at the level of ambassadors as agreed upon earlier.

The moment of truth came when Carter spoke about the controversy over Article 6 – the 'priority of obligations' clause. Why, he asked, did we attach so much importance to this? I had to repeat, as I had had to time and again, that if our peace treaty did not have priority over Egypt's commitments to her earlier treaties with the Arab States, she would have to go to the help of Syria, for example, if that country launched an attack on the Golan Heights. To this the President replied: 'But the Egyptians don't claim that'; and he turned to Khalil for confirmation. Khalil remained silent, refusing to endorse Carter's statement. He would give no undertaking that Egypt would not join Syria in such an event.

I went on to say that my disappointment was not only with the increased extremism shown by Egypt but also with the espousal by the United States of Sadat's doctrine. On this issue of Article 6, for example, the proposal brought by Secretary Vance to Israel some weeks earlier on behalf of Egypt, which we had rejected, was exactly the same, word for word, as the one we had just been handed as the proposal of the United States! This time it was Vance who remained silent. He could not very well deny it.

Carter abandoned the point and said he had it in mind to invite Begin to Washington on 1 March 1979 'since you lack the authority to decide on behalf of your Government. Khalil has such authority. I shall ask Begin to come so that it will be possible, with his participation, to end the negotiations.' He added that there were also bilateral subjects which had to be concluded between Israel and the United States.

The hour-long meeting was largely a presidential monologue. It was evident that this time, unlike previous occasions, Carter's intention was to utter and demand rather than listen and learn. He spoke of ending the clarifications in terms of days, with the urgency of a mariner expecting a tempest and determined to reach harbour in time.

Carter's invitation to Begin for a Washington summit meeting was handed to us before we left Camp David. The Americans had also wanted Sadat to come, but he refused, and said that Prime Minister Khalil had full authority to take decisions. I recognized, of course, that a summit conference in which Begin's counterpart would be Khalil was something of a slight to us, for Begin was head of our Government, and though Khalil also bore the title of Prime Minister, the head of his Government was Sadat. But I saw no alternative. During our talk, the President had asked me if the Israeli Government would be willing to grant me decision-making authority, and I replied that there was not the slightest chance of that. We both smiled. In these circumstances, and also in the light of the political situation in the Middle East and America's perception thereof, I felt that Begin should accept the presidential invitation. This was also the view of the other members of our delegation. I telephoned Begin and told him so. He said he would think it over.

It came up, and under fire, at the regular Cabinet meeting in Jerusalem that Sunday, my last day in Washington. Many ministers expressed reservations about Begin's attending such a meeting. They resolved to wait until my return to Israel the following day and take a decision at the special Cabinet session scheduled for the day after, Tuesday, 27 February.

Rosenne and I gave detailed reports at that session of our negotiations at Camp David II and my talk with the President. I had also brought to this meeting the latest versions of the American proposal which I had asked Vance to give me before my departure. They consisted of the seventh draft of the proposed joint Sadat–Begin letter, as well as the 'agreed minutes' which were designed to explain, interpret and solve the problems of the controversial clauses in the treaty. Neither the Egyptians nor we had given our final replies to these proposals. Rosenne read the two documents to the Cabinet, and clarified their meaning. In most instances, the Americans had accepted the Egyptian position.

We had not agreed to anything at this Camp David II Conference, and had made no recommendations, and so my fellow Cabinet ministers had no cause for complaint. However, when it came to my recommendation that the Prime Minister should accept Carter's summit invitation, they rejected it out of hand. It was put to the vote and only two of us favoured acceptance. All the rest voted against.

The Cabinet discussion ended with the following decision:

The Government heard a report on the deliberations at Camp David from the Foreign Minister and members of the delegation. It was made clear to the Government that in these discussions no progress was made towards an Egypt–Israel agreement but, on the contrary, the Egyptian stand has become more extreme. To her earlier proposals which Israel considered unreasonable, Egypt has added demands which are not in line with the Camp David Agreement of last September, and which in fact nullify the meaning of the peace treaty between the two countries.

The Israel delegation presented counter-proposals which were rejected by the other party. Prime Minister Dr Khalil insisted on the Egyptian proposals as described above. In these conditions the Government decided that the Prime Minister was unable to go to the meeting with Dr Khalil at Camp David.

The Prime Minister was authorized to write to President Carter giving the detailed reasons for the Government's decision.

The Prime Minister is ready at any time convenient to the President of the United States to meet with him to discuss the problems connected with the peace process, the problems in the region against the background of the latest events, and bilateral questions between the United States and Israel.

When news of the Government's decision reached Washington, the President did not give up. He put a personal telephone call through to Begin and urged him to come – to be in Washington on Thursday, 1 March 1979, as planned. If Begin was unwilling to discuss matters with Khalil, he said, then the meeting would be with just the two of them – the President of the United States and the Prime Minister of Israel. Begin asked to postpone his arrival for a few days, but the President was insistent. Another Cabinet meeting was convened within the next twenty-four hours and Begin's visit to Washington was approved. At my urging, the Cabinet also gave the Prime Minister the authority, at his discretion, to agree, reject or pass on for a Government decision any proposal that might be raised during his talk with the President. At least Begin's hands would not be tied.

CHAPTER TWENTY-ONE

Half the Battle

Begin flew to Washington with two legal experts among his entourage, Meir Rosenne and Yehuda Blum, and started his talks with President Carter on 1 March. Three days later, in Jerusalem, acting Prime Minister Yigael Yadin convened the Cabinet to consider a report by Begin. It consisted of page after page of dialogue between the Prime Minister and the President, read out to the assembled ministers by Ben-Elissar. The lion's share of the dialogue was Begin's. No decisions were yet required at this stage.

The Cabinet was called into session again the following day. This time it was to hear from Begin that there had been a complete turnabout in the American position. He had reached agreement with Carter on the two delicate clauses in Article 6 which dealt with the problem of conflict of obligations, as well as on the joint letter on autonomy. He recommended that the Government approve the new drafts.

I had read them before the Cabinet meeting, and I could see nothing new in them that was of significance. In the joint letter, for example, the term 'target date' had been changed to 'goal'. The Cabinet sat for several hours, during which Yadin spoke to Begin on the telephone to clear up some of the obscurities. The meeting ended with the Government's decision to authorize the Prime Minister to approve the proposals he had recommended concerning Article 6, as well as the goal for ending the autonomy negotiations within one year. The Cabinet vote on the decision was nine in favour, three against, with four ministers abstaining. I supported the motion. Even if the new formulae were not substantially different from their predecessors, that was not a reason for torpedoing the chance of an agreement.

Begin informed Carter of the Government's decision, and the President thanked him. Half the job was done – but only half. Begin had not wished to sit with Khalil; Sadat had not come to Washington to meet with Begin; and the agreement that had been reached so far was only between the United States and Israel.

Carter informed Begin that he had decided to accept his and Sadat's invitations and would be visiting Jerusalem and Cairo. He wanted to finish the job, to reach a formula agreed upon by Egypt and Israel on the outstanding controversial items and also, he hoped, to add his signature to the peace treaty in both capitals. He would be leaving Washington on Wednesday, 7 March, for Cairo, which he would reach the following morning, stay three days, and come on to Jerusalem at 8.30 p.m. on Saturday night, 10 March.

Presidential protocol was in spectacular evidence at Israel's Ben Gurion airport on that Saturday night for the arrival of Carter and his party – army guard of honour, twenty-one gun salute, red carpet, flags and speeches. Everyone of note in both the coalition and Opposition parties was there. One element alone was lacking – emotion. After Sadat's landing at that airport a year and a half earlier, it was difficult not to be blasé about the arrival of anyone else.

When we reached Jerusalem the parties split up. The President and his wife were the private dinner guests of the Prime Minister and Mrs Begin, and Ezer and I gave an informal dinner at the King David Hotel to the others in the presidential group, Secretary of State Vance, Defense Secretary Brown, and their aides.

The formal discussions in which I took part began next morning. Vance asked me to see him at 9.30 a.m. With him were Atherton and Saunders. I had Eli Rubinstein with me to take a record of our talk, which was very general, and covered several topics. Vance gave me America's proposal for our bilateral 'Memorandum of Understanding'. I read it and said I did not think it was specific enough. I asked him whether Egypt also wanted a similar agreement between the United States and herself, and Vance said she did not.

Vance then read out the American proposal on the joint letter on autonomy. I asked for a copy, but Vance refused. However, even at first hearing I noticed that it contained no mention of the term 'administrative council', and it was also clear that the Gaza District had been given an honoured place. It spoke of liaison officers between Egypt and Gaza; of the start of autonomy to be made in Gaza; and the five-year transition period was to commence from the day autonomy was established in Gaza.

I told Vance this did not seem to me to be acceptable. To which he replied that the Egyptians were also turning it down.

On oil supplies, the American administration, he said, wished to propose a ten-year agreement with Israel: Egypt would sell to the United States the production from the Sinai oilfields at the market price, and America would sell this oil to Israel as part of its obligation to ensure that Israel's oil needs would be met for the next ten years.

On the thorny clauses of Article 6, Vance said the Egyptians did not agree to the formulae reached in Washington with Begin. They wanted to change certain words, and add others, which would have the effect of cancelling the Camp David accords.

Vance finally got around to the main point of our meeting. During the talk the previous evening between the President and the Prime Minister, said Vance, Begin had given negative answers to everything. Moreover, Begin had said he would not sign the peace treaty until the Knesset had discussed and approved it. Carter, for his part, had taken this most unusual step of coming to Cairo and Jerusalem expressly to get the treaty signed. If he were now to return to Washington without it, it would affect him adversely. Furthermore, a Knesset debate could complicate matters. Who knew what speeches would be made there, and what interpretations given to the treaty, and what Cairo's reaction to them might be. Washington had faced a similar situation over the treaty with Panama, and the President had decided to sign the treaty first and only later was it debated in the Senate.

I did not ask for details of the Begin–Carter meeting. From the little that Vance said, I understood that it had been difficult and disappointing.

While I was sitting with Vance, Carter was paying visits to our President Yitzhak Navon, to the Yad Va'Shem Holocaust Memorial, and to Mount Herzl. At 11.15 a.m. we all gathered for a working session. The Americans were there in full force. Apart from the President and Secretaries Vance and Brown, there were Brzezinski, Atherton, Saunders, Quandt, Hansell, Samuel Lewis, Hamilton Jordan, Jody Powell, and three other White House aides. Begin had an equally inflated company of attendants. His team consisted of Ministers Yadin, Weizman, Ehrlich, Burg, Shostak, Sharon, and myself, as well as ten officials. Begin and Carter exchanged congratulatory greetings. Begin, in a characteristic courteous gesture, proposed that his guest conduct the proceedings. Carter thanked him, jokingly rapped the table, and opened by saying that he hoped we were all conscious of the importance of those few days. We had travelled a long road together, and we had not given up even when there seemed to be no chance of succeeding. This was the most difficult of all the negotiations he had ever known. He had just come from Egypt, he said, and there he had witnessed an emotional overflow of the masses who wanted peace. He wished now to conclude all the required conditions for the signing of the treaty. President Sadat was as anxious to end the negotiations as he was. It was almost certain, he added, that if we failed to do so during this visit, it would be very difficult to do so later. Sadat was under heavy pressure from the Arab States who were opposed to peace; but if we were able to resolve our differences, he would be ready to come here to Jerusalem immediately, sign the peace treaty, and invite Begin to do the same in Cairo.

Carter said he had promised to telephone Sadat that evening to tell him whether or not he had succeeded.

Begin quickly poured cold water on the proposal. He reminded Carter of what he had explained the previous evening, that before we could sign, the Cabinet had to hold basic deliberations on the autonomy programme, and the Knesset had to debate the peace treaty. Both these would take time. He therefore suggested that we hear from the President and the Secretary of State the proposals put forward by Cairo on all the items directly and indirectly relating to the treaty.

Begin's general displeasure was apparent as he told the gathering that in Washington he had reached agreement with President Carter on the formulae for Article 6 and on the target goal of one year for ending the autonomy negotiations. He had sought his Government's approval and received it by a majority vote. Of course, Sadat had the right to put up counter-proposals and our friends the Americans could change their minds and support them. We would hear them, said Begin, and he would then present Israel's stand.

I did not know whether Carter was aware of the accusing finger, but the purport of Begin's remarks should have been evident. What indeed had been the point of the Prime Minister's having to go to Washington, make concessions to Carter, secure the Israeli Government's approval, if now he was asked to make further concessions to meet Cairo's demands?

Vance read out the suggested Egyptian changes in Article 6. Begin took the floor to give his reactions, speaking in sharp and angry tones. We, too, were a free people, he said, and could either accept or reject the Egyptian proposals. We rejected them, and he took time to explain why. Carter tried to cut him short, but Begin would have none of it. He quoted from articles in the Egyptian press attacking Israel, dubbing her a transient phenomenon and a creature of imperialism. That, said Begin, was the spirit prevalent in Egypt, and therefore they did not wish to commit themselves unequivocally to making peace with her.

Carter, too, got angry. Did we, he asked curtly, have any counter-proposals? Begin shook his head, but he then thought better of it and said we would think about it. Carter pressed for an answer. Begin said we needed time, and reminded the President that in Washington they had found a solution in two days. Carter replied harshly that he did not have two days. Vance intervened with the suggestion that we move on to consider the joint Sadat–Begin letter. Carter said that the draft they were submitting had been reached after lengthy and tough arguments with the Egyptians. The draft letter was read out to the gathering, and Begin expressed his reservations. Our principal objections were to starting the autonomy in Gaza and having Egyptian liaison officers there, and we wanted to add in brackets the words 'admin-istrative council' after the term 'self-governing authority'.

Three other ministers, Yadin, Sharon and I, spoke after Begin, and at 1.30 we broke off for lunch. We resumed at 3, when Vance submitted suggestions for resolving our differences over Article 6 and the joint letter. Yadin and I took issue with them. After half an hour, Carter requested that we stop for a while and meet again later. To prepare us for the next session, he launched into an analysis of the situation in the Middle East and the policy of the United States. Washington regarded the peace treaty as an important basis for her relations both with the Arab States and with Israel. In his talks in Egypt, he had found Sadat generous and open to compromise. He hoped this would also be Israel's approach.

We resumed our meeting at 5 p.m. Carter wished to continue the efforts to resolve the differences so that we could arrive at an agreement. But Begin thought we should stop, since he had to bring the issues before the Cabinet. He was prompted not only by fatigue and pressure but also by the limitation of his authority. Begin was neither willing nor able to accept changes in texts which had already been approved by the Government.

The situation was now paradoxical. The Israeli Government found itself in conflict with President Carter, who had come specially to mediate and work towards securing peace between Egypt and ourselves – the same goal we were aiming to reach. The conflict, now, was not really over substance. It was caused by two technical problems. One was that in order to reach agreement, the Government of Israel would need to retract certain decisions it had taken in the past – some of them only a week earlier. The second was the limited time. Begin said the heavens would not fall if it took longer than a few days to arrive at an agreement. Carter thought differently. The United States President, both for reasons of personal prestige and fear of the collapse of the negotiations, was demanding that all the problems be solved and the treaty signed during his visit.

It must be said that we ourselves were not innocent of any mistakes. When Carter spoke to Begin in Washington about his visits to Cairo and Jerusalem, it was indicated that in the course of his stay there would also be a ceremonial signing of the treaty. If Begin had it in mind to hold discussions in the Cabinet and the Knesset before the signing, he should have told Carter in Washington, and not surprised him in Jerusalem. This was also true of the proposed changes in the formulae of certain Articles in the treaty. When Begin preferred to negotiate with Carter without the participation of Khalil, he should have known that that was not the end of the road. He should have expected that the Egyptians would not accept as Holy Writ, any more than we would, a text agreed upon between the Americans and the other party. The peace to be established was between us and the Egyptians, and it was with them that we had to reach agreement.

Between the afternoon meeting with Carter and the night session of the Cabinet, the Prime Minister gave a dinner party for the President. It was a festive affair in the Chagall hall of the Knesset building, with artistic offerings by violinist Isaac Stern, pianist Pnina Salzman and the Inbal ballet group. The after-dinner speeches were hardly inspiring. Carter talked of the United States' special relationship and commitments to Israel. Begin spoke of difficulties in the negotiations, but expressed confidence that they would be overcome. The mood at the top table was flat. Those who had taken part in the talks were tired and tense. Such gala dinners should be given with the successful termination of deliberations, otherwise they are a waste of good food and pretty dresses.

The Cabinet met immediately after the dinner, starting at 11.30 and going on until 5.30 in the morning. Though ministers strongly criticized the American position, they did not now renew their approval of the Government's previous decision. What they did, at the suggestion of the Prime Minister and the legal advisers, was agree to the Egyptian request to change a word ('derogate' to 'contravene') in the 'interpretative note' to Article 6 (5). On the question of establishing autonomy first in Gaza, it was decided not to include this in the joint letter; but if Egypt should propose it, Israel would be ready to consider it during the autonomy negotiations. On oil supplies, the decision, at my suggestion, was to notify Vance that we were interested in buying from Egypt the total oil production from the wells we had drilled. Should Egypt fail to honour this commitment, we would receive the oil from the United States in accordance with her guarantee. This suggestion was a combination of our request and a proposal made by Vance.

The principal step taken by the Government towards a compromise with the Egyptians was over the exchange of ambassadors. It decided to inform the President of the United States that he could in turn inform the Egyptians that the withdrawal of our forces from Sinai would be carried out in stages. Put simply, this meant that we would withdraw from El Arish at an earlier stage than was called for in the treaty, on condition that Egypt would stick to what it had agreed to, and what Sadat had promised Carter, that an exchange of ambassadors would be effected one month after our forces withdrew to the Ras Mohammad–El Arish line. Thus, the Government was now agreeing to the very proposal which Defence Minister Ezer Weizman had flown specially from Blair House to put before it, and which it had at that time turned down.

The Government decisions were transmitted to the Americans, but they were dissatisfied. Vance said he saw no point in going to Egypt unless we agreed to the stationing of Egyptian liaison officers in Gaza.

At 10.30 on Monday morning, 12 March, there was a further meeting in the Prime Minister's office with Carter and his aides. We were represented this time by the entire Cabinet. The atmosphere was bleak. Both Begin and Carter were tired and impatient. Both were due to deliver speeches at a special session of the Knesset which was to open at noon. Begin had had almost no sleep for the past two nights, and Carter saw time slipping by without the progress he had expected. He was scheduled to leave Israel the following day, and if the situation remained unchanged he would be returning to Washington empty-handed. The chief obstacle, and almost the only one, was Gaza. Carter demanded with brutal insistence that we should agree to Egyptian liaison officers in Gaza so that Egypt could influence her people to support the autonomy programme. Just as the Americans had free entry into Gaza, he said, so should the representatives of Egypt. Begin interpreted Carter's insistence as a virtual command to us to carry out his wish, and he replied coldly that we would sign only what we agreed on, and not on anything with which we disagreed. The Camp David accords had made no mention of Egyptian liaison officers in Gaza, and we would not agree to have them there.

We also discussed the problem of oil supplies. Cabinet ministers rejected the American proposal that we receive Egyptian oil through an American company. This would signify a continuation of the Arab boycott against Israel. After the signing of the peace treaty and the establishment of normal relations, Israel had the right to buy oil directly from Egypt and transport it in her own tankers through the Gulf of Suez. This was not only a practical matter but also one of principle.

The meeting ended, and we all hurried over to the Knesset.

There were only three speakers, Carter, Begin, and Opposition leader Shimon Peres, and all three were short. Yet this parliamentary session lasted two hours, prolonged by non-stop interruption during the speeches of Begin and Peres. This was not the Knesset's finest hour. As soon as Begin rose to his feet, he was shouted down by the vigorous heckling of Geulah Cohen and Moshe Shamir (who thought the Premier had conceded too much) and by the Communist members (who thought he had not conceded enough). It was true, as Begin observed to Carter, that this was a sign of our lively democracy; but there were other democracies in the world where all political parties were careful to uphold the dignity of their parliament. This was not the case with us. The removal of Geulah Cohen from the hall and the incessant exchanges between the Knesset Speaker and the heckling members proved a dismal spectacle. I felt sorry and ashamed. If only to respect the demands of civilized hospitality to our guests, we should have shown our better side and behaved with common courtesy.

In his address, Carter concentrated on the importance of establishing peace in our region. And he also gave a hint of his inner feelings when he said that the nations were ready for peace, but 'we, the leadership, have not yet shown that we are ready'.

Begin picked up the gauntlet. We, he said, wanted a peace treaty that had meaning, and we had therefore not consented to the nullification of Articles which were the very core of the treaty.

This special session of the Knesset happened to be held during the most difficult hours of our negotiation. That, I thought, was not the moment to talk about peace, but to make it.

At 2 p.m., when the session ended, the ministers returned to the Prime Minister's office for a Cabinet meeting. Vance had refused to go to Cairo, on the plea that he could not 'sell' our Government decisions to the Egyptians.

The Cabinet sat until 4.30, and a quarter of an hour later the ministers were joined by Vance, Brzezinski and their aides. Nothing new emerged. Each side repeated its arguments and explanations. During the meeting with the Americans we received word that President Carter had decided to leave the following morning. Begin prepared the draft of a joint statement by Carter and himself which he handed to Vance. It spoke of fruitful discussions, progress gained, and the need to continue negotiations. Vance read it and said he would pass it on to the President. We broke up at 6.30 p.m., the Americans returning to the King David Hotel, the Prime Minister to his home. No further meetings had been scheduled.

Several ministers remained round the Cabinet table, dispirited over the apparent dead end and trying to find a way out. The problem of conflict of obligations had been solved, at least in part, and the questions of the phased withdrawal and the exchange of ambassadors had been settled. Two tough obstacles remained: oil supplies and liaison officers in Gaza. All present agreed that the President's visit and his efforts to bridge the gap should not end in failure. One of the ministers proposed a formula on the oil problem which seemed to me to have a chance of American acceptance. I telephoned Begin, catching him as he was about to go to bed, and told him of the proposal which had come up. I suggested that another minister and I should talk about it to Vance. Begin said I should go alone, for I, as Foreign Minister, was entitled to try out new possibilities despite the Government's decision, but not, of course, to commit myself. Only the Government had the right to change its decision.

I telephoned Vance, went over to his hotel suite, and the two of us sat together for the next few hours trying to clear things up. We had had dealings with each other over quite a long period, and I believe we had found a common tongue and enjoyed mutual trust. I urged Vance to try to persuade the Egyptians to accept our view on Gaza and to allow no mention in the joint letter of liaison officers. And I repeated what we had said earlier about the Egyptians being able to bring up their proposal of advancing elections in Gaza at the autonomy negotiations. As for what the President had said about Egyptian representatives having the same freedom to enter Gaza as Americans, this was unjustified. With withdrawal from El Arish and the inauguration of normal relations, any Egyptian could travel to Gaza on an Israeli visa, just as any Israeli would be able to go to Cairo on an Egyptian visa. It seemed to me that Vance accepted this argument. He, too, was looking for a way to resolve the issue. He promised to try to persuade the President and the Egyptians.

On oil supplies, I told him I understood that at this stage it was not possible to compel the Egyptians to undertake to sell us oil on a long-term contract. Egypt had no such arrangement with any other country. If, therefore, we accepted the American proposal for the oil to be supplied to us through an American oil company, we would need, I said, two commitments. One was an American guarantee ensuring that our oil needs would be satisfied for the next twenty years, not ten. The other was a clause in the treaty stating that we had the right to buy oil directly from Egypt. Without such a clause, the Egyptian boycott of Israel would remain in force, despite the peace treaty, and this was the most sensitive element when it came to oil.

During our talk, Vance was on the telephone several times to President Carter, and after the last call his spirits rose. He said that his aides would prepare the draft of an appropriate clause, incorporating my suggestion, to be added to the treaty. As for the long-term American guarantee, he would need to examine it with the President, but he thought they would come towards us on this matter. I left him to return to my hotel, and found Rahel waiting up for me. To her I could boast: 'The crisis is over.'

I telephoned Begin early next morning and reported on my talk with Vance. Any new proposals, he said, would need to be brought before the Government.

Shortly afterwards, at 7 a.m., Vance telephoned to ask whether I could join him for an early breakfast. When I arrived, he showed me the draft that had been prepared as an addendum to Appendix C of the treaty. It stated that the peace treaty and the Appendix determined the establishment of normal economic relations between the parties. Accordingly, it was agreed that these relations also included the commercial sale of oil by Egypt to Israel; Israel would have the absolute right to submit proposals for the purchase of oil from an Egyptian source which was not required for Egyptian internal consumption; and Egypt and concession owners would also receive proposals for the purchase of oil by Israel, and on the same basis and the same conditions which applied to all potential purchasers.

On the American guarantee, Vance said the United States would be prepared to give such a guarantee for fifteen years. If for any reason Israel should be unable to secure the oil she required from other sources, the United States would supply it. I asked, part jokingly, part not, what was expected to happen after fifteen years. Vance laughed. Oh, he said, if only someone would guarantee oil supplies to the United States for fifteen years! He then added that in another ten years there would be additional sources of energy.

Vance said he had asked me to come at that early hour as the President had invited the Prime Minister for breakfast, and had requested Vance and me to join them. When we entered the President's suite, Begin was already there. The talk was amiable. Carter presented, as his own proposal, the clause covering oil supplies to be added to the Appendix, and the US guarantee for fifteen years. Begin said he would bring it to the Cabinet for approval.

Carter then asked about Gaza. I repeated what I had already told Vance – that with normalization there would be free movement between Egypt and Israel, including Gaza, in accordance, of course, with the relevant arrangements laid down in the peace treaty. The President then raised a further question – about the 'gestures' Egypt was requesting from Israel in order to create a favourable atmosphere among the inhabitants of the territories. These were of subsidiary interest. Begin asked to receive the request in writing and promised to consider it sympathetically.

As we rose to leave, the President said he would be discussing with Sadat what we had decided in his talks with us and would let us know the result. Though he made no promises, his expression indicated that we had cleared the last hurdle.

The President and his party left at 1 p.m. that day, after brief speeches by Carter and Begin at the airport. Both were restrained but optimistic. The Prime Minister told Carter: 'You have succeeded. It is now Egypt's turn to reply.' Carter thanked the Government and people of Israel for their kindness, and added that there had been good progress. The previous night, he said, there had been lengthy discussion between the Israeli and United States delegations on the three stubborn outstanding problems, and that morning, on the basis of those deliberations, he and the Prime Minister had succeeded in making substantial progress.

The presidential plane took off for Cairo, and in a few hours we would have Egypt's answer. As I drove home to Rahel and the promised black coffee, the rain, which had held off for about an hour, came down in torrents, a boon to the blossoming orange groves and the ripening crops, a blessing to every planted seed and every spring and well.

The Cabinet met at 10 next morning, Wednesday, 14 March, and Begin reported that Carter had telephoned him from Cairo airport, after he had seen Sadat and shortly before taking off for Washington, to say that all was well. This had been followed by a letter from the President, which had been brought to him that morning by the US Ambassador, giving the details. Sadat had agreed to the new text of the conflict of obligations, as worked out in Israel, and had approved the draft of the joint letter which made no mention of Egyptian liaison officers in Gaza. If the Israeli Government approved the plan of withdrawal in stages, as first proposed at Blair House, Sadat would send a letter to Carter agreeing to an exchange of ambassadors one month following the completion of the first withdrawal stage. Sadat also accepted the proposed addendum to Appendix C of the treaty concerning the sale of oil, and declared himself satisfied with the proposed opening of the border between Egypt and Israel after Israel's evacuation of El Arish.

Begin and I also reported briefly to the Cabinet on the chain of developments on the Monday night and Tuesday morning. There was no need to report at length, since these developments had been widely reported in the press and over the air in Egypt, Israel and the United States, each in its own way. A short statement at the end of the meeting announced that the Prime Minister had informed the President of the United States that the two remaining problems had been solved by the positive decision of the Israeli Government.

CHAPTER TWENTY-TWO

Celebration at the White House

When Sadat changed his mind about going to Jerusalem to sign the peace treaty and Begin signing it in Cairo, it was arranged that the joint signing ceremony would take place in Washington at the White House on 26 March 1979 at two o'clock in the afternoon.

A few matters still remained to be cleared up, the most important of which were the Memorandum of Understanding between us and the United States, and the subject of oil supplies. Oil was handled by the Prime Minister and the Minister of Energy. The Memorandum of Understanding was dealt with by me. I reached Washington on 23 March, having two days in which to complete my negotiations with the State Department. There was an air of finality in the corridors of the American administration, and with the treaty itself completed and ready for signature at the scheduled time, there was little disposition to spend night and day on discussion and bargaining. The attitude seemed to be that any ancillary items that remained could be settled after the signing. To my regret, my own Prime Minister contributed to this mood. While I was saying in a television interview that Israel would not sign the treaty until all the outstanding problems had been solved, Begin was telling another television interviewer that the treaty would be signed on time.

I did not know whether Vance took heed of what I had said, but after a talk with him the attitude changed. He rolled up his sleeves, mobilized his legal experts, and we got down to work. The Americans accepted several of our proposals but not all. Since it had been decided in Jerusalem that the responsibility for the final wording of the Memorandum of Understanding lay with the Israeli Government, I asked Vance to meet the Prime Minister. He did so, and after their talk, Begin informed me that he accepted the United States position.

On the oil question, Begin spoke directly to Sadat, calling on him at the residence of Egyptian Ambassador Gorbal, where he was staying. The two reached an agreement whereby we would advance the date of our withdrawal from the Sinai oilfields and El Arish, and Egypt would sell us oil from those fields at the market price and on a permanent basis. Israeli tankers would carry the oil directly from the Gulf of Suez, and we would not go through the annual competition with other countries for this oil.

Sadat had asked Begin to rely on his word and not to seek a written agreement on this matter. But in consultations with our delegation, I urged that there had to be an official document. I proposed that, as in the case of the exchange of ambassadors, we should receive a letter from the US President in which he confirmed this arrangement on oil supplies. I telephoned Vance and he was good enough to come over to the hotel, where I explained the request. He took it upon himself to get it settled.

Next morning Secretary Vance telephoned and suggested that the signing of the Memorandum of Understanding as well as the President's letter on oil should be left until after the signing of the peace treaty. I did not ask him the reason, but it was clear enough: neither document was welcome to the Egyptians, and it was thought best that the peace treaty should become an accomplished fact before these were published.

I have never had a liking for ceremonial. Throughout my years in the army, when I had to attend formal functions and parades, whether as a private in the ranks or a general on the podium, I felt no contact with the event, and would keep looking at my watch, willing it to go faster. In Israel, the most impressive parade is the annual Independence Day march, and I took part in most of them. But the most memorable, for me, was the parade that never was! This happened on our first anniversary of the State, in May 1949. The fighting had ended only a few weeks earlier, and we were too busy organizing the country's services and reorganizing our lives to spend much time on arrangements for the great parade. When the first units appeared, the joyful and unrestrained crowds flocked, or were pushed by those in the rear, onto the parade route; and to top it all, some of the hastily erected stands behind the saluting base collapsed. Ben Gurion promptly called off the march – and he did not seem to be much put out. I had had no part in the organization of this event, and so I was able to vanish happily and quickly and make for home, using side alleys to avoid the crowds.

I recalled this experience with nostalgia at every ceremonial event thereafter – including the open-air signing ceremony for the Egypt–Israel peace treaty in Washington, though undoubtedly it was an outstanding happening. While the invited guests jostled each other to get to their seats, and Palestinian Arabs demonstrated some distance away denouncing the peace, at precisely 2 p.m. the three leaders strode onto the platform that faced the

White House, received copies of the treaty from their aides, and signed. The guests applauded, the demonstrators shouted their slogans, and the television cameras – without which an event would become a non-event – went into action. The speeches were mediocre. All three, Carter, Sadat and Begin, had spoken so much during the protracted negotiations about the importance of peace that there was almost nothing left to say. Nevertheless, this was indeed a momentous occasion, not for the pageantry, nor for the speeches, but for the deed itself that was being celebrated – the signing of a peace treaty between Egypt and Israel, officially witnessed by the President of the United States. (A few hours after this signing ceremony, another document was signed without pomp and without publicity at the State Department. This was the Memorandum of Understanding, one of the most important agreements between the United States and Israel.)

The White House put on a gala dinner in the evening, the President and his wife playing host to Sadat and Begin and their wives – and another sixteen hundred invited guests. We sat at small tables inside a huge marquee that had been erected on the White House lawn. I was seated at the table of Secretary Cyrus Vance and his wife, and with us were Arthur Goldberg and his wife, and Israel's outgoing President, Ephraim Katzir, who was in the United States at the time. Many of the guests were leading members of the American Jewish community. Everyone was in festive mood, the tent adding something to the carnival atmosphere, and the drink flowed. I happened to be sitting close to the entrance gangway, and the legs of my chair stuck out, so that some who tried to pass stumbled over them, mumbled a curse, suddenly recognized me, and irritation melted into friendship. The Jews called me 'Moishe', the Gentiles 'General'. All asked something or other, and I answered something or other, but the noise was such that no one could catch a word. Food was served, the band played, and the heat inside the marquee soon conquered the winter cold outside. This heat, and the fatigue – not only of the previous two days and nights – began to tell on me. Gay Vance noticed and sympathized. 'You look tired and bored,' she said. Because of my friendship with the Vances and their understanding, I knew I could ask their forgiveness if I left quietly and returned to the hotel. I bade farewell to them and my other table companions, and drifted out.

With the noisy marquee behind me, my head cleared in the winter night, I was alone again with my thoughts, thoughts about the treaty, of the clauses written on paper which had now to be transformed into reality. I recalled what others and I had said at the emotional Knesset debate only a few days earlier. The Washington signing ceremony and the festive evening had been preceded by an anguished moral stock-taking in Israel's legislative assembly. The Cabinet decision on 14 March approving the treaty had been followed a week later by the longest and perhaps the most critical session of the Knesset. It had lasted ten hours on 20 March, continued for another six hours the following day, and ended with a decisive majority in favour of the treaty. Of the 120 members in the Knesset, 118 took part. 95 voted for, 18 against, 2 abstained, and 3 declared that they were not participating in the vote.

The Prime Minister opened the debate with a detailed account of the final moves, climaxed by Carter's visit to Cairo and Jerusalem and its results. At the end of his address, which was interrupted by repeated heckling, Begin called upon the Knesset for a vote of approval for the peace treaty with its appendices and accompanying letters.

Opposition leader Shimon Peres followed with an opening announcement that his Ma'arach group of Labour parties had taken a decision to vote in favour of the peace treaty. They had resolved to support the treaty because it was the only realistic programme that existed at that time. He concluded by promising that the Labour movement would do its best to persuade our friends and enemies that there was no other true path to peace than the one decided upon by the Government of Israel and the Arab Republic of Egypt, with the help of the United States.

I was the last to speak in the debate before the winding up speech by the Prime Minister. I usually avoid rhetoric and highflown phrases, and I was particularly careful to do so on that occasion. There is nothing easier than to slide into flowery and bombastic language when talking about peace. I tried my hardest to present the treaty as I saw it, in cold and sober terms.

The Egypt–Israel peace treaty, I told the House, was not a pastoral idyll full of sweetness and sunshine and repose in lush meadows. It was not the fulfilment of Isaiah's end-of-days vision when swords would be beaten into ploughshares, and nation would not lift up sword against nation any more. This was a peace treaty which contained military clauses, a treaty which called for the construction of air bases, and held guarantees for the strengthening of Israel's armed forces. It was also a political treaty. But above all it was a realistic peace treaty, set in the context of current realities, and designed to bring about relations between two neighbouring countries, Egypt and Israel, as normal as those between any other two countries in the world.

This was an honest treaty which did not paper over the cracks or ignore the facts and circumstances of our lives. It also included a trial period of two years during which we would continue to remain in the eastern half of the Sinai peninsula, after the inauguration and fulfilment of normalization in Egypt–Israel relations. These relations would be tested during those two

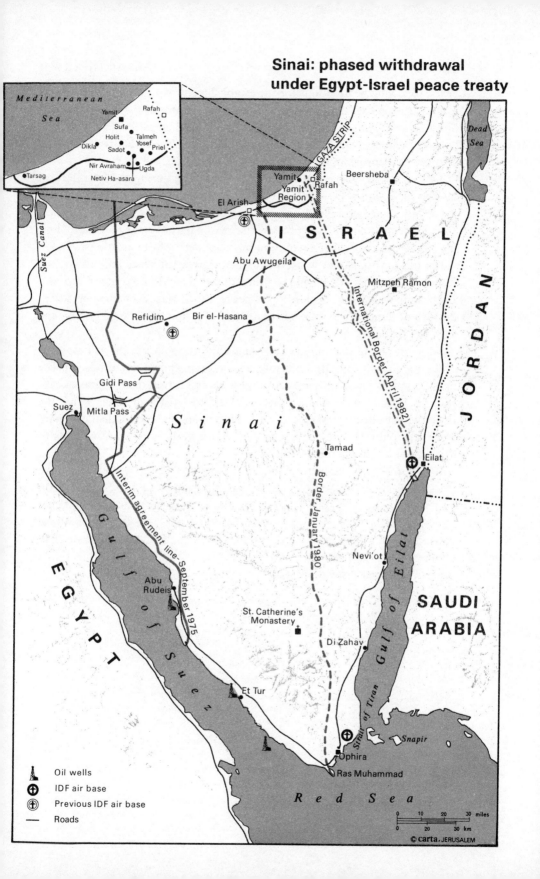

Sinai: phased withdrawal under Egypt-Israel peace treaty

Mediterranean Sea

Rafah
Yamit
Sufa
Dikla
Holit
Talmeh
Sadot
Yosef Priel
Nir Avraham
Ugda
Tarsag
Netiv Ha-asara

El Arish

GAZA STRIP

Yamit
Rafah
Yamit Region

Beersheba

I S R A E L

Abu Awugeila

Mitzpeh Ramon

Refidim
Bir el-Hasana

International Border (April 1982)

J O R D A N

Gidi Pass

Suez
Mitla Pass

S i n a i

Interim agreement line–September 1975

Tamad

Eilat

Border, January 1980

Dead Sea

Gulf of Suez

G U L F   O F   S U E Z

E G Y P T

Abu Rudeis

Nevi'ot

St. Catherine's Monastery

SAUDI ARABIA

Di Zahav

Gulf of Eilat

Et Tur

Strait of Tiran

Snapir

Ophira

Ras Muhammad

R e d   S e a

Oil wells
IDF air base
Previous IDF air base
Roads

0   10   20   30 miles
0   20   40 km

© carta, JERUSALEM

years, following negotiations for the establishment of autonomy in the territories. True, in that period we would not be in control of the whole of Sinai; but we would remain in Sharm e-Sheikh, in our Sinai air bases, and in our Sinai settlements. And if we gave up the Sinai oilfields, we had an American guarantee to ensure our oil supplies for fifteen years.

This, as I said, was a realistic treaty. At no time during our negotiations did the Egyptians seek to evade or even modify any detail or clause which would guarantee completely normal relations between our two countries. They made no attempt, either by an interim or a partial arrangement, to limit the impact of a complete revolution in the pattern of our relations.

For the Egyptians this was a dual treaty: a treaty of peace and a treaty of reconciliation. Its purpose was to bring about an end to the state of war and establish in its stead a relationship of peace. Egypt was reconciling herself to the idea of Israel's existence. Therein lay vindication – for Israel and for the path she had chosen.

I did not ignore the military campaigns and their part in the achievement of this agreement. But after our military victories we had not imposed peace upon Egypt. We had not seized Arab capitals and forced them to make peace with us. What those wars gave us – those four hard campaigns which the Israel Defence Forces fought against the Egyptians – was the defeat of Egypt, and every one of those campaigns had ended with Israel's army closer to Cairo than it had been before.

If we did not impose peace upon them, we did force the Egyptians to take stock of the situation and of their future. It had to be said to Sadat's credit that after the Yom Kippur War, he abandoned Nasser's concept that 'What has been taken by force will be returned by force.' He also rejected the Nasserist – and Egyptian – concept that 'If we have failed this time we shall plan anew for the next war.' Sadat turned in a totally different direction – peace with Israel instead of war.

CHAPTER TWENTY-THREE

Cancer

I had been feeling out of sorts for more than a year, but I had done nothing about it, having always believed that the best way to cure an illness was to ignore it. As usual, it worked. I did my job in my customary way, pursued my archaeological interests in leisure hours, ate, alas, with unjaded appetite, and rose at my usual hour of five in the morning after going to bed at midnight.

Eventually, however, I was unable to disregard what was happening to me. Physical effort in the garden, which I had formerly done with ease and satisfaction, I now found arduous. Walking up flights of stairs set my heart pumping outrageously. And where before I would scramble up hills in top gear, I now climbed them puffing like an old steam engine, and arrived at the top breathless.

I finally called Professor Boleslaw ('Bolek') Goldman, head of the Sheba hospital and an old family friend, and we agreed that I would come in for a general check-up. The problem was *when*. I was busy at the time on the peace talks with Egypt, which were approaching conclusion, and I simply could not absent myself from crucial meetings in Jerusalem and Washington. I then had to go off on official visits to several Asian countries, which had been scheduled months earlier after complicated co-ordination, and could not be postponed. We therefore decided that I would have the medical examination upon my return from the Far East.

My itinerary included Nepal, Burma, Singapore and Thailand, and I also managed to take in Hong Kong. I left on 23 April 1979 and got back on 10 May. One purpose of the trip was to explain the Israel–Egypt peace treaty to my hosts. (Egypt's Vice-President Hosni Mubarak had paid a visit to the same region shortly before, and for the same purpose.) I also wished to find out more about Vietnam's military operations in Cambodia and Laos, and more about China. I also sought to renew personal contact with some of the leaders in the area, among them my friends Ne Win, President of Burma, General Kriangsak Chomanan, Prime Minister of Thailand, and Dr Goh Kengswi, Deputy Prime Minister of Singapore. My fourth purpose was to

settle a number of bilateral matters in the economic and political fields which
our ambassadors had had difficulty in concluding.

I was well satisfied with the visits and got what I wanted. The political talks
were constructive; the renewal of friendships was helpful; practical solutions
were found for the economic subjects of common concern; and the background information and judgments I received from the statesmen in the host
countries enabled me to understand much better the developments in the Far
East, and especially the policy of China. An additional 'bonus' was the
arrival in Hong Kong, shortly after I got there, of Dr Kissinger. He was on
his way back to Washington after visiting Peking, and a breakfast meeting
contributed further to my grasp of what was happening, and what was
expected, in the conflict between China and Vietnam.

Due to the nature of the trip, the timetable was crowded, and we were on
the go all the time, flying from one country to the next, rushing from one
meeting to another, with lots of ceremony and speeches, tours of the interior,
and very little sleep. I could have done without the ceremonial, but not the
tours. On no account would I forego visits to some exotic spot, or inspection
of some interesting farm project, and thanks to the kindness of my hosts I
was able to see a great deal. By plane, helicopter and jeep, I was taken to
areas far from the capital where I could see the villagers following the
primitive ways of their forefathers. But on these trips, whenever I had to walk
through rough fields and climb rugged hills, my heart and my breathing
seemed to rebel.

It was in Thailand that I felt I had reached the limits of endurance, when
visiting the region of Chang Mei. Our objective was a mountain top more
than twenty miles east of the city, home of the Maew tribe. Close by is an
experimental farm, run by overseas experts, among them several Israelis,
who are trying to introduce new crops into the region.

The season of the monsoons was not far off, and the weather was hot and
humid. To get to the top of the mountain, our jeeps crawled in four-wheel
drive up a winding, pitted and pot-holed track, bouncing and swaying so that
we had to hold tightly to the sides of the vehicle to avoid being flung out. We
reached our first stop, the experimental farm, at noon, with the sun at its
hottest. There we were treated to tea and a lecture on the function of the
farm.

The principal speaker was a young American, the son of missionary parents, who had spent the last eighteen years in Thailand, spoke several of the
local dialects and, above all, was utterly devoted to his work. He and his
colleagues told us that the people in the region grew opium, which found its
way to many parts of the world. The experts at the experimental farm,

financed by the World Bank, were trying to persuade the Maew tribe to grow coffee instead, which would bring them greater revenues. I listened to the speakers with profound sympathy. It was a pleasure to meet this group of idealistic young men, passionate believers in the idea for which they laboured. I was sorry not to be able to share their belief. I could not avoid the thought that the local inhabitants, long accustomed to growing – and smoking – opium, might well agree to grow coffee trees, but that would be in addition to, not instead of, opium, which would continue to be their priority crop.

After the tea and the explanations, we were invited to inspect the farm. Rahel and the other ladies in the party preferred to stay behind and rest. But I was anxious to see their work, and we went out to the coffee plantation. To get there, we had to climb a steep stretch of the mountainside, and at times negotiate long and thick tree trunks serving as bridges across the broad clefts in the slope. This was no effort for my hosts, who were used to the track and walked barefoot, and since they were anxious to show me all their farming experiments, they quickened their step. I found it difficult to keep up, and after a few hundred yards I was suddenly overcome by a great weakness. I did not wish to cut short the visit, but my heart simply was not supplying the required fuel. I stopped, and asked them a few questions so that I could rest a little, and got back my breath while they were giving their answers.

We returned to the rest of the party, and then went on to the Maew tribal village, which is on the mountain peak. We were taken to the house of the village chief, a tall, lean and withered old man with a wrinkled face who, I was told, smoked opium from morning to night. Control of most of the land and all the villagers was in his hands.

The house consisted of one huge room, which was multi-functional. A group of infants in cots filled one corner, sacks of corn and rice another. Despite the stifling weather, pots were steaming over a fire in the centre of the room. I tried to leave quickly, but my guide, the young American, drew my attention to a broad shelf on one of the walls. This was an altar, and on it lay gift offerings – bowls of rice, flowers in vases, boxes with spices, strings of primitive beads, and other objects which I could not quite make out. The young American, familiar with the customs of this tribe, said these people were 'spiritualists' – they believed they were ruled by spirits, and these were offerings to their 'rulers'. There were two kinds of spirits: demonic and angelic. The evil ones brought disaster, and had to be appeased; the good ones brought blessings, and had to be kept well-disposed.

In addition to the altar and its offerings, the spirits also had to be provided with the means of access. Accordingly, two thin cords were strung from the altar-shelf to the window, and my guide explained that each was a 'one-way path': the spirits came into the house along one cord and left by the other.

With all the absurdity of this practice, with its strange devices, so bizarre to the Western mind, I could well feel how much their belief and their ritual meant to these people. For them, the spirits were an unquestionable reality, infinitely more powerful than all the efforts of the American to persuade them to adopt the teachings of Jesus, and to raise coffee rather than opium. This reality was also stronger than the laws of a distant government sitting somewhere in the lowlands, in Bangkok. It was stronger than anything else because they had imbibed it as infants and believed in it with all their hearts. Nor did the smoking of opium do anything to weaken their determination not to change their ways.

The suffocating heat in the room, the altitude, and the sheer fatigue were telling on me. I suggested that we get out in the fresh air and go down the slopes to our vehicles. I stole a backward glance at the altar-shelf and was amused by the thought that if I did not leave quickly, my soul would depart from my body and decamp along one of the two cords to the world of the spirits.

Upon my return to Israel I got in touch, as promised, with Dr Goldman, and he arranged for me to receive a comprehensive examination by his team of specialists. I accordingly presented myself at the hospital on 14 May 1979. The preliminary, general probe was performed by Dr Goldman himself, and after comparing the results with those of his previous tests two years earlier, he found there were only two slight changes for the worse, something to do with my pulse and pallidity. From him I was passed, as on a conveyor belt, to the other departments. The orthopaedist examined my injured spine, the result of an archaeological mishap some years before when a cave collapsed on top of me, and he saw no deterioration. The chest man inspected my lungs and found them in order. The heart specialist detected a weakening in the muscles. An analysis of the blood showed I was suffering from anaemia and a lack of iron.

At this stage the prime cause of my indisposition was obscure. I was given injections and a variety of pills, but the anaemia persisted. At the beginning of June, during consultations among the medical team, it was suggested that the colon be X-rayed, as that might provide the reason for the loss of blood. But this could not be done immediately as I had meetings in Egypt to negotiate the implementation of the peace treaty. It was not until 21 June that the radiological examination was carried out, by Professor Hertz, and it was then that the cause was discovered.

When I went into Dr Goldman's room after the X-ray, awaiting me were coffee and company. With him were two colleagues, Dr Wolfstein, the hospital's chief surgeon, and Dr Hertz, all three trying hard to appear composed. Without any preliminaries, and affecting a matter-of-fact tone, Dr Goldman told me the results. 'We've found a growth in your colon,' he said, 'and it needs to be removed as quickly as possible.'

'When you say growth,' I asked, 'do you mean cancer?'

'We'll know that only after we've operated and had it analysed,' he replied. 'All we know for the moment is that the X-ray shows a blockage of the colon.'

I asked to telephone my home, and when Rahel came on the line I told her that the doctors had confirmed what I had suspected – cancer. An operation would be necessary almost immediately. Dr Goldman was not happy with my unvarnished words, and took the telephone to speak to her directly and soften the news. But Rahel had understood, and it was with evident difficulty that she tried to keep her voice calm.

There was no point in dilly-dallying over what was to be done, and I asked the doctors how soon they could operate. It was now 11 o'clock on a Thursday, and they said it could be done on the Sunday. I could return to my office at the Foreign Ministry in Jerusalem, deal with the more urgent matters for the rest of the day, then go home, have the next two days free, and enter the hospital on Saturday evening for my operation on the morrow.

The significance of the test results was not lost upon me, yet it produced no depression. In some ways I felt a sense of ease: I now knew what was wrong. The cause had been correctly diagnosed, and the doctors were to remove it.

I was given more coffee and we then returned in a sober and unemotional mood to the subject of the illness and the operation. The question, according to the doctors, was whether the cancer was concentrated in one place, or whether additional growths had sprouted in other organs. This could not be known from the X-rays. Only after they opened me up could they carry out a precise examination. They therefore hoped that after the operation they would be able to tell me if the trouble had spread, or if I was lucky and it was concentrated in one spot. If the latter, then the operation would be relatively simple: they would cut out the growth and part of the colon, leaving it several inches shorter, and I would be back home and at work in a few weeks. If, however, the cancer had spread, additional operations might be required, as well as radiological and other treatment, in an effort to arrest it.

There was little purpose to continued speculation. We would know in another three days. Nevertheless, in the course of our exchange, somehow or other the subject of death slipped in. For me this subject was neither new nor disturbing. I have long been prepared psychologically to depart from life, to close my eyes and 'be gathered unto my fathers'. If I were to know that I would die in another two hours or two weeks, I do not think I would be particularly shocked or discomposed. Death, after all, is the absolute end and, like most people, I am ready for it at any time. There have been moments in my life which I had good reason to believe were my last, and I know that the thought did not worry me. I suppose this tendency of ours to ignore death springs from the counterweight in the scales: to avoid the danger of losing our lives, we would have to forego actions which we feel are essential, as on a battlefield, or are driven to do by a compelling inner urge, and we are simply not prepared to relinquish such actions for the sake of safety. At all events, over the years, anxiety about mortality ceased to occupy any part of my consciousness. The prospect of death was of no interest to me, and had no effect on my way of life. The guiding forces of that way of life were yearning, ambition and faith.

So there we were, in Dr Goldman's hospital office, talking about death, albeit obliquely. The doctors were explaining the continued treatment if other organs were found to be affected. I preferred not to think of it.

To end the talk on a cheerful note, I told them I had turned sixty-four the previous month, had led a pretty full life, and had no complaints. I did not feel as the patriarch Jacob had felt in hoary old age. And since my medical friends might not be too familiar with the Bible, I told them what Jacob had said to the Pharaoh, after being introduced by his son Joseph, and the Pharaoh had asked him 'How old art thou?' Jacob sighed in reply, complaining that he was about to die prematurely: 'The days of the years of my sojourning are a hundred and thirty years: few and evil have been the days of the years of my life, and have not attained to the days of the years of the life of my fathers in the days of their sojourning' (Gen. xlvii:9). Poor father Jacob. One hundred and thirty years had not sufficed. Well, when he died, the Egyptians embalmed him, as they did their kings, and thereby ensured him eternal life even after death!

Time was running on, and my office in Jerusalem had telephoned several times asking when I would arrive. The doctors gave me the diet to be followed until I returned on Saturday evening for the Sunday morning operation. And then they handed me a gift: I could have Friday as a free day, to do whatever I wished.

I was overjoyed. With all the banter as I sat with the medical men, I was ever conscious of the fact that I had a growth in my colon, which I was sure was cancerous, large enough to cause serious anaemia, and it had to be cut out before it blocked the colon completely. But I had no wish to think of the future. At this moment my only thought was that next day I would be free from dawn to dusk, and I had no doubt what I would do: I would drive south to the dry and desolate region beyond Beersheba which in mid-summer is abandoned even by the Bedouin flocks. I would scrabble about in the wadis, the dry river beds, and search for the remains of dwellings and artefacts of the people who lived there six thousand years ago, during the Chalcolithic period.

In the car on our way to Jerusalem, I sensed that there was no need to tell my bodyguards the medical news. They had been with me for many years, and they had a way of getting to know everything – as they did now, including the hospital ward to which I had been assigned and the number of the telephone that would be installed there!

On arrival at my office, I telephoned the Prime Minister, told him my news, and said that if all went well at the operation, I hoped to be back at work in three or four weeks. I asked him if he wished to appoint another minister in my place during my absence, and he said he preferred to take over the portfolio himself. He was sure it would not be for long. I thanked him for his good wishes, but added, and made it very clear, that if it transpired that I was unable to return in a short time to work at full capacity, I would resign from the Government. Public service in the Government of Israel required total and strenuous devotion day and night to one's job. That was how I had worked up to now, and only if I could continue to work without handicap and without limitation would I permit myself to remain in the Cabinet.

I cancelled or postponed all the meetings scheduled for the next few weeks. There was one item, however, which needed immediate attention and which I wished to deal with myself. It concerned the entrance examination to Egyptian universities for students in the Gaza District. There were some seven thousand of them, young men and women, and the procedure had been for them to be examined in Gaza under the supervision of Unesco representatives who came from Paris, and who then transmitted the examination papers from Gaza to Egypt. There was, in addition, the question of summer vacation visits to Gaza by Gaza students already studying in Egypt which had been arranged previously through the Red Cross. We had now informed the Egyptians and the people of Gaza that since we had signed a peace treaty with Egypt, there was no longer any need for the intermediary services of these international bodies, Unesco and the Red Cross. It should be done directly between us and the Egyptians.

Unfortunately, Egypt did not think so. She insisted on the continuation of the earlier procedure, since in her view Gaza had a special status, and in any case we had not reached the point where we could begin normal relations between our two countries.

I knew that Egypt had her own considerations, connected with her relationship to the other Arab States; but I was not prepared on any account to change our position. Under the peace treaty, Israel had committed herself to withdraw from the whole of Sinai, and even to remove Israeli settlements which had been established just beyond our border. We had agreed to such far-reaching concessions primarily because we had regarded the peace treaty as an absolute end to the state of war and the establishment of normal relations. Thus, the case of a student leaving Gaza to study in Egypt, a foreign country, was exactly the same as that of an Israeli student who left Tel Aviv to study in Italy. Neither Unesco nor the Red Cross nor any other intermediary was required – or would be allowed – to arrange this.

After receiving the Prime Minister's backing for my stand, I sent the appropriate cable to Egypt's Butros Ghali, and I also ordered my ministry officials who dealt with Israel-Egypt relations to carry out my instructions meticulously, and not submit to any pressure. (The military governor had informed me that demonstrations against us on this issue were being planned in Gaza.)

I wanted my words to be clear also to the citizens of Gaza, and wished them to understand that it was not we, the Israelis, but the Egyptians who were holding up the summer visits of their children and the entrance examinations for the new academic year. I picked up the telephone and rang Dr Haidar Abdul Shafi in Gaza. I knew him well, though I had not seen him for several years. He was one of the most extreme radical nationalist and pro-PLO leaders in the Gaza District, highly intelligent, well educated, and frank. On one occasion during my term as Minister of Defence, when there had been a mounting series of terrorist acts in the Gaza District, we had expelled him. He was later allowed to return, and he resumed his medical work and his nationalistic preaching. Latterly he had been chosen by the people of Gaza to head the Red Crescent, an organization which in practice provided a framework for extremist political activity under a humanitarian cover.

He seemed not only surprised but rather pleased to hear my voice, and after the usual exchange of greetings, I got to the point. I told him that as far as we were concerned, all the students could return to Gaza from Egypt, and all who wished to could leave to study in Egypt. But we would not allow either Unesco or the Red Cross to be the intermediaries in this happy enterprise. Even with Jordan, with whom we had no peace treaty, more than one hundred thousand Arabs a year, including students, came and went between our two countries, and all without the involvement of a single person from the Red Cross or Unesco.

Dr Haidar said he knew our views, but it was not the people of Gaza but the Egyptians who insisted on the participation of the international bodies. I told him that all I wished him to know was that it was not we who were the cause of the suffering for the students, and we would not change our position. If the Egyptians remained unmoved, the young men and women in Gaza would stay at home, and those students already in Egypt would stay there forever. Dr Haidar broke in with a laugh. 'You don't have to tell me that,' he said. 'I know you well. I'll try to do the best I can on this matter.'

We arranged that the next day Yossi Hadas, the man in my office who was dealing with this subject, would proceed to Gaza and see the Mayor and other notables, including Dr Haidar. The meeting would be held in the office of the military governor, and the message I had delivered to Dr Haidar on the telephone and to Butros Ghali in a cable would be explained to the Gaza leaders face to face. I had no doubt that in the end they would accept our terms, not only because we were justified but mainly because the problem was pressing and a solution had to be found.

I gathered up the remaining papers on my desk, said *Shalom* to my aide and secretaries, and left for home. I was glad the hour was late, and the general office empty. I was in no mood to talk to anyone.

I took a sleeping pill that night, hoping to sleep late. But I awakened, as usual, at dawn. It would be an unusually hot day, according to the forecast, but when I set out in the morning there was still a light and pleasant breeze. The traffic was heavy as we drove through the outskirts of Tel Aviv, but thinned as we reached the coastal road on our way south, and by the time we reached the Ashdod crossroads we had left the teeming world behind us, and with it the world of newspaper headlines. For a moment I wondered whether to continue south or turn left to the limestone quarry between biblical Yav-neh and the settlement of Benaya. I had once spotted the remains of Canaan-ite graves in the quarry, as well as a cave with parts of a Chalcolithic burial urn. But work in the quarry had then been abandoned, and I had found nothing on a second visit. Since then, however, work might have been re-sumed, and perhaps additional graves had been exposed.

On any other day, I would assuredly have turned off to find out; but not now. The area that I was anxious to inspect, south-west of Beersheba, was rather far, and there was no time to spend on other places. What drew me to the southern spot was the report I had received that the army had con-structed there, for training purposes, a model military outpost, complete with

communication trenches, dugouts and firing positions. If there were no training that day, I could inspect the earthworks in the hope that signs of ancient
remains had been turned up during the digging and had gone unnoticed by
the troops.

We passed through Beersheba, skirted the airfield, and continued south,
following the tracks of tanks and other military vehicles until we reached the
training area. To my delight, there was no sound of firing, and not a living
soul in the mock outpost: the training that day was elsewhere. I got out of the
car, went into the trenches and examined the walls. I found nothing, not even
a single potsherd. The outpost had been erected on a barren hill which had
never been settled by man.

No matter. There were other hills to explore. I walked towards a wadi in
the west, scanning the terrain for any evidence of early settlement. I suddenly
noticed heaps of stones on a mound, but when I came closer I saw they
belonged to an abandoned Bedouin compound. Some had been used to peg
the tents, and others to shelter the cooking fires.

On reaching the lip of the wadi near the foot of the hills, I found what I was
looking for. There were isolated bits of pottery lodged in the fissures of the
slopes, having been swept there by the flash floods that roar through the dry
river beds of the desert, carrying the waters from the north during the rainy
season. The potsherds were not numerous, but I saw they were all from the
Chalcolithic period – about three to four thousand years BC. Their brown,
rough surface bore small black and white blobs, which the ancient potters had
failed to smooth out when preparing the clay for manufacturing the vessels.

I soon found that these potsherds were indeed on the edge of an ancient
dwelling enclosure that had been established on the slope of the hill above the
wadi. Near by, I noticed the tips of stones protruding from the ground, and
when I cleared the earth around them I came upon a layer of black ashes.
Here, six thousand years ago, stood a house, part of it above ground, but its
walls and roof, no doubt of clay and reeds, had long vanished. What was left
was the level below ground, which the wind and rain over the centuries had
covered with a layer of earth. Mixed among the earth and the ashes were the
scattered remains of pottery vessels, flint implements with razor-sharp edges,
pebbles from the dry river bed used as a platform for the cooking fire, and
flat stones on which they pounded the seeds and roots which served them as
flour.

Only very rarely have I found a complete pottery vessel which had remained intact from those times. But I did not search for them because it
meant serious digging, and I was in no state to do any tough physical work.
The doctors had ordered me to eat very little before the operation, and that

morning I had taken nothing but a cup of tea. It was now high noon, and I had trudged several miles in the heat, so that it was with difficulty that I managed to move the stones.

But it was not only weakness which kept me from trying to dig up the resistant earth. I was looking for something special – for stones and pebbles which the ancient inhabitants of this region used to fashion into the shapes of animal heads, or even birds or a human head. For some years now, my main archaeological interest has been the early Chalcolithic period. The antiquities dealers in the Old City of Jerusalem already know this, and whenever stone objects, pottery vessels or other artefacts from this period come into their hands – mostly originating in the Jericho area or the region of Bab el-Dara on the eastern shore of the Dead Sea – they let me know. They are pleased to do so, for the items which interest me have little attraction for the general tourist. They are for the most part blemished, without colour, and lacking in conventional form. The vessels were made before the invention of the potter's wheel, so they are asymmetrical and their handles are crooked.

I had acquired three such vessels the previous week from different dealers, one from Haji Baba, another from Kandu, and the third from an Armenian named Moumingian but known as Abu-Salah. The one I bought from the Armenian was the most interesting. The vessel was splintered, and Abu-Salah, who was utterly absorbed in his game of backgammon and did not wish to be interrupted, warned me that many of the pieces were missing, particularly from the base. I worked on all three vessels at the weekend, cleaned them with nitric acid, filled in the missing parts with gypsum, strengthened the cracked parts with glue, and they then looked as they had when they were fashioned. They are not things of beauty in the accepted conventional sense, but I am very fond of them. I think that even if I had not known their age, and not learned that these were the first pottery artefacts the early inhabitants of this country had discovered how to make, I would recognize them from their appearance. When I took at them, I see their originality. I see a handful of mud being kneaded and moulded, then dried in the sun or over a fire, and turned into a dish, a vessel looking as much like a concave block of natural clay as the creation of man.

On my trips in search of the dwelling places of these early Canaanites, I began to be interested in the peculiar stones found at the bottom of their houses or near by. The truth is that to this day I am not certain whether it is my imagination that sees in these stones the heads of animals, complete with eyes and nostrils, or whether they really have been sculptured. I now have in my home twenty such stones. Some show definite signs of human touch, as though someone had tried to carve certain lines on them with a flint tool, or gouge out pieces to accentuate eye-sockets. Did they do this to make them look like what I see in them – the form of an animal, a man, a bird? Or am I reading something into random pebbles that were simply used in the house as hearthstones for the cooking pots?

On that Friday morning, too, I collected several stones and then, too, I could not tell for certain whether they were the work of some ancient sculptor or whether they were shaped by nature. I was tired, and I laid them out in a row and sat and looked at them. As a matter of fact I had already stopped struggling over the question of whether they were natural or sculptured. They were what they were. The Canaanites who lived on this hill saw in them what they saw, and I, on that Friday, saw what I wished to see. They were stones in the form of sheep's heads, clearly designed to bring fruitfulness to the flocks, for why else would the good Lord have given them that shape?

I had intended at first to cross to the other side of the wadi to see what that had to offer; but when I rose, I suddenly felt near collapse. I rested a little and then walked back towards the car with dragging feet, thinking, as I went, that I would probably get home by the late afternoon. That should give me enough daylight time to immerse the stones I had collected into a cleansing solution and remove the layers of dirt and limestone that had collected over the millennia. When I reached the car, I curled up on the back seat, closed my eye and was dead to the world, undisturbed by the bumping and swaying of the vehicle as we drove for miles over the rough track before joining the main road. I dreamed.

I cannot be certain whether I fell asleep the moment I shut my eye and only then started dreaming, or whether I began to picture a dream scene while still awake, and dropped off only later. In general, I am one of those people who dream when they sleep, and the dreams are truncated, fast-changing, often associated with the day's events, and promptly forgotten upon awakening. That is, we remember that we have dreamt, but the details vanish. For about a year, however, I had been frequently visited by one particular dream, and its details have remained with me during my conscious hours. It would come to me when I had gone to bed very tired, yearning for the moment when I could put my head on the pillow and cut myself off body and soul from the tense and wearing burdens of the day. It was this strange dream that I now dreamt in the car on my way home from the visit to the southern desert site of antiquity.

In this dream, I am evading pursuit, climbing a hill and trying desperately to reach the top where I know I shall find a haven. I am exhausted, and the going is hard, but I continue to climb without pause. The track I follow is known to me, and so is my objective. I am clambering up the hillside just north of my village of Nahalal, the site of the village cemetery overlooking the Haifa–Nazareth road. To my left is the hill of Shimron, and to my right Migdal Ha'Emek. The track leads to the cemetery; but that is not what I am aiming for. My objective is the peak above and just north of it, what the children of Nahalal in my time used to call 'the forest'. It is covered with rich foliage, terebinth and oak, with cyclamen, anemone and Star of Bethlehem sprouting between the rocks in winter. Even in summer, the withered plants have enough left in them to give food to the cattle and goats of the El-Mazarib tribe of Bedouin who dwell in the wadi beyond the hill.

I finally get to the top, and close to the track which turns westwards is a cave scooped out of the rock. Its entrance is hidden by branches of terebinth, but since I know it I go straight to it and crawl inside. It has just space enough for me to lie down comfortably. The ground is not hard. Indeed, it is 'upholstered' by a mixture of dust from the peeling walls and ceiling, and earth and leaves swept into it by the wind and rain. I lie on my right side, shift about to get the right depression in the 'mattress' beneath me, close my eye, and sink into the calmness and tranquillity for which I yearn.

I have climbed the hill to get to this hideaway, but not out of fear. I know that I wished to escape from where I came, but not because I was being pursued by someone who meant me harm. Even now, as I lie relaxed, slowly breathing the limpid air and listening to the rustling of the leaves in the wind, the feeling of peacefulness is prompted not by the safety of my refuge, but by the achievement of my aim – cut off from the world which I have left behind. To lie thus is what I wanted, on a blanket of soft earth and rotting leaves, in a cave hidden among bushes somewhere on a hill that looks out over the Valley of Jezreel; to lie quietly, to rest, to forget all, to think of nothing; just to sense the softness of the ground and listen to the light whispers that come in from afar.

On the Saturday evening I drove to the hospital and delivered myself into the hands of the doctors and nurses, who put me through all the preparatory procedures of the night before an operation. They were all very amiable, throwing me from side to side and doing with me what they willed, punctuating it with frequent smiles and enquiries of how I felt.

In the morning I was put through additional tests, told that they were satisfactory, and taken to the operating theatre, which I just managed to glimpse before the anaesthetic took effect. I awoke at noon to find myself back in my room, with Rahel at the bedside telling me 'All is well, all is well'. I wanted to ask whether they had found anything more than the growth that had shown up on the X-ray, but decided to postpone it; I imagined I was probably too befuddled by the anaesthetic to register what I would be told. I noticed various tubes sticking out of my nose and arms, and a cardiograph recording my heart movements in wavy green lines. My mouth was dry, but I was only allowed a moistening of the tongue. Drowsy, and feeling I was about to go under again, I just had time to ask Rahel to remind me, when next I awoke, to tell her what I had dreamed while undergoing the operation. The words I managed to get out before falling asleep were: 'Imagine, of all places in the world, I dreamt I was back in Nepal! In Katmandu ...'

When I opened my eye the second time I was myself, fully conscious, aware of pains in my stomach, my voice extremely hoarse, my belly bandaged and bound by a wide belt.

I now wished to know my state, and whether the growth had spread. Dr Goldman and Dr Wolfstein assured me faithfully that apart from the lump which they had taken out, together with a portion of the intestine, they had discovered no sign of any growth in any other of my abdominal organs. As to the exact nature of the growth they had extracted, they would know this only in another few days after completing the laboratory tests.

This did not change my outlook, since I was certain it was cancer, and its particular form and its Latin name were of no interest. We exchanged a few words on the public announcement that had to be made, and I insisted that they tell the unadorned truth – 'without blue paint and without rouge', as we say in Hebrew.

Physically, I felt well, though weak. My digestive organs worked as they should, unbothered by the shortened intestine.

Next morning, after I had shaved, Rahel reminded me that I had promised to tell her of my Katmandu dream. I told her that while waiting to be brought to the operating theatre, my mind went back to some of the experiences on our visit to the Far East. From the personal point of view, my most interesting talk was with Ne Win in Burma. But there was a diverting episode in Nepal, which I was visiting for the first time, that I had forgotten, and it suddenly came back to me.

Among the guests at a reception given for me by our Ambassador in Katmandu was a young Jewish couple from the United States. The husband was a computer expert, employed by the World Bank, who had served in several developing countries and was now stationed in Nepal. His wife, Brooklyn-born, spent her time raising two daughters and giving Yoga lessons to the wives of diplomats. She had been to Israel, spent two years at the Hebrew University in Jerusalem, and spoke Hebrew. We had a very pleasant talk. They were well-mannered, intelligent, and had a keen sense of humour.

Nevertheless, the chasm between us was wide and deep. We were in two different worlds.

They told me that before their children were born, they had travelled and got to know many countries; and despite their Jewish origin, study at the Hebrew University, and their advanced cultural level, they had decided that they wished to spend the rest of their lives in a distant corner of the world. The wheel of fortune had stopped at Katmandu. They were happy there. The crowd they mixed with were young Europeans from various countries who had cut their ties with their lands of origin. The wife told me that she took drugs – but only to the point where it induced good spirits. They were also involved with the local Hindus and Buddhists who spent their time meditating in pagodas and making pilgrimages to holy places. Their outward lives seemed primitive, and Katmandu, in Western terms, could not be called a cultural centre of the world. But it gave them an inner satisfaction and they were contented. This young Jewish couple from America were not nostalgic for their country or for Europe, and they had no share or interest in the aspirations of Israel. Neither the Jewish heritage of the past nor the dramatic events of the Jewish present meant anything to them.

After the reception, they suggested that we join them for a trip to a part of Katmandu that, according to them, would assuredly not be included in the itinerary of our official visit. To the disquiet of our Nepalese security men, we accepted. The place they took us to, not far from the capital, was the bank of a river that flows into India's holy Ganges. The mounds above were studded with numerous pagodas, and milling around them were Hindu pilgrims and emaciated, almost naked, wild-haired yogis. Sitting or stretched out in niches at the sides of the pagodas were men and women holding out a rice bowl and begging for alms.

As we walked between the pagodas, we saw a funeral group walking towards the river, bringing one of their sect to his eternal peace. They took a few paces into the water, opened the casket containing his ashes, and scattered them over the surface of the river. They floated for a while and then vanished, carried off by the current to the Ganges.

The young couple with whom we had come seemed greatly impressed, and could not stop talking about it as we drove back to the hotel. The sight was indeed affecting but on no account did it help me to understand why these two young Jews should find this place the ideal of their lives. Perhaps I was incapable of understanding what I saw. It may be that certain people get attached to the faith of the local population, and even though they themselves do not become Buddhists or Hindus, they prefer the atmosphere surrounding this spot to life in the West.

I did not talk to them again on this subject, but it saddened me. I thanked them for the trouble they had taken, and I imagined that the whole episode would be wiped off the memory slate in a few days. But apparently not. Some time or other under deep anaesthesia on the operating table, I found myself back in Katmandu, hovering over the river and rising steadily skywards. I had not turned into ashes, yet I was no longer a physical being. Even when I awoke, I remembered that the higher I rose, the more the world below me shrank, until it eventually disappeared. At that point I, too, somehow or other ceased to exist. I simply became part of the air around me. A strange dream.

A few days later, though still in bed, I was able to hold work sessions with senior members of my office staff, and a week after the operation I left the hospital. After all, my arms, legs and head were unaffected, and the stomach had been sewn and re-sealed. Why, then, should I stay cooped up in a hospital room when I could be walking around at home, and start getting back into the swing of office affairs? Moreover, there was an exciting basketball match scheduled for the Saturday night between the select Israeli amateur team and the American champion professionals. Of course the American professionals were expected to win, but how could I not be present to shake the hands of our players, as usual, before the game? Dr Kishon, the cardiologist, was not enthusiastic over my proposed programme. I would need to climb a lot of stairs, he said, and furthermore, in the course of the game I was likely to get overexcited. I reassured him. I would take the stairs one at a time, and as for the excitement, it was Rahel who yelled herself hoarse cheering our team, not I; and it was she who shouted the bravos whenever our star scorer Micky Berkowitz dropped an impossible ball through the basket.

As I began to recover, the events of my Far East visit preceding hospitalization began to recede. Only a few small islands in the sea of memory stood out boldly, unblurred and unfaded. One was the visit to the Shveh Dagon pagoda in Burma. In itself the event was of slight importance, but it had significance for me. We were touring Rangoon and were, of course, taken to this pagoda, the most magnificent and impressive I have ever seen. It is probably unmatched for size, splendour and beauty. The outside of the building is plated with gold, and its dome studded with precious stones. Gold, silver and precious stones also adorn the interior halls, where statues of Buddha abound.

But the hall which captured our hearts – Rahel was with me at the time – was the one which displayed the gift offerings for Buddha and the pagoda.

We were told that devout pilgrims from far-off places brought valuable objects, and, indeed, ranged round the hall were cupboards full of exquisite treasures, figurines and vessels of gold, silver and ivory, lengths of brocade, and delicately embroidered fabric. All very opulent. But our eye was caught by a doll that stood alone on a shelf in one of the cupboards. It bore a necklace and its dress was embroidered, but it was a simple doll that could be bought anywhere for a few cents. The monk who accompanied us saw our surprise as we stopped to look at it, and he explained that it was on display because the child who brought it said it was her most precious possession. She loved it more than anything in the world, and she therefore wished to offer it to Buddha.

The outstanding recollection from Burma, of course, was my meeting with Ne Win. The two main subjects we discussed were China's reaction to Vietnam's invasion of Cambodia, and Burma's domestic policy. The visitor immediately notices one significant difference between this country and nearby countries like Thailand, Singapore or the Philippines: there are few foreigners in Burma. Its standard of living is low, and the patterns of the West have not penetrated its shores. Ne Win explained his policy with utter frankness. Not only did his Government not encourage tourism or capital investment from abroad, but they worked actively to keep both out. Visas to foreigners were given very sparingly, and those that were granted were limited to seven days. Ne Win knew the economic boons that tourism brought, but imagine, he said, what it would do to the character of Burma and its people. There would be a rash of nightclubs and fancy restaurants; the young men and women would dance attendance on the foreigners to make quick money; villagers would leave their fields and stream into the towns; the streets would be crowded with American cars; and the traditional Burmese dress would give way to jeans and gaudy shirts. Burma would cease to be Burma. So long as he, Ne Win, was in control, he would do his utmost to preserve the character and independence of Burma. It was up to the Burmese to grow their own food, and they had a country rich in water and cultivable land to do so. They had to grow rice by their own labours, raise their own cattle, bring in their own fish, cut down and export their much-wanted teak trees. Ne Win told me that thousands of elephants were at work in the teak forests in the service of the Government, hauling the timber to the rivers from where it was floated down to the port. That, said Ne Win, was Burma, and he wanted no strangers, no tourists, no foreign investors, and no development, if that meant turning Burma into a Western satellite and losing her traditions and her political, economic and cultural independence.

When I rose to leave, he shook my hand, looked me in the eye, and said:

'My dear friend General Dayan, all my life I dreamed of Burmese indepen-dence. Now we have it. Never will I allow it to be lost. Certainly not through easy money.' Not being in Ne Win's shoes, it was not for me to judge whether his approach was sound or not. But I could not help being deeply moved by his words. After all, I come from Israel, and who knows better than I what has happened in my country since the early days of the pioneers in kibbutz Deganiah on the Sea of Galilee, where I was born, and the co-operative village of Nahalal in the Valley of Jezreel, where I grew up.

On Sunday, 15 July, exactly three weeks after the operation, I was back at full-time work. I drove to Jerusalem in the morning to attend the regular weekly meeting of the Government, shook hands with my colleagues as though I had just returned from a trip abroad, and reported on the major current issues of foreign affairs. From the Cabinet session I went to my office where, as usual, much work awaited me, and had lunch, as usual, on my return home to Zahala in the early evening.

As to my state of health, there were three problems. My body had been weakened, and the doctors considered whether to strengthen it artificially through injections and pills, or to let it fend for itself. They decided on the second course, which pleased me, since I preferred Rahel's cooking to injec-tions, and I never did have faith in pills.

The second problem was my hoarseness. Dr Rubinstein was very familiar with my throat and vocal cords, which had been damaged at the time of my archaeological mishap. They had now suffered further bruising by the plastic tubes inserted during the operation. Dr Rubinstein was reassuring. All would be well, he said. I had lost my voice once and regained it after several months. This time, too, it would take some months, but I would get it back.

The third problem, over which the doctors were most concerned, was my blood. They explained that a cancerous growth secretes a certain element into the blood, and this element should therefore be absent after the extrac-tion of the growth. I cannot claim that I grasped all the details expounded by the medical profession, but what pleased me was their verdict after the final test: 'The blood is clean.'

Dr Wolfstein continued to visit me for several days after I left the hospital. He probed my belly, took my blood pressure, and removed the last of the stitches. He then stopped coming, and showed no further interest. Asked why, he said simply: 'I treat sick people, not healthy ones!'

CHAPTER TWENTY-FOUR

Resignation

In October 1979 I told the Prime Minister I was resigning. Begin said he was sorry, but I fancied he would now breathe more freely. With the negotiations concluded and the peace treaty signed, we both knew we could not work together as we had in the past. I had also had enough of the continued carping by my ministerial colleagues, who always thought I was exceeding my authority and was too ready to compromise and give in to the Egyptians and the Americans. Begin, too, wanted me to operate under a tighter rein, and was always insisting that I obtain his approval before making any proposals or putting forward new ideas.

Now that we were about to start the autonomy negotiations, he had even more reason to be relieved by my departure, for on this issue we differed fundamentally in our basic concept. Our relationship grew more distant, and Begin relied on me less and less. He now appeared to display a sense of intellectual superiority, as though he harboured not the slightest doubt that if he himself dictated every move in our foreign policy, he would do it more successfully. I did not share this estimate of his capacities, but he was, after all, the Prime Minister. It was he who bore responsibility for the Government, and so he had every right to exercise full authority in the conduct of its policies.

We might have drawn apart even if we had not been embarking on autonomy talks. But that clinched it, for the gap between our respective approaches towards the future of the Arabs in Judea, Samaria and the Gaza District was too wide to bridge. Begin and his party wanted these territories to be under Israeli sovereignty, though I doubted whether they had crystallized their views on what would be the status of the Arab inhabitants. From statements made by Begin, I gathered he was prepared to grant them autonomy within the framework of the State of Israel. I, on the other hand, did not believe that Israeli sovereignty could be imposed on these Arabs against their will. Moreover, even if all or some of them requested it, a government structure was required which ensured that the Arab element would not deprive Israel of her distinctive Jewish character.

It was my view that we had to establish a pattern of relationship between us and the Palestinians that would preserve our vital interests, and at the same time enable the Arabs to lead their lives as they wished. For our part, we had to make certain that no Palestinian State would arise west of the River Jordan; that we would have the right to maintain military units and installations in that territory; and that we would be entitled to establish settlements there providing this was not done at the expense of the Arabs – settlement would be confined to uncultivated State land or land bought by us from its Arab owners.

I did not believe the solution lay in 'territorial compromise' – the division of the area between Israel and Jordan. On the contrary, I felt that the region between the State of Israel and the River Jordan should hold a mixed population of Arabs and Jews living side by side. The Jewish settlements would be linked to the Government of Israel, and the Arabs could decide whether they wished to have ties with the Government of Jordan or of Israel, or to run their own institutions. At the moment, it seemed to me that they would prefer to benefit from all three worlds. In certain spheres, such as agriculture and health, they would probably choose the Israeli connection, since it brought them greater rewards than they could derive from Jordan. In other spheres, they would almost assuredly wish to maintain independent institutions, in addition to links with Jordan.

I attached double importance to the Israeli settlements in these areas. Judea and Samaria are part of our historic homeland, and we had to do everything possible to prevent an arrangement whereby Jews would be considered strangers there. Even if these territories were not to come under Israeli sovereignty, on no account should we agree to their being handed over to foreign rule. Furthermore, civilian Jewish settlement in this territory was also essential for Israel's security. We needed to maintain there early-warning systems and other military installations, as well as army units, for the sole purpose of protecting the adjacent narrow strip of Israel with its dense population along the Mediterranean. We had no wish to deploy our units in the midst of the populated Arab centres of the West Bank. Thus, if we had sizable Jewish settlement blocs, such as the Jordan Valley, the Etzion region south of Jerusalem, and the ridges in Samaria, those would be the places where we could maintain a military presence; and our troops there would not be regarded as foreign conquerors but as a defence element to safeguard Israel.

It was possible that in time the Arabs and Israel might reach some other arrangement. But whatever that might be, it would have to be by mutual agreement. Until then, the territory was neither to be turned into a Palestinian State nor to come under Israeli sovereignty.

When the government first drew up its autonomy proposals, it held that the question of sovereignty should remain open. The relevant paragraph read: 'Israel stands by its right and its claim of sovereignty to Judea, Samaria and the Gaza District. In the knowledge that other claims exist, it proposes, for the sake of the agreement and the peace, that the question of sovereignty in these areas be left open.'

However, after the Camp David accords and the signing of the peace treaty with Egypt, with the requirement that we start autonomy talks, the Government changed its position. The Prime Minister did not wish now to repeat the earlier text, and a new version was substituted. This one read: 'At the end of the five-year transitional period, Israel will continue to maintain its claim to the right of sovereignty in the Land of Israel territories – Judea, Samaria and the Gaza District.' No longer was it stated that the sovereignty question would remain open. To recognize the full significance of this change, this clause had to be read together with the one preceding it, which stated that Israel would not agree to the establishment of a Palestinian State. Put plainly, what we were saying to the Arabs was that there would be no Palestinian State for we would prevent it. On the other hand, they had to know that it was our aspiration to exercise sovereignty over the entire territory west of the River Jordan.

I, too, was firmly opposed to the rise of a Palestinian State, but I thought the only way to maintain a dialogue with the Palestinian Arabs was to tell them this, and to add at the same time that neither would we annex the territories without their agreement. In the Cabinet vote on this question, as on the subject of appropriating private Arab land for the benefit of Israeli settlers, I was in the minority, and the formula proposed by the Prime Minister was adopted.

I did not feel I could remain in the Government where there were such differences of view on so grave a subject. These differences would be marked throughout the autonomy negotiations and in the Government's proposals for a permanent arrangement. Moreover, it was clear to me that the Palestinians would refuse to send official representatives to the negotiations; but I believed we should find unofficial ways to meet with them, both the moderates and the extremists, talk to them, find out their views, seek out points of agreement, and use such points as a basis for our policy and our actions. Even if we failed to reach mutual agreement, I personally was prepared unilaterally to abolish our military administration in the territories and maintain a civilian relationship with the Arabs through our Government ministries, such as the Ministries of Health, Agriculture and Police. I had expected that once we had put forward our autonomy proposal, we had taken a new direction from which there was no turning back.

*   *   *

During the course of my last year as Foreign Minister, I had met privately with a considerable number of leading Arab personalities in Judea, Samaria and the Gaza District, representing different political views and outlooks. They included moderates like Aziz Shahada of Ramalla, Elias Freij, the Christian Mayor of Bethlehem, and Dr Hatem Abu Gazala of Gaza, as well as extremists such as Dr Ahmed Hamze al-Natshe of Hebron and Dr Haidar Abdul Shafi of Gaza. Anwar al-Hatib and Hikmat al-Masri were among those who supported the Jordanian connection, while Fahd Kawasme, Mayor of Hebron, was opposed to Hashemite rule. These and others to whom I talked reflected the entire spectrum of opinion among the Arab inhabitants of the administered territories, and I must say they all spoke frankly. Not one, incidentally, refused my request that we meet.

I was encouraged by these talks. I could find a basis for dialogue even with those who held the most extreme views. Even with them, I saw prospects of a mutual arrangement, at least for a transition period, which conformed to the principles of the Camp David accords and were in keeping with my own approach.

My encouragement would no doubt surprise anyone who had overheard or read the minutes (if there had been any) of our conversations and put a literal interpretation on the Arab statements. After all, every one of them said he wanted a Palestinian State; their authorized leadership was the PLO; our settlements had to be removed – or at least agree to be subject to an Arab Government, Palestinian or Jordanian; and our army would eventually have to withdraw and return to the May 1967 borders. These were indeed the views expressed by the men of the left and the men of the right, as well as the pro- and the anti-Jordanians, and I was not surprised. These were their aspirations. But one had to distinguish between what they wished to happen and what they were prepared to accept in the given circumstances.

I found their attitude to the PLO enlightening. The ones who were most insistent that any agreement we reached would require the approval of the PLO were the moderates, mostly the heads of distinguished families, the men of property, with sons and brothers in Jordan, Lebanon, the Gulf States and Europe. They were prompted not by ideology but by the fear of exposing themselves to acts of terrorism. They told me privately that they simply could not afford to risk their own lives and those of their kin. Fourteen Arab States had agreed at the Rabat Conference that the PLO was the sole representative of the Palestinians. Even King Hussein found himself compelled to support this resolution, though it was the last thing he wanted. How then, they asked, could they be expected to flout it? Some of the extremists went further. They wanted their meetings with me to be held in the offices of the military administration, so that they could claim to the PLO people that they had been ordered to talk to me by the Military Governor!

I did not belittle the impact of PLO threats. However, these had not always been effective in the past. When faced, for example, with the alternative of electing their own mayors or having their cities administered by Israeli officers, the Arabs in the territories chose the former. They did this despite contrary instructions by the PLO, who wanted army officers in the job as demonstrative symbols of Israel's military occupation. There was a similar development in the case of Arabs in the territories finding employment in Israel. The PLO opposed it vehemently – and not only in words. Terrorist squads shot up buses taking the Arabs to work, and this went on for some time. But the terror did not stop the process, and eventually the attacks ceased.

Thus, the determining factors, to my mind, would be the wishes of the Arabs in the territories, and what Israel would do. These Arabs wanted a leadership of their own choosing from among their own people in the main cities – Nablus, Hebron, Jenin and Gaza – and did not wish to be subject to Yasser Arafat or George Habash. True, they would not appoint an official delegation to join our autonomy talks; but I was convinced that the mayors they themselves had elected would be prepared to meet together over their affairs, and even agree to negotiate with us on practical matters.

Time and events leave their mark. The Arab notables to whom I spoke before we signed the treaty with Egypt believed that Sadat would not make peace with Israel without an arrangement between us and the Palestinians. They were also confident that the United States and Egypt would ultimately force us to return to the May 1967 frontiers, and agree to Egyptian and Jordanian forces being stationed in the Gaza District, Judea and Samaria during the five-year transitional period. What materialized was the reverse of their hopes – a separate treaty with Egypt, no arrangement with the Palestinians, and a continued Israeli (not an Egyptian and Jordanian) military presence in the territories. They saw themselves being bypassed by history, and changed their approach. If their aspirations were not fulfilled, they would reconcile themselves to what they could reasonably accept.

Therein, I thought, lay the key to a *modus vivendi* with the Palestinian Arabs. Even without their joining the autonomy talks, Israel on her own could take action to create a new reality by abolishing her military administration, and the Arabs would then fall in with the new regime even if Israeli settlements and military units remained in the territories.

I also found in my talks with the Arabs that, in their attitude to Jordan, a distinction had to be drawn between their basic position on the right to establish a Palestinian State and the realities they recognized when they spoke of their links with Amman. All stressed the vital need to preserve these links but not out of love for Hussein. The left-wing leaders were critical of the monarchy in general and of Hussein in particular; and even the right-wingers who were reluctant to speak ill of the King thought the Jordanian regime should be made democratic. The ties between the administered territories and Jordan were essential, they said, and the two could not be kept apart, because of the characteristics of their populations and their economies. There was hardly a family in Judea, Samaria and Gaza, rich or poor, urban resident or Bedouin, that did not have a relative living in Jordan. And Jordan constituted the principal market for their produce, from dressed building-stones to olive oil, soap, grapes. Moreover, Jordan was the bridge to the more distant Arab States – Iraq, Saudi Arabia, Syria and Lebanon.

When I asked them how they saw their constitutional links with the Hashemite Kingdom, they spoke of a federation, or possibly direct ties between Jordan and individual districts in the territories. Under such a scheme, the districts of Jerusalem, Gaza, Nablus and the Hebron hills would each be linked separately to Jordan. This was clearly in contradiction to the concept of a Palestinian State. I had no doubt that their association with Jordan was a living reality and vital to their future, whereas a Palestinian State was more of a slogan, expressive of their heartfelt sentiments. But these sentiments sprang from dissatisfaction with their existing condition – subject to Israel, with fellow Palestinians living in refugee camps and lacking citizenship and social status – and did not reflect thoughtful planning for independent statehood.

What I found constructive in my talks with these Arabs were the ties they wished to maintain with Israel, and their horror of another Arab-Israel war. No one wanted a return to the pre-1967 sealed borders, with their barbed wire and minefields, and their people cut off from the benefits they enjoyed from the Israeli association. And none wanted Jerusalem to be redivided: it was one city, and its Arabs and Jews now mingled freely. The inhabitants of the Gaza District were particularly anxious for the border to remain open. There were not enough local sources of livelihood, and if they were unable to work in, and sell their produce to Israel, many would find themselves back on the pre-1967 poverty line, living solely on UNRWA relief. Moreover, today, an Arab in Gaza travels freely through Israel to get to Jerusalem, Hebron, Nablus and Jordan. With the frontiers closed, he would be isolated. There was talk once of a corridor from Gaza to Jordan, but the Arabs now realized it was both impractical and undesirable.

At our meetings, the Arab notables made very clear their view that the way to reach a settlement with us was through political negotiation and not through war. This approach had been evident in the 1973 Yom Kippur War, when they carefully refrained from making any move against us even in the opening days when they – and many others in the world – thought we were going down to defeat and the Egyptians and Syrians were winning. They had cause to remember the 1948 war experience, with the initial victories of the Arab invasion armies; and they knew that if there were another war, when battle reached their population centres, their buildings would be destroyed and they themselves would become refugees. In all the wars launched by the neighbouring Arab States against Israel, they had gained nothing and lost much. Syria had not recaptured the Golan Heights, nor Egypt the Sinai peninsula, which they had lost in the 1967 Six Day War. Indeed, when they tried to do so in their surprise attack on Yom Kippur 1973, that war ended with Israeli forces closer to Damascus and Cairo than they had ever been.

When I heard these facts recited by the Arabs, I knew that they, too, were aware of the practical significance of what they were saying. They understood that not only would we not give up Beersheba, we would also not abandon our Etzion group of settlements in Judea's Hebron hills, nor the East Jerusalem suburb of Ramot Eshkol, nor our settlements in the Jordan Valley. If they were ready to live together with us side by side, they knew that this would apply not only to Tel Aviv and Haifa but also to Kiriat Arba and Ma'aleh Adumim in Judea. They also knew the implications of eschewing war as a means of attaining their ends. Whoever did so had to choose the path of negotiations. At present, the Arabs in the administered territories had neither independent leadership nor the power or ability to cut themselves off from the PLO. It was up to Israel, therefore, to take appropriate action. We should establish a regime that would be acceptable to them, one that would not give them a status inferior to our own, but would enable them to conduct their lives as they wished.

I had talks with two of the Arabs with extremist views after the peace treaty with Egypt had been signed and was being implemented, and when the autonomy negotiations were already in progress. They were Dr Natshe and Dr Haidar Shafi. Dr Haidar was the pro-PLO Gaza doctor to whom I had telephoned about the Gaza students on the eve of my hospitalization. I have already mentioned that when I was Minister of Defence I expelled him from Gaza (and allowed him to return after two and a half months) in order to prevent the encouragement of acts of terror. That was in 1970, and it was his second expulsion. The first was in 1969. In that year, I decided to improve the electricity service to the inhabitants-of the Gaza District by linking it to the Israeli network. Up to then, they had had to suffer frequent power cuts and

weak current supplied by the old and decrepit generators installed by the
Egyptians, who had ruled Gaza before 1967. Haidar protested against my
action, claiming that though it benefited the Arabs in Gaza, it was a political
move designed to induce them to accept the Israeli occupation. I had had
several talks with him at the time, but failed to change his opinion. Fearing
that his open opposition to the 'Israeli connection' would encourage sabotage of the new power line, I expelled him from Gaza and sent him to the
Bedouin village of Nahal in Sinai. But I allowed him to return to Gaza three
months later, after the broken-down generators had been cast away and the
new service was in operation. I judged that he would now call off his saboteur
friends, as the sole victim would be not the Israeli Government but the
people of Gaza, who would be without lighting and without power for the
pumps supplying water to their vegetable plots and orange groves. I was
right. Haidar did not change his opinion, but he became reconciled to using
Israeli electricity.

I had considerable personal admiration for him. When he talked to me and
to other members of the administration, he did not hide his opinions. Nor did
he cease to express them openly even at the risk of being penalized. He may
have been connected directly with groups who carried out acts of terrorism,
but we had no knowledge of this. I could therefore assume that his activities
were limited to the expression of opinion alone.

My talk with him now, after the signing of the Egypt–Israel peace treaty,
was not disappointing. His views were unchanged. He still wanted an end to
our administration, and its replacement by Palestinian independence. But
just as he had once found it realistic to accept the Israeli electricity network,
so now he did not ignore today's realities. He said he favoured open borders
between Israel and a Palestinian State – if it were to emerge. And though he
showed satisfaction that the doctors in the Gaza District were now Arabs, he
said this did not prevent them from seeking the help of Israeli physicians and
hospitals when the need arose. This, however, was done not under duress but
of their own free will. 'If special medical treatment is required which is not
available in Gaza, why should the patient suffer?' he asked.

'You are right,' I replied. 'Just like the electric power. If all you have are
outmoded generators, why not get a better service from us?'

'It was not so bad in Nahal,' he said with a smile.

I had not seen him for several years, but he looked much the same. His hair
was thinner, but his swarthy face was still unwrinkled, and his smile was as
amiable as ever. There is an old Armenian proverb: 'Be good to your enemies; remember it is you who made them.' I did not know what Haidar Shafi
felt about me. But I have found on occasion – and this may have been one –

that a wedge that separates two parties may sometimes also serve as a bridge between them.

With Dr Natshe it was my first meeting. I had not known or even heard of him before. But General Danny Matt, the commanding officer of the military administration in the territories, told me he was a man of considerable influence in the Hebron and Bethlehem region, and thought I should meet him. He was well thought of by the intellectuals, and commanded particular respect among the people of Hebron as the leading member of a local family of tribal proportions – numbering some five thousand! I was told that if there were municipal elections and he stood for mayor, he would have a good chance of being elected.

He had been for a long time a Soviet-oriented communist, and held a senior position in the Palestinian Communist Organization of the West Bank. In 1976, during the Rabin Government, he was exiled to Jordan for subversive activities against the military administration. He was allowed to return two years later but forbidden to engage in politics. During his exile, he was appointed by the PLO to membership of the Palestinian National Council.

In manner and appearance, he was not the typical Arab. He had a fair complexion, a chubby face, wore European clothes, and spoke with the dogmatism and inflexibility of a hard-line communist. He had studied in France, married a Frenchwoman, practised as a physician in Morocco for several years, returned home, and was now director of a hospital in Bethlehem. During his exile in Amman, his wife would visit him from time to time, and they both abhorred the monarchic regime of the Hashemite family. They were the worst two years of his life, he said, not because of any material hardships, but because he simply could not stand Hussein's rule. He recognized the special links between the Arabs of the administered territories and Jordan, and these could not be ignored or cut. But if this relationship were to be given political expression, he said, one would first need to change the Jordanian regime. The monarchy, of course, would be abolished.

With Israel, he was firmly of the opinion that no matter what the circumstances, the borders had to remain open, as they were now. As an example of the mutual benefits that flowed therefrom, he told me that many Jews from Jerusalem went to Bethlehem for dental treatment because it was far less costly. Conversely, his own Bethlehem hospital used the services of a Jewish radiologist from Jerusalem, a certain Dr Cohen, since there was no specialist in this field on his staff.

He had nothing good to say about the Camp David accords. Both the Americans and Sadat had sold out the Palestinians for an Egypt-Israel peace. The only way to bring about an overall and true peace was to revive the Geneva Conference, with the participation of all the Arab States together with the PLO, and co-chaired by an American and a Russian. Without the involvement of the Soviet Union, he concluded, there would be no permanent peace in the Middle East.

Dr Natshe differed from any other Palestinian Arab I had met. There were moments during our talk when I thought I was in Romania, the only communist country I had visited, speaking to one of its leaders. I did not know whether he really believed that future developments in the region would match his forecast. But as a veteran communist, he could not ignore the significant fact that the United States, Egypt and Israel had reached a framework agreement on the administered territories. He would not change his political outlook, and he would continue to be moved, ideologically, by what he hoped would happen. But on practical day-to-day matters, he would fall in with the realities of Bethlehem and Jerusalem, and of Jews and Arabs following their lives without barriers between them.

For me, the most enlightening part of our talk was his observation that he and his family preferred to live in Bethlehem under 'Israeli occupation' than in Jordan, Morocco, or any other Arab or European country. This was not only because he wanted to fight for the liberation of his homeland, but because here, in spite of everything, he was better off!

When Prime Minister Begin invited me to discuss the composition of the Israeli team to the autonomy negotiations, we both knew that the decisive moment had arrived. He opened without any preliminaries and without prevarication. 'Are you prepared to head the team?' he asked. I said I was not. 'Are you sure you won't regret it?' 'Quite certain,' I replied.

The candidate he preferred in my place had already been selected. 'What do you think of Dr Burg [Minister of the Interior]? He is a wise man.' I told Begin that for my part he could have Dr Burg or any other minister. With that our talk ended, and we both recognized its implications.

I wrote to him on 2 October 1979 recalling what I had said in a later conversation about my reservations over the way in which the autonomy negotiations were being conducted. I had then told him that in the present circumstances I saw no point in remaining in the Government as Foreign Minister. I now wished to set down my reasons on paper.

Throughout the years since the Six Day War, I had considered that our relationship with the Arabs of the administered territories (not with the PLO) was a key issue, and I had had no difficulty in explaining our policy during that period. Now, no question was more topical, both on the domestic and particularly the foreign affairs fronts. Our talks with leaders in Europe, the Far East and especially the United States, always revolved round this issue. Thus, the Foreign Minister could not discharge his duties effectively without being personally involved in determining our policy and in associating himself with it.

It was no secret, I wrote to the Prime Minister, that I disagreed with the manner in which we were conducting the autonomy negotiations, as well as with our policy line. The same was true of some of our actions in the territories. There was no need for me to go into details. I had objected to the Committee of Six which was entrusted with the negotiations (and I had seen no point in participating). And regrettably I had had to vote against some of the fundamental Cabinet decisions: the expropriation of 'rocky land', the establishment of the Eilon Moreh settlement, and the 'clarifications of Israel's position on the suggested principles for autonomy arrangements'.

When the autonomy negotiations began, I considered the possibility that I might be wrong, and that my assumption of the sterility of the negotiations in their current form would prove false. They had been going on now for four months, and to my sorrow I felt they were largely fruitless. But whether I was right or wrong, this was my view, and it prevented me from taking part in them. In such a situation, a Foreign Minister could not fulfil his function since he would be dealing with marginal matters and not with a central issue.

It was therefore my intention to tender my resignation from the Government – after discharging certain prior commitments (including official visits to Strasbourg and Mexico) – about the middle of December. If, of course, the Prime Minister wished to advance this date, I would resign at any time he decided. I signed the letter 'In great friendship and deep appreciation'.

We had a final talk on this subject a week later. It was brief, as I told Begin that I had nothing to add to what he already knew. I could put it all in one sentence: The things that interested me, I did not handle; and what I dealt with held no interest for me. I had not entered his Government in order to meet ambassadors and attend diplomatic cocktail parties. The main subject that interested me was the pattern of co-existence with the Arabs. I reminded him that I had once suggested resigning from the Foreign Ministry and serving as his assistant in charge of this area, even without Cabinet rank. But this matter was now being conducted quite differently – with the Interior Minister, Dr Burg, handling a central policy issue, and the Foreign Minister inactive. This was patently absurd, on any objective rating. I was well aware of the circumstances which had led to the appointment of Dr Burg, leader of the National Religious Party, to head the Israeli team in the autonomy negotiations. Neither Begin's Likud nor Burg's Religious Party had been enamoured of the way in which I had conducted talks during the peace negotiations with Egypt. The truth was that this Government did not have complete confidence in me. I was not recommending a 'palace revolt' – firing Burg and appointing me in his place to head the autonomy talks. I simply wished to resign.

Begin expressed his regret, and said I was making things difficult for him. But there was no hint in his words of any readiness to change the situation. He asked me not to talk to anyone of my intention to resign until the forthcoming Cabinet meeting on Sunday, 21 October.

Two days after that meeting, at the end of a night session of the Knesset, the Prime Minister officially announced my resignation from the Government. He read out the relevant paragraph in the Law pertaining to minister-ial resignations, and added words of praise for my service in the Government and my part in securing the peace treaty with Egypt. When he left the rostrum, I went up to him, shook hands warmly, and we exchanged mutual thanks and good wishes.

I would now no longer be sitting at the Government table, which was in the centre of the horse-shoe Knesset chamber. The seating of members is determined in accordance with the numerical strength of their parties. The larger the party, the more seats it is allotted in the front rows closest to the Cabinet table. During the period when I was a rank-and-file member, after the resignation of Golda Meir's Government and before I joined Begin's Government, I had a seat in the last row, in the left wing of the chamber, as befitted the Labour Party. The Prime Minister was Yitzhak Rabin, and I was far removed – also in opinion – from his Government. My immediate neigh-bour, then, was the Bedouin Hamad Abu-Rabia, Sheikh of the Abu-Rabia tribe in the Negev, south of Beersheba. We were very friendly – and he was very helpful. Whenever it was time to vote, and I was supporting the Govern-ment, Hamad would nudge me and whisper *'Arpa idek'* – raise your hand!

I was seated once again in the last row, but this time in the right wing of the chamber. Next to me sat Moshe Shamir, and next to him Geulah Cohen. Both had left the Likud and set up an independent extreme nationalist party. I shook my neighbour by the hand, but this time I could get no help from him. I told him that despite the proximity, there was no danger I would vote as he did. 'Thank the Lord,' he replied, which amused us both.

The location of my seat fitted my approach to my future political activities. This would be my last Knesset. I did not expect to run in the next elections, nor would I serve in a future Government. Although in political and social outlook I belonged to the Socialist Labour movement, I would no longer be

included in the Labour Party. They would not have me back, after my
'treacherous' acceptance of a ministerial post in the Begin Government, and I
would not ask them to. I had not joined any of the Likud parties even when I
was a member of the Likud coalition, and I had no wish to form an independent list or join one of the small parties.

I had begun public life in the army, and had run the gamut from private
and sergeant through officers' course to Chief of Staff. At the end of my four-
year term, a few months after the 1956 Sinai Campaign, I started a new life as
a civilian. I went into politics, fought an election, entered the Knesset, and
served in Ben Gurion's Government as Minister of Agriculture. When Ben
Gurion retired, I continued to serve in subsequent Labour coalitions, including a seven-year stint as Minister of Defence. I was first appointed to that
office by Levi Eshkol in May 1967, just before the Six Day War. When
Eshkol died, I continued in the same post under Golda Meir. After the Yom
Kippur War, I again stood for election to the Knesset on the list she headed,
and when she formed her new Government I was again appointed Defence
Minister. I did not join the Rabin Government, but returned to office under
the Begin administration. When I resigned two and a quarter years later, I
had behind me a record of more than twenty years in politics, most of them
as a Cabinet Minister.

These two periods of public service, in the army and the Government,
seemed to me to be sufficient, and it was time for me to leave. I would
continue to express my views from time to time whenever I had anything
special to say; I would write, lecture, and meet with the Jewish communities
of the Diaspora; but I would no longer hold office. I had seen our great
leaders – Chaim Weizmann, Ben Gurion, Golda Meir – trying to cling to
power until they failed. I did not want to do the same. I had never pushed
myself to the fore, had never put my name forward for any position, and had
never organized supporters to do so for me. Every office I had held had been
by invitation. I had long ago resolved that when I withdrew from public life,
it would be at my choosing. I would not be ousted. The new seat allotted me
in the Knesset was appropriately located – near the exit.

It was nearing midnight when I left the Knesset after the announcement of
my resignation. The official car and driver were still at my disposal, and
though I usually dozed on the drive home, I was kept awake by mixed
feelings – relief tinged with disappointment.

Rahel was waiting for me when I reached Zahala, and had a pot of soup
simmering on the stove. We ate, and decided to postpone to the morning the
practical decisions of a private life. After supper I strolled into the garden,

and was calmed by its tranquillity and the joy of the pines and rose-beds against the background of illuminated ancient mosaics. The silence of the night was broken only by the occasional hum of distant cars.

Back in the house all was peaceful, the antiquities lying serenely on the shelves. Only one figure disturbed the stillness. When I came close, it stared back at me with angry eyes, and its pursed lips were expressive of resentment. It was what I called the 'Egyptian Governor', a life-size stone head dating from the time of Rameses II, who is believed to have been the thirteenth-century BC Pharaoh at the time of Exodus. It had been discovered at Rafah, and I had bought it in Jerusalem from the dealer Haj Omar. When I went to see him and asked if he had anything interesting for me, he walked over to a corner of the store and drew from a cardboard box the head wrapped in an Arab newspaper. It had not been put on display as it was not the kind of object that attracted his usual tourist customers. At first sight it appeared to be a slovenly piece of primitive sculpture, the head set directly on the shoulders without the linking neck, the eyes sunken, the mouth wide and tightly closed. The nature of the stone prevented the sculptor from giving it delicate features, and the surface was rough. When Haj Omar placed it on the counter, I felt a sudden quickening of the pulse. Here indeed was an ancient piece of sculpture, probably Egyptian and originating in the Gaza Strip. I was convinced that it was not a fake. I recalled that this type of stone – *Jiri* in Arabic, though referred to locally as 'sea-stone' – was used as headstones on Egyptian graves discovered at Dir-el-Balah, near Gaza. It was also from this stone that the celebrated Rameses II stele was fashioned – an upright slab inscribed with that Pharaoh's name, which had been found on the seashore at Tel Akluk, also in the Gaza Strip.

I asked Haj Omar to bring a bucket of water, and we washed the sculpture. We then found why it had given the appearance of having no neck. The head was covered by a cloth in the typical Egyptian fashion at the time, draped on both sides of the face and running down to the chest. Even after the perfunctory wash in ordinary water, it bore no signs of recent chisel marks. I asked Haj Omar where he had acquired it. He replied without hesitation that he had bought it from Bedoui – an antiquities dealer in Rafah whom I knew well. Bedoui had told him that the head had been found at Tel Zuarub. I was quite sure this information was accurate, for Haj Omar knew I could always check with Bedoui.

Bargaining over the price did not take long. Haj Omar asked for ten thousand Israeli pounds. I was in a quandary. If the head was a fake, it was not worth a penny. If it was genuine, it was very valuable. I told him I could not pay more than five thousand. The words were hardly out of my mouth when he seized me by the hand and cried *'Mabruk'* (Arabic for 'with blessing'). That clinched the deal. I could, of course, have got it for less had I gone on bargaining, but I liked the bust too much for that.

I planned to inspect the site where it had been found. But before that I asked my friend Gibeon, Professor of Egyptology at the University of Tel Aviv, to inspect my purchase. He came round immediately, gave it a thorough examination while I stood by full of suspense, and delivered his verdict. The head, he said, was 'excellent. Genuine Egyptian. Very interesting.' As far as he knew, it was the only one of that size ever found in Israel. Many small Egyptian figurines had come to light, but no life-size stone bust. 'To tell you the truth,' he added, 'when I heard you describe it over the telephone, I was sure you had been fooled and the head was a fake. On my way to you, I had prepared a whole lecture to prove it, and to warn you to be more careful in the future. I am glad to say I was wrong. The head is genuine.' I consoled him by saying that his lecture was not wasted – it would keep for the next time, for in my next acquisition I would undoubtedly be tricked.

A week later, on the day of Id-el-Fitr, the Moslem feast marking the end of the fast of Ramadan, I set off for Tel Zuarub. I had known the site for some time. The name does not appear on the map, but it derives from the name of the wealthy owner of the land on which it is located, Sheikh Zuarub. I arrived in Rafah at noon and called on the Sheikh, who gave me a warm welcome. I had not seen him for some years. We had first met when I was Minister of Defence, and responsible for the administered territories. We had proposed to train the Arab farmers in the Gaza Strip to introduce progressive agricultural methods. Sheikh Zuarub eagerly accepted our advice that he grow early-ripening strawberries. We told him how, and also how to package for export. Some months later, on one of my visits, he proudly showed me the results. His labourers were busy packing the fruit intended for the markets of Europe. The price he was getting exceeded his wildest dreams. These were not strawberries, he told me. They were gold! The delight was not only in the price. They looked delicious – large, red and juicy. Climate and sandy soil make the Gaza Strip ideal for spring crops.

The Mayor and other town notables began gathering in the Sheikh's spacious salon, and we were treated to fruit, cakes and coffee. I told the Sheikh the purpose of my visit, and he summoned his son, Yihye, who was familiar with everything that went on in the area. When he heard my story, he said that Bedoui the dealer was out of town that day, but he had got the stone head from children who had been playing on the Tel and digging around.

Though I was eager to get off, I stayed for another round of coffee to talk to the Sheikh and his guests about conditions in the town. They had no complaints. They all earned a comfortable livelihood, selling their fruits and vegetables in Tel Aviv at good prices. The Rafah Arabs who worked in Israel also received good wages. The only trouble, they said, was that our money was 'no good', and kept dropping in value, so they changed it for Jordanian dinars or Egyptian pounds – but mostly they bought gold. Gold bracelets covered the wrists and arms of almost every woman and girl in Rafah.

I asked them about conditions in El Arish, now that we had evacuated that town in advance of the date laid down in the Camp David accords, and it was under Egyptian rule. They all avoided direct answers, but from what they did say I gathered that the people of El Arish were far from satisfied. The President of Egypt had promised them development projects and the establishment of local industrial plants, but there was no sign of them. And anyone from El Arish who had worked with the Israeli authorities was called 'traitor' by the Egyptian officials. When the frontier was closed, those from El Arish who had found employment in Israel were now out of work. Many were therefore crossing surreptitiously to return to their jobs.

After fond farewells, I left for Tel Zuarub. I found signs of excavation and in the upper strata there were fragments of a marble tablet from the Roman period. Canaanite potsherds were scattered in the lower levels. I went to the spot where the children had said they had found the Egyptian head, and scrabbled about until I came upon parts of a typical Egyptian jar, with a narrow top decorated by a blue stripe. I gathered the fragments and left the mound in high spirits. The day's experiences – locating the 'birthplace' of the 'Egyptian Governor', meeting the Sheikh, talking to the notables – were all of a piece, past merging with present – we, the Arabs, and ancient Israel.

The relations between us – Israel and the Palestinian Arabs – were not idyllic in the past, nor are they in the present. We have basic differences of opinion on the future of the administered territories and the rise of a Palestinian State. On the personal plane, there is no brotherly – or even cousinly – love between all the Palestinians and all the Israelis. It is not only in Lebanon that the PLO, the National Front and other terrorist organizations have a foothold. They have one in Judea, Samaria and the Gaza District, too. The explosives in the markets of Jerusalem and Tel Aviv, on the railway lines and in buses, are placed there by Arabs who live close to us. It is fair to assume that the families and friends of the terrorists are aware of their activities. Nevertheless, the overwhelming majority of the Arabs in the administered territories live at peace with the Israelis. Between 70,000 and 100,000 come into Israel daily to work or to sell their produce. The 100,000

Arab residents of Jerusalem live among, or adjacent to, the Jews of Jerusalem without quarrel, conflict or political murders – which was not the case during the British Mandatory period.

There is also voluntary co-operation between the two peoples in the fields of agriculture, health and other economic and social services (the Arabs for the most part being aided by Israeli experts). Whenever I visit an Arab settlement in the territories, I feel a sense of satisfaction and pride that, following the Six Day War, we succeeded in doing away with all the barriers, and establishing 'open bridges' with Jordan. In industrial plants, in building, in the large hotels, I frequently meet Arabs who speak fluent Hebrew, and many of them occupy positions of responsibility. I, of course, am closer to the men who work the land than I am to others, and whenever I meet an Arab farm labourer out in the fields, sit and chat with him under a fig tree, visit his home, I feel even more confident that we can live together amicably.

On my way home from Rafah and Tel Zuarub through the Gaza Strip, I stopped at Dir-el-Balah and turned off the main road along a track that took me to 'the grove of the Judge'. This was the site excavated by Israeli archaeologist Dr Trude Dothan, where she unearthed anthropoid coffins of Egyptian governors buried in a Canaanite cemetery. While I wandered round the excavation area, I saw an old Bedouin acquaintance, Hammed, walking towards me. He lived in the nearby dunes, and he had been fetched by one of his children who had spotted me. We exchanged the customary three kisses on the cheek, and greetings. Hammed is a remarkable man. I know no one, Jew or Arab, with his genius for ferreting out antiquities. A Bedouin through and through, his vast tracking experience since childhood to retrieve a straying goat or follow the trail of a thief has given him a sharpness of eye and an exquisite sense for detecting the presence underground of the remains of ancient settlements and burials.

I have a soft spot for him. He is not only a 'professional'; he is also something of a character. As a rule he never lies to me; but never does he tell me the whole truth, nor does he pretend to. He prefers 'perhaps' to 'certainly'.

I asked him what he was doing these days. He had recently been working with Dr Dothan, but now he was just 'mooching around'. The next day, for example, he was going to Jordan. Then, as though there was no connection, he switched subjects. The Bedouin in the Gaza Strip and Sinai, he said, had hit upon good times since there was now a frontier between Israel and Egypt. He, of course, did not engage in such activities, but the smugglers were raking in the money. Who could stop them from using the Sinai tracks at night to carry such items as television sets and electrical appliances between El Arish, which was now Egyptian, and Gaza, which was under Israeli rule?

I could only smile. Our desire to bring about normalization in our relations with Egypt was still far from being realized, but the 'international link' was as lively as ever.

Before we parted, Hammed drew a small scarab from his pocket, bearing the inscription in Egyptian hieroglyphs 'Amon Ra Lord of Life'. He wanted no payment. 'It's a gift,' he said. I thrust a banknote in his pocket, muttering 'for the children', and promised to visit him one day. I returned to my car, and Hammed went back to his dunes.

Back at home, I made room for the stone head of the Egyptian on a bookshelf close to my desk. The usual Egyptian figures are much alike, delicate, well-featured, expressionless. This head was different. It was undoubtedly the likeness of a real person, strong, virile, ugly, and full of power. I dubbed him 'The Egyptian Governor of Rafah'. Somewhere in the bowels of that mound of Zuarub lies the torso of the complete figure, perhaps holding a sceptre, as was common with the rulers of those times. There, more than three thousand years ago, lived the Canaanites; but it was the Egyptians who controlled the ancient 'Way of the Sea', the Mediterranean coastal route. And this man, whose angry likeness was in my study, was without doubt the tough representative of his king, Pharaoh Rameses II, who had had such trouble with the Children of Israel.

On the night of my resignation, as I sat at my desk before retiring to bed, the harsh gaze of the 'Governor of Rafah' did not trouble me. But nor was I overjoyed by my departure from office. I would not need to go to Jerusalem in the morning. I would no longer bear the burden of public responsibility. I would be free of the frequent distressing moments I had experienced as a member of this Government. But was that what I wanted?

My mind wandered over the recent events, the growing distance between the Prime Minister and myself, our differences over the relations between us and the Palestinian Arabs. It was not to secure relief from the burden and the anguish that had prompted my decision to resign. It was my refusal to acquiesce in a policy with which I disagreed that had tipped the scales. No, it had not been a day of joy, but it was a day of truth.

Appendix 1

THE CAMP DAVID ACCORDS

The Framework for Peace in the Middle East

Mohamed Anwar el-Sadat, President of the Arab Republic of Egypt, and Menachem Begin, Prime Minister of Israel, met with Jimmy Carter, President of the United States of America, at Camp David from 5 Sept. to 17 Sept. 1978, and have agreed on the following framework for peace in the Middle East. They invite other parties to the Arab-Israeli conflict to adhere to it:

Preamble

The search for peace in the Middle East must be guided by the following:

The agreed basis for a peaceful settlement of the conflict between Israel and its neighbours is UN Security Council Resolution 242 in all its parts.

After four wars during 30 years, despite intensive humane efforts, the Middle East, which is the cradle of civilization and the birthplace of three great religions, does not yet enjoy the blessings of peace. The people of the Middle East yearn for peace, so that the vast human and natural resources of the region can be turned to the pursuits of peace and so that this area can become a model for co-existence and co-operation among nations.

The historic initiative by President Sadat in visiting Jerusalem and the reception accorded to him by the parliament, government and people of Israel, and the reciprocal visit of Prime Minister Begin to Ismailia, the peace proposals made by both leaders, as well as the warm reception of these missions by the peoples of both countries, have created an unprecedented opportunity for peace which must not be lost if this generation and future generations are to be spared the tragedies of war.

The provisions of the Charter of the United Nations and the other accepted norms of international law and legitimacy now provide accepted standards for the conduct of relations between all states.

To achieve a relationship of peace, in the spirit of Article 2 of the UN Charter, future negotiations between Israel and any neighbour prepared to negotiate peace and security with it, are necessary for the purpose of carrying out all the provisions and principles of Resolutions 242 and 338.

Peace requires respect for the sovereignty, territorial integrity and political independence of every state in the area and their right to live in peace within secure and recognized boundaries free from threats or acts of force. Progress towards that goal can accelerate movement toward a new era of reconciliation in the Middle East marked by co-operation in promoting economic development, in maintaining stability and in assuring security.

Security is enhanced by a relationship of peace and by co-operation between nations which enjoy normal relations. In addition, under the terms of peace treaties, the parties can, on the basis of reciprocity, agree to special security arrangements such as demilitarized zones, limited armaments areas, early warning stations, the presence of international forces, liaison, agreed measures for monitoring, and other arrangements that they agree are useful.

Taking these factors into account, the parties are determined to reach a just, comprehensive, and durable settlement of the Middle East conflict through the conclusion of peace treaties based on Security Council Resolutions 242 and 338 in all their parts. Their purpose is to achieve peace and good neighbourly relations. They recognize that, for peace to endure, it must involve all those who have been most deeply affected by the conflict. They therefore agree that this framework as appropriate is intended by them to constitute a basis for peace not only between Egypt and Israel, but also between Israel and each of its other neighbours which is prepared to negotiate peace with Israel on this basis.

With that objective in mind, they have agreed to proceed as follows:

A. West Bank and Gaza

1. Egypt, Israel, Jordan and the representatives of the Palestinian People should participate in negotiations on the resolution of the Palestinian problem in all its aspects. To achieve that objective, negotiations relating to the West Bank and Gaza should proceed in three stages.

(A) Egypt and Israel agree that, in order to ensure a peaceful and orderly transfer of authority, and taking into account the security concerns of all the parties, there should be transitional arrangements for the West Bank and Gaza for a period not exceeding five years. In order to provide full autonomy to the inhabitants, under these arrangements the Israeli military government and its civilian administration will be withdrawn as soon as a self-governing authority has been freely elected by the inhabitants of these areas to replace the existing military government.

To negotiate the details of a transitional arrangement, the government of Jordan will be invited to join the negotiations on the basis of this framework. These new arrangements should give due consideration to both the principle of self-government by the inhabitants of these territories and to the legitimate security concerns of the parties involved.

(B) Egypt, Israel, and Jordan will agree on the modalities for establishing the elected self-governing authority in the West Bank and Gaza. The delegations of Egypt and Jordan may include Palestinians from the West Bank and Gaza or other Palestinians as mutually agreed. The parties will negotiate an agreement which will define the powers and responsibilities of the self-governing authority to be exercised in the West Bank and Gaza. A withdrawal of Israeli armed forces will take place and there will be a redeployment of the remaining Israeli forces into specified security locations.

The agreement will also include arrangements for assuring internal and external security and public order. A strong local police force will be established, which may include Jordanian citizens. In addition, Israeli and Jordanian forces will participate in joint patrols and in the manning of control posts to assure the security of the borders.

(C) When the self-governing authority (administrative council) in the West Bank and Gaza is established and inaugurated, the transitional period of five years will begin. As soon as possible, but not later than the third year after the beginning of the transitional period, negotiations will take place to determine the final status of the West Bank and Gaza and its relationship with its neighbours, and to conclude a peace treaty between Israel and Jordan by the end of the transitional period.

These negotiations will be conducted among Egypt, Israel, Jordan and the elected representatives of the inhabitants of the West Bank and Gaza. Two separate but related committees will be convened, one committee, consisting of representatives of the four parties which will negotiate and agree on the final status of the West Bank and Gaza, and its relationship with its neighbours, and the second committee, consisting of representatives of Israel and representatives of Jordan to be joined by the elected representatives of the inhabitants of the West Bank and Gaza, to negotiate the peace treaty between Israel and Jordan, taking into account the agreement reached on the final status of the West Bank and Gaza.

The negotiations shall be based on all the provisions and principles of UN Security Council Resolution 242. The negotiations will resolve, among other matters, the location of the boundaries and the nature of the security arrangements.

The solution from the negotiations must also recognize the legitimate rights of the Palestinian people and their just requirements. In this way, the Palestinians will participate in the determination of their own future through:

(1) The negotiations among Egypt, Israel, Jordan and the representatives of the inhabitants of the West Bank and Gaza to agree on the final status of the West Bank and Gaza and other outstanding issues by the end of the transitional period.

(2) Submitting their agreement to a vote by the elected representatives of the inhabitants of the West Bank and Gaza.

(3) Providing for the elected representatives of the inhabitants of the West Bank and Gaza to decide how they shall govern themselves consistent with the provisions of their agreement.

(4) Participating as stated above in the work of the committee negotiating the peace treaty between Israel and Jordan.

2. All necessary measures will be taken and provisions made to assure the security of Israel and its neighbours during the transitional period and beyond. To assist in providing such security, a strong local police force will be constituted by the self-governing authority. It will be composed of inhabitants of the West Bank and Gaza. The police will maintain continuing liaison on internal security matters with the designated Israeli, Jordanian and Egyptian officers.

3. During the transitional period, the representatives of Egypt, Israel, Jordan and the self-governing authority will constitute a continuing committee to decide by agreement on the modalities of admission of persons displaced from the West Bank and Gaza in 1967, together with necessary measures to prevent disruption and disorder. Other matters of common concern may also be dealt with by this committee.

4. Egypt and Israel will work with each other and with other interested parties to establish agreed procedures for a prompt, just and permanent implementation of the resolution of the refugee problem.

B. Egypt–Israel

1. Egypt and Israel undertake not to resort to the threat or the use of force to settle disputes. Any disputes shall be settled by peaceful means in accordance with the provisions of Article 33 of the Charter of the United Nations.

2. In order to achieve peace between them, the parties agreed to negotiate in good faith with a goal of concluding within three months from the signing of this Framework a peace treaty between them, while inviting the other parties to the conflict to proceed simultaneously to negotiate and conclude similar peace treaties with a view to achieving a comprehensive peace in the area. The Framework for the conclusion of a peace treaty between Egypt and Israel will govern the peace negotiations between them. The parties will agree on the modalities and the timetable for the implementation of their obligations under the treaty.

C. Associated Principles

1. Egypt and Israel state that the principles and provisions described below should apply to peace treaties between Israel and each of its neighbours – Egypt, Jordan, Syria and Lebanon.

2. Signatories shall establish among themselves relationships normal to states at peace with one another. To this end, they should undertake to abide by all the provisions of the Charter of the United Nations. Steps to be taken in this respect include:

(A) Full recognition,

(B) Abolishing economic boycotts,

(C) Guaranteeing that under their jurisdiction the citizens of the other parties shall enjoy the protection of the due process of law.

3. Signatories should explore possibilities for economic development in the context of final peace treaties, with the objective of contributing to the atmosphere of peace, co-operation and friendship which is their common goal.

4. Claims commissions may be established for the mutual settlement of all financial claims.

5. The United States shall be invited to participate in the talks on matters related to the modalities of the implementation of the agreements and working out the timetable for the carrying out of the obligations of the parties.

6. The United Nations Security Council shall be requested to endorse the peace treaties and ensure that their provisions shall not be violated. The permanent members of the Security Council shall be requested to underwrite the peace treaties and ensure respect for their provisions. They shall also be requested to conform their policies and actions with the undertakings contained in this Framework.

For the Government of the   For the Government of Israel:
Arab Republic of Egypt:

Witnessed by:

Jimmy Carter, President of the United States of America

A Framework for the Conclusion of a Peace Treaty between Israel and Egypt

In order to achieve peace between them, Israel and Egypt agree to negotiate in good faith with a goal of concluding within three months of the signing of this framework a peace treaty between them.

It is agreed that:

The site of the negotiations will be under a United Nations flag at a location or locations to be mutually agreed.

All of the principles of UN Resolution 242 will apply in this resolution of the dispute between Israel and Egypt.

Unless otherwise mutually agreed, terms of the peace treaty will be implemented between 2 and 3 years after the peace treaty is signed.

The following matters are agreed between the parties:

(a) The full exercise of Egyptian sovereignty up to the internationally recognized border between Egypt and Mandated Palestine;
(b) The withdrawal of Israeli armed forces from the Sinai;
(c) The use of airfields left by the Israelis near El Arish, Rafah, Ras-en-Naqb and Sharm e-Sheikh for civilian purposes only, including possible commercial use by all nations;
(d) The right of free passage by ships of Israel through the Gulf of Suez and the Suez Canal on the basis of the Constantinople Convention of 1888 applying to all nations; the Strait of Tiran and the Gulf of Aqaba are international waterways to be open to all nations for unimpeded and non-suspendable freedom of navigation and overflight;
(e) The construction of a highway between the Sinai and Jordan near Eilat with guaranteed free and peaceful passage by Egypt and Jordan; and
(f) The stationing of military forces listed below.

Stationing of Forces

A. No more than one division (mechanized or infantry) of Egyptian armed forces will be stationed within an area lying approximately 50 km east of the Gulf of Suez and the Suez Canal.
B. Only UN forces and civil police equipped with light weapons to perform normal police functions will be stationed within an area lying west of the international border and the Gulf of Aqaba, varying in width from 20 km to 40 km.
C. In the area within 3 km east of the international border there will be Israeli limited military forces not to exceed 4 infantry battalions and UN observers.
D. Border patrol units, not to exceed 3 battalions, will supplement the civil police in maintaining order in the area not included above.

The exact demarcation of the above areas will be decided during the peace negotiations.

Early warning stations may exist to insure compliance with the terms of the agreement.

UN forces will be stationed:
A. In part of the area in the Sinai lying within about 20 km of the Mediterranean Sea, and adjacent to the international border, and
B. In the Sharm e-Sheikh area to insure freedom of passage through the Strait of Tiran; and these forces will not be removed unless such removal is approved by the Security Council of the UN with a unanimous vote of the five permanent members.

After a peace treaty is signed, and after the interim withdrawal is complete, normal relations will be established between Egypt and Israel, including: Full recognition, including diplomatic, economic and cultural relations; termination of economic boycotts and barriers to the free movement of goods and people; and mutual protection of citizens by the due process of law.

Interim Withdrawal

Between 3 months and 9 months after the signing of the peace treaty, all Israeli forces will withdraw east of a line extending from a point east of El Arish to Ras Mohammad, the exact location of this line to be determined by mutual agreement.

For the Government of the   For the Government of Israel:
Arab Republic of Egypt:

Witnessed by:

Jimmy Carter, President of the United States of America

Annex to the Framework Agreements – United Nations Security Council Resolutions 242 and 338

Resolution 242 of 22 November 1967

The Security Council,
  Expressing its continuing concern with the grave situation in the Middle East,
  Emphasizing the inadmissibility of the acquisition of territory by war and the need to work for a just and lasting peace in which every State in the area can live in security,
  Emphasizing further that all Member States in their acceptance of the Charter of the United Nations have undertaken a commitment to act in accordance with Article 2 of the Charter,
  1. *Affirms* that the fulfilment of Charter principles requires the establishment of a just and lasting peace in the Middle East which should include the application of both the following principles:
    (i) Withdrawal of Israeli armed forces from territories occupied in the recent conflict;

(ii) Termination of all claims or states of belligerency and respect for and acknowledgement of the sovereignty, territorial integrity and political independence of every State in the area and their right to live in peace within secure and recognized boundaries free from threats or acts of force;

2. *Affirms further* the necessity

(a) For guaranteeing freedom of navigation through international waterways in the area;

(b) For achieving a just settlement of the refugee problem;

(c) For guaranteeing the territorial inviolability and political independence of every State in the area, through measures including the establishment of demilitarized zones:

3. *Requests* the Secretary-General to designate a Special Representative to proceed to the Middle East to establish and maintain contacts with the States concerned in order to promote agreement and assist efforts to achieve a peaceful and accepted settlement in accordance with the provisions and principles of this resolution.

4. *Requests* the Secretary-General to report to the Security Council on the progress of the efforts of the Special Representative as soon as possible.

Resolution 338 of 22 October 1973

The Security Council

1. *Calls upon* all parties to the present fighting to cease all firing and terminate all military activity immediately, no later than 12 hours after the moment of the adoption of this decision, in the positions they now occupy;

2. *Calls upon* the parties concerned to start immediately after the cease-fire the implementation of Security Council Resolution 242 (1967) in all of its parts;

3. *Decides* that, immediately and concurrently with the cease-fire, negotiations start between the parties concerned under appropriate auspices aimed at establishing a just and durable peace in the Middle East.

Exchanges of Letters

All letters from Mr Carter are dated 22 September 1978, all the other letters are dated 17 September 1978

The President
Camp David
Thurmont, Maryland

17 September 1978

Dear Mr President:

I have the honour to inform you that during two weeks after my return home I will submit a motion before Israel's Parliament (the Knesset) to decide on the following question:

If during the negotiations to conclude a peace treaty between Israel and Egypt all outstanding issues are agreed upon, 'are you in favour of the removal of the Israeli settlers from the northern and southern Sinai areas or are you in favour of keeping the aforementioned settlers in those areas?'

The vote, Mr President, on this issue will be completely free from the usual Parliamentary Party discipline to the effect that although the coalition is being now supported by 70 members out of 120, every member of the Knesset, as I believe, both of the Government and the Opposition benches, will be enabled to vote in accordance with his own conscience.

Sincerely yours,
Menachem Begin

His Excellency
Anwar El-Sadat
President of the Arab Republic of Egypt
Cairo

22 September 1978

Dear Mr President:

I transmit herewith a copy of a letter to me from Prime Minister Begin setting forth how he proposes to present the issue of the Sinai settlements to the Knesset for the latter's decision.

In this connection, I understand from your letter that Knesset approval to withdraw all Israeli settlers from Sinai according to a timetable within the period specified for the implementation of the peace treaty is a prerequisite to any negotiations on a peace treaty between Egypt and Israel.

Sincerely,
Jimmy Carter

Enclosure:
Letter from Prime Minister Begin

His Excellency Jimmy Carter
President of the United States

17 September 1978

Dear Mr President:

In connection with the 'Framework for a Settlement in Sinai' to be signed tonight, I would like to reaffirm the position of the Arab Republic of Egypt with respect to the settlements:

1. All Israeli settlers must be withdrawn from Sinai according to a timetable within the period specified for the implementation of the peace treaty.

2. Agreement by the Israeli Government and its constitutional institutions to this basic principle is therefore a prerequisite to starting peace negotiations for concluding a peace treaty.

3. If Israel fails to meet this commitment, the 'framework' shall be void and invalid.

Sincerely,
Mohamed Anwar El-Sadat

His Excellency
Menachem Begin
Prime Minister of Israel

22 September 1978

Dear Mr Prime Minister:

I have received your letter of 17 September 1978, describing how you intend to place the question of the future of Israeli settlements in Sinai before the Knesset for its decision.

Enclosed is a copy of President Sadat's letter to me on this subject:

Sincerely,
Jimmy Carter

Enclosure:
Letter from President Sadat

His Excellency Jimmy Carter
President of the United States

17 September 1978

Dear Mr President:

I am writing you to reaffirm the position of the Arab Republic of Egypt with respect to Jerusalem.

1. Arab Jerusalem is an integral part of the West Bank. Legal and historical Arab rights in the city must be respected and restored.

2. Arab Jerusalem should be under Arab sovereignty.

3. The Palestinian inhabitants of Arab Jerusalem are entitled to exercise their legitimate national rights, being part of the Palestinian People in the West Bank.

4. Relevant Security Council resolutions, particularly Resolutions 242 and 267, must be applied with regard to Jerusalem. All the measures taken by Israel to alter the status of the City are null and void and should be rescinded.

5. All peoples must have free access to the City and enjoy the free exercises of worship and the right to visit and transit to the holy places without distinction or discrimination.

6. The holy places of each faith may be placed under the administration and control of their representatives.

7. Essential functions in the City should be undivided and a joint municipal council composed of an equal number of Arab and Israeli members can supervise the carrying out of these functions. In this way, the city shall be undivided.

Sincerely,
Mohamed Anwar El-Sadat

The President
Camp David
Thurmont, Maryland

17 September 1978

Dear Mr President:

I have the honour to inform you, Mr President, that on 28 June 1967 Israel's parliament (the Knesset) promulgated and adopted a law to the effect: 'the Government is empowered by a decree to apply the law, the jurisdiction and administration of the State to any part of Eretz Israel (Land of Israel – Palestine), as stated in that decree'.

On the basis of this law, the government of Israel decreed in July 1967 that Jerusalem is one city indivisible, the capital of the State of Israel.

Sincerely,
Menachem Begin

His Excellency
Anwar El-Sadat
President of the Arab Republic of Egypt
Cairo

22 September 1978

Dear Mr President:

I have received your letter of 17 September 1978, setting forth the Egyptian position on Jerusalem. I am transmitting a copy of that letter to Prime Minister Begin for his information.

The position of the United States on Jerusalem remains as stated by Ambassador Goldberg in the United Nations General Assembly on 14 July 1967, and subsequently by Ambassador Yost in the United Nations Security Council on 1 July 1969.

Sincerely,
Jimmy Carter

His Excellency
Jimmy Carter
President of the United States
The White House
Washington, D.C.

17 September 1978

Dear Mr President:

In connection with the 'Framework for Peace in the Middle East', I am writing you this letter to inform you of the position of the Arab Republic of Egypt, with respect to the implementation of the comprehensive settlement.

To ensure the implementation of the provisions related to the West Bank and Gaza and in order to safeguard the legitimate rights of the Palestinian People, Egypt will be prepared to assume the Arab role emanating from these provisions, following consultations with Jordan and the representatives of the Palestinian People.

Sincerely,
Mohamed Anwar El-Sadat

His Excellency
Menachem Begin
Prime Minister of Israel

22 September 1978

Dear Mr Prime Minister:

I hereby acknowledge that you have informed me as follows:

A. In each paragraph of the Agreed Framework Document the expressions 'Palestinians' or 'Palestinian People are being and will be construed and understood by you as 'Palestinian Arabs'.

B. In each paragraph in which the expression 'West Bank' appears it is being, and will be, understood by the Government of Israel as Judea and Samaria.

Sincerely,
Jimmy Carter

Appendix 2

THE PEACE TREATY WITH EGYPT

Treaty of Peace between the Arab Republic of Egypt and the State of Israel

The Government of the Arab Republic of Egypt and the Government of the State of Israel;

Preamble

Convinced of the urgent necessity of the establishment of a just, comprehensive and lasting peace in the Middle East in accordance with Security Council Resolutions 242 and 338;

Reaffirming their adherence to the 'Framework for Peace in the Middle East Agreed at Camp David', dated 17 September 1978;

Noting that the aforementioned Framework as appropriate is intended to constitute a basis for peace not only between Egypt and Israel but also between Israel and each of its other Arab neighbours which is prepared to negotiate peace with it on this basis;

Desiring to bring to an end the state of war between them and to establish a peace in which every state in the area can live in security;

Convinced that the conclusion of a Treaty of Peace between Egypt and Israel is an important step in the search for comprehensive peace in the area and for the attainment of the settlement of the Arab-Israeli conflict in all its aspects;

Inviting the other Arab parties to this dispute to join the peace process with Israel guided by and based on the principles of the aforementioned Framework;

Desiring as well to develop friendly relations and co-operation between themselves in accordance with the United Nations Charter and the principles of international law governing international relations in times of peace;

Agree to the following provisions in the free exercise of their sovereignty, in order to implement the 'Framework for the Conclusion of a Peace Treaty Between Egypt and Israel';

Article I

1. The state of war between the Parties will be terminated and peace will be established between them upon the exchange of instruments of ratification of this Treaty.

2. Israel will withdraw all its armed forces and civilians from the Sinai behind the international boundary between Egypt and mandated Palestine, as provided in the annexed protocol (Annex I), and Egypt will resume the exercise of its full sovereignty over the Sinai.

3. Upon completion of the interim withdrawal provided for in Annex I, the Parties will establish normal and friendly relations, in accordance with Article III (3).

Article II

The permanent boundary between Egypt and Israel is the recognized international boundary between Egypt and the former mandated territory of Palestine, as shown on the map at Annex II, without prejudice to the issue of the status of the Gaza Strip. The Parties recognize this boundary as inviolable. Each will respect the territorial integrity of the other, including their territorial waters and airspace.

Article III

1. The Parties will apply between them the provisions of the Charter of the United Nations and the principles of international law governing relations among states in times of peace. In particular:
   (a) They recognize and will respect each other's sovereignty, territorial integrity and political independence;
   (b) They recognize and will respect each other's right to live in peace within their secure and recognized boundaries;
   (c) They will refrain from the threat or use of force, directly or indirectly, against each other and will settle all disputes between them by peaceful means.

2. Each Party undertakes to ensure that acts or threats of belligerency, hostility, or violence do not originate from and are not committed from within its territory, or by any forces subject to its control or by any other forces stationed on its territory, against the population, citizens or property of the other Party. Each Party also undertakes to refrain from organizing, instigating, inciting, assisting or participating in acts or threats of belligerency, hostility, subversion or violence against the other Party, anywhere, and undertakes to ensure that perpetrators of such acts are brought to justice.

3. The Parties agree that the normal relationship established between them will include full recognition, diplomatic, economic and cultural relations, termination of economic boycotts and discriminatory barriers to the free movement of people and goods, and will guarantee the mutual enjoyment by citizens of the due process of law. The process by which they undertake to achieve such a relationship parallel to the implementation of other provisions of this Treaty is set out in the annexed protocol (Annex III).

Article IV

1. In order to provide maximum security for both Parties on the basis of reciprocity, agreed security arrangements will be established including limited force zones in Egyptian and Israeli territory, and United Nations forces and observers, described in detail as to nature and timing in Annex I, and other security arrangements the Parties may agree upon.

2. The Parties agree to the stationing of United Nations personnel in areas described in Annex I. The Parties agree not to request withdrawal of the United Nations personnel and that these personnel will not be removed unless such removal is approved by the Security Council of the United Nations, with the affirmative vote of the five Permanent Members, unless the Parties otherwise agree.

3. A Joint Commission will be established to facilitate the implementation of the Treaty, as provided for in Annex I.

4. The security arrangements provided for in paragraphs 1 and 2 of this Article may at the request of either party be reviewed and amended by mutual agreement of the Parties.

Article V

1. Ships of Israel, and cargoes destined for or coming from Israel, shall enjoy the right of free passage through the Suez Canal and its approaches through the Gulf of Suez and the Mediterranean Sea on the basis of the Constantinople Convention of 1888, applying to all nations. Israeli nationals, vessels and cargoes, as well as persons, vessels and cargoes destined for or coming from Israel, shall be accorded non-discriminatory treatment in all matters connected with usage of the canal.

2. The Parties consider the Strait of Tiran and the Gulf of Aqaba to be international waterways open to all nations for unimpeded and non-suspendable freedom of navigation and overflight. The Parties will respect each other's right to navigation and overflight for access to either country through the Strait of Tiran and the Gulf of Aqaba.

Article VI

1. This Treaty does not affect and shall not be interpreted as affecting in any way the rights and obligations of the Parties under the Charter of the United Nations.

2. The Parties undertake to fulfil in good faith their obligations under this Treaty, without regard to action or inaction of any other party and independently of any instrument external to this Treaty.

3. They further undertake to take all the necessary measures for the application in their relations of the provisions of the multilateral conventions to which they are parties, including the submission of appropriate notification to the Secretary General of the United Nations and other depositaries of such conventions.

4. The Parties undertake not to enter into any obligation in conflict with this Treaty.

5. Subject to Article 103 of the United Nations Charter, in the event of a conflict between the obligations of the Parties under the present Treaty and any of their other obligations, the obligations under this Treaty will be binding and implemented.

Article VII

1. Disputes arising out of the application or interpretation of this Treaty shall be resolved by negotiations.

2. Any such disputes which cannot be settled by negotiations shall be resolved by conciliation or submitted to arbitration.

Article VIII

The Parties agree to establish a claims commission for the mutual settlement of all financial claims.

Article IX

1. This Treaty shall enter into force upon exchange of instruments of ratification.

2. This Treaty supersedes the Agreement between Egypt and Israel of September 1975.

3. All protocols, annexes, and maps attached to this Treaty shall be regarded as an integral part hereof.

4. The Treaty shall be communicated to the Secretary General of the United Nations for registration in accordance with the provisions of Article 102 of the Charter of the United Nations.

Annex I – Protocol Concerning Israeli Withdrawal and Security Agreements

Article I: Concept of Withdrawal

1. Israel will complete withdrawal of all its armed forces and civilians from the Sinai not later than three years from the date of exchange of instruments of ratification of this Treaty.

2. To ensure the mutual security of the Parties, the implementation of phased withdrawal will be accompanied by the military measures and establishment of zones set out in this Annex and in Map 1, hereinafter referred to as 'the Zones'.

3. The withdrawal from the Sinai will be accomplished in two phases:

(a) The interim withdrawal behind the line from east of El Arish to Ras Mohammad as delineated on Map 2 within nine months from the date of exchange of instruments of ratification of this Treaty.

(b) The final withdrawal from the Sinai behind the international boundary not later than three years from the date of exchange of instruments of ratification of this Treaty.

4. A Joint Commission will be formed immediately after the exchange of instruments of ratification of this Treaty in order to supervise and co-ordinate movements and schedules during the withdrawal, and to adjust plans and timetables as necessary within the limits established by paragraph 3, above. Details relating to the Joint

Commission are set out in Article IV of the attached Appendix. The Joint Commission will be dissolved upon completion of final Israeli withdrawal from the Sinai.

Article II: Determination of Final Lines and Zones

1. In order to provide maximum security for both Parties after the final withdrawal, the lines and the Zones delineated on Map 1 are to be established and organized as follows:

a. Zone A

    (1) Zone A is bounded on the east by line A and on the west by the Suez Canal and the east coast of the Gulf of Suez, as shown on Map 1.

    (2) An Egyptian armed force of one mechanized infantry division and its military installations, and field fortifications, will be in this Zone.

    (3) The main elements of that Division will consist of:

        (a) Three mechanized infantry brigades.

        (b) One armoured brigade.

        (c) Seven field artillery battalions including up to 126 artillery pieces.

        (d) Seven anti-aircraft artillery battalions including individual surface-to-air missiles and up to 126 anti-aircraft guns of 37 mm and above.

        (e) Up to 230 tanks.

        (f) Up to 480 armoured personnel vehicles of all types.

        (g) Up to a total of twenty-two thousand personnel.

b. Zone B

    (1) Zone B is bounded by line B on the east and by line A on the west, as shown on Map 1.

    (2) Egyptian border units of four battalions equipped with light weapons and wheeled vehicles will provide security and supplement the civil police in maintaining order in Zone B. The main elements of the four border battalions will consist of up to a total of four thousand personnel.

    (3) Land based, short range, low power, coastal warning points of the border patrol units may be established on the coast of this Zone.

    (4) There will be in Zone B field fortifications and military installations for the four border battalions.

c. Zone C

    (1) Zone C is bounded by line B on the west and the international boundary and the Gulf of Aqaba on the east, as shown on Map 1.

    (2) Only United Nations forces and Egyptian civil police will be stationed in Zone C.

    (3) The Egyptian civil police armed with light weapons will perform normal police functions within this Zone.

    (4) The United Nations Force will be deployed within Zone C and perform its functions as defined in Article VI of this Annex.

    (5) The United Nations Force will be stationed mainly in camps located within the following stationing areas shown on Map 1, and will establish its precise locations after consultations with Egypt:

MAP 1
Sinai Peninsula

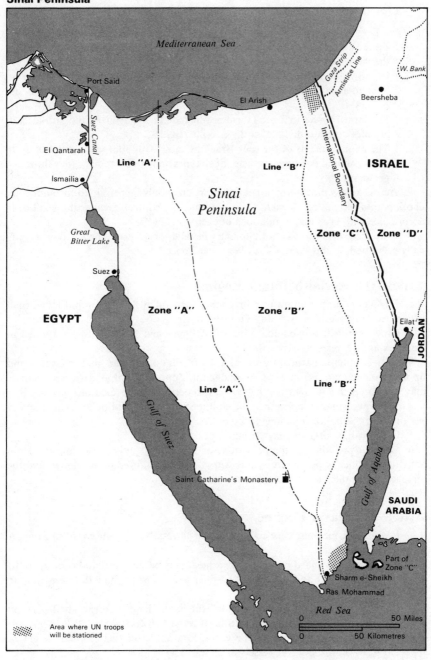

Mediterranean Sea

Port Said

El Arish

Gaza Strip

Armistice Line

W. Bank

Beersheba

Suez Canal

El Qantarah

Line "A"

Line "B"

International Boundary

ISRAEL

Ismailia

*Sinai
Peninsula*

Zone "C"

Zone "D"

*Great
Bitter Lake*

Suez

Zone "A"

Zone "B"

Eilat

JORDAN

EGYPT

Line "A"

Line "B"

Gulf of Suez

Saint Catharine's Monastery

Gulf of Aqaba

**SAUDI
ARABIA**

Part of
Zone "C"

Sharm e-Sheikh

Ras Mohammad

Red Sea

Area where UN troops
will be stationed

0   50 Miles

0   50 Kilometres

(a) In that part of the area in the Sinai lying within about 20 km of the Mediterranean Sea and adjacent to the international boundary.

(b) In the Sharm e-Sheikh area.

d. Zone D

(1) Zone D is bounded by line D on the east and the international boundary on the west, as shown on Map 1.

(2) In this Zone there will be an Israeli limited force of four infantry battalions, their military installations, and field fortifications, and United Nations observers.

(3) The Israeli forces in Zone D will not include tanks, artillery and anti-aircraft missiles except individual surface-to-air missiles.

(4) The main elements of the four Israeli infantry battalions will consist of up to 180 armoured personnel vehicles of all types and up to a total of four thousand personnel.

2. Access across the international boundary shall only be permitted through entry check points designated by each Party and under its control. Such access shall be in accordance with laws and regulations of each country.

3. Only those field fortifications, military installations, forces, and weapons specifically permitted by this Annex shall be in the Zones.

Article III: Aerial Military Regime

1. Flights of combat aircraft and reconnaissance flights of Egypt and Israel shall take place only over Zones A and D, respectively.

2. Only unarmed, non-combat aircraft of Egypt and Israel will be stationed in Zones A and D, respectively.

3. Only Egyptian unarmed transport aircraft will take off and land in Zone B and up to eight such aircraft may be maintained in Zone B. The Egyptian border units may be equipped with unarmed helicopters to perform their functions in Zone B.

4. The Egyptian civil police may be equipped with unarmed police helicopters to perform normal police functions in Zone C.

5. Only civilian airfields may be built in the Zones.

6. Without prejudice to the provisions of this Treaty, only those military aerial activities specifically permitted by this Annex shall be allowed in the Zones, and the airspace above their territorial waters.

Article IV: Naval Regime

1. Egypt and Israel may base and operate naval vessels along the coasts of Zones A and D, respectively.

2. Egyptian coast guard boats, lightly armed, may be stationed and operate in the territorial waters of Zone B to assist the border units in performing their functions in this Zone.

3. Egyptian civil police equipped with light boats, lightly armed, shall perform normal police functions within the territorial waters of Zone C.

4. Nothing in this Annex shall be considered as derogating from the right of innocent passage of the naval vessels of either party.

5. Only civilian maritime ports and installations may be built in the Zones.

6. Without prejudice to the provisions of this Treaty, only those naval activities specifically permitted by this Annex shall be allowed in the Zones and in their territorial waters.

Article V: Early Warning Systems

Egypt and Israel may establish and operate early warning systems only in Zones A and D, respectively.

Article VI: United Nations Operations

1. The Parties will request the United Nations to provide forces and observers to supervise the implementation of this Annex and employ their best efforts to prevent any violation of its terms.

2. With respect to these United Nations forces and observers, as appropriate, the Parties agree to request the following arrangements:

   (a) Operation of check points, reconnaissance patrols, and observation posts along the international boundary and line B, and within Zone C.

   (b) Periodic verification of the implementation of the provisions of this Annex will be carried out not less than twice a month unless otherwise agreed by the Parties.

   (c) Additional verifications within 48 hours after the receipt of a request from either Party.

   (d) Ensuring the freedom of navigation through the Strait of Tiran in accordance with Article V of the Treaty of Peace.

3. The arrangements described in this article for each zone will be implemented in Zones A, B, and C by the United Nations Force and in Zone D by the United Nations Observers.

4. United Nations verification teams shall be accompanied by liaison officers of the respective Party.

5. The United Nations Force and observers will report their findings to both Parties.

6. The United Nations Force and Observers operating in the Zones will enjoy freedom of movement and other facilities necessary for the performance of their tasks.

7. The United Nations Force and Observers are not empowered to authorize the crossing of the international boundary.

8. The Parties shall agree on the nations from which the United Nations Force and Observers will be drawn. They will be drawn from nations other than those which are permanent members of the United Nations Security Council.

9. The Parties' agree that the United Nations should make those command arrangements that will best assure the effective implementation of its responsibilities.

Article VII: Liaison System

1. Upon dissolution of the Joint Commission, a liaison system between the Parties will be established. This liaison system is intended to provide an effective method to assess progress in the implementation of obligations under the present Annex and to

resolve any problem that may arise in the course of implementation, and refer other unresolved matters to the higher military authorities of the two countries, respectively, for consideration. It is also intended to prevent situations resulting from errors or misinterpretation on the part of either Party.

2. An Egyptian liaison office will be established in the city of El Arish and an Israeli liaison office will be established in the city of Beersheba. Each office will be headed by an officer of the respective country, and assisted by a number of officers.

3. A direct telephone link between the two offices will be set up and also direct telephone lines with the United Nations command will be maintained by both offices.

Article VIII: Respect for War Memorials

Each Party undertakes to preserve in good condition the War Memorials erected in the memory of soldiers of the other Party, namely those erected by Israel in the Sinai and those to be erected by Egypt in Israel, and shall permit access to such monuments.

Article IX: Interim Arrangements

The withdrawal of Israeli armed forces and civilians behind the interim withdrawal line, and the conduct of the forces of the Parties and the United Nations prior to the final withdrawal, will be governed by the attached Appendix and Map 2.

Appendix to Annex I – Organization of Movements in the Sinai

Article I: Principles of Withdrawal

1. The withdrawal of Israeli armed forces and civilians from the Sinai will be accomplished in two phases as described in Article I of Annex I. The description and timing of the withdrawal are included in this Appendix. The Joint Commission will develop and present to the Chief Co-ordinator of the United Nations forces in the Middle East the details of these phases not later than one month before the initiation of each phase of withdrawal.

2. Both Parties agree on the following principles for the sequence of military movements.

(a) Notwithstanding the provisions of Article IX, paragraph 2, of this Treaty, until Israeli armed forces complete withdrawal from the current J and M Lines established by the Egyptian–Israeli Agreement of September 1975, hereinafter referred to as the 1975 Agreement, up to the interim withdrawal line, all military arrangements existing under that Agreement will remain in effect, except those military arrangements otherwise provided for in this Appendix.

(b) As Israeli armed forces withdraw, United Nations forces will immediately enter the evacuated areas to establish interim and temporary buffer zones as shown on Maps 2 and 3, respectively, for the purpose of maintaining a separation of forces. United Nations forces' deployment will preceded the movement of any other personnel into these areas.

MAP 2
Sinai Peninsula

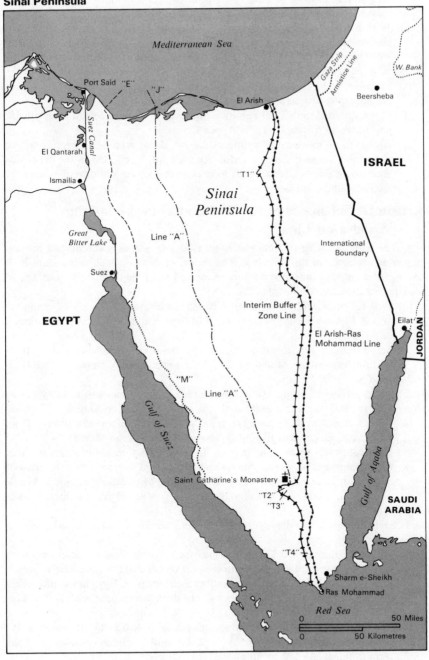

Mediterranean Sea

Port Said "E"

"J"

El Arish

Gaza Strip

Armistice Line

W. Bank

Beersheba

Suez Canal

El Qantarah

ISRAEL

Ismailia

"T1"

Sinai Peninsula

Great Bitter Lake

Line "A"

International Boundary

Suez

Interim Buffer Zone Line

EGYPT

El Arish-Ras Mohammad Line

Eilat

JORDAN

"M"

Line "A"

Gulf of Suez

Gulf of Aqaba

Saint Catharine's Monastery

"T2"

"T3"

SAUDI ARABIA

"T4"

Sharm e-Sheikh

Ras Mohammad

Red Sea

0   50 Miles

0   50 Kilometres

(c) Within a period of seven days after Israeli armed forces have evacuated any area located in Zone A, units of Egyptian armed forces shall deploy in accordance with the provisions of Article II of this Appendix.

(d) Within a period of seven days after Israeli armed forces have evacuated any area located in Zones A or B, Egyptian border units shall deploy in accordance with the provisions of Article II of this Appendix, and will function in accordance with the provisions of Article II of Annex I.

(e) Egyptian civil police will enter evacuated areas immediately after the United Nations forces to perform normal police functions.

(f) Egyptian naval units shall deploy in the Gulf of Suez in accordance with the provisions of Article II of this Appendix.

(g) Except those movements mentioned above, deployments of Egyptian armed forces and the activities covered in Annex I will be effected in the evacuated areas when Israeli armed forces have completed their withdrawal behind the interim withdrawal line.

Article II: Subphases of the Withdrawal to the Interim Withdrawal Line

1. The withdrawal to the interim withdrawal line will be accomplished in subphases as described in this Article and as shown on Map 3. Each subphase will be completed within the indicated number of months from the date of the exchange of instruments of ratification of this Treaty.

(a) First subphase: within two months, Israeli armed forces will withdraw from the area of El Arish, including the town of El Arish and its airfield, shown as Area I on Map 3.

(b) Second subphase: within three months, Israeli armed forces will withdraw from the area between line M of the 1975 Agreement and line A, shown as Area II on Map 3.

(c) Third subphase: within five months, Israeli armed forces will withdraw from the area east and south of Area II, shown as Area III on Map 3.

(d) Fourth subphase: within seven months, Israeli armed forces will withdraw from the area of El Tor-Ras El Kenisa, shown as Area IV on Map 3.

(e) Fifth subphase: within nine months, Israeli armed forces will withdraw from the remaining areas west of the interim withdrawal line, including the areas of Santa Katrina and the areas east of the Gidi and Mitla Passes, shown as Area V on Map 3, thereby completing Israeli withdrawal behind the interim withdrawal line.

2. Egyptian forces will deploy in the areas evacuated by Israeli armed forces as follows:

(a) Up to one-third of the Egyptian armed forces in the Sinai in accordance with the 1975 Agreement will deploy in the portions of Zone A lying within Area I, until the completion of interim withdrawal. Thereafter, Egyptian armed forces as described in Article II of Annex I will be deployed in Zone A up to the limits of the interim buffer zone.

(b) The Egyptian naval activity in accordance with Article IV of Annex I will commence along the coasts of Areas I, III, and IV, upon completion of the second, third, and fourth subphases, respectively.

MAP 3
Sub-Phases of Withdrawal to the El Arish-Ras Mohammad Line

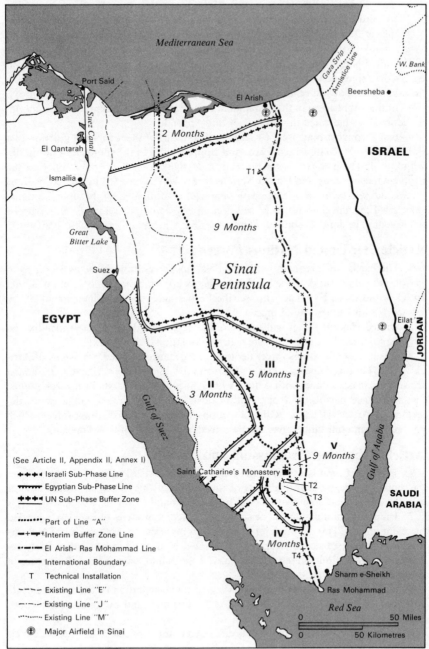

Mediterranean Sea

Port Said

El Arish

Gaza Strip Armistice Line

W. Bank

Beersheba ●

El Qantarah

Suez Canal

ISRAEL

Ismailia ●

T1

Great
Bitter Lake

V
9 Months

Suez ●

*Sinai
Peninsula*

EGYPT

Eilat ●

JORDAN

Gulf of Suez

III
5 Months

II
3 Months

V
9 Months

Gulf of Aqaba

(See Article II, Appendix II, Annex I)

Saint Catharine's Monastery

T2
T3

**SAUDI
ARABIA**

┿┿┿┿ Israeli Sub-Phase Line

┯┯┯┯ Egyptian Sub-Phase Line

┿┿┿┿ UN Sub-Phase Buffer Zone

•••••• Part of Line "A"

━+━+ Interim Buffer Zone Line

━•━•━ El Arish- Ras Mohammad Line

━━━ International Boundary

T   Technical Installation

━ ━ ━ Existing Line "E"

━•━•━ Existing Line "J"

•••••• Existing Line "M"

✈ Major Airfield in Sinai

IV
7 Months

T4

Sharm e-Sheikh

Ras Mohammad

Red Sea

0	50 Miles
0	50 Kilometres

(c) Of the Egyptian border units described in Article II of Annex I, upon completion of the first subphase one battalion will be deployed in Area I. A second
battalion will be deployed in Area II upon completion of the second subphase.
A third battalion will be deployed in Area III upon completion of the third subphase. The second and third battalions mentioned above may also be deployed
in any of the subsequently evacuated areas of the southern Sinai.

3. United Nations forces in Buffer Zone I of the 1975 Agreement will redeploy to
enable the deployment of Egyptian forces described above upon the completion of the
first subphase, but will otherwise continue to function in accordance with the provisions of that Agreement in the remainder of that zone until the completion of interim
withdrawal, as indicated in Article I of this Appendix.

4. Israeli convoys may use the roads south and east of the main road junction east
of El Arish to evacuate Israeli forces and equipment up to the completion of interim
withdrawal. These convoys will proceed in daylight upon four hours notice to the
Egyptian liaison group and United Nations forces, will be escorted by United Nations
forces, and will be in accordance with schedules co-ordinated by the Joint Commission. An Egyptian liaison officer will accompany convoys to assure uninterrupted
movement. The Joint Commission may approve other arrangements for convoys.

Article III: United Nations Forces

1. The Parties shall request that United Nations forces be deployed as necessary to
perform the functions described in this Appendix up to the time of completion of final
Israeli withdrawal. For that purpose, the Parties agree to the redeployment of the
United Nations Emergency Force.

2. United Nations forces will supervise the implementation of this Appendix and
will employ their best efforts to prevent any violation of its terms.

3. When United Nations forces deploy in accordance with the provisions of Articles I and II of this Appendix, they will perform the functions of verification in limited
force zones in accordance with Article VI of Annex I, and will establish check points,
reconnaissance patrols, and observation posts in the temporary buffer zones described in Article II above. Other functions of the United Nations forces which
concern the interim buffer zone are described in Article V of this Appendix.

Article IV: Joint Commission and Liaison

1. The Joint Commission referred to in Article IV of this Treaty will function from
the date of exchange of instruments of ratification of this Treaty up to the date of
completion of final Israeli withdrawal from the Sinai.

2. The Joint Commission will be composed of representatives of each Party headed
by senior officers. This Commission shall invite a representative of the United Nations
when discussing subjects concerning the United Nations, or when either Party requests United Nations presence. Decisions of the Joint Commission will be reached
by agreement of Egypt and Israel.

3. The Joint Commission will supervise the implementation of the arrangements
described in Annex I and this Appendix. To this end, and by agreement of both
Parties, it will:
(a) co-ordinate military movements described in this Appendix and supervise their
    implementation;

(b) address and seek to resolve any problem arising out of the implementation of Annex I and this Appendix, and discuss any violations reported by the United Nations Force and Observers and refer to the Governments of Egypt and Israel any unresolved problems;

(c) assist the United Nations Force and Observers in the execution of their mandates, and deal with the timetables of the periodic verifications when referred to it by the Parties as provided for in Annex I and in this Appendix;

(d) organize the demarcation of the international boundary and all lines and zones described in Annex I and this Appendix;

(e) supervise the handing over of the main installations in the Sinai from Israel to Egypt;

(f) agree on necessary arrangements for finding and returning missing bodies of Egyptian and Israeli soldiers;

(g) organize the setting up and operation of entry check points along the El Arish-Ras Mohammad line in accordance with the provisions of Article 4 of Annex III;

(h) conduct its operations through the use of joint liaison teams consisting of one Israeli representative and one Egyptian representative, provided from a standing Liaison Group, which will conduct activities as directed by the Joint Commission;

(i) provide liaison and co-ordination to the United Nations command implementing provisions of the Treaty, and, through the joint liaison teams, maintain local co-ordination and co-operation with the United Nations Force stationed in specific areas or United Nations Observers monitoring specific areas for any assistance as needed;

(j) discuss any other matters which the Parties by agreement may place before it.

4. Meetings of the Joint Commission shall be held at least once a month. In the event that either Party or the Command of the United Nations Force requests a special meeting, it will be convened within 24 hours.

5. The Joint Committee will meet in the buffer zone until the completion of the interim withdrawal and in El Arish and Beersheba alternately afterwards. The first meeting will be held not later than two weeks after the entry into force of this Treaty.

Article V: Definition of the Interim Buffer Zone and Its Activities

1. An interim buffer zone, by which the United Nations Force will effect a separation of Egyptian and Israeli elements, will be established west of and adjacent to the interim withdrawal line as shown on Map 2 after implementation of Israeli withdrawal and deployment behind the interim withdrawal line. Egyptian civil police equipped with light weapons will perform normal police functions within this zone.

2. The United Nations Force will operate check points, reconnaissance patrols, and observation posts within the interim buffer zone in order to ensure compliance with the terms of this Article.

3. In accordance with arrangements agreed upon by both Parties and to be co-ordinated by the Joint Commission, Israeli personnel will operate military technical installations at four specific locations shown on Map 2 and designated as T1 (map central co-ordinate 57163940), T2 (map central co-ordinate 59351541), T3 (map

central co-ordinate 59331527), and T4 (map central co-ordinate 61130979) under the following principles:

   (a) The technical installations shall be manned by technical and administrative personnel equipped with small arms required for their protection (revolvers, rifles, sub-machine guns, light machine guns, hand grenades, and ammunition), as follows:

       T1 – up to 150 personnel
       T2 and T3 – up to 350 personnel
       T4 – up to 200 personnel.

   (b) Israeli personnel will not carry weapons outside the sites, except officers who may carry personal weapons.

   (c) Only a third party agreed to by Egypt and Israel will enter and conduct inspections within the perimeters of technical installations in the buffer zone. The third party will conduct inspections in a random manner at least once a month. The inspections will verify the nature of the operation of the installations and the weapons and personnel therein. The third party will immediately report to the Parties any divergence from an installation's visual and electronic surveillance or communications role.

   (d) Supply of the installations, visits for technical and administrative purposes, and replacement of personnel and equipment situated in the sites, may occur uninterruptedly from the United Nations check points to the perimeter of the technical installations, after checking and being escorted by only the United Nations forces.

   (e) Israel will be permitted to introduce into its technical installations items required for the proper functioning of the installations and personnel.

   (f) As determined by the Joint Commission, Israel will be permitted to:

      (1) Maintain in its installations fire-fighting and general maintenance equipment as well as wheeled administrative vehicles and mobile engineering equipment necessary for the maintenance of the sites. All vehicles shall be unarmed.

      (2) Within the sites and in the buffer zone, maintain roads, water lines, and communications cables which serve the sites. At each of the three installation locations (T1, T2 and T3, and T4), this maintenance may be performed with up to two unarmed wheeled vehicles and by up to twelve unarmed personnel with only necessary equipment, including heavy engineering equipment if needed. This maintenance may be performed three times a week, except for special problems, and only after giving the United Nations four hours notice. The teams will be escorted by the United Nations.

   (g) Movement to and from the technical installations will take place only during daylight hours. Access to, and exit from, the technical installations shall be as follows:

      (1) T1: through a United Nations check point, and via the road between Abu Aweigila and the intersection of the Abu Aweigila road and the Gebel Libni road (at Km 161), as shown on Map 2.

      (2) T2 and T3: through a United Nations check point and via the road constructed across the buffer zone to Gebel Katrina, as shown on Map 2.

      (3) T2, T3, and T4: via helicopters flying within a corridor at the times, and

according to a flight profile, agreed to by the Joint Commission. The helicopters will be checked by the United Nations Force at landing sites outside the perimeter of the installations.

(h) Israel will inform the United Nations Force at least one hour in advance of each intended movement to and from the installations.

(i) Israel shall be entitled to evacuate sick and wounded and summon medical experts and medical teams at any time after giving immediate notice to the United Nations Force.

4. The details of the above principles and all other matters in this Article requiring co-ordination by the Parties will be handled by the Joint Commission.

5. These technical installations will be withdrawn when Israeli forces withdraw from the interim withdrawal line, or at a time agreed by the Parties.

Article VI: Disposition of Installations and Military Barriers

Disposition of installations and military barriers will be determined by the Parties in accordance with the following guidelines:

1. Up to three weeks before Israeli withdrawal from any area, the Joint Commission will arrange for Israeli and Egyptian liaison and technical teams to conduct a joint inspection of all appropriate installations to agree upon condition of structures and articles which will be transferred to Egyptian control and to arrange for such transfer. Israel will declare, at that time, its plans for disposition of installations and articles within the installations.

2. Israel undertakes to transfer to Egypt all agreed infrastructures, utilities, and installations intact, inter alia, airfields, roads, pumping stations, and ports. Israel will present to Egypt the information necessary for the maintenance and operation of these facilities. Egyptian technical teams will be permitted to observe and familiarize themselves with the operation of these facilities for a period of up to two weeks prior to transfer.

3. When Israel relinquishes Israeli military water points near El Arish and El Tor, Egyptian technical teams will assume control of those installations and ancillary equipment in accordance with an orderly transfer process arranged beforehand by the Joint Commission. Egypt undertakes to continue to make available at all water supply points the normal quantity of currently available water up to the time Israel withdraws behind the international boundary, unless otherwise agreed in the Joint Commission.

4. Israel will make its best effort to remove or destroy all military barriers, including obstacles and minefields, in the areas and adjacent waters from which it withdraws, according to the following concept:

(a) Military barriers will be cleared first from areas near populations, roads, and major installations and utilities.

(b) For those obstacles and minefields which cannot be removed or destroyed prior to Israeli withdrawal, Israel will provide detailed maps to Egypt and the United Nations through the Joint Commission not later than 15 days before entry of United Nations forces into the affected areas.

(c) Egyptian engineers will enter those areas after United Nations forces enter to conduct barrier clearance operations in accordance with Egyptian plans to be submitted prior to implementation.

Article VII: Surveillance Activities

1. Aerial surveillance activities during the withdrawal will be carried out as follows:

  (a) Both Parties request the United States to continue airborne surveillance flights in accordance with previous agreements until the completion of final Israeli withdrawal.

  (b) Flight profiles will cover the Limited Forces Zones to monitor the limitations on forces and armaments, and to determine that Israeli armed forces have withdrawn from the areas described in Article II of Annex I, Article II of this Appendix, and Maps 2 and 3, and that these forces thereafter remain behind their lines. Special inspection flights may be flown at the request of either Party or of the United Nations.

  (c) Only the main elements in the military organizations of each Party, as described in Annex I and in this Appendix, will be reported.

2. Both Parties request the United States operated Sinai Field Mission to continue its operations in accordance with previous agreements until completion of the Israeli withdrawal from the area east of the Gidi and Mitla Passes. Thereafter, the Mission will be terminated.

Article VIII: Exercise of Egyptian Sovereignty

Egypt will resume the exercise of its full sovereignty over evacuated parts of the Sinai upon Israeli withdrawal as provided for in Article I of this Treaty.

Annex III – Protocol Concerning Relations of the Parties

Article 1: Diplomatic and Consular Relations

The Parties agree to establish diplomatic and consular relations and to exchange ambassadors upon completion of the interim withdrawal.

Article 2: Economic and Trade Relations

1. The Parties agree to remove all discriminatory barriers to normal economic relations and to terminate economic boycotts of each other upon completion of the interim withdrawal.

2. As soon as possible, and not later than six months after the completion of the interim withdrawal, the Parties will enter negotiations with a view to concluding an agreement on trade and commerce for the purpose of promoting beneficial economic relations.

MAP 4
Sinai Peninsula

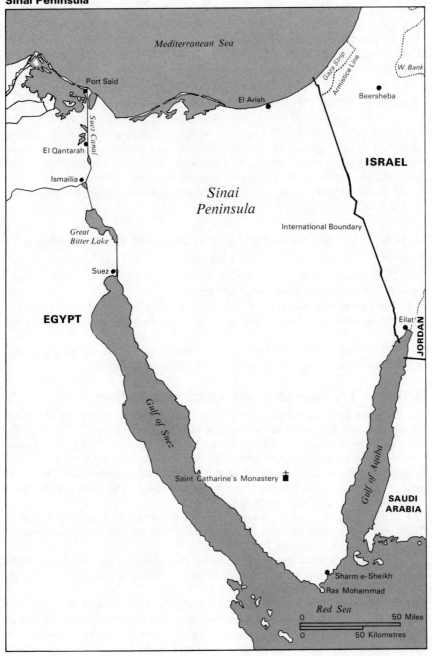

Mediterranean Sea

Port Said

El Arish

Gaza Strip

Armistice Line

W. Bank

Beersheba

Suez Canal

El Qantarah

Ismailia

Sinai
Peninsula

ISRAEL

International Boundary

Great
Bitter Lake

Suez

EGYPT

Eilat

JORDAN

Gulf of Suez

Gulf of Aqaba

Saint Catharine's Monastery ✝

SAUDI
ARABIA

Sharm e-Sheikh

Ras Mohammad

Red Sea

0   50 Miles

0   50 Kilometres

Article 3: Cultural Relations

1. The Parties agree to establish normal cultural relations following completion of the interim withdrawal.

2. They agree on the desirability of cultural exchanges in all fields, and shall, as soon as possible and not later than six months after completion of the interim withdrawal, enter into negotiations with a view to concluding a cultural agreement for this purpose.

Article 4: Freedom of Movement

1. Upon completion of the interim withdrawal, each Party will permit the free movement of the nationals and vehicles of the other into and within its territory according to the general rules applicable to nationals and vehicles of other states. Neither Party will impose discriminatory restrictions on the free movement of persons and vehicles from its territory to the territory of the other.

2. Mutual unimpeded access to places of religious and historical significance will be provided on a non-discriminatory basis.

Article 5: Co-operation for Development and Good Neighbourly Relations

1. The Parties recognize a mutuality of interest in good neighbourly relations and agree to consider means to promote such relations.

2. The Parties will co-operate in promoting peace, stability and development in their region. Each agrees to consider proposals the other may wish to make to this end.

3. The Parties shall seek to foster mutual understanding and tolerance and will, accordingly, abstain from hostile propaganda against each other.

Article 6: Transportation and Telecommunications

1. The Parties recognize as applicable to each other the rights, privileges and obligations provided for by the aviation agreements to which they are both party, particularly by the Convention on International Civil Aviation, 1944 ('The Chicago Convention') and the International Air Services Transit Agreement, 1944.

2. Upon completion of the interim withdrawal any declaration of national emergency by a Party under Article 89 of the Chicago Convention will not be applied to the other Party on a discriminatory basis.

3. Egypt agrees that the use of airfields left by Israel near El Arish, Rafah, Ras El Nagb and Sharm e-Sheikh shall be for civilian purposes only, including possible commercial use by all nations.

4. As soon as possible and not later than six months after the completion of the interim withdrawal, the Parties shall enter into negotiations for the purpose of concluding a civil aviation agreement.

5. The Parties will reopen and maintain roads and railways between their countries and will consider further road and rail links. The Parties further agree that a highway will be constructed and maintained between Egypt, Israel and Jordan near Eilat with guaranteed free and peaceful passage of persons, vehicles and goods between Egypt

and Jordan, without prejudice to their sovereignty over that part of the highway which falls within their respective territory.

6. Upon completion of the interim withdrawal, normal postal, telephone, telex, data facsimile, wireless and cable communications and television relay services by cable, radio and satellite shall be established between the two Parties in accordance with all relevant international conventions and regulations.

7. Upon completion of the interim withdrawal, each Party shall grant normal access to its ports for vessels and cargoes of the other, as well as vessels and cargoes destined for or coming from the other. Such access shall be granted on the same conditions generally applicable to vessels and cargoes of other nations. Article 5 of the Treaty of Peace will be implemented upon the exchange of instruments of ratification of the aforementioned treaty.

Article 7: Enjoyment of Human Rights

The Parties affirm their commitment to respect and observe human rights and fundamental freedoms for all, and they will promote these rights and freedoms in accordance with the United Nations Charter.

Article 8: Territorial Seas

Without prejudice to the provisions of Article 5 of the Treaty of Peace each Party recognizes the right of the vessels of the other Party to innocent passage through its territorial sea in accordance with the rules of international law.

Agreed Minutes

(relating to Articles I, IV, V and VI of the Peace Treaty, and Annexes I and III)

Article I

Egypt's resumption of the exercise of full sovereignty over the Sinai provided for in paragraph 2 of Article I shall occur with regard to each area upon Israel's withdrawal from that area.

Article IV

It is agreed between the Parties that the review provided for in Article IV (4) will be undertaken when requested by either Party, commencing within three months of such a request, but that any amendment can be made only with the mutual agreement of both Parties.

Article V

The second sentence of paragraph 2 of Article V shall not be construed as limiting the first sentence of that paragraph. The foregoing is not to be construed as contravening the second sentence of paragraph 2 of Article V, which reads as follows:

'The Parties will respect each other's right to navigation and overflight for access to either country through the Strait of Tiran and the Gulf of Aqaba.'

Article VI (2)

The provisions of Article VI shall not be construed in contradiction to the provisions of the framework for peace in the Middle East agreed at Camp David. The foregoing is not to be construed as contravening the provisions of Article VI (2) of the Treaty, which reads as follows:

'The Parties undertake to fulfil in good faith their obligations under this Treaty, without regard to action or inaction of any other Party and independently of any instrument external to this Treaty.'

Article VI (5)

It is agreed by the Parties that there is no assertion that this Treaty prevails over other Treaties or agreements or that other Treaties or agreements prevail over this Treaty. The foregoing is not to be construed as contravening the provisions of Article VI (5) of the Treaty, which reads as follows:

'Subject to Article 103 of the United Nations Charter, in the event of a conflict between the obligations of the Parties under the present Treaty and any of their other obligations, the obligations under this Treaty will be binding and implemented.'

Annex I

Article VI, paragraph 8, of Annex I provides as follows:

'The Parties shall agree on the nations from which the United Nations Force and Observers will be drawn. They will be drawn from nations other than those which are permanent members of the United Nations Security Council.'

The Parties have agreed as follows:

'With respect to the provisions of paragraph 8, Article VI, of Annex I, if no agreement is reached between the Parties, they will accept or support a US proposal concerning the composition of the United Nations Force and Observers.'

Annex III

The Treaty of Peace and Annex III thereto provide for establishing normal economic relations between the Parties. In accordance therewith, it is agreed that such relations will include normal commercial sales of oil by Egypt to Israel, and that Israel shall be fully entitled to make bids for Egyptian-origin oil not needed for Egyptian domestic oil consumption, and Egypt and its oil concessionaries will entertain bids made by Israel, on the same basis and terms as apply to other bidders for such oil.

For the Government of the   For the Government of Israel:
Arab Republic of Egypt:

Witnessed by:

Jimmy Carter, President of the United States of America

Joint Letter from President Sadat and Prime Minister Begin to President Carter

The President
The White House   **26 March 1979**

Dear Mr President:
This letter confirms that Israel and Egypt have agreed as follows:
The Governments of Israel and Egypt recall that they concluded at Camp David and signed at the White House on 17 September 1978 the annexed documents entitled 'The Framework for Peace in the Middle East Agreed at Camp David' and 'A Framework for the Conclusion of a Peace Treaty between Israel and Egypt'.

For the purpose of achieving a comprehensive peace settlement in accordance with the above-mentioned Frameworks, Israel and Egypt will proceed with the implementation of those provisions relating to the West Bank and the Gaza Strip. They have agreed to start negotiations within a month after the exchange of the instruments of ratification of the Peace Treaty. In accordance with the 'Framework for Peace in the Middle East', the Hashemite Kingdom of Jordan is invited to join the negotiations. The Delegations of Egypt and Jordan may include Palestinians as mutually agreed. The purpose of the negotiation shall be to agree, prior to the elections, on the modalities for establishing the elected self-governing authority (administrative council), define its powers and responsibilities, and agree upon other related issues. In the event Jordan decides not to take part in the negotiations, the negotiations will be held by Israel and Egypt.

The two Governments agree to negotiate continuously and in good faith to conclude these negotiations at the earliest possible date. They also agree that the objective of the negotiations is the establishment of the self-governing authority in the West Bank and Gaza in order to provide full autonomy to the inhabitants.

Israel and Egypt set for themselves the goal of completing the negotiations within one year so that elections will be held as expeditiously as possible after agreement has been reached between the parties. The self-governing authority referred to in the 'Framework for Peace in the Middle East' will be established and inaugurated within one month after it has been elected, at which time the transitional period of five years will begin. The Israeli military government and its civilian administration will be withdrawn, to be replaced by the self-governing authority, as specified in the 'Framework for Peace in the Middle East'. A withdrawal of Israeli armed forces will then take place and there will be a redeployment of the remaining Israeli forces into specified security locations.

This letter also confirms our understanding that the United States Government will participate fully in all stages of negotiations.

Sincerely yours,

For the Government of Israel: For the Government of the
                                        Arab Republic of Egypt:

Menachem Begin   Mohamed Anwar El-Sadat

Letter from President Carter to Prime Minister Begin about the Deployment of a UN or an Alternate Multinational Force

His Excellency
Menachem Begin
Prime Minister of the
State of Israel   **26 March 1979**

Dear Mr Prime Minister:

I wish to confirm to you that subject to United States Constitutional processes:

In the event of an actual or threatened violation of the Treaty of Peace between Israel and Egypt, the United States will, on request of one or both of the Parties, consult with the Parties with respect thereto and will take such other action as it may deem appropriate and helpful to achieve compliance with the Treaty.

The United States will conduct aerial monitoring as requested by the Parties pursuant to Annex I of the Treaty.

The United States believes the Treaty provision for permanent stationing of United Nations personnel in the designated limited force zone can and should be implemented by the United Nations Security Council. The United States will exert its utmost efforts to obtain the requisite action by the Security Council. If the Security Council fails to establish and maintain the arrangements called for in the Treaty, the President will be prepared to take those steps necessary to ensure the establishment and maintenance of an acceptable alternative multinational force.

Sincerely,
Jimmy Carter

Exchange of Letters between President Carter and Prime Minister Begin Regarding the Exchange of Ambassadors between Egypt and Israel

His Excellency
Menachem Begin
Prime Minister of the
State of Israel   **26 March 1979**

Dear Mr Prime Minister:

I have received a letter from President Sadat that, within one month after Israel completes its withdrawal to the interim line in Sinai, as provided for in the Treaty of Peace between Egypt and Israel, Egypt will send a resident ambassador to Israel and will receive in Egypt a resident Israeli ambassador.

I would be grateful if you will confirm that this procedure will be agreeable to the Government of Israel.

Sincerely,
Jimmy Carter

The President,
The White House   **26 March 1979**
Dear Mr President:
  I am pleased to be able to confirm that the Government of Israel is agreeable to the procedure set out in your letter of 26 March 1979 in which you state:

'I have received a letter from President Sadat that, within one month after Israel completes its withdrawal to the interim line in Sinai, as provided for in the Treaty of Peace between Egypt and Israel, Egypt will send a resident ambassador to Israel and will receive in Egypt a resident Israeli ambassador.'

                                              Sincerely,
                                              Menachem Begin

Appendix 3

II MEMORANDA OF AGREEMENT

Memorandum of Agreement between the Governments of the United States of America and the State of Israel

26 March 1979

Recognizing the significance of the conclusion of the Treaty of Peace between Israel and Egypt and considering the importance of full implementation of the Treaty of Peace to Israel's security interests and the contribution of the conclusion of the Treaty of Peace to the security and development of Israel as well as its significance to peace and stability in the region and to the maintenance of international peace and security; and

Recognizing that the withdrawal from Sinai imposes additional heavy security, military and economic burdens on Israel;

The Governments of the United States of America and of the State of Israel, subject to their constitutional processes and applicable law, confirm as follows:

1. In the light of the role of the United States in achieving the Treaty of Peace and the parties' desire that the United States continue its supportive efforts, the United States will take appropriate measures to promote full observance of the Treaty of Peace.

2. Should it be demonstrated to the satisfaction of the United States that there has been a violation or threat of violation of the Treaty of Peace, the United States will consult with the parties with regard to measures to halt or prevent the violation, ensure observance of the Treaty of Peace, enhance friendly and peaceful relations between the parties and promote peace in the region, and will take such remedial measures as it deems appropriate, which may include diplomatic, economic and military measures as described below.

3. The United States will provide support it deems appropriate for proper actions taken by Israel in response to such demonstrated violations of the Treaty of Peace. In particular, if a violation of the Treaty of Peace is deemed to threaten the security of Israel, including, inter alia, a blockade of Israel's use of international waterways, a violation of the provisions of the Treaty of Peace concerning limitation of forces or an armed attack against Israel, the United States will be prepared to consider, on an

urgent basis, such measures as the strengthening of the United States presence in the area, the providing of emergency supplies to Israel, and the exercise of maritime rights in order to put an end to the violation.

4. The United States will support the parties' rights to navigation and overflight for access to either country through and over the Strait of Tiran and the Gulf of Aqaba pursuant to the Treaty of Peace.

5. The United States will oppose and, if necessary, vote against any action or resolution in the United Nations which in its judgment adversely affects the Treaty of Peace.

6. Subject to Congressional authorization and appropriation, the United States will endeavor to take into account and will endeavor to be responsive to military and economic assistance requirements of Israel.

7. The United States will continue to impose restrictions on weapons supplied by it to any country which prohibit their unauthorized transfer to any third party. The United States will not supply or authorize transfer of such weapons for use in an armed attack against Israel, and will take steps to prevent such unauthorized transfer.

8. Existing agreements and assurances between the United States and Israel are not terminated or altered by the conclusion of the Treaty of Peace, except for those contained in Articles 5, 6, 7, 8, 11, 12, 15 and 16 of Memorandum of Agreement between the Government of Israel and the Government of the United States (United States–Israeli Assurances) of 1 September 1975.

9. This Memorandum of Agreement sets forth the full understandings of the United States and Israel with regard to the subject matters covered between them hereby, and shall be implemented in accordance with its terms.

Memorandum of Agreement between the Governments of the United States and Israel – Oil

26 March 1979

The oil supply arrangement of 1 September 1975, between the Governments of the United States and Israel, annexed hereto, remains in effect. A memorandum of agreement shall be agreed upon and concluded to provide an oil supply arrangement for a total of 15 years, including the 5 years provided in the 1 September 1975 arrangement.

The memorandum of agreement, including the commencement of this arrangement and pricing provisions, will be mutually agreed upon by the parties within sixty days following the entry into force of the Treaty of Peace between Egypt and Israel.

It is the intention of the parties that prices paid by Israel for oil provided by the United States hereunder shall be comparable to world market prices current at the time of transfer, and that in any event the United States will be reimbursed by Israel for the costs incurred by the United States in providing oil to Israel hereunder.

Experts provided for in the 1 September 1975 arrangement will meet on rquest to discuss matters arising under this relationship.

The United States administration undertakes to seek promptly additional statutory authorization that may be necessary for full implementation of this arrangement.

M. Dayan   Cyrus R. Vance
For the Government of Israel   For the Government of the United
                                                 States

Annex to the Memorandum of Agreement concerning Oil

Annex

Israel will make its own independent arrangements for oil supply to meet its requirements through normal procedures. In the event Israel is unable to secure its needs in this way, the United States Government, upon notification of this fact by the Government of Israel, will act as follows for five years, at the end of which period either side can terminate this arrangement on one-year's notice.

(a) If the oil Israel needs to meet all its normal requirements for domestic consumption is unavailable for purchase in circumstances where no quantitative restrictions exist on the ability of the United States to procure oil to meet its normal requirements, the United States Government will promptly make oil available for purchase by Israel to meet all of the aforementioned normal requirements of Israel. If Israel is unable to secure the necessary means to transport such oil to Israel, the United States Government will make every effort to help Israel secure the necessary means of transport.

(b) If the oil Israel needs to meet all of its normal requirements for domestic consumption is unavailable for purchase in circumstances where quantitative restrictions through embargo or otherwise also prevent the United States from procuring oil to meet its normal requirements, the United States Government will promptly make oil available for purchase by Israel in accordance with the International Energy Agency conservation and allocation formula, as applied by the United States Government, in order to meet Israel's essential requirements. If Israel is unable to secure the necessary means to transport such oil to Israel, the United States Government will make every effort to help Israel secure the necessary means of transport.

Israeli and United States experts will meet annually or more frequently at the request of either party, to review Israel's continuing oil requirement.

Appendix 4

Self-rule for Palestinian Arabs, Residents of Judaea, Samaria and the Gaza District, which will be instituted upon the Establishment of Peace

The following programme was submitted by Prime Minister Begin to President Sadat, as announced by Mr Begin in the Knesset on 28 December 1977:

1. The administration of the Military Government in Judaea, Samaria and the Gaza District will be abolished.
2. In Judaea, Samaria and the Gaza District administrative autonomy of the residents, by and for them, will be established.
3. The residents of Judaea, Samaria and the Gaza District will elect an Administrative Council composed of eleven members. The Administrative Council will operate in accordance with the principles laid down in this paper.
4. Any resident, 18 years old and above, without distinction of citizenship, or if stateless, will be entitled to vote in the elections to the Administrative Council.
5. Any resident whose name is included in the list of candidates for the Administrative Council and who, on the day the list is submitted, is 25 years old or above, will be entitled to be elected to the Council.
6. The Administrative Council will be elected by general, direct, personal, equal and secret ballot.
7. The period of office of the Administrative Council will be four years from the day of its election.
8. The Administrative Council will sit in Bethlehem.
9. All the administrative affairs relating to the Arab residents of the areas of Judaea, Samaria and the Gaza District will be under the direction and within the competence of the Administrative Council.
10. The Administrative Council will operate the following Departments:
(a) The Department of Education;
(b) The Department of Religious Affairs;
(c) The Department of Finance;
(d) The Department of Transportation;

(e) The Department for Construction and Housing;

(f) The Department for Industry, Commerce and Tourism;

(g) The Department of Agriculture;

(h) The Department of Health;

(i) The Department for Labour and Social Welfare;

(j) The Department for Rehabilitation of Refugees;

(k) The Department for the Administration of Justice and the Supervision of Local Police Forces;

- and promulgate regulations relating to the operation of these Departments.

11. Security and public order in the areas of Judaea, Samaria and the Gaza District will be the responsibility of the Israeli authorities.

12. The Administrative Council will elect its own chairman.

13. The first session of the Administrative Council will be convened 30 days after the publication of the election results.

14. Residents of Judaea, Samaria and the Gaza District, without distinction of citizenship, or if stateless, will be granted free choice (option) of either Israeli or Jordanian citizenship.

15. A resident of the areas of Judaea, Samaria and the Gaza District who requests Israeli citizenship will be granted such citizenship in accordance with the citizenship law of the State.

16. Residents of Judaea, Samaria and the Gaza District who, in accordance with the right of free option, choose Israeli citizenship, will be entitled to vote for, and be elected to, the Knesset in accordance with the election law.

17. Residents of Judaea, Samaria and the Gaza District who are citizens of Jordan will elect, and be eligible for election to, the Parliament of the Hashemite Kingdom of Jordan in accordance with the election law of that country.

18. Questions arising from the vote to the Jordanian Parliament by residents of Judaea, Samaria and the Gaza District will be clarified in negotiations between Israel and Jordan.

19. A committee will be established of representatives of Israel, Jordan and the Administrative Council to examine existing legislation in Judaea, Samaria and the Gaza District, and to determine which legislation will continue in force, which will be abolished, and what will be the competence of the Administrative Council to promulgate regulations. The rulings of the committee will be adopted by unanimous decision.

20. Residents of Israel will be entitled to acquire land and settle in the areas of Judaea, Samaria and the Gaza District. Arabs, residents of Judaea, Samaria and the Gaza District who, in accordance with the free option granted them, will become Israeli citizens, will be entitled to acquire land and settle in Israel.

21. A committee will be established of representatives of Israel, Jordan and the Administrative Council to determine norms of immigration to the areas of Judaea, Samaria and the Gaza District. The committee will determine the norms whereby Arab refugees residing outside Judaea, Samaria and the Gaza District will be permitted to immigrate to these areas in reasonable numbers. The rulings of the committee will be adopted by unanimous decision.

22. Residents of Israel and residents of Judaea, Samaria and the Gaza District will be assured freedom of movement and freedom of economic activity in Israel, Judaea, Samaria and the Gaza District.

23. The Administrative Council will appoint one of its members to represent the Council before the Government of Israel for deliberation on matters of common interest, and one of its members to represent the Council before the Government of Jordan, for deliberation on matters of common interest.

24. Israel stands by its right and its claim of sovereignty to Judaea, Samaria and the Gaza District. In the knowledge that other claims exist, it proposes, for the sake of the agreement and the peace, that the question of sovereignty in these areas be left open.

25. With regard to the administration of the holy places of the three religions in Jerusalem, a special proposal will be drawn up and submitted that will include the guarantee of freedom of access to members of all the faiths to the shrines holy to them.

26. These principles will be subject to review after a five-year period.

Index

Aaron, David, 219
Abdullah, King of
    Transjordan, 60
Abu-Rabia, Hamad, 314
Administered Territories, see
    Occupied Territories
Agranat Commission, 2
Al-Arabi, Nabil, 182
Al-Baz, Oasama, 111, 138,
    141–2, 252; at Camp David,
    173, 182; at Blair House,
    199; at Camp David II
    Conference, 260
Al-Hatib, Anwar, 150–2
Al-Natshe, Dr Ahmed
    Hamze, 306, 311–12
Ali, General Kamal Hassan,
    199, 229
Allon Plan, 60, 68, 144, 146,
    196
Alterman, Nathan, 189–90,
    247
American guarantees, see
    under United States
Arafat, Yasser, 28, 33, 145
Arian, Professor, 199
Assad, President, 19, 41, 48,
    57, 88; Hassan on, 42
Aswan Declaration, 110, 166,
    173
Atherton, Alfred, 22, 67, 98,
    202, 226–7; talks with
    Sadat, 129–30; replaces
    Vance, 211; mission to
    Jerusalem and Cairo,
    256–8; at Camp David II
    Conference, 260

Baghdad Conference, 205,
    240, 249; shock to Egypt,
    235
Bar-On, Hanan, 122
Barak, Aharon, 25, 101, 103,
    112, 122–9 passim, 138, 154,
    164, 173; Carter's respect
    for him, 156; replies to US
    proposals, 174; at Blair
    House, 199, 210; appointed
    to Supreme Court Bench,
    209–10; and Egypt's
    treaties with Arab States,
    219–20
Begin, Menachem: offers
    Dayan Foreign Ministry
    post, 1, 5; on Israeli
    sovereignty, 4–5; forms
    Cabinet, 7; Carter's appeal
    for peace negotiations, 16;
    leaves for US, 18; talks with
    Carter, 18–21; personal tie
    with Carter, 21; meeting
    with Vance, 24–5; approves
    Dayan's peace proposals,
    53; reservations on joint
    US–Israel proposals, 71;
    invites Sadat to Israel,
    75–6; reply to Sadat's
    Knesset speech, 82–3;
    friendship with Sadat, 89;
    invites Hassan to Israel, 96;
    Washington trip, 101–2;
    proposals for Palestinian
    autonomy, 101; meets
    Sadat at Ismailia, 102–5;
    reports to Knesset, 105;

Knesset approves peace
    plan principles, 105–6; and
    Egyptian complaints after
    Ismailia, 109–10; and
    Kamel's reaction, 113–14;
    speech at Political
    Committee dinner, 113;
    visits Washington, 122–9;
    strained relations with
    Carter, 128; in US for State
    of Israel anniversary,
    133–4; welcomes Vance to
    Israel, 149; relation with
    Carter, 156; report on first
    meeting at Camp David,
    160–1; replies to Sadat's
    Framework proposal,
    161–2; replies to American
    proposals, 173–4; signs
    Framework Agreement,
    179–80, 188–9; speech to
    Knesset on Framework
    Agreement, 192–3;
    disagreements with Dayan,
    210, 253–4; awarded Nobel
    Peace Prize, 228; discusses
    treaty changes with Vance,
    232–3; requests loan for
    Sinai withdrawal, 232;
    Washington visit en route
    to Canada, 233; requests
    grant for Sinai withdrawal,
    234; meeting with Vance at
    Kennedy Airport, 244–6;
    returns to Israel, 246;
    agreement reached with
    Carter, 268; talks with

Carter in Washington, 268; shouted down in Knesset, 274; reaches agreement with Sadat on oil, 279–80; signs peace treaty, 281; texts of letters, 327–30, 353–5

Ben Gurion, David, 3, 4, 195, 202–3

Ben-Elissar, Eliyahu, 100, 256

Ben Meir, Yehuda, 194

Bentov, Mordechai, 31

Black September movement, 14

Blair House Conference, 199–246; preliminary talks, 205–7; official opening, 207; Dayan's disagreement with Begin, 210; Egypt's treaties with Arab States, 211–12, 218–19, 219–20; diplomatic relations, 212–13; Palestinian problem, 205–6, 212, 216, 220; Israeli oil revenue from Gulf of Suez, 214–15; US financial aid, 214; problem of Egypt's missiles, 218; Suez Canal to be open to Israel, 219; agreement on draft treaty, 220–1; Israeli Cabinet vote on agreement, 225; Ghali brings Sadat's instructions, 234–7; military negotiations, 234; hostility of Israeli Cabinet, 238; deterioration in mood, 239; withdrawal from El Arish, 241–2; dates for leaving oilfields, 241; Palestinian autonomy, 242, 244; Begin–Vance meeting at Kennedy Airport, 244–6; Israeli Cabinet position after, 248–9

Blum, Yehuda, 260

Brown, Harold, 164, 166, 217

Brussels meeting, 252–5; Israeli Cabinet response, 255–6

Brzezinski, Zbigniew, 55, 56, 58, 67, 123, 157, 164, 166; Blair House Conference, 206, 211, 213, 218

Burg, Dr (Israeli Interior Minister), 312, 313

Burg, Yosef, 24

Cairo Preparatory Conference, 99–101; positive effects of, 100–1

Camp David Conference (see also Framework Agreements), 153–80; informality, 155; first tripartite meeting, 160–1; Palestinian problem, 161, 167, 173, 174, 175; Israeli reply to Sadat's Framework proposal, 162–3; US Framework proposals, 163–7; Sinai, 167; West Bank, 167; Gaza, 167; Jerusalem, 167, 177; display by Marines, 169–70; Gettysburg visit, 170–1; second US proposal, 173–4; Framework agreement signed, 179–80, 188–9; conflicting interpretations of settlement details, 181–8; final talks before signing, 182–8

Camp David II Conference, 259–67; Egypt's treaties with Arab States, 260–1, 265; Gaza autonomy, 262; diplomatic relations, 263; Carter meets Dayan and Khalil, 264–5; Khalil's estimate of progress, 264–5; Dayan's estimate of progress, 265

Carter, President, 10; appeal to Begin for peace negotiations, 16; talks with Begin, 18–21; on Palestinian refugees, 19; personal tie with Begin, 21; anger over occupied territories, 59; first meeting with Dayan, 59; on Palestinian problem, 60; further meeting with Dayan, 66–70; personality, 67; criticizes Israeli 'rigidity', 69; meets Sadat at Aswan, 110; meeting with Dayan, 119–20; invites Begin to Washington, 120, 266; disappointment over Israeli stand, 125; negative view of Israeli case, 126; strained relations with Begin, 128; indefatigability, 155; relations with Begin, 156; relations with Sadat, 156; talks with Dayan, 173; anger with Begin, 173; final talks at Camp David, 182–8; signs Framework Agreement, 179–80, 188–9; replies to Hussein's questionnaire, 202; preliminary Blair House discussions with Dayan, 205–6; refuses financial aid for moving Israeli settlements, 214; and Egypt's treaties with Arab States, 219–20; agreement reached with Begin, 268; negotiations in Israel, 269–77; addresses Knesset, 275; leaves for Cairo, 278; signs peace treaty, 281; texts of letters, 328–31, 353–5

Carter, Rosalynn, 156

Ceausescu, President Nicolae, 47, 87

Cohen, Geulah, 192–3, 274, 314

Czechanower, Yosef, 122

Dayan, Ehud (Udi), 134
Dayan, Moshe: offered post
of Foreign Minister, 1, 5;
opposes sovereignty over
captured territories, 1;
leaves Labour Party, 4;
reaction to his appointment
as Foreign Minister, 5-6;
first speech as Foreign
Minister, 7-8; first Cabinet
meeting under Begin, 9-10;
letter to Begin on issues for
Geneva Conference, 11-16;
discussions with Vance,
22-5, 55-9; negotiations in
India, 26-32; purpose in
meeting Desai, 27;
discussions with Desai,
27-30; talks with Shah of
Iran, 32-4; meeting with
Hussein, 35-7; invited to
Morocco, 38; in
Marrakesh, 39-40; initial
meeting with King Hassan,
40-2; initial meeting with
Tuhami, 44-53; on
Palestinian problem, 51;
three moves agreed with
Tuhami, 51-2; Begin
approves his peace
proposals, 53; invites
Tuhami to Israel, 53;
doubts value of American
security guarantee, 56; first
meeting with Carter, 59;
resumes talks in
Washington, 64; tensions
with Israeli Government,
66; attitude to Americans,
66; further meeting with
Carter, 66-70; speech to
UN General Assembly, 72;
defends working paper in
Knesset, 73-4; discussions
with Ghali, 77-8, 84-6; first
meeting with Sadat, 79-80;
reactions to Sadat's speech,
82; relationship with Sadat,
89; further visit to

Morocco, 91-7; further
meeting with Tuhami,
91-7; doubts Tuhami's
status, 97; reflections on
Sinai, 104; further visit to
Shah of Iran, 106-8; visits
antiquities dealer in
Teheran, 107-8; and
Egyptian complaints after
Ismailia, 110; impression of
Egyptian behaviour,
112-13; lectures in US,
117-18; talks at US State
Department, 119; meeting
with Carter, 119-20; puts
Israeli position to
Americans, 130-3; his
mother, 134-5; visits
Nahalal, 134-6; arrives in
Britain for Leeds Castle
Conference, 138-9;
formulates position at
Leeds Castle, 146; reports
to Knesset on Leeds Castle
Conference, 147-8;
discussion with al-Hatib,
150-2; disagreements with
Begin, 153-4, 210; morning
walk at Camp David,
157-8; in Haganah, 170;
Gettysburg visit, 170-1;
talks with Carter, 171-2,
176; speech to Knesset on
Camp David agreement,
194-8; leaves for Blair
House Conference, 200;
addresses UN General
Assembly, 203-4; talk with
Waldheim, 204;
preliminary discussion with
Carter on Blair House,
205-6; reservations about
El Al captains, 222-3;
reports to Begin in
Toronto, 238; at Madison
Hotel, 246-7; love of Bible,
247-8; meeting with Kahlil
in Brussels, 252-5; at Camp
David II Conference,

259-66; negotiating status
at Camp David, 261-2;
complains about Khalil's
attitude, 263-4; reports to
Israeli Cabinet on Camp
David II, 266-7; reaches
agreement on oil supplies
and Gaza, 276-7; dislike of
ceremonial, 280-1;
addresses Knesset on peace
treaty, 282-4; visits Far
East, 285-8; cancer
diagnosed, 289; attitude to
death, 289-90;
archaeological trip to
Beersheba, 293-7; recurrent
dream, 296-7; cancer
operation, 297-8;
Katmandu visit and dream,
298-300; Burma visit,
300-1; returns to full-time
work, 302; differences with
Begin, 303, 313-14; on
status of Arabs in
administered territories,
303-13; resigns from
Government, 303, 313-14;
political career, 315
Dayan, Rahel, 2, 5, 134, 224
Dayan, Zohar (Zurik), 134
Declaration of Principles,
128, 129; Kreisky's, 140
Desai, Moraji, 27; discussions
with Dayan, 27-30;
personality, 29-30
Dinitz, Simcha, 22, 67, 122,
199, 211
Dinstein, Zevi, 218
Dothan, Dr Trude, 319

Eban, Abba, 140
Eban-Kreisky Declaration,
140
Egnaf, Azriel, 26-7
Egypt: border with Israel (see
also Sinai), 19-20, 57, 96;
attitude to Soviet Union,
47; opposed to united Arab
delegation, 65-6; boycott

by Arab States, 100;
treaties with Arab States,
211-12, 218-19, 260-1, 265;
diplomatic relations with
Israel, 212-13; Saudi
Arabia cuts financial aid,
230; growing isolation from
Arab States, 236, 249, 253
Egypt-Israeli Committee,
Political, 110-14
Egypt-Israeli Committee,
Military, 103
Ehrlich, Simcha, 24, 34, 233
Eilat, Gulf of (*see also* Sharm
e-Sheikh), 12, 57
Eitan airfield, 12
El Al (national airline), 9-10
El Arish, 205, 208, 241-2
Eshkol, Levi, 3, 59
Ethiopia: Israeli aid to, 52
Etzion airfield, 12
Evron, Ephraim, 22
Eytan, General Raphael, 25

Fahmi, Ismail, 94
Framework proposals:
Sadat's, 161-2; US, 163-7
Framework Agreements:
signed, 179-80; Israeli
Cabinet vote, 192; Knesset
debate, 192; texts, 321-7
Freij, Elias (Mayor of
Bethlehem), 58, 306

Gamassi, General Abd-el-
Ghani, 103, 130, 199
Gandhi, Indira, 26, 27
Gaza Strip, 11, 274, 275-6;
refugees in, 14; Begin's
proposals, 20; Egyptian
view, 48; Sadat wants
independence for, 85-6;
Israeli position, 92-3, 209;
proposed visit by Egyptian
delegation, 211; and
international border, 224;
status of, 224-5; autonomy,
262; students' entrance to
Egyptian universities,

291-2; Framework
Agreements, 322-3
Gazala, Dr Hatem Abu, 306
Geneva Conference, 2-3, 5;
American memorandum as
basis for, 21-2; Arab
demand for participation of
PLO, 23; Arab view on
preliminary talks, 24;
preparatory talks, 55-74;
procedural questions, 61-2;
American working paper
on, 65; US-Israel joint
working paper, 70-1
Gettysburg, 170-1
Ghali, Butros, 77-8, 79, 84-6,
86-7, 111, 211, 229;
reservations about Sadat's
moves, 182; at Blair House,
199, 207-8; brings
instructions to Blair House
Conference, 234-7; at
Camp David II Conference,
260
Gibeon, Professor, 317
Golan Heights (*see also*
Syria), 10, 12
Goldberg, Arthur, 281
Goldman, Professor
Boleshaw ('Bolek'), 285
Guber, Rebecca, 198
Gur, Motta, 25
Gush Imunim, 117, 118

Habib, Philip, 22, 55, 98
Hadassah Hospital, 36
Haig, General Alexander, 43
Hansell, Herbert: mission to
Jerusalem and Cairo, 256-8
Hassan, King of Morocco, 92,
93, 94, 96-7; initial meeting
with Dayan, 42; arranges
Egypt-Israel meeting, 42;
on Palestinians, 42;
working dinner with Dayan
and Tuhami, 44-53; Begin
invites him to Israel, 96
Hermon, Mount, 12
Herut Party, 87

Hussein, King of Jordan, 19,
24, 48; attitude to
Palestinians, 35-6; meeting
with Dayan, 35-7; on
division of West Bank, 36;
on Palestinian State, 37;
questionnaire to US, 201;
declines to join peace talks,
216
Hussein, Saddam, 143

India: Dayan's talks in,
26-32; diplomatic relations
with Israel, 28-9
Iran: Dayan's talks in, 32-4;
diplomatic relations with
Israel, 32; industrial project
with Israel, 33;
deteriorating situation in,
203; revolution in, 249, 260,
261
Iran, Shah of: talks with
Dayan, 32-4; on Saudi
Arabia, 33-4; on PLO, 33;
on America, 34; on
Iranian-Israeli relations,
106; Dayan visits, 106-8;
on Soviet-American
struggle, 107
Ismailia summit meeting,
102-5; Egyptian reactions,
109-10
Israel: border with Egypt, *see
under* Egypt; border with
Syria, *see under* Syria;
diplomatic relations with
India, 28-9; diplomatic
relations with Iran, 32;
diplomatic relations with
Arabs, 56-7

Jarring, Gunnar, 50
Jerusalem, 11, 15, 16, 46;
status of Holy Places, 20;
Egyptian view, 48-9;
problems of religion, 51;
Israeli view, 58-9, 158; need
for alternative to
sovereignty, 85; as Israeli

Jerusalem (*continued*)
  capital, 177, 203–4; US
  view, 177, 198–9
Jordan, Hamilton, 63, 64, 211
Jordan: refugees in, 14, 37;
  relation with PLO, 58; and
  representation of
  Palestinians, 74; attitude of
  Palestinians, 307–8
Judea, *see* West Bank

Kamel, Muhammad Ibrahim,
  102–3, 111; negotiations at
  Leeds Castle, 143–5; resigns
  as Egyptian Foreign
  Minister, 182
Katz, Shmuel, 21, 25
Katzir, Ephraim (Israeli
  President), 9, 77, 281
Kawasme, Fahd, 306
Khalil, Mustapha, 79, 249;
  meeting with Dayan in
  Brussels, 252–5; at Camp
  David II Conference, 260–4
Khartoum, three Noes of,
  60–1
Khomeini, Ayatollah, 203, 261
Kissinger, Henry, 55, 286;
  Sadat's disappointment
  with him, 90
Knesset Foreign Affairs and
  Defence Committee, 72, 73
Krim, Arthur, 233

Labour Party, 1–2, 3, 4;
  opposition to US–Israel
  working paper, 72–3;
  attitude to peace proposals,
  106; favour territorial
  compromise over West
  Bank, 147
Lapidot, Professor Ruth, 257
Lavie, Naftali, 67
Lebanon: refugees in, 14, 37
Leeds Castle Conference,
  138–48; Egyptian proposal
  on occupied territories, 141;
  Palestinian issue, 142–3
Letters, exchanges of: texts,
  327–31, 353–5

Lewis, Samuel (US
  Ambassador to Israel), 17,
  21, 22, 98
Likud Party, 3, 4
Lipson, Professor L., 219
Litani, Operation, 121–2

McDougal, Professor M.S.,
  219
Magdub, General Taha, 199
Magnes, Judah, 202–3
Majid, Abd el, 111
Marrakesh, 39–40; Dayan's
  meeting with Tuhami in,
  91–7
Meir, Golda, 3, 5, 59, 88–9
Memorandum of Agreement,
  279–80, 357–8; oil, 358–9
Minervi, Yitzhak, 252
Mondale, Vice-President
  Walter, 60, 63, 123, 164,
  211; first meeting with
  Dayan, 59
Morocco; Dayan in, 38–54,
  91–7
Mubarak, Hosni, 41, 45, 86,
  103; visits Washington, 249

Nahalal, Dayan visits, 134–6
Naot-Sinai settlement, 22
Nasser, President, 42, 45;
  Tuhami on, 52
National Religious Party,
  191, 313
Natshe, *see* Al-Natshe
Navon, Yitzhak, 270
Ne Win, President, 301–2
Nehru, Jawaharlal, 31

Occupied territories (*see also*
  Palestinian problem;
  Palestinian refugees;
  Palestinian State; *and
  individual territories*):
  Egyptian view, 48–9;
  problems of Israeli
  withdrawal, 50–1; Sadat's
  requirement of Israeli
  withdrawal, 50; Carter's

anger over, 59; settlements
  in, *see* settlements in
  occupied territories; public
  security in, 127; question of
  sovereignty after five years,
  132–4, 136–7; Egyptian
  proposal at Leeds
  Conference, 141
Oil supplies, 218, 274;
  American proposals, 269;
  new formula on, 275–6;
  Sadat reaches agreement
  with Begin, 279–80
Oilfields: dates for leaving,
  241
Omar, Haj, 316
Operation Litani, 121–2
Orli, General Avraham, 152

Palestine Liberation
  Organization (PLO),
  12–14; participation at
  Geneva Conference
  demand, 23; recognition by
  Arab States, 24, 35; Shah of
  Iran on, 33; relation with
  Jordan, 58; and Geneva
  Conference proposals, 71,
  72; coastal road massacre,
  120–2; atrocities committed
  by, 121–2; attitude of
  Arabs, 306–7
Palestinian Arabs, 125; Israeli
  view, 127; relations with
  Israelis, 318–19
Palestinian autonomy, 120,
  124, 132; Begin's proposals,
  101; Knesset approves
  Begin's plan, 105–6; Leeds
  Castle Conference, 142–3;
  Palestinian view, 150–1;
  proposed timetable, 235–6,
  238–9; Blair House
  Conference, 242, 244;
  Israeli Government
  statement, 250; text of
  agreement, 359–61
Palestinian Council, 235,
  236

Palestinian problem: Hassan on, 46-7; Dayan on, 51; Carter on, 60; Camp David Conference, *see under* Camp David Conference; Blair House Conference, 208-9, 212, 216, 220, 236-7

Palestinian refugees, 12-16, 144-5; homeland problem, 15; Carter on, 19; Katz' ideological arguments, 21

Palestinian State, 304; Israeli view, 4, 58, 93, 116, 162-3, 174; Desai on, 28; Hussein on, 37; Soviet view, 65; American view, 68, 126; Sadat on, 76; Sadat's speech in Knesset, 81; Arab view, 115-16; Egyptian view, 161-2

Peace treaty: negotiations on Article 6, 265, 269-70, 271, 272, 273; signed, 281; Knesset vote, 282; Dayan's address to Knesset, 282-4; preamble, 332; text, 332-5

Peres, Shimon, 73, 83, 106, 140, 193-4, 282

PLO, *see* Palestine Liberation Organization

Poran, Froike, 260

Powell, Jody, 238

Presidents' Club, 117-18

Quandt, William, 22, 67, 150, 211

Rabat Conference, 24

Rabin, Yitzhak, 4, 5

Rachel (poetess), 158

Rafi Party, 4

Refugees, Palestinian, *see* Palestinian refugees

Rodman, Peter, 55

Rogers Plan, 59, 185

Rosenne, Meir, 67, 100, 122, 129, 138, 154; at Blair House, 199, 207-8, 210, 211;

at Camp David II Conference, 260

Rostow, Eugene, 219-20

Rubin, Gail, 120

Rubinstein, Eliakim, 67, 122, 129, 154, 211

Sadat, President of Egypt, 19; need for Begin's commitment to Israeli withdrawal, 50; offers to visit Israel, 75; co-ordinates position with Assad, 76; arrives in Israel, 77; Arab reactions to his peace initiative, 77-8, 94; first meeting with Dayan, 79-80; attitude to negotiations, 79-80; speech to Knesset, 80-2; aim of his visit, 80, 86-8; disappointed with Begin's speech, 83; announcement on return to Egypt, 84; wants independence of Gaza, 85-6; friendship with Begin, 89; American view of Jerusalem visit, 89-90; relationship with Dayan, 89; friendship with Weizman, 89, 156; disappointment with Kissinger, 90; personality, 90; attitude to Soviet Union, 90; convenes Cairo Preparatory Conference, 99-100; meets Begin at Ismailia, 102-5; attacks Israel in *October* weekly, 109; meets Carter at Aswan, 110; offended by Begin's speech, 114; visits Washington, 115-17; disappointed at Israeli attitude, 119; talks with Weizman, 129; gravity of his position, 130; American support for his position, 130; relationship with

Carter, 156; Framework proposals, 161-2; signs Framework agreements, 179-80, 188-9; returns from Camp David, 191; awarded Nobel Peace Prize, 228; agrees to new text, 278; reaches agreement with Begin on oil, 279-80; signs peace treaty, 281; texts of letters, 328-30, 353

Salem, Mamduk, 103

Samaria, *see* West Bank

Saudi Arabia: Shah of Iran on, 33-4; cuts financial aid to Egypt, 230

Saunders, Harold, 98, 201, 225

Scopus, Mount, 36

'Secure boundaries', 16

Security Council, *see* United Nations

Settlements in occupied territories, 63, 64, 66, 115, 130-3; US plan for 'freeze' on, 165; conflicting interpretations of Camp David agreements, 181-8; Carter refuses financial aid, 214; their extension causes storm in Washington, 226-7; Israeli request for loan, 232; request for grant, 234

Shafi, Dr Haidar Abdul, 292-3, 306, 308-11

Shahada, Aziz, 306

Shamir, Moshe, 274, 314

Sharett, Moshe, 31

Sharm e-Sheik, 57, 93, 94, 95, 96, 176

Sharon, Arik, 9, 24, 60; Egyptian complaints after Ismailia, 110

Shiloh settlement, 117

Sinai, 57; demilitarization, 93; Israeli withdrawal from, 93-4, 98-9, 180, 283 (*map*); Dayan's reflections

Sinai (*continued*)
on, 104; UN force in, 213;
cost of Israeli withdrawal,
217; timetable of Israeli
withdrawal, 233
Sisco, Joseph, 55
Sivan, Amiram, 218
Six Day War: borders after
(*map*), 13
Soviet Union: proposed joint
declaration with US, 65;
Sadat's attitude to, 90;
Shah of Iran on, 107
Suez Canal: reopening, 11;
Israeli withdrawal from,
88–9; Egypt agrees to
passage of Israeli ships,
219
Syria: border with Israel, 12,
20, 57; attitude to Israel, 24

Tamir, Major-General
Avraham, 100
Thailand, Dayan in, 286–8
Tripoli Conference of Arab
States, 100
Tubin, Yehuda, 5–6, 200
Tuhami, Dr Hassan: initial
meeting with Dayan,
44–53, attitude to Israeli
victories, 45; presents
Egypt's case to Dayan,
47–9; three moves agreed
with Dayan, 51–2; on
Nasser, 52; Sadat on his
talks with Dayan, 88;
further meeting with
Dayan, 91–7; obscurity of
his status, 97

United Nations: Resolution
242 (1967), 7, 18, 19, 20, 60,
62, 67, 68, 83, 110, 119, 124,
129; Resolution 338,

(1973), 10, 20, 67, 68, 83,
110, 327 (text); Dayan's
speech to General
Assembly, 72
United States: security
guarantees by, 11–12, 56,
62, 64–5; Dayan proposes
defence treaty with, 12;
proposed joint declaration
with Soviet Union, 65, 67;
superficial grasp of the
Middle East, 166–7;
financial aid for Israeli
withdrawal, 214, 240, 245
Urquhart, Brian, 204–5

Vance, Cyrus, 31, 55, 56, 63,
67, 70, 123, 146, 164, 231;
discussions in Israel, 22–5;
meeting with Begin, 24–5;
visits Sadat in Cairo, 98;
visits Jerusalem, 98–9;
sessions with Political
Committee, 110–11;
condemns Israeli
settlements in Sinai, 115;
Israeli protest at his
remarks, 116; talks in
Israel, 149–50; anger at
Israeli rejection, 174; at
Blair House Conference,
203, 206; denounces
extension of settlements,
226; concern over Blair
House disagreements, 239,
240–2; meeting with Begin
at Kennedy Airport, 244–6;
visits Egypt and Israel,
249–51; at Brussels talks,
252–4; at Camp David II
Conference, 260; reaches
agreement on oil supplies
and Gaza, 276–7

Vance, Gay, 139, 231, 281
Vardi, Joseph, 218

Waldheim, Kurt, 204
Weizman, Ezer, 9, 24, 83, 98,
205, 211; friendship with
Sadat, 89, 157; and
Egyptian complaints after
Ismailia, 110; talks with
Sadat, 129; at Blair House,
199
West Bank (*see also*
Palestinian autonomy; P.
problem; P. State),
significance for Israel, 15;
interim arrangement for,
15–16; Begin's proposals,
20; Hussein on division of,
36; Egyptian view, 48;
Dayan's discussions with
Vance, 58; proposed
autonomy of, 58; Israeli
view, 61, 68, 70; proposes
discussions about co-
existence, 73–4; Vance's
remarks bring Israeli
protest, 116; and
Resolution 242, 124;
United States position,
125–6; Egyptian view at
Leeds Castle Conference,
141; negotiations at Leeds
Castle, 143–4; Framework
Agreements, 322–3

Yacobi, Gad, 6
Yadin, Professor Yigael, 24,
79, 98, 268
Yom Kippur War, 2

Zamir, Yitzhak, 256; at Camp
David II Conference, 260
Zuarub, Sheikh, 317